Wanted Women

Also by Deborah Scroggins

Emma's War

Wanted Women

Faith, Lies, and the War on Terror:
The Lives of Ayaan Hirsi Ali and Aafia Siddiqui

Deborah Scroggins

HARPER
An Imprint of HarperCollins*Publishers*
www.harpercollins.com

HarperCollins books may be purchased for educational, business, or sales promotional use. For information, please write: Special Markets Department, HarperCollins Publishers, 10 East 53rd Street, New York, NY 10022.

FIRST EDITION

Designed by Ashley Halsey

Library of Congress Cataloging-in-Publication Data
Scroggins, Deborah.

Wanted women : faith, lies, and the war on terror : the lives of Ayaan Hirsi Ali and Aafia Siddiqui / by Deborah Scroggins. — 1st ed.

p. cm.

ISBN 978-0-06-089897-7

1. Hirsi Ali, Ayaan, 1969– 2. Siddiqi, 'Afiyah, 1972– 3. Muslim women—Social conditions. 4. Muslim women—Political activity. I. Title.
HQ1170.S35 2011
305.48'697—dc23
2011022153

12 13 14 15 16 OV/RRD 10 9 8 7 6 5 4 3 2 1

For my mother,
Gloria Baker Scroggins

and in memory of my father,
Frank William Scroggins (1933–2010)

Pledge, O Sister
To the sister believer whose clothes the criminals have stripped off.
To the sister believer whose hair the oppressors have shaved.
To the sister believer who's body has been abused by the human dogs.
To the sister believer whose . . .

Pledge, O Sister
Covenant, O Sister . . . to make their women widows and their children orphans.
Covenant, O Sister . . . to make them desire death and hate appointments and prestige.
Covenant, O Sister . . . to slaughter them like lambs and let the Nile, al-Asi, and Euphrates rivers flow with their blood.
Covenant, O Sister . . . to be a pick of destruction for every godless and apostate regime.
Covenant, O Sister . . . to retaliate for you against every dog who touch you even with a bad word.

—Introduction to a military manual found in the home of an al-Qaeda member in Manchester, England, May 10, 2000

Man is a child wandering lost in the forests of symbols.

—Charles Baudelaire, "Correspondences," *Flowers of Evil*, 1861

Contents

Principal Characters

Aafia Siddiqui's Story

Ali Abdul Aziz Ali (aka Ammar al-Baluchi): Aafia's second husband, the nephew of Khalid Sheikh Mohammed

Ijaz ul-Haq: Minister of religious affairs from 2004 to 2008; family friend of the Siddiquis'; son of Pakistan's military dictator Muhammad Zia ul-Haq

General Muhammad Zia ul-Haq: Ruler of Pakistan from 1977 to 1988; friend and patron of the Siddiqui family

Aga Naeem Khan: Amjad Khan's father; Aafia's former father-in-law

Majid Khan: The computer programmer from Baltimore for whom Aafia is alleged to have opened a U.S. post office box in order to further Khalid Sheikh Mohammed's 2003 plan to attack gas stations and other targets

Dr. Mohammed Amjad Khan: Aafia's first husband, a Pakistani anesthesiologist who did his residency in Boston

Zahera Khan: Amjad Khan's mother; Aafia's former mother-in-law

KHALID KHAWAJA: A former Pakistani Air Force and Inter-Services Intelligence (ISI) officer who became an advocate for Aafia and other allegedly missing persons in Pakistan

KHALID SHEIKH MOHAMMED (aka KSM): The al-Qaeda mastermind who planned the 9/11 attacks as well as the 2003 plot to attack gas stations and other targets with which Aafia is alleged to have assisted

SAIFULLAH PARACHA: Uzair Paracha's father, currently a prisoner at the U.S. base in Guantánamo Bay, Cuba, accused by U.S. military prosecutors of having helped KSM and al-Qaeda

UZAIR PARACHA: A young businessman convicted of providing material support to terrorists after being found to have helped Majid Khan and Aafia in their scheme to bring Khan back to the United States

YVONNE RIDLEY: A British journalist and convert to Islam who held a press conference in July 2008 alleging that Aafia might be "Prisoner 650" secretly held at the U.S. air base in Bagram, Afghanistan

GRAND MUFTI MUHAMMAD SHAFI: The highest religious authority in Pakistan and Ismat Siddiqui's religious teacher

DR. FOWZIA SIDDIQUI: Aafia's sister, a U.S.-trained neurologist

ISMAT JEHAN SIDDIQUI: Aafia's mother

MUHAMMAD ALI SIDDIQUI: Aafia's brother, a Houston architect

DR. MUHAMMAD SUALEH SIDDIQUI: Aafia's father, a neurosurgeon

GRAND MUFTI MUHAMMAD RAFI USMANI: A son of Grand Mufti Muhammad Shafi and spiritual adviser to the Siddiqui family

MUFTI MUHAMMAD TAQI USMANI: A son of Grand Mufti Muhammad Shafi, the leading authority on Islamic finance and member of Muhammad Zia ul-Haq's Council of Islamic Ideology

Ayaan Hirsi Ali's Story

Asha Artan: Ayaan's mother

Mohamud Mohamed Artan: A cousin whom Ayaan says she secretly married while in Somalia in 1990

Mohammed Bouyeri: The murderer of Theo van Gogh

Sinan Can: A researcher for the *Zembla* television program that nearly cost Ayaan her Dutch citizenship

Leon de Winter: A Dutch novelist and friend of Ayaan

Niall Ferguson: A bestselling British historian and Ayaan's lover

Leo Louwé—A Dutch volunteer who befriended Ayaan and Haweya in Lunteren

Hirsi Magan Isse—Ayaan's father, a Somali politician and rebel leader

Arro Hirsi Magan: Ayaan's half sister, a gynecologist

Haweya Hirsi Magan: Ayaan's sister

Ijaabo Hirsi Magan: Ayaan's half sister

Mahad Hirsi Magan: Ayaan's brother

Herman Philipse: A philosophy professor at Utrecht University who was Ayaan's friend and lover; later defended her in the wake of the controversy over van Gogh's murder

Osman Musse Quarre: A Canadian man who paid for Ayaan's ticket to Europe after she married him in 1992

Jos van Dongen: A correspondent for the television program *Zembla* who made the television program that nearly cost Ayaan her Dutch citizenship

THEO VAN GOGH: The Dutch filmmaker who made "Submission" with Ayaan and was murdered by Mohammed Bouyeri

MARCO VAN KERKHOVEN: A science journalist who lived with Ayaan from 1996 to 2001

RITA VERDONK: A Liberal Party member and minister of immigration and integration; ruled in 2006 that Ayaan was no longer Dutch

MARYAN FARAH WARSAME: Ayaan's stepmother, one of the first Somali women to gain a Western university education and enter government

INTRODUCTION:
Why I Followed Them

It began with a coincidence. On November 3, 2004, I was standing in line for a security check at the Atlanta airport when I read in the newspaper that the Dutch filmmaker Theo van Gogh had been murdered in Amsterdam.

The article said van Gogh had been bicycling to work when a younger, bearded man wearing traditional Arab clothes and a prayer cap cycled up next to him. Brandishing a pistol, the stranger fired eight shots and then pulled two knives from his robe. With the larger knife he sawed off the filmmaker's head. With the smaller one he pinned a five-page letter to van Gogh's body.

The letter was addressed to a Dutch-Somali politician named Ayaan Hirsi Ali, who had collaborated with van Gogh to produce a short film about how Islam mistreated women. In a kind of incantation, the murderer predicted that Ayaan Hirsi Ali would be destroyed, the Netherlands would be destroyed, Europe would be destroyed, and finally the United States would fall before the might of Islam.

The words made me shiver, and not just because such lurid crimes weren't supposed to happen in easygoing Amsterdam. The fate of Theo van Gogh, a great-great-grandnephew of the nineteenth-century painter Vincent van Gogh, recalled the beheading two years earlier of Daniel Pearl, a reporter in Pakistan for the *Wall Street Journal*. The U.S. government had recently announced that Khalid Sheikh Mohammed, the "superterrorist" who was said to have planned the 9/11 attacks, had also murdered Pearl. I happened to be on my way just then to the very city where Pearl had been killed. My assignment for *Vogue* magazine was to discover more about a mysterious Pakistani woman named Aafia Siddiqui, whom the FBI had accused of working for Khalid Sheikh Mohammed (or "KSM," as books and newspapers often called him, after the shorthand of the world's intelligence services).

There was also something else about the story from Amsterdam that focused my attention. The treatment of women in Islam—the subject of the film that was said to have sparked van Gogh's murder—was a topic I had followed for a long time. I had felt for years that the suppression of women was as basic to the ideology of radical Islam as racism had been to the old American South or as anti-Semitism was to Nazi Germany. Whenever political Islam took power, as I had seen as a reporter in Africa and the Middle East, women were the first victims. Under the banner of Islam, women lost much of the freedom they had once possessed to dress as they pleased, to marry whom they chose, and to travel, work, and generally order their lives without male permission. Men, meanwhile, gained the right, wherever the new theocracies flourished, to police and control women.

Men often welcomed the changes. It was only later, typically, that the puritanical Islamists made it clear that they also claimed a God-given right to rule other *men*—sometimes, indeed, while supposedly hastening an apocalypse that the most fanatical Islamists believed in dearly. Any serious struggle against such people, I believed, would have to be based on the principle that universal human rights must not be canceled in the name of some allegedly higher law.

Yet I knew very well that ordinary Muslims were deeply suspicious of Westerners who claimed to want to liberate them. In the nineteenth century, Western imperialists had cited the emancipation of Muslim women as an excuse to invade and conquer Muslim lands. When President George W. Bush's wife, Laura Bush, said after the

United States invaded Afghanistan that "the fight against terrorism is also a fight for the rights and dignity of women," many Muslims rejected her rhetoric as more of the same. And in fact, neither male nor female Muslims outside the United States seemed to have any inalienable rights in the shadowy war that Vice President Dick Cheney called "the dark side."

This darkness seemed to have swallowed Aafia Siddiqui alive. The woman I was going to Pakistan to investigate had been born in Karachi, and she was said to be brilliant as well as pious. She had lived in Boston for a decade while earning degrees at the Massachusetts Institute of Technology and Brandeis University. She had married a Pakistani doctor and eventually had three young children by him. But she had also returned to Pakistan and divorced him. And after the FBI named her in 2003 as the only known female operative of al-Qaeda, Aafia and her children had vanished.

Sometimes her family said they thought she was dead. Or they said they believed the United States was holding her and her children in a secret U.S. prison. Washington denied this and kept issuing warnings, some of which mentioned Aafia by name, that Osama bin Laden's followers might start using women to attack the West and that future attacks might involve weapons of mass destruction.

In a photograph that her family released, Aafia seemed the image of sweet triumph as she graduated from MIT in 1995. She wore a scholarly cap and gown and held a bouquet of red roses as her long black hair blew prettily against her heart-shaped face. Why, I wondered, would a woman who had the freedom to be whatever she wanted join a hate-filled, all-male movement dedicated to controlling women—*if* she actually had joined al-Qaeda? Why would a first-class scientist with a Ph.D. from a university founded by Jews go to work for a man and a movement who apparently delighted in chopping off Jewish heads—if in fact she had? And why would a woman who had everything that most Pakistani women only dream about choose to throw all that away in order to massacre Americans? Could the FBI's charges possibly be true?

Muslims, meanwhile, seemed unafraid of Aafia Siddiqui. Instead, it was Ayaan Hirsi Ali who filled them with fear and rage.

Like Aafia, Ayaan was small, even delicate. But while Aafia Siddiqui was demurely attractive, the Somali-born Ayaan Hirsi Ali had a striking, pantherlike beauty. The newspaper article about van Gogh's murder said that she had written the script for the ten-minute film that had apparently gotten him killed. In it, some fictional Muslim women tell God about the rapes, beatings, and incest they have suffered at the hands of Muslim men. Beneath transparent veils, the actresses' naked bodies are inscribed with verses from the Quran that are used to justify women's submission.

For the average Dutch viewer, the idea that such verses were still taken seriously probably came as a greater shock than the fact that they were painted on female flesh. But Muslims regard the Quran as the literal word of God, and some very conservative Muslims believe they are forbidden to depict the human body. Most Islamic religious art tries to glorify the written Quran, and from a Muslim standpoint it was deeply disrespectful of Ayaan to portray the holy scriptures on naked human skin. As a born Muslim herself, moreover, Ayaan must have known that to use such scenes to blame the Quran for rape and incest would be nothing less than incendiary.

What sort of rage, I wondered, had provoked her to make the film? What kind of bravery, or foolishness, had made her promise to produce a sequel?

Some reports attributed her anger to the traditional female circumcision she had undergone as a child and to the forced marriage she said had led her to seek asylum in the Netherlands. I had spent enough time in Somalia to feel sure that such an explanation couldn't be the whole story. Nearly *every* Somali woman is circumcised, yet most of them would defend their religion and their customs to the death—at least against outsiders. What made Ayaan Hirsi Ali different?

She and the pious Aafia Siddiqui seemed, at first, to have nothing in common. But when I looked closer, I discovered more and more similarities. They were both in their early thirties. They were both fiercely intelligent. They both came from politically ambitious families. They had both been tossed about among Africa, Asia, Europe, and the United States ever since childhood. Both had landed in the West from the periphery of Islam just as the Cold War was ending. And while Westerners were congratulating themselves on "the end of history" and talking about building a "new world order," Ayaan and Aafia had already experienced the Muslim world's new order of failed states and wars without end. When it came to dealing with the crises of Islam, they were mirror opposites, but there were hints in their complicated backgrounds that each woman *might* have gone in a very different direction, perhaps even to the extent of Aafia Siddiqui becoming a Westernizing feminist and Ayaan Hirsi Ali becoming a militant Islamist.

Ayaan, a self-described atheist, had flirted with political Islam as a teenager. Aafia, a fervent Muslim, had studied feminist theory at one of the United States' finest universities. They shared a kind of warrior mentality. Both prized fearlessness. They were both rebels, though Ayaan rebelled against Islam while Aafia said she rebelled to serve Islam more completely. Both had been indoctrinated at an early age into the obsessive anti-Semitism that is such a disturbing feature of modern political Islam. Ayaan ultimately rejected it; Aafia embraced it. And both women would later speak out about something equally strange in the rise of modern jihadi thought—an elaborate and fantastic millenarian strain that, alas, has escaped the notice of all but a few Westerners.

Once I noticed their weird symmetry, I couldn't stop comparing them. Hirsi Ali and Siddiqui seemed to occupy the poles of the global war on terror. They were opposites, yet related. Like the bikini and the burka or the virgin and the whore, you couldn't quite understand one without understanding the other.

And if you *could* understand both, maybe you'd get close to what drove this whole awful conflict. So I decided to follow them and find out.

I flew to Pakistan. And later I traveled to the Netherlands to write an article about Ayaan. In 2005, I moved to Amsterdam with my family. I finally returned to the United States in 2009 to finish this book.

For a while, Ayaan's star rose as Aafia remained invisible. Later the spotlight of celebrity focused on Aafia, while Ayaan had to strive to maintain a certain level of visibility. Only one thing remained constant: neither woman would speak to me.

When I first decided to write their parallel lives, I may have been the only person anywhere to see a powerful connection between Ayaan Hirsi Ali and Aafia Siddiqui. Ayaan was becoming famous, while on the other side of the world Aafia seemed little more than a face on a wanted poster. But as each woman came to be seen under threat, they both took on an exaggerated political significance. In the West, people rallied around Ayaan and the Enlightenment values they felt she represented. Later, in Pakistan and elsewhere, Muslims mobilized around the figure of Aafia and the Islamic purity she was felt to stand for. Flags were burned, governments fell, presidents and prime ministers were implored to save these idols. And the names, loved or hated, of these two previously unknown women rose to the lips of millions of people like the syllables of some powerful magic.

They became icons of the war on terror. "She's an innocent victim!" the followers of each woman cried on talk shows and in the streets. "She's a monster!" the followers of the other muttered in return.

From a distance, anyway—and I came to see my enforced distance from both women as a blessing in disguise—the mythology surrounding both figures became increasingly obvious. And as I tried to sort the truth from a remarkable collection of lies, smoke, and mirrors, I grew more curious about how these two women got under other people's skin. Countless people followed their stories—breathlessly and furiously at times. They were like Rorschach tests. People saw utterly different things in them, and what they saw told you how they saw the war on terror. I came to believe that if I could crack the code of that dreamlike power, I might understand the deep structure of the defining conflict of our time.

PART I

Regarding the West

One

When Aafia Siddiqui's name first appeared on the FBI's Most Wanted list, in 2003, few Pakistanis had ever heard of her. But within a tight circle of bearded Karachi clerics and retired generals there were smiles of recognition. They knew that Aafia's mother had raised her to be a hero of Islam.

Her mother, Ismat Jehan Siddiqui, was born in 1939 in the north Indian town of Bulandshahr. Before the British arrived in India, high-ranking Muslim women of Ismat's class had lived in purdah, veiled and secluded. Men outside their families weren't even supposed to know their names or hear their voices. But in the nineteenth century, Muslim reformers such as Sir Syed Ahmad Khan began arguing that the isolation of Muslim women had contributed to the backwardness of their whole community. And by the time Ismat was born, upper-caste families like hers had begun sending their daughters to school.

The burning question for many Muslim thinkers, dating back to the expansion of Europe's modern empires, was why Islam, which had once dominated the world, had yielded to the West. Didn't the Quran proclaim that the Muslim *ummah*, or community, was "the best community brought out for mankind"? Sir Syed's answer was that Muslims had forgotten the Quranic injunction to "Go and learn, even if it takes you to China." He urged Muslims to learn from the British and to master Western science and technology. Ismat's brother, Shams Ul-Hassan Faruqi, accordingly studied geology at Aligarh Muslim University, the "Muslim Cambridge" that

Sir Syed founded in 1875 near Bulandshahr. And Ismat attended Sir Syed Girls College in Karachi after their family left their home and traveled west to Pakistan, "the Land of the Pure," established in 1947 as a homeland for India's Muslims.

She and Aafia's father, Muhammad Sualeh Siddiqui, were married in an arranged match. Ismat was a small, bustling person of ferocious intensity. Aafia's father was a scholarly, retiring doctor. Not long after their wedding, Ismat and Sualeh (who like many Pakistanis named Muhammad was called by his second name) moved to Britain so he could study neurosurgery. Their first child—Muhammad Ali, but called Ali in the family—arrived in 1961. A girl they named Fowzia followed in 1966. And Aafia, the baby of the family, was born in 1972, after they returned to Pakistan.

Islam, believers emphasize, is a total way of life, and that was how the Siddiquis practiced it. The first words the infant Aafia heard were the verses of the call to prayer that her father whispered in the newborn's ear. Her parents later impressed on her that the purpose of life was to submit to the will of Allah the exalted and to be grateful for his bounty. They kept the Holy Quran in a high, safe place and never let the name of God's messenger, the Prophet Muhammad, pass their lips without adding the blessing, "Peace be upon him." Islam determined what they ate (no pork, no alcohol, only correctly butchered meat), how they ate (with the right hand, not greedily, and with thanks to Allah), and when they ate (after sunset during the holy month of Ramadan, with invocations to God); what they wore (for females, a tunic over baggy trousers with a scarf to symbolize modesty); how they slept (on the right side); how they should treat one another (with respect for elders and love and kindness for all); what they said of their neighbors (no gossip, no backbiting); and what they tried to avoid (pride, arrogance, television, music, romantic novels). They worried about washing properly and getting into just the right position for prayer. They knew that Allah did not accept the prayers of the unclean. And whether greeting people or saying good-bye, expressing sympathy or wishing someone well, they never forgot to thank God, from whom all things flow.

Aafia and her siblings also memorized vast stretches of the Quran and the hadiths, or sayings of the Prophet, and recited them to their parents. The child who did the best job received a prize. By the age of seven, Aafia could perform her five daily prayers. Even before that, she learned to examine her intention before committing any act. Was it to please Allah? If so, she should offer her deed to him with the words "In the name of God, the compassionate, the merciful." But if her action wasn't intended or likely to please Allah, she simply shouldn't do it. Charity is one of the pillars of Islam, and Aafia and her siblings were taught to spend their free time helping others. There were rules for everything, but behind the rules stood the unity of Allah and of Islam. Eventually this great system flowed into sharia, "the straight path" of Islamic law, that defined what was right and wrong, pure and impure, and to what degree. Those who followed the path were rewarded with blessings in this life and paradise in the next. Those who failed made themselves and those around them miserable as they headed straight for hell.

All this was fairly standard for observant Muslims. But the Siddiquis went further. They were followers of an Islamic movement known as Deobandism.

The Deobandis began as an anticolonial movement in the nineteenth century. A group of Sunni scholars founded the sect after instigating the rebellion against the British that they called "the Jihad of 1857" and that British historians called the Sepoy Mutiny. The uprising failed spectacularly, costing 200,000 Muslim lives and causing the British to expel the last Mughal emperor and tighten their hold on India. The scholars, however, were undeterred. They retreated to the town of Deoband, in Uttar Pradesh, not far from where Ismat grew up, to survive "the dark night of British imperialism," as they put it, "and to ensure that the torches of the religion of Islam remain alight."

Like Sir Syed, the Deobandis wanted to know why Islam had fallen under Western rule. But they rejected the view that Muslims needed to learn from the West. Instead, they argued that Muslims, in their haste to imitate unbelievers, had forgotten Allah and his law, and they sought to purify the religion and return it to its roots.

Most Indian Muslims were not Deobandis. The mostly illiterate Sunni peasant majority belonged rather to the mystical sect of the Barelvis. They worshipped at the shrines of Sufi saints and followed hereditary religious leaders known as pirs. The feudal landlords, for their part, who ruled over the Sunni masses, were usually Shiite—a legacy of Iran's ancient influence. The Deobandis, who tended to come from the urban middle classes, looked down on both those groups.

Although the Deobandis were few in number their sect was favored by army officers, professionals, and small-business men. Before partition, India's highest Muslim religious authority, the grand mufti, was the Deobandi mufti Muhammad Shafi. After partition, the same cleric became Pakistan's first grand mufti, based in Karachi.

Aafia's mother, Ismat, was a restless, ambitious woman, and rarely content unless she was organizing people. As a rule, Grand Mufti Muhammad Shafi believed that women should stay at home, under the strict control of men. He once wrote, in fact, that at least half of the world's "disorder, bloodshed, and internecine wars" was caused by "woman and her unbridled freedom." Yet somehow, during her young married life, Ismat persuaded this exalted cleric to let her study under his personal tutelage. The religion that had kept generations of Indian Muslim women locked in purdah became, for her, a means of self-assertion.

Under the grand mufti's guidance, Ismat studied Islamic jurisprudence and the life of the Prophet. But she also read the works of twentieth-century writers such as Pakistan's Abu al-A'la al-Maududi and Egypt's Hassan al-Banna. Western intellectual historians call thinkers like Maududi and Banna, whose goal has been to create a modern Islamic state, "Islamists." Maududi had a secular education but came from a Deobandi background. In the 1930s, he began arguing that a "gigantic flood" of Western ideas and customs threatened to obliterate Islam. But Islam was more than a religion, he contended; it was also a revolutionary political ideology and an economic and political system. He also sought to revive the idea of jihad, a religious imperative that Maududi defined as the struggle for political power. "A total *Deen*," or religion, he wrote, "whatever its nature, wants power for itself. The prospect of sharing power is unthinkable."

Like many other Islamists, then and now, Maududi was especially bothered by Western-style efforts to place the sexes on a more equal footing. Asked what had set him on his political path, Maududi once mentioned an incident from the 1930s: "I saw Muslim *shurafa* [honorable] women walking the streets without *purdah* [veil], an unthinkable proposition only a few years before. This change shocked me so greatly that I could not sleep at night, wondering what had brought this sudden change among Muslims." In 1941, Maududi formed a political party, Jamaat-e-Islami, which aimed to return women to the strict guardianship of men. Paradoxically, it also offered women from conservative families a socially acceptable way of entering public life, and by the 1970s, Jamaat-e-Islami had more female activists than any other party.

While Aafia was still a baby, her family left Pakistan for Africa. Dr. Siddiqui had been offered a job at the new University Teaching Hospital in Lusaka, Zambia's capital. The Siddiquis quickly became active in the city's small but lively Asian community, and Ismat began holding religious classes for women, often taking little Aafia along.

When Aafia was two years old, Ismat formed a group she called the United Islamic Organisation, or UIO. Its aim was to unify Lusaka's Muslims and steer their worship into channels favored by the Deobandis. They also aimed, more falteringly, to convert the country's Christian majority to Islam. Aafia later told a friend that one of her earliest memories was sitting cross-legged on the floor as her mother lectured a rapt audience of African and Asian women dressed in colorful veils and head wraps, her voice rising and falling with the cadence of a revivalist. For Aafia, who was still a small child, her mother exemplified the respect and admiration that a woman could gain through her command of religion. It was a lesson Ismat would reinforce when the family moved back to Pakistan in 1980.

Two

After Theo van Gogh was murdered in 2004, the classically Somali face of Ayaan Hirsi Ali flashed across television screens all over the world. Few Somalis could claim to know her, but nobody was surprised to learn that she was causing a stir. Her father was famous for his audacity.

Ayaan's mother, Asha Artan, met him at a literacy class in 1966. Asha was born in the white-hot light of Somalia's northern desert in the late 1940s. She was the daughter of a tribal judge who herded camels and could find rain by smelling the air. At the age of fifteen, Asha walked out of the desert and crossed the Gulf of Aden to find work as a housecleaner for a British woman. After a brief marriage and divorce, she returned to Somalia not long after it gained independence in 1960. With help from the U.S. Agency for International Development, Somalia's new government was sponsoring classes in the new capital of Mogadishu for adult Somalis to learn how to read. Asha signed up for a class and promptly fell in love with her teacher, a dashing thirty-one-year-old writer and politician named Hirsi Magan Isse.

The parliamentary government that the British handed Somalia before sailing away was entirely new to its people. Traditionally, the Somalis were camel-herding nomads whose only form of government was the clan.

Even today, a typical Somali child grows up memorizing the names of his or her ancestors, stretching back hundreds of years. Armed with this knowledge, a Somali can determine how closely he is kin to any other Somali by placing him on his mental genealogical tree. Under the clan system, close relatives have a duty to support one another against outsiders according to the logic of the old Bedouin proverb, "I against my brother; I and my brother against my cousin; I and my brother and my cousin against the world." Without an enemy to unite them, Somalis often fell to quarreling among themselves. Bravery and a readiness to fight were the virtues they esteemed. Weakness and cowardice were the worst sins.

Both Asha and Hirsi belonged to the high-caste Darood clan, whose women are legendary for their beauty. (The Somali supermodels Iman, Waris Dirie, and Yasmin Warsame all come from the Darood clan.) Hirsi also belonged to a particularly fierce subclan called the Majerteen, warriors who lived on the northern coastline opposite Aden. Within this subclan, the members of Hirsi's lineage group, known as the Osman Mahamud, were the traditional rulers.

Hirsi's father—Ayaan's paternal grandfather—was one of the clan's leading warriors. His given name was Ali, but everyone called him Magan, or "He Who Protects Those He Conquers." He was considered great on account of all the men he had killed and the women and camels he had stolen from rival clans.

Ayaan's father, Hirsi, the youngest son of Magan's youngest wife, was born in 1935 in Nugaal Province, near the Eyl oasis, when his mother was in her teens and the old warrior Magan about seventy. As a young boy, Hirsi had a gift for memorizing poetry that attracted the attention of the scholar of the clan, who taught him to read and write and had him sent to school.

The clan later sent Hirsi, at the age of twenty-five, to Mogadishu to represent it in the Somali Youth League, a political party organized by the British. In a browned photograph from the period Hirsi has exchanged the traditional Somali sarong for a shirt and tie and a Western suit with wide lapels. He wears a Somali Youth League pin and the bright optimism of a man with a future.

Washington was offering scholarships to young Africans to study in the United States, and in 1960, the year Somalia became a nation, Hirsi left for Ohio University.

He sailed through an anthropology program there and also attended a training course for teachers of literacy at Columbia University in New York. He moved back to Mogadishu in 1966, and he taught there in one of the new schools that the Somali Youth League was setting up. It was there that he met Asha.

Hirsi had already started writing the satirical short stories about Somali politics that later won him acclaim, and people who knew him during those days in Mogadishu remember how charismatic he was, with his urgent talk and flashing wit. Asha was a poet, too, and, like Hirsi, had some knowledge of Arabic. The mutual attraction grew quickly, and within a few months they were married.

For Hirsi, it wasn't the first time. In fact, he was already married to a woman named Maryan Farah Warsame. Maryan was one of a tiny number of Somali women who had gone to school in the colonial period and continued studying. Indeed, she was studying at Syracuse University, in upstate New York, when her husband married Asha in Somalia, and she had borne Hirsi a daughter, Arro, the year before. Taking a second wife, as Hirsi did, seldom made for a happy household, but there was no stigma attached to it. Islam allows men to marry up to four wives, and Africa has an even older tradition of polygamy.

Asha gave birth to Ayaan's older brother, Mahad, in 1968, and Ayaan herself was born at Mogadishu's Digfeer Hospital in 1969.

The name Ayaan means "lucky." But 1969 was anything but a lucky year for her family. Hirsi had come home from the United States three years earlier feeling that Somalia could become a superpower. As Ayaan has written, he thought that if the Americans had achieved what they had in two hundred years, "then we Somalis, with our endurance and resilience—we can make America in Africa." But after just a few years the country's democracy was faltering, and in October 1969 a military officer named Mohamed Siad Barre overthrew the elected government and set up a military dictatorship. Ayaan was born twenty-three days later, on November 13.

Hirsi's first wife, Maryan, returned from the United States with her bachelor's degree that same year. She had heard nothing about his marriage to Asha, and she evidently did not take the news well. For a while, Hirsi tried to divide his time between the two women. Maryan's youngest daughter, Ijaabo, and Asha's youngest daughter, Haweya, were both born in 1971. But Ayaan claims that eventually Maryan ordered Hirsi to choose between her and Asha. When he refused, she went to live with her children by herself.

A few months later, in April 1972, Somalia's strongman, Siad Barre, threw Hirsi into prison. Hirsi had mocked the dictator in his poems and short stories, and no Somali leader would stand for that. "Hirsi does not mince his words when it comes to talking," Mahmoud Yahya, a Somali banker friend, said years later, chuckling. "Hirsi is capable of saying what he thinks without fear or favor." Ayaan's father was taken to Mandera prison in the north.

Siad Barre called himself a socialist, and Somalia sided with the Soviet Union. He banned political parties and arrested members of the former government. He also made some changes in the name of "scientific socialism" that elevated Somalia's women. For example, he granted women equal rights of inheritance and divorce, and when religious leaders opposed the changes, calling them un-Islamic, he had ten of them executed. He opened public schools for girls that Ayaan and her sister, Haweya, attended. And, with Barre's blessing, Ayaan's stepmother, Maryan, who belonged to the dictator's Marehan subclan, and other professional women began campaigning to end the traditional Somali practice of female genital mutilation, or, as it was called then, female circumcision.

Like girls in parts of Ethiopia and Sudan, Somali girls were commonly infibulated, meaning that the clitoris and labia were cut off and the genitals stitched shut. Infibulation was thought to ensure that girls would remain virgins until their fathers married them off. Often it caused lifelong pain and health problems. In Somalia, female circumcision was justified as Islamic, though the practice seems to have originated in Africa long before Islam. As Ayaan's half sister

Arro later wrote, it was called "pruning" in the Somali language and regarded as a sign of cleanliness and beauty.

Hirsi, however, like his first wife, Maryan, became convinced that the custom was not Islamic, and before he left for prison, he left strict instructions that Ayaan and Haweya should not be "pruned" while he was gone. But their grandmother, Asha's mother, feared the girls would be ostracized as freaks if they weren't cut. So one day, while Asha was away, she had both girls and their brother, Mahad, circumcised.

Ayaan was five at the time, and she has written that her operation, though extremely painful, was less severe than some other girls experienced. She has never complained in public about the urinary and menstrual blockages that torment some infibulated women. She has said that she enjoys sex. In her autobiography she says her sister suffered far worse. "Haweya was never the same afterward."

Ayaan says that her grandmother did it out of love. When Ayaan's mother complained, her grandmother flew into such a rage that Asha ended up apologizing to the older woman. Hirsi and Asha disapproved, but they probably didn't regard female genital mutilation with the revulsion many Westerners felt. Nearly every woman they knew was infibulated, and Ayaan's grandmother didn't have to remind them how hard it was for an uncircumcised girl to find a husband.

In 1975, after three years in prison, Hirsi escaped with the help of the warden, a member of Hirsi's lineage who was later caught and executed. Ayaan's father made his way to Saudi Arabia and then to Ethiopia, Somalia's traditionally Christian neighbor and rival. There, in the Ethiopian mountain capital of Addis Ababa, he helped found a group of mostly Majerteen rebels against Siad Barre. They called themselves the Democratic Front for Salvation of Somalia.

In April 1978, when Ayaan was eight, Hirsi told Asha to leave the country with the children and meet him in Saudi Arabia. The Majerteen were organizing a coup. Asha managed to get passports, and they boarded an airplane for the first time in their lives. After a nerve-racking journey, they landed safely in Jeddah—but Hirsi failed to meet them at the airport. Under Saudi Arabia's strict Islamic laws, women weren't allowed to travel except under the supervision of a male relative. Asha feared that if the Saudis noticed her husband's absence they would send her and the children back to Somalia, where Siad Barre might have them punished for conspiring against him. Fortunately, a Somali man who was one of Asha's own clan members happened to see her at the airport, and he offered to take them home to stay with his family. Days passed before Hirsi's kinsmen tracked them down.

The coup had failed, and all over Somalia Majerteen were being killed. In Ayaan's telling, the disappointment Asha felt about the way in which Hirsi let them down during those first few days in Saudi Arabia became a bitterness that eventually permeated Asha's life. "Something inside her seemed to snap," Ayaan writes of her mother. "She cried and cursed and hit at us in a kind of frenzy."

Hirsi's clansmen moved her and the children to Mecca, where they rented a two-room flat in one of the shabby cinder-block walk-up buildings inhabited by Saudi Arabia's legions of guest workers. Being in Islam's holiest city was some consolation for the devout Asha, but mostly she and the children were miserable. Ayaan remembers the period for its family fights. "Ma saw us pretty much as camels: to tame us, she yelled and hit a lot."

Months later, Hirsi appeared. It was the first time Ayaan could remember seeing her father. Hirsi picked her up and swung her around, cuddled her, and told her she was pretty. No one had ever done that before, and Ayaan instantly adored him. Hirsi moved the family to Riyadh, the capital, where he got a job in a government ministry.

He was as hard on his only son as he was soft on his daughters. He would mock Ayaan's brother, Mahad, belittle him, and call him a coward. Ayaan became his favorite. "You are my only son," he would croon to her.

But Ayaan wasn't a son, and, as a girl, there were many things she wasn't allowed to do. Their father argued that Islam honored women as highly as men, and he quoted the hadith that says, "Paradise is at the feet of your mother." Ayaan drily observed that her father's feet were shod in expensive Italian shoes while her mother's bare feet were cracked from washing floors. "There were two examples, my father's life and my mother's. My father's life was more exciting. He was always going out, he did important things, he gave his life for the country. My mother was always toiling away—cooking, cleaning, taking care of us, being taken for granted." Ayaan decided she didn't want to be like her; she wanted to be like her father.

Politically, the American-educated Hirsi was fairly pro-Western before he went to prison. But one of his fellow prisoners at Mandera was a dissident sheikh from the Society of the Muslim Brotherhood, the oldest modern Islamist group in the Arab world and the counterpart of Pakistan's Jamaat-e-Islami. This sheikh introduced Hirsi to Islamism, which was just beginning to spread.

It began in the Arab world as it did on the Indian subcontinent, as an anticolonial movement. The Egyptian teacher Hassan al-Banna founded the Muslim Brotherhood in 1928. Banna later described his rage at what Great Britain had done to his country. The British lived in walled cantonments of "beautiful bungalows," he wrote. They treated Egyptians "like slaves" and raised a "tide of atheism and lewdness." Like Maududi, the founder of Pakistan's Jamaat-e-Islami, Banna and the Brotherhood called on Muslims to establish new states based on Islamic law, or sharia. Membership in the group was secret, and members pledged: "Allah is our way. His Messenger is our leader. The Quran is our law. Dying in the way of God is our highest hope. Jihad is our way." During World War II, the Brothers received support from Nazi Germany because of their anti-British activities, and, when the war ended, they led the popular Egyptian and Arab resistance to the state of Israel. They became obsessed with the idea that the Jews had laid siege to Islam itself.

The Saudis discovered their form of Islamism by another and

older route. Since the eighteenth century, the ruling Saud family of central Arabia had been allied with the followers of an earlier puritan, the Arabian preacher Muhammad Ibn abd al-Wahhab. They called their interpretation of Islam Salafism, but other people called it Wahhabism and still do. Like the early Deobandis, with whom they became close, the Wahhabis were intent on destroying what they saw as idolatry. They wanted Muslims to return to imitating the *salaf*, or Companions of the Prophet, right down to such details as how the *salaf* cleaned their teeth and used the toilet. Keeping women out of sight and under the control of men was another preoccupation.

When the al-Saud conquered most of the Arabian Peninsula in the 1920s, they imposed the Wahhabi-Salafist faith on what soon became the Kingdom of Saudi Arabia. At the time, Wahhabis made up less than 1 percent of the world's Muslims. But as custodians of the sacred Kaaba (which every Muslim was and is expected to visit), the Saudis multiplied their influence by preventing other sects from teaching their versions of Islam at Mecca. Then oil was discovered. By the time Ayaan and her family arrived, in the 1970s, the Saudis were earning billions of dollars a year, and they used part of their enormous wealth to try to mold Islam everywhere according to their Wahhabi beliefs. A political scientist, Alexi Alexiev, later called this project "the largest worldwide propaganda campaign ever known." The kingdom spent more than $75 billion on it between 1970 and 2001, trying to convert the Muslim world to its doctrine.

One tool the Saudis used was the Muslim Brotherhood. The many schools, for example, that the Saudis built were staffed by teachers who were Muslim Brothers. The Deobandi religious movement was another tool and ally in the Saudis' vast missionary effort. To reach the workers from Pakistan, India, Bangladesh, and elsewhere who began flocking to the Persian Gulf for jobs, the Saudis built Deobandi mosques and schools and financed the Deobandis' missionary group, Tablighi Jamaat. The South Asian targets of this largesse learned to view Salafi Islam as "true Islam" and their own more eclectic and forgiving traditions (such as Sufism) as heretical.

One writer whose books the Saudis printed in many languages was Sayyid Qutb, the Brotherhood's most radical thinker. If Banna and Maududi might be called the Marx and Engels of revolutionary Islamism, perhaps Qutb was its Lenin. This sensitive and withdrawn Egyptian began his career as a secular poet and literary critic. But after Egypt's defeat in the Arab-Israeli War of 1948, he gravitated toward the Muslim Brotherhood. In 1955, Egypt's president, Gamal Abdel Nasser, had Qutb and hundreds of other Brothers arrested. Qutb was convicted of treason in 1966 and hanged. But before he died, his sisters managed to smuggle his jihadist manifesto, *Milestones*, out of prison. These sisters and Qutb's brother, Muhammad, later moved to Saudi Arabia, where Muhammad Qutb gave weekly lectures at King Abdul Aziz University in Jeddah. The future al-Qaeda leader Osama bin Laden was an occasional student of Muhammad there. So was Ayaan's father, Hirsi, according to his friend Mahmoud Yahya.

In 1979, however, the Saudis asked Hirsi to leave. Somalia's dictator, Siad Barre, had switched sides in the Cold War and joined with Saudi Arabia in the anti-Communist, pro-U.S. camp. The Saudis no longer wanted to support Siad Barre's enemies, including Hirsi's rebel group. As Ayaan's brother, Mahad, later told a reporter, "They asked him to take his war activities elsewhere, not to use Saudi [Arabia] as a staging camp."

The family moved to Ethiopia. But Asha had a miscarriage there, and Mahad says she asked their father to take them to Nairobi, in nearby Kenya. Other members of their father's clan had already settled in Nairobi, where the schools were better than Ethiopia's. So they moved again in July 1980 and settled in Nairobi's Eastleigh area—a raucous, formerly Asian suburb that had been built in the 1920s by Indian workers under the British. Now it was fast becoming known as "Little Mogadishu." Eastleigh would be Ayaan's home for the next ten years. It would also be the scene of her family's unraveling.

Three

A new century dawned for Islam before Aafia Siddiqui's family returned from Zambia to Pakistan. By the Muslim calendar, the West's 1979 was really 1400, and events surrounding that year did seem to portend momentous changes. In neighboring Iran, a revolutionary Islamist government had taken power. In Pakistan, General Muhammad Zia ul-Haq, a fellow Deobandi, had seized the government two years earlier with a promise to put Pakistan under "the system of the Prophet." The Siddiquis were soon swept up in the fervor.

They had left for Africa in a very different mood. The year before they left, in 1971, the Bengali-speaking provinces of East Pakistan had risen up against the country's military dictatorship. With the help of Pakistan's nemesis, India, the Bengalis won independence for a new country they called Bangladesh. The citizens who remained in what was left of Pakistan, especially those like the Siddiquis who had left their homes in India for the new Muslim homeland, were badly shaken. Each one of them had sacrificed to make Pakistan a reality. Now they saw their dream collapsing

After the loss of East Pakistan, the military called elections in 1973. The prime minister who was elected, Zulfikar Ali Bhutto, was a wealthy feudal landlord. His wife was a Shiite and thus a heretic in Deobandi eyes. His campaign slogan—"food, clothing and shelter"—had nothing to do with serving Allah. He tried to appease the country's religious parties, but they were unmoved. Then, in 1977, their prayers were answered when General Zia took power in a military coup.

Grand Mufti Muhammad Shafi had died by then, but his son Mufti Muhammad Taqi Usmani became a member of the Council of Islamic Ideology, which Zia established to make the country's laws conform to the Quran and the hadiths. Later another son, Mufti Muhammad Rafi Usmani, was named Pakistan's grand mufti. Zulfikar Ali Bhutto was jailed and later hanged, elections were canceled, and political parties were banned except for Maududi's Jamaat-e-Islami.

One of Zia's first pledges was to return Pakistani women to "chador and chardiwari," or the veil and the home's four walls. Since Mufti Taqi Usmani agreed that the worst development of recent times was "the modernity that had engulfed the whole world in a tornado of nudity and obscenity and provided an excuse for fornication," he agreed to help Zia write a set of laws meant to unwind the tornado.

Called the Hudood, or "Lawful Boundary," Ordinances, the laws that Mufti Taqi Usmani helped write were a fundamental legacy of Zia's rule. They redefined sexual crimes. *Zina*, or sex outside marriage, became a crime against the state, whether consensual or not. To prove rape henceforth required the testimony of four male Muslim witnesses.

The implications were sweeping. The new law made it possible for the male guardians of a woman who engaged in sex without their permission to charge her with *zina*, which was punishable by lashing, imprisonment, or death. To be sure, Pakistan's authorities had never really barred Pakistani men from deciding whom their female relatives married or how they behaved. The idea that men had the right to control the sexuality of the women in their families was too deeply ingrained in the culture for that. But what had been custom now gained the force of law. As the Pakistani sociologist Afshan Jafar wrote, "The message was clear—women were men's property and men could do with them as they pleased."

The new sex laws went on the books in February 1979, along with a host of other Deobandi innovations. Within months the world was experiencing so many Muslim-related crises that Pakistan's clerics began speculating that the new Islamic century might portend the coming of the Last Day. In Iran, Islamic fundamentalists overthrew the shah and took U.S. diplomats hostage. In Saudi Arabia, Muslim radicals briefly seized the Kaaba at Mecca's Grand Mosque. In Pakistan, Islamist students assumed that the United States and Israel had plotted the attack on the Grand Mosque and burned Islamabad's U.S. Embassy to the ground. Then, in July, the U.S. National Aeronautics and Space Administration announced that its Skylab satellite would fall to earth; Pakistani television announcers began issuing bulletins on the satellite's progress, along with pleas for prayers suggesting that this object from the skies might herald Armageddon. By December, the Soviet army had invaded Afghanistan.

The U.S. government had originally disdained Pakistan's new strongman, and it briefly suspended aid to the country. But by the end of that pivotal year it changed its mind. Zia seemed to offer an opportunity to help block the Soviet threat in Afghanistan, while Washington's Saudi allies saw Zia, an authoritarian fellow Sunni, even more positively. Pakistan had already sheltered some of Afghanistan's Islamist leaders, and now it would promote the first major religious jihad of modern times. The United States could bloody its Cold War enemy while currying favor with the Muslim world, while Saudi Arabia's royal family pumped up its religious authority, which Iran's Ayatollah Ruhollah Khomeini and his Shiite radicals were challenging.

Thus the United States and the Saudis struck a deal to create a semicovert Afghan resistance movement. They would provide the money and arms, while Zia's Directorate for Inter-Services Intelligence, better known as the ISI, would manage the program. It ended up costing more than $8 billion a year. To make sure the jihad was truly Islamic, moreover, Pakistan's Deobandi scholars would dictate its ideological content.

Aafia Siddiqui was seven when her family returned to Karachi in this charged atmosphere.

They bought a spacious two-story bungalow in the prestigious

E section of Gulshan-e-Iqbal, a new area that was attracting professionals and military officers linked to Zia's regime. The brother of Zia's chief of staff, General Mirza Aslam Beg, lived next door. Like others in the neighborhood, the Siddiquis' house was surrounded with a high "purdah wall" intended to protect the family's privacy. They planted bougainvillea and built a fountain, and, like other Pakistani upper-middle-class families, they kept a cook, a watchman, and a driver for the family car. Aafia's mother, Ismat, who considered herself an Islamic feminist, was free to expand the kind of preaching she had taken up in Zambia. Mufti Taqi Usmani and Grand Mufti Rafi Usmani became the family's spiritual guides, as well as patrons of the UIO women's organization, which Ismat brought with her to Karachi. Dr. Siddiqui would become so close to Mufti Taqi that he eventually translated the cleric's book *Islam and Modernity* into English.

There was plenty for a woman of Ismat's skills to do. From a population of about 435,000 at the time of independence, Karachi by 1980 had grown to more than five million. Its new arrivals included millions of poor and illiterate women, mainly from Punjab and Sindh, who often came to work as cooks and maids. Aafia would later write that her mother's UIO set up schools to offer those women and their children an Islamic education. The group also provided them with sewing machines, sewing lessons, and vending carts so they could support themselves by working at home. For more prosperous women, Ismat's organization put on an annual conference at Karachi's Sheraton Hotel. This conference in its heyday attracted delegates from Afghanistan, Somalia, the Philippines, Nigeria, Saudi Arabia, and elsewhere.

Today, fashionably conservative female preachers such as Dr. Farhat Hashmi are an established feature of Pakistan's social landscape. But when Ismat started holding her religious classes and conferences for women, she was a pioneer, and President Zia noticed. The country's most prominent feminists opposed the Hudood laws that called for the stoning and flogging of wicked women, yet here was an educated woman who said that women should seek their rights through Islam, not against it. Zia's shy, retiring wife, Begum Shafiq, began attending Ismat's classes. Zia's son Ijaz ul-Haq told me that in time his whole family came to respect Ismat as a religious scholar. Eventually Zia took the unusual step of appointing her to a government board he set up to collect and distribute *zakat*, the annual 2.5 percent tithe required in the Quran for charity.

Ismat's membership on the board made her one of a very few women linked with the early efforts to produce mujahideen, or "fighters in the way of Allah," for Afghanistan. The *zakat* money helped support a Deobandi system of seminaries, charities, and militant groups that would become the engine of jihad. Grand Mufti Muhammad Rafi Usmani called the growing seminaries "fortresses of Islam," and soon many of them were literal fortresses, stocked with weapons and ammunition and offering military training. Pakistan's intelligence agencies, the Deobandi clergy, Jamaat-e-Islami, and some smaller Islamist groups were all deeply involved. Donors in Saudi Arabia and the other Persian Gulf states also contributed. A few numbers tell the story. When Zia came to power in 1977, there were about seven hundred seminaries across Pakistan. But by 2004, Karachi alone had at least 1,800 seminaries, of which 1,500 were Deobandi institutions even though Deobandis made up less than a quarter of Pakistan's population. Nationwide, some seven thousand Deobandi seminaries were registered as of 2009.

Pakistan's Shiites, who dominated the feudal class that Zia had sidelined, so fiercely opposed the new *zakat* system that eventually they were excused from paying it. The Shiites, like the Deobandi Sunnis, made up a quarter of the population, but Shiites weren't allowed to join the jihad or build new seminaries—and in 2004 they had only thirty-six religious schools in Karachi. In time, the Deobandi-dominated state, military, and religious institutions became known as Pakistan's establishment, and the jihadi militias that this new establishment nurtured became a whip held over the country's non-Deobandi majority. Back in 1981, however, when some of Pakistan's first jihadis left for Afghanistan from the giant Binori Town Mosque, not far from the Siddiquis' house, most Pakistanis saw them as heroes.

Aafia was only a small girl, yet she was caught up in the fever for jihad. The Siddiquis' neighbors still remember how Ismat used to send her walking around the neighborhood, knocking on doors and handing out religious leaflets. Well-bred young Pakistani girls didn't usually expose themselves to the view of strange men. But Aafia seemed so innocent and sincere that her neighbors found it hard to object. After all, she was doing it for Islam.

The girl's hobby was caring for pets. Years later, when visiting reporters asked her sister, Fowzia, about Aafia's childhood, Fowzia would pull out photo albums and show them page after page of dark-haired little Aafia cuddling her pet rabbit or feeding her goat. Fowzia said that Aafia, at one time or another, kept dogs, ducks, cats, a turtle, a fish, a lamb, geese, goats, pigeons, and parrots. She called her sister a happy child, sweet and eager to please. She once wrote me, "Aafia loved school, had lots of friends, [and] her favorite pastime was to play with dolls and pets."

Aafia attended the local English-language school for girls in Gulshan. Ismat told audiences that if Muslims wanted to revitalize Islam, they needed to raise children capable of succeeding in the secular realm as well as in religion. As Aafia later summarized her mother's views, "Unless our younger generation is given a well-rounded Islamic education, geared both toward material and spiritual success, the problems facing the Muslim world may not be solved. Our youth need to be transformed, Insha'Allah, into exemplary Muslims with knowledge of their rights and obligations, while being the world's leading scientists, artists, economists and philosophers capable of standing up to all the challenges facing Islam in this secular world."

She studied English, science, and math as well as Arabic, the Quran, and the Sunna. "She was always very good in school and responsibly did her work," according to her sister. "She could not bear being yelled at and so was very obedient." Aafia's teachers were so impressed that they named her head girl, with responsibility for giving speeches and representing the school at public events.

Like the rest of Pakistan, she and her classmates celebrated the Soviet pullout from Afghanistan in 1988 as a great victory for Islam. It was the first in centuries, but Pakistanis felt certain it wouldn't be the last. The ISI began laying plans to transform the ongoing struggle against India for the disputed province of Kashmir from a nationalistic fight into a holy jihad. Some of Zia's officials, such as the ISI chief, General Hamid Gul, saw in the Soviet decline and the opening of Central Asia an opportunity for Pakistan to become the nucleus of a revived caliphate.

At sixteen Aafia enrolled in Karachi's most prestigious secondary school for girls, St. Joseph's College for Women, founded by Catholic nuns in 1948. The campus of St. Joseph's, with its neo-Mughal architecture, green lawns, and long open walkways, was a bit of old Karachi in a city being swallowed by slums and skyscrapers. The wife of Pakistan's future president Pervez Musharraf had gone to school at St. Joseph's, and so had other leading Pakistani academics, doctors, and journalists. Of course, in Sehba Musharraf's day, the students were unveiled, but in 1972 the school was nationalized, and its students began wearing head scarves.

Then, in August 1988, tragedy struck. The Siddiquis' patron and the Deobandis' most powerful friend, General Zia ul-Haq, was killed in a still-unsolved plane crash along with several generals and the U.S. ambassador. The CIA put out the view that the Soviets had killed Zia in revenge for their defeat. But some members of Zia's inner circle blamed the United States, India, and Israel, which, they believed, wanted to stop Zia from expanding the jihad beyond Afghanistan. For them, the year that had begun in joy ended in gloom.

Despite years of propaganda against democracy, the military agreed to hold elections. Benazir Bhutto, the glamorous thirty-five-year-old daughter of Zulfikar Ali Bhutto, the prime minister whom Zia had hanged, decided to run. Mufti Muhammad Rafi Usmani and assorted other divines waxed apoplectic, warning that no country ruled by a woman ever came to good. But in a stunning rejection of everything that they and Zia stood for, the Pakistanis elected Bhutto's Pakistan Peoples Party, and she became prime minister. The country that Zia and his men had hoped might spawn a new caliphate instead became, in 1988, the first modern Muslim nation to be led by a woman.

Benazir Bhutto's success, though, gave Aafia's mother an idea.

All three Siddiqui children were gifted students, but Aafia was the star. She would graduate from St. Joseph's in 1989 with an A-I degree in pre-engineering. Like her mother, Aafia was small in stature—at five foot three, as tall as she would ever be—and fair-skinned, with a wide face and brown eyes set under sweeping black eyebrows. Her father wanted her to become a doctor. But Ismat hesitated to send her to a Pakistani university. Girls came under great pressure in Pakistan to marry as soon as they finished secondary school. Ismat wanted Aafia to avoid that trap, and Aafia's brother, Ali, offered an alternative. Ali himself had gone to university in the United States and was now working as an architect in Houston. Aafia could live with him and attend the University of Houston, a state college with reasonable fees and many students from Pakistan.

Other religious Pakistani families might have balked at sending an unmarried daughter to the United States. But Ismat often reminded listeners that the Quran commanded women, as well as men, to "seek knowledge, even if it takes you to China." Ismat knew that one reason simple Pakistanis looked up to Bhutto was her degrees from Harvard and Oxford. If Aafia could be armed with similar prestige, she might set an example for a new type of modern Muslim woman—not a corrupt princess like Benazir Bhutto but a true mujahida, after the model of the Prophet Muhammad's wives. The Siddiquis decided to send her to Houston.

Four

Asha loathed Eastleigh from the start. Hirsi had installed her and the three children in a concrete two-bedroom flat near the busy Juju Road, with its shoddy little bars and gambling halls. Asha had nothing but contempt for the Christians and pagans who made up most of Kenya's population, and she feared the impact of Eastleigh's boozing and prostitution on her children.

Kenya was tacitly supporting Somalia's opposition groups, including Hirsi's SSDF, and the United Nations High Commissioner for Refugees gave the Magan family official refugee status. Hirsi wanted all three children to go to the Muslim Girls Secondary School, which allowed boys to attend through the primary grades, and UNHCR agreed to pay their tuition. But only the boy, Mahad, passed the exam. Ayaan and Haweya had to go to the local Kenyan primary school on Juju Road.

Ayaan was ten and started in the fourth grade. Her formal education had been sketchy until then, and she would never make up for what she'd missed in math. But she and her siblings quickly learned English, the lingua franca of educated Kenyans and Somalis. English opened a world of reading for her and Haweya. Ayaan's first book was *Chicken Licken*. From there, she moved on to fairy tales, detective stories, and Nancy Drew mysteries. Asha couldn't afford to buy them books, so Ayaan and her friends passed whatever books they found from hand to hand. Often pages would be torn out, and Ayaan recalled later that she and Haweya would go into bookstores, find new copies of the books, and stand there surreptitiously reading the pages they'd missed.

Her mother tried to teach her children the traditional skills of memorizing and composing Somali verse. All three of them had inherited their father's phenomenal memory. Relatives later recalled that Haweya could hear a poem just once and know it by heart, making her the quickest of the bunch. But Ayaan could recite a poem after reading it once, and Mahad could recite it after reading it twice. Yet urban Kenya was far from the world of camels and deserts, and Asha found it hard to keep them interested in Somali poetry.

Mahad could do well in school when he made the effort. Their mother wanted him to succeed. "Reach for the stars!" she told him. But she had only the vaguest notion of how one excelled in school. Her ambitions for the boy were traditionally Somali. He should be a warrior, a leader of men, a prince of the clan. He should conquer unbelievers and free Somalia from oppression. She impressed upon all three children the Somali lessons of always being suspicious and ready to fight. She even sent Ayaan out on "fighting practice." With a female cousin as her coach, Ayaan learned to bite, hit, and scratch an opponent. She also learned how to trick and deceive one, as by pretending to apologize and then hitting back. She was encouraged to pick fights with classmates. If she won, she was surrounded by cheering relatives. If she lost, her coach would hit and criticize her.

But Somalia's confrontational methods, which could mean survival in the desert, backfired at school in Kenya. After a disagreement with a teacher, Ayaan's brother, Mahad, set fire to his primary school. He was behaving as he had been taught, but it got him expelled. Later he scored highly enough on a national exam to win a scholarship to the Starehe Boys Centre & School, a British school that was one of the best in Kenya. Yet he was already on the road to trouble.

Ayaan's father had the authority and knowledge of schools and urban life that her mother lacked. Asha wanted her husband to stay and help raise their children, especially Mahad. But Hirsi would not leave the SSDF, and he kept going back to Addis Ababa, returning to see the family only on short visits. The group's new leader belonged to Hirsi's own subclan, and he gave Ayaan's father the task of broadcasting anti–Siad Barre invective in an hour-long nightly program on the SSDF's radio station, which was known as Radio Kulmis, or Radio Unity.

In January 1983, Hirsi arranged for his family to rent a large house in a nearby but more affluent area called Kariokor. The new house had a kitchen, a big living room, three upstairs bedrooms used by Asha and the children (Ayaan and Haweya shared a room), and a downstairs bedroom with a separate toilet for Asha's mother, as well as a garden large enough for the children to play badminton in. By the standards of Eastleigh the house was grand; by the standards of the Somali desert, it was positively palatial. It stood just across the street from a sports field and around the corner from the home of Jinni Boqor, a Somali businessman from Hirsi's Osman Mahamud lineage who agreed to take care of Asha and the children while their father was away.

"It was the ideal home," Mahad said. "Easily maintained, close to town, close to schools and to the city center." The house even included a dining table with matching chairs. These were novelties for Asha and the children, whose only experience of furniture at home had been Somali stools and sleeping mats.

Hirsi was still at loggerheads with his son, and the tension made him and Asha quarrel. One night Asha smashed the dining table to pieces. Later she told Hirsi not to come back. So he returned to Ethiopia when Ayaan was twelve, and he didn't reappear in Eastleigh for ten years.

He kept sending Asha money through Jinni Boqor, and Jinni's nephew Guled Ahmed Yusuf claims that Ayaan never lacked material things. "She was given a lot of love," Guled said. "The SSDF was taking care of her and her brother and sister because her father was a freedom fighter and we all supported the cause." But soon thirteen-year-old Ayaan and her siblings learned that Hirsi had taken a new wife in Ethiopia and fathered another daughter. Ayaan says her mother retreated into angry depression: "She began to beat us for the slightest misdemeanor, grabbing our hair, hitting us until she couldn't lift her hand anymore." Mahad's memory of his mother is different, but he agrees that "as a family, we had broken up." Mahad began skipping school so much that he got expelled. Ayaan later told a reporter that from the age of thirteen to twenty she was "angry at everyone and everything."

After Ayaan and Haweya finished primary school, they were accepted at the Muslim Girls Secondary School. Ayaan was fourteen. Founded by ethnic Indian Muslims in the 1930s, the school was an oasis of serenity in the middle of Eastleigh's mayhem. It occupies stone buildings around a neatly trimmed lawn shaded by yellow flowering trees, all surrounded by a wall. The buildings are painted with maxims from the Quran, such as "The best person is the one who benefits others," "Allah is not merciful to him who is not merciful to others," and "Do not hate one another."

At home, though, the situation was deteriorating. Ayaan has written that her mother and grandmother had no concept of adolescence. In the nomadic world of their youth, people were forced to become adults by the time they were fifteen or so. But Asha's children were in school, an alien world to her. By the time Hirsi left and the children were old enough to evade their mother's beatings, Asha's authority had vanished.

Fifteen-year-old Mahad began drinking in Eastleigh's bars. Haweya dropped out of Muslim Girls and started wearing short skirts and hanging out in afternoon discos. Even Ayaan began sneaking forbidden kisses with a friend of her brother. Terrified that Haweya was going to shame the family, Asha enlisted Mahad to discipline the girl. He would haul Haweya out of bars, tie her up, and beat her. "Sometimes in those teenage years, the house would almost explode with the rage it contained," Ayaan later wrote. To other Somalis, the Magan teenagers were simply running wild. They got a reputation for being brilliant but also stubborn and disobedient. Ayaan says that Haweya "made friends but always ended up fighting with them." An uncle told me that that was true of all Asha's children. "This is a genius family," the uncle said, "very intelligent. But remember, genius is very close to madness."

Ayaan and Haweya still loved to read. From Nancy Drew they moved on to Charles Dickens and Fyodor Dostoyevsky, but they also read Jacqueline Susann, Barbara Cartland, and Harlequin romances. "What we learned was that white people were always having these wonderful adventures that we couldn't have, either because we weren't allowed or because we couldn't afford to," Ayaan later said. If their mother had known they were reading such racy stories, she surely wouldn't have approved. Once, when Ayaan made fun of her Quran teacher, the teacher and Asha beat her so badly that she ended up in the hospital. Haweya was even more rebellious. When Hirsi stopped sending money for a while and Asha was evicted from the Kariokor house, she sent Haweya and Mahad to live with relatives in Somalia. Ayaan stayed with her mother and grandmother in a small apartment on Park Road.

A new teacher of Islamic studies arrived at Muslim Girls. She was Sister Aziza, the product of a new Saudi school for female religious teachers. She was a pretty woman and seemed very kind, and she talked about Islam in a way that Ayaan hadn't heard before. Sister Aziza said that Islam wasn't just a religion—it was a blueprint for life, and if a girl wanted to be a real Muslim she had to follow it down to the last detail.

Ayaan, now sixteen, had never been especially religious, though Nairobi swarmed with preachers of every type. Muslim or not, most Africans believed in the occult. For 30 Kenyan shillings you could buy a pamphlet that described how to discover devil worshippers. Sister Aziza naturally opposed all that, and she invited Ayaan and some other girls to meet after school at a community center across the road, and at her house. There she taught them about "true Islam."

Following Sister Aziza's example, Ayaan began praying five times a day, paying careful attention to the way in which she prayed. She experimented with a head scarf and later with a long black cloak like the one Sister Aziza had come back from Saudi Arabia wearing. Nowadays Somali girls who don't swathe themselves in such garb are liable to be harassed or worse, but Ayaan was one of the first women in Nairobi to wear one. She later wrote that "it sent a message of superiority: I was the one true Muslim. All those other little girls with their white head scarves were children, hypocrites. I was the star of God."

Spiritually, Islam didn't do much for Ayaan. She once told an interviewer that she had never felt exalted by prayer. "I never reached a transcendental state; there was no inner light." But as a path to power and glory it had an immediate appeal.

Sister Aziza told Ayaan and her classmates that Muslims were obliged to wage jihad. Jihad, she told them, had many meanings. It meant the struggle within a person to submit to Allah's will, and it meant defending Muslims against unbelievers. She showed the girls gruesome pictures of Muslims being killed and tortured in Kashmir, Afghanistan, and other dangerous places. She told Ayaan and her classmates that a cabal of Jews, Christians, and other unbelievers had done those things to the Muslims. She said the same "Zionist-Crusader" conspiracy had worked for centuries to weaken Islam. To regain its rightful place as the one true religion, Muslims needed to restore sharia law and re-create the caliphate.

Ayaan had never met a Jew; she barely knew any white people. Now, in high school, Sister Aziza encouraged her to hate Jews. "Suddenly we hated Israel with a passion. We didn't even know where Israel was. I was 16, and I had never seen an Israeli, but we hated them because it was 'Muslim' to hate them." She has often said how deeply the message sank in. "I must confess to a deep emotional hatred of Jews that I felt as a 15-, 16-, 17-year-old living in Kenya. You almost can't help it. You become part of something bigger." Hatred became the fire that fueled her religious fervor. "It was when I was most devout that I was most full of hate," she later told *The Spectator.*

Sister Aziza's classes were only one instance of the way political Islam, stirred up in Saudi Arabia and elsewhere, was beginning to be felt in other countries. The Muslim Brotherhood, or al-Ittihad al-Islami, as its Somali branch was called, had already reached Eastleigh in the person of a man named Boqol Sawm, a gaunt Somali preacher who, like Sister Aziza, had been given a scholarship to study in Saudi Arabia. Ayaan began attending lectures sponsored by the Brotherhood at the community center near her school. Boys and girls sat separately on folding chairs or on factory-made Persian rugs. Very solemnly they discussed the law that God had laid down for them in the Quran and the Sunna. But Ayaan never became a true believer. For one thing, she was too interested in boys. Even at the height of her infatuation with Sister Aziza and the Brotherhood, she still slipped away with her brother's Kenyan friend. And, after Haweya returned from Somalia and started cracking jokes about her veil, Ayaan's zeal began to fade.

One of the last events she attended at the community center took place in 1989. Salman Rushdie, a British author of Indian Muslim descent, had satirized the life of the Prophet in his novel *The Satanic Verses*, and all over the Islamic world politicians were vying to show their commitment to Islam by denouncing Rushdie. In Iran, the Ayatollah Khomeini issued a fatwa, or religious ruling, that required Muslims to kill the writer. Sister Aziza invited Ayaan to join a group that planned to burn *The Satanic Verses* outside the community center. Although Ayaan went along, the book burning failed to move her. She didn't doubt that Rushdie deserved to die, but the small crowd and the way the damp book smoldered struck her as pitiful.

Ayaan finished high school in 1988. Her scores were too low to qualify for the A level exams required for university, but she was very pretty, with creamy brown skin and her father's sparkling eyes and narrow forehead.

Haweya talked her into training to become a secretary. The Valley Secretarial College was several bus rides away from Eastleigh, in Kilimani, a smart section of villas and hotels favored by Westerners. Watching the European and U.S. diplomats and aid workers who zipped into and out of Kilimani's shopping centers and restaurants in their four-wheel-drive vehicles as she trudged along on foot toward her bus gave Ayaan a window into a Western lifestyle that she had read about and seen in movies.

Very soon, though, another bright future seemed possible in Somalia.

The waning of the Cold War meant that the United States felt free to withdraw its long support from Siad Barre, which left him unable to pay his soldiers. Several important clans in northern Somalia, meanwhile, joined Hirsi's SSDF in rising up against the dictator. When Ayaan and Haweya finished their secretarial course in the spring of 1990, Asha and the clan's elders agreed that they should join their brother, Mahad, in Somalia's capital and look for jobs.

The move seemed tantalizing. If their father and his rebel group succeeded in overthrowing Somalia's government, the girls wouldn't need to work. They'd be princesses.

Five

It was snowing when seventeen-year-old Aafia arrived in Houston at the end of 1989, a freak event that seemed to illustrate the sheer strangeness of her new surroundings. Not that Aafia didn't know about the United States. Ever since she could remember, the arrogant superpower had loomed, interfering in Pakistani politics and luring Muslims off the straight path. One lament of religious leaders such as Grand Mufti Muhammad Rafi Usmani was that so many ambitious Pakistanis wanted to go there. The United States might be the Great Satan, but having a foothold in either America or the United Kingdom virtually defined membership in Pakistan's achieving middle class.

Aafia's architect brother, Ali—a trim, quiet man with a neat beard who in the United States went by his first name, Muhammad—had become a pillar of Houston's 50,000-strong Muslim community since he'd arrived twelve years earlier. By the time Aafia started classes, Ali was busy designing a huge new mosque for the Islamic Society of Greater Houston.

Pakistani and Indian immigrants dominated the Islamic Society, which was known for its strict adherence to the same Hanafi school of Islamic law espoused by the Deobandis. They were also numerous on the 550-acre campus of the University of Houston, where Aafia started classes in the spring semester of 1990. Aafia wanted to study political science, but her parents insisted that she enroll in the premed program. Like most UH students, she commuted to classes, in her case from Ali's apartment.

Houston's humid climate and flat brown landscape weren't unlike

Karachi's, but other things took getting used to: the shameless mingling of the sexes, the sinful consumption of alcohol, the forbidden scenes blaring from TV sets even in public places—and, above all, the careless wealth. The average American income was forty times higher than the average Pakistani income. The lack of poverty also made it very costly to hire servants, which meant that American women had to do chores that middle-class Pakistani women didn't. Aafia had to learn how to cook, clean, and drive a car.

Several other Siddiqui relatives lived in Houston. All were aspiring professionals—earnest, hardworking, upwardly mobile. One of her brother's American friends, who felt he knew the local Siddiquis well, said they reminded him of Victorians. "Think of *Mary Poppins* and throw in a few headscarves," he wrote years later in an e-mail to the Human Rights Commission of Pakistan that appeared on Web sites supporting Aafia. Aafia didn't drink, she didn't dance, and heaven forbid that she should date. She read no novels, avoided movies, and stayed away from television except for the news. Ali's American friend said she wouldn't have it any other way: "Her interests were pretty much limited to her schoolwork and religion." The friend saw her roughly once a week at her brother's house. Her conversation usually centered on Islam. "The living and vibrant Islam she talked about, the Islam of mercy and redemption, the Islam of forgiveness and love, sounded very much like the Catholicism that my mother talks about," said the friend, who identified himself only as Andrew.

Her only extracurricular activity was to join the university's branch of the Muslim Students Association of the U.S. and Canada. Then, as now, the Muslim Students Association was the largest such student group in the world. Students from the Muslim Brotherhood had founded it, with Saudi money, at the University of Illinois at Urbana-Champaign in 1963. The University of Houston had opened an early chapter in the 1970s. It was dominated by Islamists who argued that the Muslim world's nation-states were for the most part illegitimate and that their former colonizers manipulated their governments in ways that kept the *ummah* weak and divided.

Halfway through Aafia's first year in Houston, a crisis struck that seemed to prove them right. On August 2, 1990, Iraq's president, Saddam Hussein, invaded Kuwait. Within days, the United States dispatched troops to help defend neighboring Saudi Arabia. In November, the UN Security Council authorized Washington and its allies to attack Iraq if Saddam refused to withdraw from Kuwait. Saddam refused, and the United States commenced Operation Desert Storm on January 16, 1991, a day after the UN deadline expired. Soon a ground assault was launched—from Saudi Arabia—and by February Saddam's troops were in full retreat. Some were strafed and bombed as they drove the choked "Highway of Death" that led from Kuwait to Iraq. By April, the United States and its allies had won.

The Persian Gulf War was the first U.S. war to be covered on a twenty-four-hour television-news cycle, and Aafia watched as it unfolded. Before the war started, many Americans feared getting bogged down in another Vietnam. Saddam promised the United States and its allies "the mother of all battles," and there was much cautious talk about the need for the U.S. government to gain international approval and to keep the war focused on limited objectives. When the bombing of Baghdad began, Americans gathered around their TV sets, listening apprehensively to the sound of sirens. But as the pyrotechnics continued and few U.S. troops were killed, the televised war took on the aspect of a sporting event, complete with instant replays.

For Aafia and her fellow worshippers at Houston's Islamic Society, the spectacle was unbearable. Many hated the secular dictator Saddam Hussein, but landing U.S. troops in Saudi Arabia struck them as a naked grab for the region's oil. They also felt the Kuwaitis and the Saudis had violated Islam by inviting Western troops to protect them. They wished Muslims had been able to settle the conflict among themselves. Under the rule of *al wala' wal bara'*, or "love and hate in the way of Allah," Muslims were discouraged from befriending Christians and Jews and were never supposed to side with Christians and Jews against other Muslims.

The prayer leader at the Islamic Society attributed the crisis to Muslims' lack of faith. "The lands of the Muslims are splintered into small states," he sadly told his congregation, "fighting Allah and fighting each other and seeking protection from their enemies."

When some American reporters visited the society, days before the bombing of Baghdad, to ask members how they felt, angry men told them to leave. In Pakistan, the army chief of staff, Lieutenant General Mirza Aslam Beg (whose brother lived next door to the Siddiquis in Karachi) denounced the allied attack on Iraq as part of a "Zionist strategy" to undermine Islam. Many Muslims in Houston agreed. After the war ended, President George H. W. Bush gave a speech, on September 11, 1991, describing the peace as a chance to create "a new world order—a world where the rule of law, not the rule of the jungle, governs the conduct of nations." To some Muslims, the term "new world order" sounded suspiciously like the world government that some clerics saw as a sign of the Dajjal, or Antichrist, who Islamic eschatologists say will rule the earth before Jesus Christ returns to kill him and usher in a reign of peace. (Muslims regard Jesus Christ as a prophet, like the prophets of the Old Testament.)

Needless to say, Aafia didn't join the celebration that drew 300,000 Houstonians downtown during the last weekend of May 1991 to welcome home the soldiers of Operation Desert Storm. She already knew she wouldn't stay much longer in Houston. She had made straight As her first year, and she came close to winning a national prize for an essay she wrote titled "How America's Intercultural Attitudes Shape a Multicultural World." The University of Houston wasn't challenging enough for her. After much prayer and discussion with her mother, Aafia had set her sights on something higher.

The Siddiquis' spiritual guide, Mufti Muhammad Taqi Usmani, wrote that mastering Western science and technology was for Muslims "the greatest need of our time." The Massachusetts Institute of Technology seemed the very citadel of that kind of learning. Aafia applied for a transfer, and, to the delight of her family, MIT not only accepted her but offered her a scholarship.

The Siddiquis felt that Aafia had been offered a chance too good to be missed. And so, in the fall of 1991, she packed her bags and moved from Houston, Texas, to Cambridge, Massachusetts.

Six

Somalia in the spring of 1990 did not prove to be the refuge Ayaan had hoped it would.

She and Haweya went to stay with their father's first wife, Maryan Farah Warsame, and Maryan's two daughters, Arro and Ijaabo. As the mother of their half sisters, Maryan was considered their closest adult relative. The three women lived in a large white villa in Mogadishu's fashionable Casa Popolare district. Maryan treated Ayaan and Haweya with perfect courtesy, and Arro and Ijaabo welcomed them as sisters. But Ayaan found herself so jealous of Maryan and her daughters that she couldn't stand being in the same house.

In the twelve years since Asha had gone to Saudi Arabia with the children, Maryan had become one of the most influential and respected women in Somalia. She ran the department in the Ministry of Education that managed Somalia's Academy of Sciences and Arts; her group financed and published research in Somali poetry, music, and oral history. She was the foreign secretary of the Somali Women's Democratic Organization, and she represented Somali women at seminars and international conferences on women's issues. Since 1984, she had also served as one of only seven women in Somalia's 177-member Parliament.

The contrast between her purposeful life and the aimless, self-pitying life that Asha led in Nairobi was extreme. Ayaan's mother had to beg Hirsi's relatives for money; Maryan had a paying job. Asha and her mother shared a walk-up flat with a goat; Maryan had decorated her villa with imported Western furniture. Asha quarreled with everyone, while the elegant Maryan was admired even by the powerful men of her clan. Most galling of all, both of Maryan's daughters were attending university, whereas Ayaan had barely graduated from high school, and Haweya and Mahad had dropped out. Ayaan wrote in her autobiography that the unspoken hurt and envy made her feel tense whenever Maryan was around. "I always felt there was a crosscurrent of something we weren't supposed to feel, let alone voice."

Maryan's twenty-five-year-old daughter, Arro, was a top medical student at Somali National University, where more than a quarter of the students were women. Ayaan had always felt that, compared with her brother and sister, she herself was most like their father. But Arro looked like him, too, and she radiated his self-assurance. Arro was strikingly beautiful and took a keen interest in clothes. She had a large collection of pastel *direh*s, the sheer Somali dress worn over a half-slip and brassiere, and she wore her outfits with matching high heels. She liked Italian clothes, too, and she hoped to transfer to an Italian university. The cheap black nylon veil that had made Ayaan feel important in Nairobi failed to impress the stylish Arro.

"Our relationship was always strained," Ayaan later said of Arro. "That she was from another mother is in itself a source of tension: polygamy leads to enormous jealousy."

Arro's younger sister was more like the girls Ayaan knew at home in Nairobi. Seventeen-year-old Ijaabo liked the Brotherhood. She wore the all-concealing *jilbab* gown and was about to start classes at a Somali university where the Muslim Brothers exerted great influence. She saw it as her religious duty to show her newfound half sisters affection. Ayaan found her sweetness cloying and false.

She would have liked to join their father in the coastal town of Eyl, where the SSDF had set up its own administration in their clan's historic territory. But it was too dangerous. The civil war wasn't going as the rebels had planned. Rather than surrender to the SSDF and its allies, Siad Barre's army seemed to be dissolving. Soldiers from southern clans such as the Hawiye were forming their own clan militias and attacking the Darood.

Ayaan struck up a relationship with a young imam, then broke it off. "I was violating all the codes." She could belong in Somalia, as she hadn't in Kenya and other places where she had lived, but there was a price to pay for belonging. "Everyone was involved in everyone else's business. The complete lack of privacy, of individual space, and the social control were suffocating."

She and Haweya left Maryan's house to move in with an aunt on their mother's side of the family. This aunt was the director of Digfeer Hospital, where Ayaan had been born, and she found both sisters jobs as secretaries with the United Nations. Ayaan's new position was with a small office of the UN Development Program, where her boss, "a rather bewildered Englishman," gave Ayaan her first picture of Western bafflement in the Third World. Despite the warfare creeping ever closer, the Englishman was helping the government lay down rural telephone lines. He spoke no Somali, and Ayaan ended up translating for him. He couldn't understand why the Somalis kept tearing up his phone lines and selling them. Ayaan saw him as timid and unwilling to assert his authority.

Order in the capital started breaking down. As President Siad Barre's fellow Marehan clansmen came under attack in the countryside, they poured into Mogadishu looking for safety. Maryan, being a successful Marehan, was expected to house her refugee kinsmen. But it was getting dangerous to be Marehan even in Mogadishu, and Maryan's relatives brought machine guns with them and set them up outside her villa.

Some Somalis thought about getting out. Somalia was so poor that even before the civil war, thousands of Somalis drowned each year trying to reach Yemen in small boats hoping to find jobs in neighboring Saudi Arabia. The ultimate dream destinations, however, were Europe and the United States. Everyone had seen pictures of the Westerners' beautiful houses and cars.

Yet the West was unreachable for all but a handful of the richest and luckiest Africans. Western countries granted visas only to those who had scholarships, guaranteed jobs, or large overseas bank accounts. Ayaan's half sister Arro said she would get a visa through her university to study medicine in Italy. For Ayaan and Haweya, the doors to the Western paradise seemed closed.

Then one day Ayaan went to visit her mother's stepsister, Khadija. Khadija introduced her to a young man. Ayaan writes in her autobiography that he was her first cousin, the son of her mother's half brother Muhammad. The young man himself, Mohamud Mohamed Artan, denies that relationship. But, cousin or not, young Mohamud had discovered a promising route out of Africa.

He was two years older than Ayaan, and he had received a scholarship to study medicine in Russia. Many elite Somalis had been granted such scholarships during the Siad Barre years, but lately they had become more valuable. Ayaan wrote that Mohamud was "utterly gorgeous, the malest man I'd ever seen," and that she fell in love with him.

Mohamud's free pass to Russia offered him a route to the West via Finland. During the Cold War, Finland had established a rule that anyone who made it out of the Soviet Union into Finland would receive political asylum. Now the Iron Curtain was gone and the Soviet Union was about to dissolve, but the Finnish rule on automatic asylum remained in force. Somalis discovered that if they could get to Russia and make their way to Finland, they would automatically have the right to stay—along with free health care, free education, and a monthly stipend.

Years later, after Mohamud became an emergency room doctor in a hospital outside Helsinki, he recalled the allure of the West for Somalis of his generation. "All the things they like and see—the cars, the beautiful clothes, everything that is very good—are in the West. Everyone wanted to go there."

Ayaan wrote that Mohamud asked her to marry him and she agreed. But since he was leaving soon, and there wasn't time to get her father's permission, they decided to enter a secret marriage. A distant cousin named Ali Wersengeli and another man whom Ayaan didn't know were the only witnesses to the ceremony, though she says she and Mohamud had their picture taken after an imam pronounced them man and wife. Somalis disapprove of such marriages, especially in the case of virgins, who ought to be given away by their fathers. But secret marriages aren't uncommon. "As for my father's family," Ayaan wrote, "they wouldn't really like it, but nobody could really oppose a marriage between maternal cousins."

According to Ayaan, she and Mohamud spent one night together in a cheap motel. Mohamud, for his part, has told different stories. Once he told the Finnish reporter Juha-Pekka Tikka that there was more to their relationship than that. Later Mohamud told me that he and Ayaan had never married at all and she had made the whole story up. Ayaan wrote that losing her virginity was painful and disgusting, and that Mohamud dropped her off in the morning at her great-aunt Khadija's house and left for Russia the next day. She washed and prayed that she wasn't pregnant. She has said that the only people she told about her marriage were her sister and Khadija.

Her father's rebel group, meanwhile, was losing its bid to take over the country. The SSDF had weakened Siad Barre, but it couldn't take the capital. Hirsi's people saw themselves as members of the Osman Mahamud lineage and of the Majerteen subclan and thus as distinct from Siad Barre's Marehan subclan. But the rival Hawiye clan viewed both President Siad Barre *and* the Majerteen rebels as fellow members of the same big Darood clan. One or another Darood group had ruled the country since independence, and the Hawiye had had enough.

Unpaid Hawiye soldiers began robbing and killing unprotected Darood civilians on the streets of Mogadishu. One night Ayaan and Haweya were held up by a man with a knife; they got away by pretending to be members of another clan. The United Nations decided to close its offices in Mogadishu. Ayaan's boss was evacuated, and she lost her job.

Asha, in Nairobi, heard that Darood girls were being raped, and she begged her children to come home to Kenya. Their brother raised clan money for Ayaan and Haweya to ride out on the back of a pickup truck. He also found a cousin to escort them. They left in November 1990, taking a roundabout route to avoid the Hawiye. Ayaan didn't feel safe until they had crossed into Kenya. When they reached Nairobi, Asha was so glad to see them that Ayaan didn't want to spoil her mother's rare good mood, so she said nothing about her secret marriage.

Other Darood clansmen streamed out of Somalia by the tens of thousands, and soon Hawiye militias were chasing not just the Darood in the capital but also those who lived in the fertile Shabelle valley, where much of the country's food grew. The Darood exodus would strip the country of much of its educated class, and it came to a head on January 27, 1991, when Siad Barre, who had ruled Somalia since Ayaan was born, landed in Nairobi. After all the years that Ayaan's father had opposed him, Somalia's strongman ended up as another Darood refugee like Hirsi and his family.

Seven

Aafia had requested a room at McCormick Hall. The luxurious university tower overlooking the Charles River was MIT's only all-female dormitory. Her first semester whizzed by in a blur. Hoping to get quickly beyond her premed requirements (her parents were still insisting that she become a doctor), she had signed up for nine science and math courses, and she passed them all splendidly. But in the spring she reduced her load to three classes, including one on her favorite subject, Asian religions. Seemingly reserved, she impressed professors and fellow students alike as pleasant, hardworking, and superbly organized.

Conservative Christian and Orthodox Jewish women also sought out McCormick Hall, but Aafia formed no close friendships with them. Mindful of representing Islam, she was invariably polite and helpful to non-Muslims—and alert to any chance of making a convert, an act that she and other pious Muslims believed was sure to gain a believer a rich reward in paradise. Otherwise she kept her distance.

She often privately reminded other Muslims of the Quranic verse that says, "Let not the believers take unbelievers for their friends." The Americans she met liked her, though they never felt they knew her well. "She was religious, but that wasn't unusual at McCormick," one former resident told *Boston Magazine* later. Marnie Biando, who worked at McCormick's front desk, remembered Aafia as unassertive: "She was just nice and soft-spoken."

Her mother's daughter, Aafia gravitated toward volunteer work.

At MIT's Public Service Center she helped clean up public playgrounds. As a junior she received a $1,200 fellowship to work forty hours a week setting up science fairs and "discovery clubs" for a poor elementary school. She even won the center's award for public service—twice. ("They couldn't award me any more, because two times was the limit for one person," she recalled.) She was so good with computers that other residents and even the staff at McCormick turned to her for help in navigating the emerging World Wide Web, and she wrote several articles showing fellow students how to download free programs from the Internet.

In Cambridge as in Houston, though, most of her nonacademic activities revolved around the Muslim Students Association. One MSA member from neighboring Wellesley College wrote later that she became "the heart behind the MSA of Greater Boston."

On behalf of MIT's MSA, Aafia helped persuade the university to provide a separate prayer room for Muslim women next door to McCormick at Ashdown House. She also asked the cafeteria to provide a wider array of halal food. (Until then, Muslim students had been eating from the kosher menu.) She organized a Muslim study group to meet in the dorm's penthouse conference room, with its views of the Boston skyline. By the time she had finished, the MSA was recommending McCormick Hall to incoming Muslims as a comfortable environment that also "caters to your needs as a Muslim woman."

Aafia met a fellow Deobandi in the MSA who became a close friend. A slender, delicate-looking Muslim of Indian descent who was raised in Zimbabwe, Suheil Laher was an engineering student so serious about his religion that he wanted to become a Deobandi *alim*, or scholar. The MSA's executive board invited Aafia and Laher to contribute to a package of materials (which the national organization published in 1996, a year after she graduated) on how to start a new MSA chapter.

Suheil Laher described how new MSA chapters could run Friday prayers. One good topic for preaching was "supporting our suffering and persecuted Muslim brothers and sisters in other parts of the world (jihad)."

Aafia's article dealt with setting up a *dawah* or "preaching" table inviting people to learn more about Islam: "First make sure the intention for this effort is only to please Allah," she wrote. "We need to ask ourselves this question over and over again. While we may have many shortcomings, still, the power of *dua* [prayer] is great. Imagine our humble, but sincere daw'ah effort turning into a major daw'ah movement in this country! Just imagine it! And us, reaping the reward of everyone who accepts Islam through this movement, through years to come. . . . Think and plan big: Allah's powers are not to be underestimated."

She proposed making the table look attractive. The best lure, she said, would be free English translations of the Quran. Students could find places on the Internet that would mail them *dawah* literature and translations of the Quran to give away. A Muslim sitting behind the table should always "use *hikmah* (wisdom), be cheerful and friendly, and never be rude or get upset at anyone." She conceded that the topics of "jihad and women in Islam" were the hardest to explain to non-Muslims. Yet she urged MSA members not to "water down" the divine teachings to suit Western sensibilities. "Our job as da'ees is only to honestly convey the message in the best manner using hikmah, but not changing the message in doing so. It is up to Allah, and not to us, to make people accept Islam."

When she first arrived at MIT, Aafia wore the ordinary Pakistani shalwar kameez—a tunic and loose trousers, often with a scarf tossed across her shoulders. But in time she adopted the long coat and nun-like veil favored by the Muslim Brotherhood.

More liberal Pakistani students steered clear of her and her tables. The figure of the "hijabi sister" who goes around instructing Muslim slackers wasn't as common then on campus as she is now, but the Pakistanis recognized the type. One man described Aafia as "well brought up, in the manner of Pakistani girls," but a "busybody." Another recalled Aafia and her friends as people who would stop

Muslim strangers and say, "Hello, brother." "They were the ones with scarves who used to get after us to come to the association meetings," he told the BBC years later. "I remember Aafia as being sweet, mildly irritating but harmless. You would run into her now and then distributing pamphlets." Some Muslim girls at McCormick found her more than irritating. "She was a maniac," one said, recalling how Aafia used to nag her to pray and wear a head scarf.

Eight

For the first time in a long time, Ayaan's mother, Asha, felt needed. Somalia had fallen violently apart, and by the spring of 1991 she had a dozen relatives camped on the cement floor of her small Nairobi apartment. Ayaan and her siblings were also in demand, especially for their precious Kenyan residence permits and knowledge of Swahili and English. In February, Ayaan impressed the clan when she and her brother, Mahad, extracted more than twenty relatives from a UNHCR border camp and drove them to Nairobi. Ayaan also made the rounds of jails, trying to free refugees who had been caught outside the camps without permits. "She was a sweet girl, nice and caring, and she was helping the people who came from Somalia," recalled Faduma Osman, a relation on Ayaan's father's side who got to know her during this crisis.

The Somali refugees soon doubled Eastleigh's population. Rents more than doubled, from 3,000 Kenyan shillings a month to 7,500. The new arrivals included former high government officials as well as canny merchants. Those people weren't about to hang around Kenya, dodging policemen. The trickle of Somalis bound for North America and Europe turned into a flood.

As the Refugee Convention of 1951 was interpreted during the Somali crisis, a nation violated international law if it returned refugees to a place where they had "a well-founded fear of being persecuted for reasons of race, religion, nationality, membership in a particular political group or political opinion." Displaced Somalis therefore learned that if they could set foot on Western European or

North American soil, they stood a good chance of receiving asylum. As in Finland, once there, they could legally send their children to school and collect welfare benefits. But since the only safe way to reach the West was by airplane, only the wealthiest Somalis could afford to try it at first.

The Somalis who obtained asylum sent money back to their relatives and clan militias. They also served as "anchors" for other family members, who then applied for visas and residence permits that were granted to reunite families. The exact rules varied by country; they took time to understand, and they shifted unpredictably. All over Eastleigh, though, Somalis began figuring them out.

The first problem was to obtain a passport and a visa. Somalia no longer had a government, much less a passport office, and Western countries had stopped giving Somalis visas because they seemed unlikely ever to go home. Only Somalis with foreign passports, especially Western ones, were truly free to travel. And so Africa's trapped Somalis began begging their overseas relatives to "lend" their passports to other family members of roughly the same age. Then, after the borrower reached his destination, he would discard the passport or mail it back to its owner and apply for asylum as a refugee.

What started as a kind of family charity soon became an industry. For a fee, overseas Somalis known as *mukhali*, or agents, would help their countrymen in Eastleigh get fraudulent passports and visas. The agents would direct them to countries likely to grant them asylum at any given moment. They would also advise their clients what they should tell officials, procuring intelligence on effective stories by paying other Somalis who sat in on immigration interviews as government translators. The total fee for an agent's help could range from $750 for the loan of a valid passport to $10,000 for a full-service trip to the West. "If you could raise enough money, usually with the help of one of your relatives already in one of these countries, then you belong to the lucky few who will have access to a life without hunger and with free health care and housing and the opportunity to smuggle in more of your relatives now in refugee camps or some other limbo land," Ayaan wrote later in her memoir, *Nomad*.

Many Somalis who arrived that way were in fact refugees under the rules of the 1951 Refugee Convention because they had no legal right to stay in Kenya and their lives would be at risk if they returned to Somalia. But their passage to the West was often greased with fraud. Studies would later show that, of the roughly 50,000 Somalis who applied successfully for asylum in Europe during the 1990s, fewer than 10 percent arrived legally, on their own travel documents, with proper visas. Of course the Somalis felt they had no other choice, and the rules and regulations of alien Western states meant nothing to them.

Ayaan lived in the thick of all this. With her fluent English and her secretarial skills, she helped her relatives with their paperwork. The ruling Boqor family of Ayaan's father's Osman Mahamud lineage had already established a branch in Canada, while other clansmen had settled in Europe, especially in the Netherlands, which was known to be lenient toward Somali asylum seekers. One Boqor relative whom Ayaan and her brother had rescued from the border camps was a woman named Fadumo. Fadumo had a sister who lived in Switzerland who got Fadumo and her children visas and tickets. Since the sister, however, knew that Switzerland almost never granted asylum to Somalis, she arranged for Fadumo and the children to fly to Switzerland via the Netherlands. When the plane landed at Amsterdam's Schiphol Airport, Fadumo got out and asked for asylum. The plan was obviously risky, but with coaching Fadumo pulled it off, and a week or so after she left Nairobi she sent word back that she and the children were in a Dutch refugee camp.

Ayaan, at that stage, may have had a plan of her own to reach Europe. She had learned that Mohamud had made it from Russia to Finland and successfully applied for asylum there. Finnish immigration records show that in 1991 Mohamud Mohamed Artan also applied for a residence permit for his wife, "Ayan Hersi Magan," born in 1969. That was the way Ayaan spelled her name when she lived in Kenya, and 1969 was the correct year of her birth.

Ayaan, or someone, signed the Finnish documents and sent them back to await a decision in Finland.

But perhaps Ayaan felt the Finnish route was taking too long. Or perhaps she became angry with Mohamud. She says in her autobiography that she got a letter from a blond Finnish girl who wanted to marry Mohamud herself, asking whether Mohamud and Ayaan were already married. Mohamud, on the other hand, told me he had never had a blond girlfriend or written such a letter—but then he also told me he had never married Ayaan. (Obviously, someone is lying, but what exactly happened between Ayaan and Mohamud is one of those mysteries that I, at least, have not been able to resolve.)

In any case, Ayaan said nothing to her father about being married when, after a decade away, Hirsi showed up in Nairobi in April 1991. Somalia's Hawiye clan had driven the Darood out of the important town of Kismayo, and Hirsi and the SSDF were forced to retreat. Ayaan's mother still couldn't forgive him for his years of neglect, but he stayed in her apartment anyway.

At first Ayaan and Haweya were delighted to have the old lion back, and the rest of the clan revered him. Then disappointment set in. Hirsi's wars had left him penniless. He had no money to pay the agents who were finding other important people tickets and visas to get to the West, and, according to Mahad and other relatives, Asha told Ayaan to stop dreaming about foreign travel and start studying for her A levels so she could get into the University of Nairobi.

Then Maryan, Ayaan's overachieving stepmother, turned up in Nairobi with her daughter Ijaabo. Ijaabo even came to stay in Asha's crowded apartment.

Ayaan's mother had given Hirsi the silent treatment in the months since his return. Fed up with the tension, Ayaan's father took Ijaabo and moved back in with Maryan. To Asha and her children, his decision felt like a public rejection. Ayaan was especially hurt. She had always felt she was her father's favorite; now he seemed to be siding with her half sisters against her.

In the midst of these dramas she met a twenty-seven-year-old Canadian named Osman Musse Quarre. As Ayaan tells it in *Infidel*, her father appeared at her mother's apartment in a jubilant mood at the end of January 1992. He told his daughter he had met a strapping young Canadian, "fed on North American beef," who was a member of their own clan. The Canadian, Osman, had come to Nairobi to rescue his relatives—but he was also looking for a wife, and he and Hirsi had met at the mosque. Ayaan says her father offered her to Osman as his bride, and that Osman accepted.

She also says she told her father that she didn't want to marry Osman. But Hirsi wouldn't listen, and the *nikhah*, or wedding ceremony, was set for the following Saturday.

Other family members remember things quite differently. Osman himself said years later that he and Ayaan met and liked each other and that afterward their fathers arranged their marriage. Faduma Osman, a relative who later settled in the Netherlands, tells a similar story in more detail: she says Ayaan told her she met Osman when he arrived in Nairobi on his way to the Utangu refugee camp in Mombasa to look for his relatives, and that Osman then returned home to Toronto; but later he returned to Nairobi (in Faduma's account) after their fathers gave them permission to marry.

Their fellow clansmen were thrilled that this helpful young woman should be rewarded with a handsome young husband who would take her to the West.

In Nairobi, only Ayaan's sister knew that she was already married. But Ayaan claims she had decided, after receiving the letter from the Finnish girl, that actually she wasn't married. She says she reasoned that since her father hadn't given her his permission, her marriage to Mohamud wasn't valid. Not everyone agreed, however. She says in her autobiography that their cousin Ali Wersengeli, who had witnessed the Mogadishu ceremony, heard the news that she was planning to marry someone else and traveled all the way from

Somalia to intervene. She says he showed up unannounced on her mother's doorstep and informed Asha that her daughter was already married to her own half brother's son.

What happened after that is even less clear. Ayaan says her brother, Mahad, demanded to know the truth. She says that she told her brother the story and he tore up her wedding certificate from Mogadishu and rushed to her father's apartment to tell him not to listen to Ali Wersengeli, who was trying to spoil Ayaan's good fortune. Perhaps Ayaan's brother saw the family's passage to North America about to go up in flames. "Mahad's goal now," Ayaan wrote in *Infidel*, "became preventing Ali Wersengeli from intervening before the *nikhah*, which was only four days away." She doesn't explain why, if she didn't want to marry Osman, she didn't simply tell her father that she was already married. Instead, she says, she lied to him and claimed there was nothing to Ali Wersengeli's story.

Ayaan's Somali relatives would later conclude that she had lied because she saw Osman as her ticket to the West and didn't want to lose him. But the psychological truth may be more complex. Ayaan would later confess, many times, to having a propensity to lie, especially to avoid one-on-one confrontations. She would say she "mastered the art of lying" to escape the beatings that were her punishment as a young girl for the slightest defiance. She would write as an adult that she had sworn off lying. Then later she would admit that her first instinct, still, was simply to tell anyone who confronted her what they wanted to hear. "I lie to get out of conflict situations rather than tell the truth," she would write when she was forty. "If a real estate agent shows me a rental, I'm embarrassed beyond words to say I don't like it. I invent ridiculous stories to explain my way out of this rather routine and obvious situation, then take the agent to an expensive lunch to apologize." If, at the age of forty, Ayaan was afraid to say no to a real estate agent, it must have been much harder to say no, at the age of twenty-two, to a father whose love she longed for and whose anger she feared.

Ayaan's brother, Mahad, disputes her story that their father pushed her to marry Osman. Mahad also says that he and his mother and sister disapproved of the marriage and that they didn't even attend the wedding. "I personally believe girls should not marry until they are self-reliant," he later told a Dutch reporter.

Faduma Osman says Ayaan arrived at her house on the morning of the wedding. Her girlfriends had gathered to paint her hands and feet with traditional henna wedding designs. Ayaan seemed very happy, and she told the gathering how she had met Osman. "She said that this boy," Faduma recalled, "she met him when he came to Nairobi to look for his family in the Utanga refugee camp. She said that he is her boyfriend, and he has come back from Canada to marry her."

After they had decorated the bride, Faduma says, the women all went to the house of Farah Goure, a clan businessman who had taken care of Ayaan and her family while her father was gone and whose place was big enough for a large party. As is customary in Somali weddings, there were two ceremonies, one for the men and another for the women. Faduma says the women's ceremony lasted from midday until about three in the afternoon, though she herself left around 2 p.m. She says it was a big clan affair with about a hundred guests. She congratulated Ayaan before she went home. "They had a buffet with different kinds of food. It was very nice."

But Faduma noticed that Ayaan's mother wasn't present. "They said she wasn't feeling well, something like that. I thought that maybe her mother wants her to stay in Kenya and go to university and work for the family. Or maybe she doesn't want to be with Ayaan's stepmother," Maryan. Of course, Faduma didn't know what Asha had just learned—that Ayaan was already married to her nephew.

Faduma's son Mahad was at the men's ceremony next door. "It was the traditional wedding," Mahad told me. "The bride was not present because the women have their own ceremony. One room is for women, and the other is for men." The men sat on the ground with the imam, Osman, and Ayaan's father. When the imam asked whether Ayaan agreed to the marriage, her father said she did, and the ceremony was over. "After that, the women started their dance, and it was going on until the night." The way Faduma's son heard it, "Her father didn't know the guy, but she came with him and said she wanted to marry him, and he gave her his blessing."

After the *nikhah*, Osman returned to Canada. Ayaan says that the plan was for them to have a final celebration in Canada before consummating their marriage and beginning their life together. Osman, on the other hand, has said they spent six days together "as man and wife" before he left for Toronto.

But the Canadian Embassy wouldn't give Ayaan a visa. Like everyone else in her family, Ayaan had a UNHCR document showing that she was a refugee with the legal right to live in Kenya. She therefore had no right to claim asylum in a third country, as refugees from Somalia's civil war were doing. Classifying Somalis like her as potential economic migrants, Canada and other Western countries were refusing to let them visit for fear they would stay.

Ayaan has never explained just how she got around those obstacles. She says her family decided she should go first to Germany, where they had relatives. Her new husband, Osman, sent the money for her ticket and expenses. She stopped in Ethiopia on the way and was due to continue on to Canada.

What's certain is that none of this was legal. The Canadian Embassy in Germany was no more likely than the one in Kenya to grant an entry visa to a Somali who was already a legal refugee in Kenya. If Ayaan had planned to enter Canada legally, she would have had to wait for Osman's request for reunification to grind its way through the Canadian bureaucracy—just as Mohamud's request was grinding its way through the Finnish bureaucracy.

More likely, Osman paid an agent to arrange for Ayaan to travel to Germany from Ethiopia. Once in Germany, she would have had to wait for the agent to find either another Somali with a passport willing to lend it to her or a false passport.

Whatever the exact plan was, Ayaan was poised to leave Africa. She says that she and Haweya were already plotting how she might leave Osman and run away to the United States. She wrote that her mother overheard the two sisters talking and burst into their room. Asha accused Ayaan of destroying her relationship with her brother, the father of the man Ayaan had married in Mogadishu, and she begged Ayaan to tell her father the truth about her secret marriage to her cousin Mohamud.

Ayaan says she planned to do exactly that, but when she went to see her father "my tongue stuck in my throat" and she left without saying anything. When she came home, she says, her mother begged her not to leave Kenya unless she planned to be a good wife to Osman.

She couldn't do that, either, Ayaan wrote. She says that is why her mother refused to say good-bye when she finally left for Ethiopia in July 1992.

Nine

Aafia spent the summer of 1992 in Pakistan. She had won a $5,000 Carroll L. Wilson Award from MIT's Entrepreneurship Center to write a paper called "Islamization in Pakistan and Its Effect on Women." Aafia thought Western criticisms of Islam's treatment of women were pure hypocrisy. It wasn't Islam that degraded women, she believed—it was Western capitalism.

The two largest Western human rights groups, Amnesty International and Human Rights Watch, had recently come out with a report condemning the Hudood Ordinances criminalizing sex outside marriage. Called "Double Jeopardy: Police Abuse of Women in Pakistan," the report drew largely on the work of Pakistani lawyers who had been fighting the Hudood laws for more than ten years. It argued that "the criminalization of adultery and fornication in Pakistan, when coupled with the discrimination against women in law and in practice, has created an extremely adverse and precarious situation for women, especially for women victims of rape."

Those laws had been written by the Siddiqui family's spiritual guide, Mufti Muhammad Taqi Usmani, and Aafia planned to defend them.

Strange as it may sound, some of her thinking was probably influenced by American feminism. In Cambridge she had attended Take Back the Night rallies at MIT and other colleges. She had listened, appalled but fascinated, as fellow students, often in tears, testified about what activists claimed was an epidemic of date rape on U.S. campuses. The organizers meant to encourage women to stand up to male sexual violence. But to Aafia the rallies confirmed the truth of what Islamists were saying: that by failing to segregate men and women and by creating a youth culture focused on romance and sex (inflamed by alcohol, besides), Western society had horribly endangered its young women.

MIT has never released the study that Aafia wrote, so it's impossible to know exactly what she said. But she later told the FBI that American men had taken advantage of the feminist movement to make women go out to work rather than taking care of their families. Muslim women, she said, were treated with more respect. She claimed she had written a book about all this and that she had begun by interviewing American women about how they had come to be homeless.

During her 1992 summer break, she had no trouble arranging interviews in Pakistan with the authors of the Hudood laws. The mufti and others were family friends, and they remembered her from childhood. They naturally applauded her approach to the subject. "I was impressed," said Ijaz ul-Haq, Zia's son and now a parliamentarian from Lahore. "She was a very intelligent girl." Ul-Haq had asked his deputy to help Aafia collect some statistics.

Ul-Haq described her as "a beautiful girl" with a "very charming face" and "fair complexion." She was "very religious-minded" and wore "a very sort of traditional dress and hijab. She was very keen regarding her studies. She just seemed like a bright and enlightened girl and keen to know and keen to learn. She seemed like a nice, innocent girl."

It's unclear what else Aafia did that summer in Pakistan. But since, within a few months of her return, she would begin volunteering for an Islamic charity implicated in the February 1993 bombing of the World Trade Center, it seems worth exploring the extraordinary ferment in Pakistan that ultimately led to the bombing.

Benazir Bhutto, hated by the Islamists and charged with corruption, had been ousted by Pakistan's military-religious complex the year after Aafia left for the United States. Bhutto's replacement after the 1990 elections was Nawaz Sharif, a relatively pliable Punjabi industrialist. As for Pakistan's powerful intelligence agency, the ISI, its new director was Lieutenant General Javed Nasir, a fervent lay Deobandi preacher. Nasir's vision of Pakistan, as the Pakistani scholar Hassan Abbas has written, "was that of an Islamic state that was obliged to help out Muslims in distress wherever they were."

Under Nasir, the ISI's efforts included secret military aid to Bosnian Muslims who opposed a brutal attempt by Serbian Christians to "cleanse" parts of the former Yugoslavia; secret training of Muslim separatists in the Philippines; secret deliveries of cash to Islamists in the former Soviet republics of Central Asia; and support for other restive Muslims in China's Xinjiang Province.

The evolving jihad also included "Arab Afghans" operating partly out of the Pakistani frontier city of Peshawar. These were Arabs, for the most part, who with U.S. and Pakistani help had fought in Afghanistan against the Soviets. By the early 1990s, with their main objective accomplished, they were casting about to enlarge their jihad against other unbelievers and oppressors of Muslims. One key figure in their plans was a wealthy Saudi named Osama bin Laden. He had helped establish an elaborate system of financing, arming, training, attacking, and propagandizing for jihad that would become known as al-Qaeda. The group also retained close ties with Pakistan's ISI.

Less famous than bin Laden, but of great future importance both to Aafia and to the bold attacks that followed over the next decade, were the members of a single, inbred Pakistani extended family known as the al-Baluchi. The al-Baluchi originally hailed from Baluchistan, but in the 1960s the family patriarch and his brother, both of whom were Deobandi preachers, moved the family to Kuwait. The most notorious member of the al-Baluchi is the 9/11 mastermind Khalid Sheikh Mohammed, widely known as KSM, but the first al-Baluchi plotter to reach the public eye was his nephew, the man known to history as Ramzi Yousef. It's still unclear how Aafia first encountered this sinister family, many members of whom had moved back to Pakistan in the 1980s to participate in the Afghan jihad against the Soviets. But around the time she was returning to school in Massachusetts, Ramzi Yousef arrived in the United States. His mission was to coordinate the first attack on the World Trade Center a few months later. His troops in that attack were recruited from the Al-Kifah Refugee Center on Atlantic Avenue in Brooklyn, an organization that was already widely known as the main recruiting office for jihad in the United States.

Al-Kifah also had a chapter in Boston. And soon after Aafia returned to MIT from Karachi, she began volunteering to work for it.

Ten

Ayaan had an uncle in Düsseldorf who was supposed to put her up when she arrived in Frankfurt in the summer of 1992. But after one night he sent her to stay with some other relatives in Bonn. Ayaan says she walked for hours in Bonn, just taking in a world that was new to her. Everything was so clean, so rich, so peaceful. She claims that the idea of running away came to her there. She says she wanted to be free. "I wanted to be a person, an individual, with a life of my own."

Her first thought was to make it to England. That's where most Somalis wanted to go. Thanks to her Kenyan education, she spoke fluent English and felt she already knew the country. But she says the son of her Somali hosts told her she would have to get a visa first. Staying in Germany wasn't an option because Germany wasn't accepting Somali applications for asylum that summer. Meanwhile, she knew her distant relation Fadumo and many other fellow clansmen had been granted asylum in the Netherlands. She decided to go there.

Ayaan had Fadumo's telephone number with her. She called and said she wanted to visit. Then she went down to the Bonn railway station and bought a ticket to Amsterdam.

On July 24, 1992, she arrived at Amsterdam's Central Station. She was twenty-two years old. Later she would call that day her real birthday. A cousin of Fadumo, Muddah Veerman, took her in for the night. Muddah lived in the nearby town of Volendam. Ayaan says she didn't tell Muddah anything about running away from her marriage; she just asked for advice on how to seek asylum.

Ayaan spent the weekend in Volendam and then went to see Fadumo in the eastern town of Almelo, two hours' drive away. Fadumo was now an interpreter for other Somalis at a center for asylum seekers there. She knew the ins and outs of the Dutch system. Ayaan later wrote that Fadumo and Muddah told her, "You had to go as quickly as possible [to a refugee center] and say that you were running away from the civil war."

The closest refugee center was about thirty miles away, in Zwolle. Ayaan found the place, but its facility was already filled with refugees. She took the bus to another center, in the town of Zeewolde, and checked into the center on July 27. While there, she talked with some Dutch volunteers from the Refugee Aid Center who explained how the process worked. She says they told her about the kinds of residence permits an asylum seeker could get. "A status" gave a person the rights of Dutch citizens, including the right to receive help finding a job and a place to live, as well as the right to bring family members into the country. "C status," on the other hand, allowed a person to stay in Holland, but one had to renew his or her residence permit every year and received no financial aid. To receive A status, an asylum seeker had to claim to be in extreme personal danger because of his or her political views, ethnicity, or religion. "If you just told them that you had terrible things happening in the country you came from, then you would get a C status, a humanitarian status," Ayaan said later by way of clarification.

She has never said in detail what she told the immigration service when she went for her first interview on August 6. She wrote in *Infidel* that she had concocted a tale based on the experiences of the real Somali refugees she had met in Kenya, plus her own experiences leaving Mogadishu in 1991. She also told the authorities that her name was "Ayaan Hirsi Ali" rather than "Ayan Hersi Magan"—Ali being her grandfather's name before he acquired the nickname Magan. She also claimed that her date of birth was November 13, 1967, rather than November 13, 1969, which would make her twenty-four rather than twenty-two.

If Ayaan didn't already know it, she would soon discover that very few Dutch people knew anything at all about Somalia. The first Somali refugees arrived in the country in 1984. That year there were ten of them. Even in 1991, fewer than 1,800 Somalis applied for asylum. But in 1992, the number shot up to 4,246. Somalia was in chaos. More important, perhaps, from the asylum seeker's viewpoint, the West was finally beginning to hear the news.

There were so many other competing tragedies at the end of the Cold War that it had taken a while for Somalia's to penetrate Western consciousness. But the same week she landed in Germany, UN secretary-general Boutros Boutros-Ghali angrily accused Europe and the United States of "fighting a rich man's war in Yugoslavia while not lifting a finger to save Somalia from disintegration." In the weeks to come, shrunken Somali babies and attacks on international relief workers appeared frequently on Dutch television. *Time* magazine's international edition, published the very week that Ayaan had her first immigration interview, reported, "For months, the mythical Four Horsemen of the Apocalypse—Conquest, Slaughter, Famine and Death—have run wild in Somalia. After 19 months of war and a long drought, 1.5 million of the country's estimated 6 million people face imminent starvation." Newspapers everywhere, including in Holland, reported that some 300,000 Somalis had died since the civil war had started.

Dutch immigration officials had only the dimmest grasp of the clan politics behind this suffering. They had no licensed Somali translators into Dutch and therefore conducted asylum interviews in English, with English-speaking Somalis such as Ayaan's relative Fadumo translating from Somali to English. Yet Somalis seemed to know what the Dutch wanted to hear. Nearly every Somali who applied for resettlement that summer received A-status asylum. A joke went around that all a Somali had to do to get A status was to say, "Ahh."

Ayaan herself hadn't witnessed any of the terrible violence and starvation that were consuming her homeland. But she, too, seems to have known what to say.

She stayed in Zeewolde for a few weeks and then learned she was being transferred to another, newly opened asylum center in Lunteren, a small town about forty miles southeast of Amsterdam. She would have her second and final interview there.

Lunteren was a deeply Protestant little place with cobbled streets and quaint thatched houses whose shutters had hourglasses painted on them. A retired Dutch army officer named Leo Louwé lived there, and Louwé had volunteered his services to the Lunteren refugee center. He met Ayaan shortly after she arrived. He liked her instantly. "She was a very lively girl, very open," Louwé said years later. It was Louwé's job to help asylum seekers prepare for their interviews. He would tell them what questions to expect and even accompany them to the meeting, so he could help if they had trouble explaining themselves. He could also serve as a witness if they needed to appeal a decision. Naturally, he was eager to help this young Somali woman who seemed somehow special.

But Ayaan said she didn't need any help. She appreciated Louwé's offer, but she planned to handle the interview on her own. Louwé explained that this second interview was really important. If she went in without a witness and made a mistake, or if the interviewer misunderstood her, she would have no way to prove it. She could be denied a permit and could even be deported to Somalia. But Ayaan maintained that she preferred to go alone.

Louwé was puzzled. Ayaan was the first refugee to refuse his help in an interview. Yet he wasn't too worried. "We were convinced that all the Somalis got permission, anyway." So he let her go alone. "She was just so independent," he recalled.

A few days later, on September 1, which was record time even for

1992, she got word that she had been granted A status. She could stay in Europe as long as she pleased. Until she found work, she would get an unemployment benefit worth $800 a month. As long as she didn't break the law, she could do anything she liked without asking anyone's permission. For a twenty-two-year-old woman who had spent her life under the control of others, the sense of freedom and promise must have been overpowering.

Eleven

Al-Kifah was a strange organization for a young, unmarried woman to involve herself in—even for a woman like Aafia, who had grown up in a time and place that celebrated jihad.

The Al-Kifah men swaggered through the Islamist circuit of mosques and conferences dressed in what their newsletter called "jihad attire." This consisted mainly of brown Afghan porkpie hats, camouflage jackets, and combat boots. And, like the Arab Afghans of Peshawar, they exuded an air of menace.

Only two years before, the group's first director, Mustafa Shalabi, had helped bring the famous Egyptian cleric Sheikh Omar Abdel Rahman to the United States to help spread the word of the need for jihad.

Blinded as a child in Egypt, Sheikh Omar was a scholar of Islam, the spiritual leader (and more) of Egypt's outlawed al-Gama'a al-Islamiya group, and a deadly opponent of Egypt's secular presidents. In his books and speeches, which were taped and sold outside radical mosques, Sheikh Omar called upon Muslims to "hit hard and kill the enemies of God in every spot, to rid it of the descendants of pigs and monkeys who have been dining from the tables of Zionism, communism, and colonialism."

Al-Kifah was known to be violent. In November 1990, not long after the blind sheikh arrived in the United States, one of his followers, El Sayyid Nosair, an Egyptian janitor who belonged to Al-Kifah, shot and killed the leader of the anti-Arab Jewish Defense League, Rabbi Meir Kahane, at a Zionist gathering in Manhattan. Then, in May 1991, Al-Kifah's director, Mustafa Shalabi—after quarreling with Sheikh Omar over how to distribute millions of dollars that the group had been raising—was found shot, stabbed, and bludgeoned to death in his Coney Island apartment. Within the Muslim community, Al-Kifah had a reputation for taking over mosques and Islamic schools by force.

The group vehemently opposed female independence. Gulbuddin Hekmatyar, the Afghan warlord whom the group considered its *amir*, or prince, had helped launch his own career by throwing acid into the faces of unveiled women at Kabul University. In Peshawar, scholars close to Hekmatyar and a like-minded warlord, Abdul Rasul Sayyaf, issued a fatwa in 1989 forbidding women and girls to be educated except by close relatives. Another fatwa banned women from "wearing perfume or cosmetics, going out without their husband's permission, talking with men other than close relatives, walking with pride, or walking in the middle of the sidewalk." The Arab Afghans who approved such measures openly attacked Western relief workers and journalists in Peshawar, spitting on them and calling them "infidel dogs." They also assassinated secular Afghan politicians and intellectuals. Such were the models, and indeed some of the leaders, of Al-Kifah in America.

Although most Muslim men have only one wife, the Arab Afghans practiced polygamy as a matter of principle. Indeed, they argued, Muslim men had a *duty* to marry more Muslim women and produce more Muslim children.

Yet despite all this—or perhaps because of its ruthless glamour—several of Aafia's friends and MSA acquaintances had fallen under the spell of Al-Kifah, and soon she did, too. Emadeddin Muntasser, for example, a Libyan graduate of Worcester Polytechnic Institute, had been raising money for the group since at least 1991. Mohamad Akra, a doctoral candidate at MIT and an MSA member who taught a night class on Islam, was also active. So was Aafia's friend Suheil Laher, the MIT student and aspiring Deobandi scholar from South Africa.

The pride, however, of Al-Kifah's Boston branch was Bassam Kanj, a burly twenty-eight-year-old Lebanese graduate of Boston University.

Back in 1985, Kanj had received a scholarship from Lebanon's Hariri Foundation to study engineering in Boston. There he had begun attending jihadi conferences. Soon he had met Sheikh Tamim al-Adnani, an obese and apparently good-humored Palestinian preacher who traveled the country from his base in Orlando, Florida, encouraging Muslims to "join the caravan"—just as the "Godfather of Jihad," the famous Palestinian preacher and Arab-Afghan leader Abdullah Azzam, summoned Muslims to do in the title of his best-known book. Kanj was married to the former Marlene Earle, an American he had met in Boston. Marlene was a Muslim convert and as fervent as her husband.

Then, in 1989, the couple moved with their baby daughter to Peshawar, so that Kanj could work for Azzam.

Marlene, like the wives of other foreign fighters, stayed in Peshawar while her husband crossed over into Afghanistan to fight. Once installed in Peshawar, an Arab Afghan typically stopped using his or her real name and started going by a *kunya*, or Arabic nickname. They did this both in imitation of the Prophet and his companions and also as a way of foiling Peshawar's spies. Kanj and Marlene had named their baby daughter after Aisha, the Prophet's youngest wife and the first lady of Sunni Islam. The baby's parents became known as Abu and Umm Aisha, or Father and Mother of Aisha.

In Peshawar, Kanj mixed with the jihadis who coalesced into al-Qaeda, including Osama bin Laden and his future second in command, the Egyptian doctor Ayman al-Zawahiri. Kanj trained at the same Khalden camp where some of the al-Baluchi family also trained, including Ramzi Yousef, the future leader of the 1993 bombing of the World Trade Center. Marlene, meanwhile, explored the even more secluded female side of jihad.

As Abdullah Azzam's widow, Umm Mohammed, later said, "Everyone who participated in the jihad in Afghanistan brought his wife with him. They would leave them behind in Peshawar and we all lived as one family. They used to consider me a mother figure." And just as jihadi men tried to model themselves after the Prophet and his companions, so their wives tried to live as they imagined the first generation of Muslim women had lived in Medina.

In 1990, Kanj was wounded fighting in Afghanistan. He and Marlene returned to Boston for surgery, and when he recovered he was off again, in 1991, to Lebanon and then to Bosnia while Marlene stayed behind to raise their growing family.

Marlene was one of the people whom Aafia met when she started volunteering for Al-Kifah. The two women became good friends.

Marlene's husband was then fighting in Bosnia, the scene of a humanitarian crisis that transfixed Aafia as it did the MSA. Most of Bosnia's Muslims were so secular that some people found it inconceivable that Islamism could gain a foothold there. In the Bosnian capital of Sarajevo, men and women mixed freely, and alcohol was served. Even Bosnian Muslims who were more strictly observant usually followed the Sufi teachings that Deobandis and Wahhabis (who dominated the MSA) abhorred. Yet the fledgling country's president, Alija Izetbegović, was himself an Islamist with old ties to the Muslim Brotherhood. In Aafia's freshman year, as soon as war broke out between Muslims and Christians in April 1992, the MSA swung into action to support Izetbegović.

The MSA in Chicago had set up a charity, Relief International, to ship food and supplies to Bosnia's Muslims. Aafia was eager to bring Bosnia's straying Muslims back into the fold of "true Islam," and she was given the job of printing and distributing a Bosnian translation of the Quran. But she wanted to do more than deliver Qurans. She wanted Bosnia to feel the power of jihad. She therefore started raising money for an Al-Kifah program to relieve the widows and orphans of martyred Muslim fighters there.

Twelve

If Ayaan had searched the world over, she couldn't have found a country less like Somalia than the Netherlands. Somalia was yellow brown and bone-dry, and its trees were scrubby thorns. The Netherlands unfolded in a patchwork of soft, wet, gray-green fields. Somalis were historically nomadic; the Dutch were settled farmers and traders who had reclaimed the land they lived on from the sea. They had a saying: "God made the rest of the world, but the Dutch made Holland."

Instead of the warlike virtues that Somalis like Ayaan's clan espoused, the Dutch prized cooperation and being *gezellig*, or cozy. Somalia was one of the world's poorest countries, the Netherlands one of the richest. Somalis were almost entirely illiterate; the Dutch were among the best-educated people on Earth. Holland was at peace, while Somalia was stricken by war and famine. Still, Ayaan did not feel intimidated. Rather, she was enchanted.

To a Somali raised partly in Africa's open spaces, the Dutch landscape, with its tidy brick houses and tulip fields under an ever-changing sky, looked almost like a toyland. By some measures the Netherlands was the world's most densely populated country. But the Dutch managed their tight quarters with ingenious efficiency, often riding bicycles instead of driving cars and building such steep and narrow staircases that they had to haul their furniture up through house windows.

Leo Louwé and the social workers at the refugee center were the first of many Dutch to find Ayaan remarkable. "Her will to be someone was amazing, in this society or any other," one social worker said when I visited Lunteren more than a decade later. "I have not met many people with that kind of drive," said another. "I always believed she would be successful. If you meet Ayaan one time, you will remember her."

The Dutch marveled at her quickness. "Within months she was speaking perfect Dutch," one said. That was an exaggeration, but Ayaan definitely learned faster than the other refugees did. The fluent English she had learned in Kenya helped, but she also did it, the social workers said, "by bothering us. Ayaan was always with the workers, asking questions. She had a good sense of humor. We laughed a lot." The refugees at Lunteren lived in metal trailers set in a former campsite behind a mansion. When she wasn't inside the mansion with the social workers, she was outside chatting with the security guards who watched the premises from a white guardhouse at the gate. It was unusual for a refugee to take such an interest in the staff. Ayaan told them frankly that she did it because she didn't want to be like the other asylum seekers; she wanted to be like the Dutch. Her attitude astonished and flattered the staff at the center. "She was an exception. She wanted to go on to university. She wanted to do all the things that Dutch girls do."

One of the first things Ayaan did after arriving was take off her head scarf. Soon she got her hair cut in an Afro and began wearing jeans. She signed up to receive municipal housing and learned to ride a bicycle. "Ayaan always came in, every time, to discuss her plans," one social worker recalled. "The other Somalis were jealous. They wanted her to wear a head scarf and stop riding her bicycle.

"She was not like most Somali women. Somali women are very proud and self-conscious. She had a liberal approach. The Somali men were quarreling with her. They asked her, 'Why don't you have a head scarf?' She talked a lot with the Somali women, but the Somali men were against her."

She seemed unafraid to be on her own in a strange land, though the workers remember how isolated she could be. At meals in the cafeteria she sat with the social workers. "We worried about that a little bit. We said, 'It will only increase the gap between you and them.'" But Ayaan didn't seem to care. "She had political ideas, and she had the idea that she wanted to make a career, and she wanted money. She had a very clear vision of what she wanted to achieve."

Even before she left the center, she agreed to appear on a television program that the Dutch Muslim network was making about asylum seekers. Plumper than she would be later, and dressed in a puffy purple down jacket, she looked nothing like the diva that Dutch couturiers would later beg to model their clothes. But her smile dazzled the TV crew as she showed them around, and the social workers thought she enjoyed the experience. "We noticed that she likes publicity."

At first she was shocked to learn that the Dutch had no objection to homosexuality. One staff member recalls her crying out, "You can't mean it!" Being Ayaan, however, she wanted to know more. "She was very curious about how it developed that way." She asked a lot of questions about how Dutch women behaved. "Can you choose your own partner?" one social worker remembers her asking. She wanted to know about soccer—what it was, how it worked, why people liked it so much. She wondered how much money the Dutch earned and who belonged to the upper class, and why. Above all, she wanted to know how she could earn a degree and find a career.

Back in Eastleigh, Ayaan's sister Haweya had opened a post office box, perhaps to receive the letters that Ayaan had promised to write if she managed to run away. Ayaan wrote Haweya the good news as soon as she received asylum, a month after leaving Germany. Haweya wrote back, as Ayaan has described, saying that Ayaan's new husband and the family had been looking for her. Haweya also asked for "clothes and a passport so that she, too, could get out."

Osman Musse Quarre, Ayaan's husband in Canada, had been waiting for her to arrive in Toronto ever since leaving Nairobi and their big clan wedding. When he didn't hear from his bride, he feared for her safety. But soon word got back to Nairobi that Ayaan was alive and well in the Netherlands.

Her relatives Fadumo and Muddah had known where she was from the start. Clan leaders in Holland quickly got the news from them. A young prince of the Osman Mahamud lineage who lived in the Netherlands with his wife and family, Yassin Musse Boqor, had received asylum there in 1991. As the highest-ranking fellow clansman in the country, it was his duty to concern himself with new arrivals. He heard that Ayaan was in Lunteren, and he went to see her. "I told her, 'You are welcome in Holland.'"

Yassin, twenty-five, was only a few years older than Ayaan. Like her, he was slim and fine-boned, with smooth dark skin. He was living at the time in Den Helder, on the north coast, but he began traveling south a couple of times a month "to talk, to help." He knew nothing of Ayaan's marital problems. One of the things they talked about was the United States' decision to intervene in Somalia.

If the Islamists feared that President George H. W. Bush would make good on his promise to create a "new world order," the American press was afraid he wouldn't. For months, editorials had been reminding him of his promise made during the Persian Gulf War. Now they mocked him for failing to act in Bosnia and Somalia. Late in the summer of 1992, the United Nations sent military observers to Somalia to protect relief deliveries to the starving. When they failed to stop clan militias from stealing donated grain and attacking aid workers, Bush announced in December that he would send U.S. troops to stop them.

The same month the Americans entered Somalia, Ayaan's father wrote to her at the reception center. She says he asked for $300 for an operation on his eyes. A few days later, her husband, Osman, telephoned her from Toronto. Ayaan says she stalled for time. "Again I lied. . . . I pretended I had never really disappeared, just gone to Holland for a few weeks to be with my dear friend Fadumo." She says she promised to go back to Germany and asked Osman to send her father the $300. Osman's account of her letter adds that she asked him to come live in Holland with her rather than in Canada.

In January 1993, he surprised her by appearing at her trailer in

Lunteren. He was shocked to find her with short hair and no hijab. Ayaan later said that she asked if he had come to take her to Canada. "I'm not going to take you if you don't want to go," she said he answered, "but I want an explanation." Ayaan excused herself and rushed outside. She seems to have feared that Osman might report her to the Dutch immigration authorities. Bumping into one of her social worker friends, she confessed to the woman that she had lied about her asylum request. She told the social worker she had been supposed to marry a man she didn't want to marry and to live in Canada, and that the man was in her trailer.

According to Ayaan, the social worker told her not to worry. How she had gotten asylum was her business. And if the man tried to force her to go with him to Canada, the social worker would call the police.

Ayaan returned to the trailer. This time she told Osman that she had decided to stay in the Netherlands without him. Osman went off to telephone Ayaan's father.

A few days later, the clan elders in the Netherlands held a meeting with the newlyweds. Ayaan told them she didn't want to live with Osman. After that, he returned to Canada alone. Ayaan says she offered to repay the money he had given her, but he refused.

Ayaan's relative Faduma Osman remembers what a scandal erupted when the story of Ayaan's desertion got back to Nairobi. "Her father got really upset. We all thought she took [Osman's] money and used him, and that's why we were talking about it. Her husband was a relative, and he didn't deserve to be treated like that."

Faduma's son Mahad heard that Osman and his family had spent $4,000 on Ayaan's ticket and other travel expenses. Her sister Haweya wrote Ayaan that Hirsi's fellow clansmen were all blaming the sisters' mother, Asha, who they thought must have plotted Ayaan's escape in order to get revenge for Hirsi's leaving her and moving in with his first wife, Maryan. The whole clan remembered that Asha had refused to attend the wedding. Some of Osman's relatives began shunning Asha.

Ayaan wrote her father, asking for his forgiveness. Hirsi scrawled his angry reply on the top of her letter and mailed it back to her. Cursing her and calling her a "Deceitful Fox," he told her not to bother ever writing him again. When Ayaan telephoned her mother, Asha asked, "Do you know how I am being treated here?" But with the Dutch state behind her, Ayaan no longer had to rely on her clan. "I had a right to stay in Holland, and I knew I had other rights, too. Nobody could force me to go anywhere I didn't want to go."

Thirteen

In Boston, Aafia Siddiqui was hanging up posters for Al-Kifah and raising money for its Bosnian widows and orphans fund. In New Jersey, where Al-Kifah's new spiritual leader, the blind sheikh Omar, lived, the Al-Kifah men who had gathered around the Pakistani Ramzi Yousef were building a bomb.

There is no reason to believe that Aafia was in touch with Yousef while he was in the United States. But Yousef, too, was involved with Bosnia, and he and Aafia moved in some of the same circles. His uncle KSM was fighting there in the same battalion as the Lebanese Bassam Kanj, the husband of Aafia's Boston friend Marlene. Ramzi Yousef regularly phoned KSM in Bosnia. Once KSM wired $660 to another Al-Kifah member to help finance Yousef's new project.

Ramzi Yousef had set himself an ambitious goal. Armed with a fatwa from Sheikh Omar, he wanted to kill 250,000 Americans. Later he would say that he chose that figure because the United States had killed 220,000 people in the space of three days at Hiroshima and Nagasaki, yet the United States still called the Palestinians who were fighting Israel for their homeland "terrorists." Only carnage on an even greater scale, Ramzi Yousef said, would force the Americans to acknowledge their error.

In the hadiths it was written that when the Dajjal appeared, the Jews would be his allies. Sheikh Omar and his followers spoke of the United States as the epicenter of "Dajjal civilization," dominated by Jews and opposed to Muslims. And of all the symbols of the Dajjal, the tallest was clearly visible from the mosque where the blind sheikh preached in Jersey City: the twin towers of the World Trade Center. Yousef calculated that it would take a bomb weighing almost 1,500 pounds to bring them down. By February 1993, he and his crew were ready.

On February 23, Yousef bought a first-class ticket back to Karachi on a plane that would be leaving three days later. At lunchtime on February 26, he and one of his comrades drove a rented truck containing the bomb into the B-2 parking garage beneath the World Trade Center's North Tower. Yousef himself lit the fuse before jumping into a waiting getaway car. The explosion that followed could be felt throughout lower Manhattan.

Yousef made his flight to Pakistan. He also made his connection to Quetta, in his family's ancestral homeland of Baluchistan. But to his great disappointment the North Tower did not buckle at the bottom and crash into the other tower as he had hoped. Only six people were killed, and more than a thousand injured. And investigators in New York soon discovered that Brooklyn's Al-Kifah Refugee Center was involved.

Mohammed Salameh, the Palestinian who had rented the truck that had delivered the bomb, was arrested on March 4. News reports quickly identified him as a proponent of jihad and a follower of the blind sheikh Omar. Salameh was also a friend of El Sayyid Nosair, the Egyptian janitor who had shot Rabbi Meir Kahane in Manhattan, and the police announced that they were reexamining that case and two other killings. Soon they arrested several Palestinians and Egyptians.

The first World Trade Center bombing was the worst international attack on the U.S. mainland since the War of 1812, and, for anyone who knew anything about Al-Kifah, the connection was clear.

Yet the commitment of Al-Kifah's Boston branch, and of Aafia in particular, did not waver. The day after the arrests of the Al-Kifah members in New York, the banner headline in *Al-Hussam*, Al-Kifah's newsletter, read, "Boston Sends More Martyrs." The accompanying article praised the life and death of Morabit Yahya (aka Al Layth Abou Al Layth), a twenty-six-year-old Moroccan immigrant who had arrived in the United States in 1990. Yahya had first worked at a Dunkin' Donuts. Then, in Boston, he had "met some [people] who loved and worked to support jihad. He joined the mujahideen in Afghanistan in 1991, where he went to training camps and later fought different battles." The article identified this man as the fourth recruit from Boston to die in Afghanistan.

A few days later, the *Boston Globe* and other papers reported extensively on the arrests of Al-Kifah members in the New York area. The report mentioned the anti-Semitism they displayed and the "trail of strife" that Al-Kifah had blazed through mosques and Muslim gathering places. The negative publicity appears not to have dented Aafia's loyalty. She sent Muslim newsgroups an e-mail the following day asking them to sponsor a Bosnian orphan or widow for Al-Kifah. "Please keep up the spirit and motivate others as well!!!" she wrote on March 15, 1993. "The Muslims of our umma need ALL the help we can provide. Humbly, your sister, aafia."

Fourteen

The word that Ayaan most often used in her autobiography to characterize the Dutch she met during her first years in Holland is "innocent." When an administrator at Lunteren told her that women from the Hawiye clan would have to share their camper with her, Ayaan considered it "such innocence" to think that murderously hostile clans from Somalia could live together peacefully in the Netherlands. She wrote that Ellen, a Dutch friend, "very innocently" did not understand why virginity should matter so much to Muslims. Ayaan decided that the Dutch didn't know much about what went on outside their beautiful little country. And her friend, the Lunteren volunteer Leo Louwé, agreed that they had "been fooled by many stories."

Every refugee had a story, even if it wasn't the same as the one the authorities heard. Some refugees had escaped terrible danger at home but could not make themselves understood or believed. One desperate Iranian refugee at Lunteren set himself on fire after being denied asylum. This terrifying act took place on Ayaan's twenty-third birthday. "I was lucky and felt guilty for getting refugee status so quickly, on false pretenses, when so many people were being turned down."

But with everyone lying at least slightly in order to sway the authorities, the asylum seekers maintained a code of silence about the stories they told the Dutch. Ayaan, for example, met a woman on the train to Lunteren who claimed to be Somali but really came, Ayaan could tell, from the neighboring country of Djibouti. She knew that her Somali friend Yasmin wasn't really underaged and that Yasmin had asked for asylum in Holland only after her false papers had failed to get her into the United States. Ayaan didn't tell her new Dutch friends about that, and the Somalis who met Ayaan didn't tell the authorities that she had actually been raised in Kenya and not Somalia.

The Dutch system of evaluating asylum applications was in chaos. The combination of the period's post–Cold War conflicts and mass air travel had hit the Netherlands hard. In four years, the number of asylum applications nearly quadrupled, to more than twenty thousand. It would be years before the government understood the system of agents—or human smugglers, as immigration officials preferred to call them. But as early as November 1991, the Dutch ministries of Justice and Foreign Affairs issued a directive that Somalis who had refugee status in Kenya be sent back, since Kenya wasn't at war and their lives weren't threatened. Ayaan was just such a person, but she got in anyway and was never sent back.

A Dutch official later told me that most Dutch did not understand that many of the new asylum seekers were professionals at home. "It was the elite from all those countries. It was really a brain drain." Especially for older people, reception centers like Lunteren usually represented the first step toward a new life near the bottom of the social heap. Unable to speak Dutch, all new arrivals were steered toward menial work. For many of them, it was a terrible comedown.

The social workers at Lunteren didn't ask Ayaan how she had come to the Netherlands. They knew she had been married, but they didn't know the details. By the time she arrived, they had given up trying to learn the truth about any single refugee.

Ayaan, busy with her new life, tried to ignore the uproar in Eastleigh over her decision to abandon her new husband. The social workers warned her that there was more to getting along in Holland than learning to speak Dutch. Perhaps the hardest thing for Ayaan to learn would be how to deal with money. She wrote later that for most Somalis getting into the Netherlands "meant, above all, material gain." But she soon learned that amounts of money that would have been huge in Nairobi disappeared fast in Europe.

nd Yasmin applied to the city council for a two-bedroom in Ede. While they waited, the U.S.-led peacekeeping effort in war-torn Somalia was stumbling badly. Even before the troops reached the country, a bomb went off in an Aden hotel where some U.S. arrivals were staying. In June, the Hawiye militia of General Mohammed Farah Aidid attacked the Pakistani contingent of UN troops in Mogadishu. The Somalis castrated the Pakistanis they captured and gouged out their eyes. Some of the Pakistanis were also skinned. "We never expected this from our Muslim brothers," a Pakistani officer told me angrily months later.

The United States bombed a meeting that Aidid's subclan was holding in a hotel. The mob outside promptly murdered four Western journalists who rushed in to cover the scene. Some observers in the West began wondering if the United States knew what it was doing. By the time Ayaan and Yasmin got permission to move in July, the fighting between Somali militias and the foreign soldiers of what the United States called Operation Restore Hope dominated the news again. But that was all behind Ayaan. The violence, the poverty, the incessant demands of family and clan, even the refugee center—she had escaped them all.

Fifteen

The FBI put Ramzi Yousef on its Most Wanted list in April 1993, and the *New York Times* published a long article on the links between the suspects in the World Trade Center bombing and the Al-Kifah Refugee Center in Brooklyn. A few days later, the Brooklyn office of Al-Kifah closed and the officers of the Boston branch—Aafia Siddiqui's friends Emadeddin Muntasser, Mohamad Akra, and Samir al-Monla—set up a corporation they called Care International. The group's founding documents stated that Care International would "provide assistance to war refugees and war victims around the Muslim world." But federal prosecutors later maintained that Care (not to be confused with the huge aid organization CARE) was in fact a continuation of Al-Kifah. They would also charge Aafia's friends with trying to conceal its real mission: "the solicitation and expenditure of funds to support the mujahideen and promote jihad."

The FBI had quickly traced Ramzi Yousef to the jihadi underworld of Peshawar. The bomber had flown back to Pakistan on a passport issued in his real name, Abdul Basit Karim. From there he was tracked to his twin brother's house in Quetta. With the help of the Pakistani police, the FBI raided both that house and also the house of Yousef's uncle in Peshawar, Zahid al-Sheikh, an older brother of KSM who was the head of Peshawar's Islamic Coordination Council. But the men had vanished. The Pakistani police told the Americans that their targets probably had friends in the ISI who tipped them off.

In Zahid's house the raiders found a copy of an application form for another Pakistani passport in the name of Abdul Basit Karim. They also found photographs of Zahid with General Zia ul-Haq, Prime Minister Nawaz Sharif, and General ul-Haq's son Ijaz ul-Haq, one of the family friends whom Aafia had interviewed the previous summer. Bizarrely, though, Pakistan's Foreign Ministry insisted that Ramzi Yousef was not Pakistani, and the confusion over his origins would last for years.

In Cambridge, Massachusetts, meanwhile, Care International took over al-Kifah's *Al-Hussam* newsletter, and the *Al-Hussam* Web site became the Care International Web site. Hundreds of thousands of dollars began flowing through Care International, and Boston became "the de facto hub of recruitment and financing" for services "in support of the jihad in Bosnia-Herzegovina," as Evan Kohlmann, the author of *Al-Qaeda's Jihad in Europe*, later testified. Federal prosecutors would eventually estimate that the group raised $1.7 million over the next decade.

Aafia became one of Care International's most dedicated volunteers. "She was always talking jihad," a Pakistani who knew her in Boston recalls. "She would hold *iftar* [the meal eaten at sunset during Ramadan] parties and fund-raisers. Anywhere she could hold a fund-raiser, she was into it." The Western press had been flooded with reports that thousands of Bosnian Muslim women were being raped. In articles with titles such as "Bosnia Rape Horror," "A Daily Ritual of Sex Abuse," and "Mass Rape: Muslims Recall Serb Attacks," American, British, and German newspapers claimed that 50,000 Bosnian women had been raped by the Serbs. Later investigations would find those numbers wildly exaggerated. At the time, though, Western feminists especially expressed outrage at reports that the Serbian Christians had established "rape camps" as part of a genocidal campaign to rid Bosnia of its Muslims. Aafia and Care International used the reports to appeal to Muslim men to restore the lost honor of Islam by waging jihad.

Care International distributed a flier titled "A Call for Jihad in Bosnia." "Thousands of Muslim girls and women have been kidnapped and kept in Yugoslav army camps for sex," the document claimed. "Ask yourself what you are doing for these Muslims. Ask Muslim governments what they are doing for these Muslims and their freedom." It went on to solicit donations for Al-Kifah to provide "the Emerging Jihad Movement in Bosnia with more than Food and Shelter." (Even after its name change, Care International still occasionally referred to itself in 1993 as Al-Kifah.) Aafia combed the news for gruesome stories of Christian atrocities that she could use in speeches encouraging women to support the mujahideen.

Her speeches about Bosnia made her one of Al-Kifah's most successful fund-raisers. They also brought her recognition in the secretive world of American Islamism.

Sixteen

From Finland, where he still lives today, Mohamud Mohamed Artan (Ayaan's first husband, whom she called "the malest man" she'd ever seen) refuses to discuss the imbroglio of Ayaan's second marriage and flight to the Netherlands—except to claim he has "nothing in common" with her and indeed was never married to her. (He does say he's a friend of Ayaan's half sisters, Arro and Ijaabo.) But those Finnish government records remain. Finland approved a residence permit for Ayan Hersi Magan in 1993. Finnish immigration records also show that *another* Somali woman entered Finland as Mohamud's wife, obtained identification and benefits, and lived under the name of Ayan Hersi Magan. Mohamud claims it was just a coincidence that that ex-wife of his, who no longer lives in Finland, has the same name as the famous Ayaan, who just happened to write a book saying she was briefly married to him. Other Somalis speculate that after Ayaan let Mohamud know she wouldn't be joining him in Finland, he invited another relative to come in her place. Certainly no Somali in his right mind would let a European residency permit (worth hundreds of thousands of dollars over time) go to waste.

In any case, the man Ayaan called her first brief husband ended up living in Finland, where Ayaan never joined him, while her second brief husband, Osman, ended up living in Canada, where Ayaan never joined him, either. She preferred to be single in Holland.

She worked as a cleaner in the Riedel orange juice factory. Later she packed cookies at a biscuit factory. But she and Yasmin were having trouble managing. Ayaan, who barely knew what a bank account was, had borrowed the equivalent of several thousand dollars from a bank. She and Yasmin used it to decorate their flat. Ayaan wrote that the security guard they talked into taking them shopping wanted to show them some inexpensive furniture stores, but the two Somali girls wouldn't have it. "Yasmin and I held our noses and said, 'Oh no, this is not who we are, we would like something more upscale.' "

Nor did Ayaan's jobs fit her sense of who she was. Her half sister Arro had made it to Italy and enrolled in medical school. Ayaan decided she should go to university and study political science. Later she said she wanted to know why so many countries in Africa and the Middle East were in turmoil, while Europe and the Netherlands were at peace.

Curse or no curse, she would show her father who his real heir was.

Her Dutch had improved, but it wasn't yet good enough to get her into a university, and she found she wasn't speaking much Dutch while living with Yasmin. Leo Louwé, the volunteer at the refugee center, introduced her to a family who agreed to practice with her for a few hours a week. "Martin and Johanna," as she calls the couple in *Infidel* (they don't want to be named, for fear of Ayaan's enemies), would become much more than Dutch teachers to Ayaan; they would become her foster family in the Netherlands, helping her with everything from disputes with Yasmin to crises over money.

Seventeen

An Internet newsgroup that Aafia Siddiqui subscribed to reported in early June 1993 that the Muslim Brotherhood charity known as Mercy International had prepared "an effective videotape" on Bosnia for "viewing outside the United States." The e-mail added that a 1991 graduate of MIT, Yusuf Khan, was making copies available for those who wanted to show it at "gatherings in Muslim countries."

Mercy International's Pakistani director at the time was Ramzi Yousef's uncle Zahid al-Sheikh, and prosecutors in the United States and Europe later described the charity as a front for al-Qaeda. The language in the e-mail about restricting the film to Muslim audiences suggests it portrayed "jihad action," perhaps including gory scenes of combat against the Serbs. Aafia was getting ready to leave for another summer vacation in Pakistan. She wrote back immediately to say that her mother's United Islamic Organisation would show the video at its weekly gatherings in Karachi.

Aafia had no fear of showing the video in Pakistan. Jihad was as popular as ever there. Her mother, Ismat, in fact, had Aafia give her speech about Bosnia at her annual conference at the Sheraton Hotel. Aafia's fire for jihad so impressed one woman in the audience, the elegant wife of a wealthy owner of a pharmaceutical company, that she invited the MIT student to give the same talk to a group of women at her house. The woman, Zahera Khan, also happened to be looking for a bride for her son. His name was Amjad, and he was a twenty-two-year-old medical student at Aga Khan University whose family hoped he would soon be moving to the United States to begin his residency.

Like other Pakistani families, the Khans were accustomed to marrying relatives from within their extended families or clans. But this custom was changing as families began branching out around the world. Some of the Khans' relatives, for example, had moved to the United States, and young Amjad himself had studied briefly at Hamilton College in upstate New York before transferring to Aga Khan's medical school. Several of Amjad's American cousins had broken with tradition and married unrelated but highly religious women they had met through Islamist organizations in America. Those educated young wives didn't waste their time on shopping and gossip. They cared about larger issues and could help their husbands in their businesses. Aafia reminded Zahera Khan of them.

Amjad wasn't invited to attend Aafia's lecture. But Zahera asked her son to pick up Aafia and Ismat at a friend's house and drive them to the Khans' two-story bungalow in the affluent KDA Housing Scheme neighborhood. Aafia sat in back. Amjad glanced at her from the driver's seat. He noticed her soft, high voice and dainty hands—and her mother, Ismat, was certainly lively.

After Aafia gave her talk, the two mothers stepped aside and Zahera asked Ismat about Aafia's plans for marriage. Ismat replied that Aafia had received many proposals. Why, the mother of a Saudi prince who had heard Aafia speak had offered to buy much of Pakistan in return for her hand, she said. But the Siddiquis wanted Aafia to marry a Pakistani. Ismat said she thought Aafia had the potential to become an Islamic Benazir Bhutto.

Zahera took all this with a grain of salt. She knew that mothers, in such negotiations, tended to exaggerate their daughters' prospects. But she liked Aafia.

Her son Amjad had his doubts. His mother let him listen to a tape of Aafia's talk. He found it disturbing. Aafia had told his mother's friends that Serbs had cut open the womb of a Bosnian woman, pulled out her fetus, and raped the woman before leaving her to die. He agreed that that was terrible. But he found something ghoulish and unfeminine in the way Aafia dwelled on the details. He told his mother that it was too early to tell if she was right for him.

Eighteen

Ayaan's Dutch foster father, a teacher, helped her figure out a way to get into university: instead of applying directly, she should enroll in a vocational school for social workers, the Hogeschool De Horst in nearby Driebergen, and transfer from there.

But she needed to pass an exam even to get into the Hogeschool De Horst. The test would cover Dutch language, history, and civics. Ayaan signed up for a course to study for it in the autumn of 1993 at Midland College in Ede.

She learned that the Dutch had helped invent the modern idea of tolerance as a virtue so that Dutch Protestants could live together with the country's still sizable Catholic minority while winning their independence from Spain. She also studied how the ideas let loose by this new religious freedom had led to scientific discoveries, geographical exploration, commercial success, and eventually Europe's conquest of the world.

Somalia could use such lessons. Ayaan's clan had given up hope that the country would be unified anytime soon. The U.S. admiral in charge of Operation Restore Hope had been using Black Hawk helicopters to hunt down Mohammed Farah Aidid, the Somali warlord they blamed for the murder of twenty-four Pakistani peacekeepers in June. On October 2, 1993, Somalis used rocket-propelled grenades to bring down two Black Hawk helicopters in Mogadishu. The sixteen-hour battle that followed left eighteen U.S. soldiers and five hundred Somalis dead, and dancing Somalis dragged the naked white body of one of the dead Americans through the streets on a rope. The bruised and bloody face of another soldier they captured soon appeared on the cover of *Time*. "What in the World Are We Doing?" asked the headline.

Ayaan and Yasmin weren't getting along. Then Yasmin disappeared with Ayaan's A-status refugee papers, her bank card, and some money. (Yasmin later wrote Ayaan a postcard from Denmark saying that the money belonged to her because Ayaan had gotten it from the government to act as Yasmin's guardian.) Ayaan already owed thousands of dollars for the furniture and carpets that she and Yasmin had bought; after her roommate left, she discovered that Yasmin had also run up more than a thousand dollars in telephone bills.

Leo Louwé helped Ayaan sort out the messes at the telephone company and the furniture store. Obtaining copies of her papers was another headache. Once Ayaan had dealt with all that, the problem of paying for her two-bedroom apartment remained.

Nineteen

Aafia returned to MIT in the fall of 1993 more militant and politicized than ever. She signed up for a course with Noam Chomsky, MIT's famously radical political writer and professor of linguistics. Chomsky promoted a view of world affairs that was enormously popular in conspiracy-minded Pakistan. The United States' democratic institutions, he argued, were little more than a facade concealing an inner cabal of greedy elites (including many Jews) who would stop at nothing to control the world. Aafia often boasted of having been his student. Chomsky says he has no recollection of meeting her.

The professor's inattention to Aafia and her Islamist friends may have been typical of MIT's instructors. The year before, Aafia had earned a B in professor Jean Jackson's introductory course in gender studies. "She was smart, really smart, and willing to learn," Jackson, an anthropologist, recalled at first, and she thought Aafia might have taken a second reading course with her. But later she wondered whether she was confusing Aafia with another student in the early 1990s who had worn a head scarf. Jackson deduced from their attire that the girls were observant Muslims, but she never asked them about the role of Islam in their lives. "That never came up," she said. "I wondered about it, but I don't bring up issues of religion with students unless they bring it up."

In this multicultural heyday, Aafia's professors seemed to see her Islamic dress and promotion of Muslim causes as a proud assertion of cultural identity. Not until a year after she left MIT would the university hold a conference at which the American feminist Susan Moller Okin posed her famous question "Is multiculturalism bad for women?" Most Americans were barely conscious of political Islam as an organized and disciplined political movement, and they knew even less about the Islamists' involvement in a bewildering array of conflicts breaking out *within* the world of Islam.

Just up the street from MIT, Harvard's Samuel P. Huntington, a political scientist, was completing what would soon become an article in *Foreign Affairs* and later a book, *The Clash of Civilizations.* Huntington had plucked the phrase from an earlier article written by his friend and adviser on Middle Eastern issues, Bernard Lewis, a scholar of Near Eastern studies at Princeton, and he had tried out his theory a few months earlier at the American Enterprise Institute (AEI), a conservative think tank that both Huntington and Lewis frequented. Huntington's article argued that the State Department policy planner Francis Fukuyama had been wrong when he had claimed in his 1992 book *The End of History* that liberal democracy was the wave of the future. Instead, Huntington predicted clashes along civilizational lines, especially between Islam and the West.

What Huntington and Lewis were warning of was a mirror image of what the Muslim Brothers and other pro-jihad forces were actually promoting. Salman al-Ouda, for example—a rising young Saudi cleric who had been a student of Sayyid Qutb's brother Muhammad and whom Osama bin Laden regarded as a spiritual guide—had written his own rejoinder to Fukuyama. The Saudi's article (also called "The End of History") said that liberal democracy, far from being the final form of human government, was in fact in an advanced state of decay and would sooner or later collapse. Bringing about that collapse, which would also stanch Muslim suffering, "exists in one word: Jihad," Ouda wrote. Huntington, who did not read Arabic, Urdu, or Farsi, seems not to have known about Ouda and discounted the evidence of bitter conflicts *within* Islam. Muslims were killing Muslims across much of the Islamic world, and jihadists were trying to seize power from Algeria to the Philippines. But rather than recognizing those wars as the product of a specific political movement, Huntington ascribed them to "Islam."

Non-Muslims almost never attended the lectures and conferences that the MSA held at metropolitan Boston's many colleges and universities. When they did, though, they were often shocked by the naked hatred and aggression expressed toward Jews and the West.

In the same guide to starting an MSA chapter to which Aafia contributed, a Canadian convert named Katherine Bullock described a meeting in 1994 when 1,400 people had shown up at the University of Toronto to hear Imam Jamil al-Amin—the former Black Panther H. Rap Brown—speak about "Social Justice in the Americas." "The Imam mocked Westerners, Jews and Christians, alienating a large part of the audience," Bullock wrote. "He also talked about how in Islam men were above women. Naturally the 'women and Islam' topic is delicate, but comments like that made in passing without the whole Islamic context, reinforces, rather than challenges, the notion that Islam oppresses women." Organizers had directed the audience into separate sections for men and women. "Naturally Muslims expect this, but it is a shock for non-Muslims," Bullock commented. Her advice to the MSA was to warn speakers when non-Muslims would be in attendance, to use "gender-neutral language when speaking English," and to "be discreet" about seating arrangements.

Perhaps the need for discretion that Bullock mentioned was what led Aafia to form a group of her own that she called the Dawah Resource Center, which linked radical speakers to more select audiences. Her future husband later recalled that some of the speakers Aafia invited were "world names" in the field of jihad for whom "America was the enemy." Aafia also used the Dawah Resource Center to reach out to African-American Muslims and potential converts. She visited Malcolm X's old neighborhood of Roxbury and got to know the imam of its oldest house of Muslim worship, the shabby brick Mosque for the Praising of Allah on Shawmut Avenue. The imam there, Abdullah Faaruuq, also served as the Muslim chaplain to several Massachusetts prisons. Through the Dawah Resource Center, Aafia ordered hundreds of Islamic books in English, usually from Saudi Arabia, and Faaruuq distributed them to the prisoners he visited. Faaruuq said the books included works by the famous Egyptian Islamist Sayyid Qutb. "She would come and get a box of books as big as she was," the imam recalled. She also volunteered for mentoring programs that the mosque offered to poor African-American and immigrant children.

The anonymous writers of the *Al-Hussam* newsletter that Aafia distributed called for Muslims to shed "rivers of blood." It reminded readers of the so-called beheading verse in the Quran urging believers in conflict with unbelievers to "smite at their necks." Aafia did not mention violence in the e-mails she sent out under her own name. But by the end of 1993, she had begun scouring Boston's used bookstores for old U.S. military manuals and books about espionage that she could donate to the mujahideen. Arguing that women, moreover, had the same religious duty as men to train for jihad, she learned in a self-defense class how to fight hand to hand, and she took the basic National Rifle Association gun course at the Braintree Rifle & Pistol Club, south of Boston. She also organized her girlfriends to head off into the woods for a weekend of paintball games, another way to practice for jihad.

The blind sheikh Omar and Al-Kifah had been subjected to another wave of arrests in the summer of 1993 in connection with the "Landmarks Case," a plot to bomb the United Nations and New York City's tunnels. The author Evan Kohlmann feels sure that anyone with Aafia's exposure to Al-Kifah had to know by the end of 1993 that its members were prepared to kill American civilians. "Everyone at that level knew what they were doing," he said.

Yet according to Aafia's family, she sent home a sentimental poem around this time, expressing her love for Boston and the United States. Perhaps she rationalized the contradiction by looking forward to the day when the United States would convert to Islam. In the guide to *dawah* that she wrote for the MSA, she asked for the strength and sincerity "that our humble effort continues and expands . . . and more and more people come to the [religion] of Allah until America becomes a Muslim land."

Twenty

One day in January 1994, Ayaan got a call from the Frankfurt airport. To her surprise, she wrote in her autobiography, her younger sister, Haweya, was in Europe. Ayaan has told several different versions of how the twenty-two-year-old Haweya got there. In her collection of essays and lectures, *The Caged Virgin*, she said that Haweya had run away from an arranged marriage. Later, in her autobiography, *Infidel*, she said that her sister was escaping from a love affair with a married man from Trinidad. Neither book explains how Haweya got past the usual obstacles of money, passports, and visas. In *Infidel* Ayaan implied that the Trinidadian, who worked for the United Nations, paid for Haweya's passage. In any case, Haweya got to Germany, and it made Ayaan very happy.

She told Haweya to go straight to the station and catch a train to the German border. Under Europe's Schengen Accord, there were no border controls between the Netherlands and Germany. She arranged for a Dutch friend to drive there and pick her up, avoiding the police. International regulations required asylum seekers to apply in the first safe country in which they found themselves, and Ayaan wanted Haweya to claim that she had entered Europe in Holland rather than Germany. Haweya registered for asylum at the Dutch center in Lunteren.

Once again, Leo Louwé offered to help prepare her for her interview with the Dutch immigration authorities. But, like her sister before her, Haweya said she would rather go on her own. Ayaan wrote in *Infidel* that she helped Haweya "cook up a story." Whatever it was, the story worked, and Haweya quickly received A status. Soon she was allowed to share Ayaan's apartment in Ede, checking in at Lunteren once a week.

The social workers at Lunteren liked Haweya just as they had her sister. "She was as intelligent as Ayaan, but a bit different in her character," one worker remembered. "She was a little younger, a little bit softer. She was more joyful." Haweya kept her hair long and never wore blue jeans, but she was as quick to learn Dutch as Ayaan had been. She could be prickly, but when she made the effort, she won people over with her confident wit and mischievous smile. "She was a little bit spoiled," Louwé recalled. "She behaved like a Somali princess. But that was her power, too."

Yet, to Ayaan's irritation, Haweya failed to respond to the marvels of Holland as she had. Indeed, her younger sister seemed disappointed and depressed. She told Ayaan she felt guilty because her affair with the Trinidadian had gotten her pregnant and she'd had an abortion. She would lie in bed for days, watching television. She wouldn't eat and wouldn't clean the flat. "My sister, who longed for freedom more than anyone I knew when we were growing up, was appalled when she actually found it," Ayaan later observed. "She repeatedly said, 'Is this all? Is this it?' "

Haweya was shocked by Ayaan's distance from the Somali community. When Ayaan held a small party to celebrate her birthday in November 1994, Haweya couldn't help crying out, "But you have only invited Dutch people!" After several months in the Netherlands, Haweya became pregnant again, this time by a Somali man from the refugee center. Ayaan was furious. Haweya had another abortion—but not before Ayaan accused her of murder.

Ayaan went to see a social worker friend at the refugee center and learned from the man that he was already counseling Haweya. He said one problem was that Haweya feared her sister's judgmental nature. "I was always telling Haweya what I thought was wrong with her," Ayaan admitted.

Haweya stopped attending language school. She would stay home for days, crying about how guilty she felt for leaving their mother alone. She still didn't help with the housework. Ayaan sought help from her foster parents. The Dutch couple recommended that the sisters live apart. They helped Haweya move into her own place. But she was lonely there.

Leo Louwé visited her. She had started wearing a head scarf. She seemed beset by fears that made no sense to him. Once Louwé and his wife invited her to join them in Lunteren so they could all visit the Louwés' daughter, who had just given birth to their first grandchild. By the time they left the daughter's house, night had fallen. Louwé knew it was safe, but Haweya was afraid to cycle back to Ede on her own. When Louwé refused to take her by car and told her it would be inappropriate for her to ask his daughter if she could spend the night, she stopped speaking to him for two months.

Somalis who made it to the West were alarmingly prone to mental illness. A 1995 British study found that 14 percent of Somalis living in London's Tower Hamlets area, where Ayaan's father would eventually move, suffered from schizophrenia. The figures were astonishing compared with the 1 to 2 percent of the general British population who reported schizophrenic symptoms. By the end of the 1990s, the pattern of Somali mental illness was so blatant that the International Organization for Migration, a refugee assistance group, began including "stress" along with snow and women's liberation among the novel challenges for which Somalis bound from Kenya for the West needed to be carefully prepared.

The symptoms that teachers in Kenya described to their classes of refugees were just like Haweya's: "You can't sleep. You watch TV all the time." Some people even killed themselves. In Somalia, suicide was practically unheard of, and at first the refugees refused to believe that, having survived war, famine, and homelessness, one might take one's own life after reaching some of the richest countries in the world. Somalis later said of a refugee who became unbalanced in the West, "The wealth got to him." But when Haweya started feeling blue, no one knew what was wrong.

Twenty-one

By early 1994, Aafia Siddiqui was arranging events in Boston for two new charities in addition to Care International: the Global Relief Foundation and the Benevolence International Foundation. Both had recently opened in Chicago, and U.S. prosecutors would later describe both as fronts for al-Qaeda.

The director of operations of Benevolence International was Suleman Ahmer, a balding twenty-six-year-old Pakistani engineer with a raspy voice, a frizzy black beard, and thick glasses. Like Aafia, Ahmer got involved with jihad through his passion for Bosnia. In 1993, he and some fellow students from the University of Nebraska were briefly taken prisoner by Croatian militiamen after they went to Bosnia to deliver relief. Returning to the United States, Ahmer discovered a talent for public speaking on the MSA lecture circuit. Now he traveled the world for Benevolence International, overseeing relief missions to the mujahideen. Aafia arranged for Ahmer to speak in Boston. The title of his talk was "Jihad: The Misunderstood Word."

Aafia was now doing something that other jihadi women had not. She was standing up before mixed audiences and preaching the virtues of jihad. In fact, according to Rohan Gunaratna, the author of *Inside al-Qaeda*, and Evan Kohlmann, both experts on terrorism, Aafia is the only woman known to have publicly raised money for Al-Kifah this way. "She's a very interesting person," Kohlmann said. "These guys were just so misogynistic, so filled with this bizarre machismo—yet for some reason they prized this woman."

What made them accept Aafia's preaching may have been her way of playing on their macho religiosity. She got away with shaming men into discharging what Al-Kifah's newsletter, *Al-Hussam,* called "the obligation to fight the infidels." Imam Abdullah Faaruuq, the African-American spiritual leader whom Aafia got to know while distributing religious tracts, remembers how effectively she spoke. "She used to encourage Muslim men to be Muslim," Faaruuq said. "She used to say that you should take care of your families and be the best Muslim you can. She used to say, 'Where are the Muslim men? Why do I have to be the one to get up here and talk?' She wanted us to take a more proactive part in advancing the cause of Islam. Her voice was real sweet but piercingly high. Some of the brothers used to say, 'Man, that sister's tough!'"

Twenty-two

Ayaan passed her Dutch exams in the autumn of 1994 and began the classes in social work that she hoped would enable her to transfer to a university. She and Haweya had much to celebrate. But it was getting harder to make Haweya smile.

One by one, their whole family was immigrating to Europe. Even their pious half sister Ijaabo seems to have made her way to the Netherlands. Perhaps Ayaan declined to help this relative come up with a winning story for the immigration authorities; in any case, she later wrote that Ijaabo had applied for asylum in the Netherlands and failed to get it. (She eventually settled in England.)

It was while her half sister was visiting that Ayaan learned in her Dutch history class, for the first time in her life, about Nazi Germany's extermination of six million Jews. The class discussion focused on why so many Dutch people had failed to act while their neighbors were taken away. Ayaan sat quietly during the talk, thinking how similar Nazi propaganda sounded to what she had heard all her life about Jews being agents of Satan who controlled the world. Earlier, during a visit to Antwerp's Jewish neighborhood, she had been shocked to discover that Jews looked just like other people. It occurred to her in the classroom that "if I had lived in the 1930s growing up as I had done with the belief that Jews are evil . . . I might well have participated. And I know a huge number of people who would have participated." At home she tried to tell her half sister what she had learned in class, but Ijaabo refused to hear it. "It's a lie!" Ijaabo cried, according to Ayaan. "Jews have a way of blinding people. They were not killed, gassed or massacred. But I pray to Allah that one day all the Jews in the world will be destroyed."

Ijaabo's sister, Arro, was as modern and open-minded as Ijaabo was said to be closed. Arro had become a gynecologist. Like her mother, Maryan, she worked with Somali women's groups to eradicate female genital mutilation, and their father was said to be very proud of her.

Hirsi Magan still wasn't speaking to Ayaan. But she pressed on with her studies, and in May 1995 she became Holland's first licensed Somali-Dutch translator.

As an interpreter Ayaan could make good money. Her goal, though, was to attend the oldest and most famous institution of higher learning in the Netherlands, four-hundred-year-old Leiden University. Leiden was known for its department of political science. And as soon as she earned the credits she needed, she used them to transfer there.

Twenty-three

Aafia often reminded audiences of a Muslim woman's duty to wage jihad. The "Godfather of Jihad," Abdullah Azzam, had said that the modern Muslim community was in such danger that a woman did not need her husband's permission nor a son his father's permission. Now that she would soon graduate, she longed to join the action.

If she had been a man, she would have found a job like Suleman Ahmer's at one of the Islamist charities or front organizations. But the secret army against unbelief never put women in positions of leadership over men. And, as her friend Suheil Laher pointed out on his Web site, Abdullah Azzam had also written that it was impermissible for a woman to travel without a *mahram*, or close male family member.

From Ahmer, Aafia had heard the story of Kamila, a British Muslim girl who was said to have ventured alone to Bosnia. Although Ahmer admired Kamila's bravery ("she dared where men hesitated"), he disapproved of her going without a *mahram*. "I placed that on a lack of a grounded Islamic education growing up in England," Ahmer wrote in his book, *The Embattled Innocence*. The happy ending for Ahmer came when Kamila rectified her dangerously incorrect position by marrying a Sudanese aid worker and going to work for his group helping the Bosnians.

The obvious thing for Aafia to do was to marry a mujahid. The wives of these knights of Islam whispered that they made tender husbands, as soft on their families as they were hard on unbelievers. Several of the "Care brothers" were willing. Their families had written to Aafia's parents asking permission to marry her. But the Siddiquis had turned the offers down. And when they arrived in Massachusetts for her graduation, in February 1995, they told her they had received a more attractive offer at home.

The family of the medical student Amjad Khan, at whose house Aafia had lectured in 1993, had approached them with an offer of marriage. Amjad was about to graduate from Aga Khan University Medical College. He was a brilliant student, at the top of his class, and he planned to do his residency in anesthesiology at Massachusetts General Hospital, in Boston. To Dr. Siddiqui, his proposal sounded ideal.

For her graduation ceremony Aafia exchanged her usual hijab for a gown and mortarboard. She was graduating summa cum laude with close to an A average, 4.4 on a 5-point scale, and that included the biology courses she had not wanted to take.

Inside, though, she seemed to be panicking. She tried to tell her mother later about her dream of finding a partner in jihad, but Ismat brushed her feelings aside.

Aafia knew that Islam gave her the right to turn down any marriage proposal. Some of her friends had used Islam as a kind of liberation theology to marry jihadis in defiance of their more secular parents. But Aafia's mother and father were neither secular nor impious, and Aafia knew that Islam also said she should obey them unless she had a good reason not to.

The only sign the Khans saw that something was wrong came when Grand Mufti Muhammad Rafi Usmani asked Amjad and his father to see him. The two men were impressed that Aafia merited the interest of Pakistan's senior religious authority. But toward the end of their conversation, the mufti asked a question that puzzled them: "If the need arises, would you be willing to go for jihad?" Amjad wasn't sure what the mufti meant. He was a doctor, not a soldier. But jihad had many meanings, all of them positive to devout Muslims. *"Inshallah,"* he answered—"God willing."

Aafia remained at McCormick Hall after she graduated and kept working for MIT's computer service. For some time now, she had felt she was being watched. She told friends later that beefy American men in suits had started showing up at some of her lectures. She suspected them of being FBI agents, and she was probably right. In 2008, the prosecution of several Care International officers for tax fraud revealed that the FBI had begun wiretapping Care International's office in November 1994.

Meanwhile, Benazir Bhutto had been reelected prime minister of Pakistan. Under pressure from the U.S. government, her government had embarked on a secret war against the Islamist radicals. One of her first acts was to fire the bearded Deobandi preacher Lieutenant General Javed Nasir as the head of ISI. The United States had given Bhutto the names of ISI officials who had helped Ramzi Yousef enter the United States in 1992 before he had bombed the World Trade Center. Under Bhutto the police had raided the homes of Yousef and his relatives several times, though the suspects were always gone by the time the police arrived. The police official in charge of the investigations, Rehman Malik, suspected that the al-Baluchi clan was being protected by higher officials. Then, just as Aafia was preparing to graduate, Bhutto and Washington finally got the break they were waiting for.

A South African student whom Yousef had tried to draw into one of his terrorist plots went to the police with the information that the world's most wanted man was staying at a guesthouse in Islamabad. Bhutto hurriedly assembled a team of U.S. and Pakistani troops answerable only to her, and they captured Yousef at the guesthouse on February 7. Bhutto waived the law forbidding the extradition of Pakistani citizens without a court order, and the Americans quickly took Yousef to New York to be tried, fearing that any delay might embolden his hidden supporters.

Aafia and her friends in Boston were stunned. For them, it was a basic tenet of Islam never to turn over a Muslim prisoner to unbelievers.

Bhutto appealed publicly on March 22—shortly before Hillary

Clinton, President Bill Clinton's wife, was to arrive on a visit—for U.S. help in uprooting the jihadi networks, which were too powerful, she said, for her to take on alone. She told the *New York Times* that police were looking for Ramzi Yousef's uncle, the Mercy International director Zahid al-Sheikh. She described the photographs the police had found of Zahid and his influential friends. "Pakistan, on its own," Bhutto said, could not just "shut down" terrorist training camps, religious schools, and other facilities used as terrorist fronts without prompting the militants to fan out across Pakistan and step up their violence.

Aafia read about Bhutto's statement, and she wrote an e-mail to a Pakistani Listserv complaining bitterly. In a comment sprinkled with mocking quotation marks, she wrote that Pakistan under Bhutto had become as cowardly as the United States' Arab allies:

> [The] Pakistani govt. has officially joined the gang of our typical contemporary govts. Of Muslim countries. I mean Egypt, Algeria, Tunisia and the likes of them. . . . Here's what I read in this friday's issue of the "Muslim News," something that was confirmed a few days earlier by some articles in local newspapers like The Boston Globe and the New York Times etc: BENAZIR ASKS FOR THE WEST'S HELP AGAINST "EXTREMISM." Benazir Bhutto, Pakistan's prime minister, called on the west to help her eradicate religious opposition. She said that Pakistan is a "moderate" Islamic country and it is the first defense line against "terrorism," and hence needs international support. She added that the arrest of Ramzi Yousef and giving him to the United States is a simple proof.

Aafia closed her e-mail with a quotation from the Quran familiar to Deobandis and Salafists: "O you who believe! Take not the Jews and Christians for protecting friends (auliyaa'). They are the protecting friends of one another. Whoever among you takes them for protecting friends is (one) of them. Indeed, Allah does not guide the wrongdoing people."

A few weeks later, on April 19, 1995—with Ramzi Yousef and his coconspirators in the World Trade Center bombing already on trial in New York—a huge bomb exploded at the Alfred P. Murrah Federal Building in Oklahoma City, killing 168 people, including 19 small children, and injuring more than 600 others. The bomb was similar in composition to Ramzi Yousef's. Like Yousef's, moreover, it was delivered in a rented truck, leading investigators to suspect at first that Yousef and Al-Kifah were behind the attack. On April 23, the FBI listened in while the officers of Care International and Global Relief held a worried meeting about the crackdown in Pakistan. "Some brothers are nervous in Boston," one man said. Aafia's MIT supervisor informed her around this time that some FBI agents had visited the university's computer office looking for her.

Aafia stayed away from work after that. She packed an assortment of U.S. military manuals she had been collecting for the mujahideen and mailed them to her mother in Pakistan. She moved out of her dorm and went to stay in Roxbury with her African-American friends.

Later she said she felt she had spent that summer "underground." Perhaps after her privileged upbringing, life in what was still a dangerous neighborhood, full of drug abusers and prostitutes, came as a shock. She evidently changed her mind about the young doctor who wanted to marry her, for the Siddiquis soon called the Khans to say they accepted the proposal.

After the FBI determined that two right-wing Americans had planted the bomb in Oklahoma City, Aafia didn't hear from them again. She went to Chicago to join her sister, Fowzia, who had recently graduated from a Pakistani medical school and was starting an internship in Chicago.

The *nikhah* ceremony linking Aafia and Amjad in marriage took place in a Chicago hotel room on October 2, 1995, the day after

Sheikh Omar and his followers from Al-Kifah were convicted in the plot to blow up New York City's landmarks. Aafia wore a white silk dress with pearls. She formally agreed to the marriage in a phone call to Karachi, where her parents were assembled with the Khans, including Amjad.

After that Amjad flew to Chicago to meet her. He and his parents all knew about Aafia's passion for jihad—the mothers, after all, had met at her speech. But it never crossed his parents' minds that the bride herself might have asked the mufti to pose his mysterious question about Amjad's willingness to go for jihad—much less that his answer, "God willing," would strike Aafia as a personal commitment to a war against unbelievers.

Twenty-four

Ayaan rented a room in a suburb of Leiden and bicycled to classes at the university. She also kept working as a translator. She was making far more money than most of her fellow students, yet she couldn't help noticing the contrast between the young Dutch she met and the immigrants for whom she translated. The Dutch students had nothing more to worry about than their grades. Ayaan was translating in police stations and hospitals for Somali girls who had been raped and beaten. She was telling refugees that the authorities had decided to send them and their families back to war zones. She was explaining to doctors that pregnant women wanted abortions. In these emergency rooms and women's shelters, "I began to notice how many dark faces looked back at me."

What made her angry was her sense that the Somali women got no support from their religion or community. "I knew many Dutch women were abused, too. But their community and their family didn't approve of it. No one blamed them for the violence or told them to obey better." She had a case in which a Somali child had been accused of beating up other children. A Dutch teacher kept trying to explain to the parents that in Holland a child wasn't allowed to hit another child, even if he was badly insulted. The Somali parents couldn't understand that. "In Somalia, you attack. You hit first. If you wait to be hit, you'll only be bullied more. I was taught that, too," Ayaan had to tell the teacher. "Where we come from, aggression is a survival tactic."

The students at Leiden knew nothing of this other world. Leiden seemed like paradise to Ayaan. "Imagine," she said. "Everybody is reasonable. Everybody is tolerant. Everybody is happy. Your biggest worries are, 'Will I get my points?' and 'Do I have a boyfriend?' and 'Did I party well last night?' And then you have vacations." One day some of her friends declared that they were going to take her drinking. "And I said, 'I can't, it's forbidden by God; I'll go to hell.' And they said, 'Wooah, that's cool.' And my first drink was a martini. After one glass, I was completely drunk."

Most students in Leiden lived in student houses, cooperatives owned and managed by groups of students. A Dutch friend suggested that Ayaan apply to live in hers. Each newcomer had to be approved by the other members of the house, and Ayaan's friend worried that she might not make it. Despite her charisma, Ayaan was just so different from the average Leiden student. But the residents proved more open-minded than Ayaan's friend had feared. Ayaan was admitted.

It was March 1996, and within days of moving in she met the man who would become her first serious boyfriend. Like her, Marco van Kerkhoven was older than the other residents. He had gone to the university but was now working as a freelance science reporter. He was slim and very pale, with a thick mop of light brown hair and what Ayaan described as "big blue innocent eyes." After their first night, Ayaan and Marco stayed together for five years. "She was a beautiful woman and very intelligent," he told me later. "We clicked instantly." He loved her joy in life, her optimism.

Marco had studied biology. He hadn't grown up with any religious belief. He found it strange to be in a relationship with a Muslim, but his immediate response was to ask questions. "I was very curious and I asked about everything."

Ayaan told him she wanted to learn about politics. "She wanted to know about power and how power works in a general way. It is an interesting subject and I got interested in her." The two of them watched the *Nova* television news nearly every night. Marco was fascinated by the way watching the same program could lead them to such variant conclusions. "The way she experiences the world is just so different," Marco said. The childhood she described to him seemed like one of utter poverty and abuse. Yet she was much more cheerful than the average dour Dutchman. "I guess if you start life with nothing," he said, "every day is a lucky day. . . . There is not a day that Ayaan does not wake up smiling. She always sees the sunny side of things. She is always laughing."

Ayaan enjoyed her studies but struggled with some subjects, statistics in particular. Still, she persevered. If she failed a course she took it again. Marco admired her all the more for her drive.

Marco's friends also liked her. She had inherited her father's gift for storytelling. Fellow students recall how Ayaan enthralled them with tales of growing up in Africa and working as a translator in a seamy immigrant underground that they hardly knew existed. They found her beautiful as well. The photographer Marc de Haan took her picture for the student magazine. He was struck by how relaxed she was about it. "Most women are a little bit shy in front of the camera. But Ayaan was nothing like a classical refugee. Posing came completely naturally to her." Eventually Marco became resigned to the fact that other men were constantly attracted to his exotic girlfriend. "If you were a lovely, baby-faced woman, people would fall in love with you," he said. "And people do fall in love with Ayaan. People fall for her instantly."

Twenty-five

"First marriage, then love." That's the motto among Muslims. Aafia believed it, and so did the shy and serious husband who flew to Chicago to meet her in October 1995. At first it seemed to work for them. Amjad had the slim frame, fair skin, and almond-shaped black eyes of a nobleman in a Persian miniature. He had grown up in a Pakistani family of three boys and wasn't used to the company of pretty young women. He was captivated by his new bride.

Amjad would later say that when he arrived in the United States he was what the Brothers called a "cultural Muslim." He prayed and fasted and considered himself Muslim, but he hadn't thought deeply about religion. He knew Aafia was what he called "ultrareligious," but that didn't bother him. Still, he didn't know what to think when his new wife confided that the FBI had come looking for her in the spring and that if anything similar happened again, she would have to leave the United States immediately.

Surely, he thought, she was exaggerating. But he noticed that other Muslim activists seemed to take her quite seriously, and as he later told the *Guardian*, it was exciting that "she was so pumped up about jihad."

After a honeymoon in Chicago, the newlyweds flew to Boston to start their new life. They rented a tiny basement apartment in Cambridge, but Amjad did not like living in a cellar, what with the constant gurgle of people upstairs flushing their toilets and draining their washing machines. He preferred a modern, larger apartment in the suburbs. Thus, in the first of many moves over the next few years, they found something he liked in the suburb of Malden, in a complex off Interstate 93.

Amjad had shaved off his beard before leaving Pakistan after hearing that since the Oklahoma City bombing Americans had become suspicious of bearded Muslims. He was in the United States for just one thing—to get his training in anesthesiology—and he didn't want some prejudice against Muslims to interfere.

Aafia, however, wanted him to wear a beard. She claimed that Islam required it. And so—in the first of many such inquiries—Amjad consulted various theological works. He learned that though beards were desirable because they set a believer apart from unbelievers, it was permissible to go beardless in the service of a larger Islamic cause—such as gaining the knowledge to save Muslim lives. Aafia, however, didn't seem to care, and he felt she was embarrassed to introduce her Islamist friends to a clean-shaven husband.

One day not long after they were married, Aafia came home with the news that she and Suleman Ahmer of Benevolence International had come up with a plan for her and Amjad to go to Bosnia. The Dayton peace accords had been signed the year before. Under the agreement, irregular foreign fighters would leave the country while U.S. troops enforced the peace. But the Global Relief Foundation had distributed a flier in the United States warning Muslims not to be fooled into thinking they should *abide* by the agreement. Mujahideen recruits were still needed. They should create "a nightmare for U.S. troops in Bosnia" and encourage the Bosnians "to stay true to their Islamic values and open their mind to love of Jihad and martyrdom for the sake of Allah." Aafia told Amjad excitedly that she could teach religion there while Amjad practiced medicine. Finally they would enter the "fields of jihad."

Amjad was startled to hear it. He told Aafia gently that he couldn't possibly leave the United States until he finished his residency. Aafia was disappointed. But she soon discovered that she was pregnant, and that settled the matter.

Twenty-six

Unfortunately for Ayaan, just as she was embracing Western culture her sister was rejecting it. There was more to it than loneliness. By the time Ayaan moved into her student house, Haweya turned her mirror to the wall. She began praying—and reading the Islamist classics by Hassan al-Banna and Sayyid Qutb. She told other Somalis she was hearing voices. She began to talk about the Dajjal and the return of Jesus Christ.

Sometimes when Leo Louwé and his wife went to see Haweya, she seemed her old self. Her eyes would flash, and she would make them laugh with her tales of her latest encounters in Holland. At other times, she refused to leave her room.

One day Haweya announced that she was moving to Nijmegen, an ancient city not far away, on the Maas River near the border with Germany. Some of her fellow clansmen already lived there. Haweya told the Louwés that she had been accepted to study public administration at Nijmegen University. "We never knew how she did that, but that was Haweya—always something new," Louwé said.

At the end of August, Louwé and his wife packed up Haweya's belongings and drove her to a student house in Nijmegen where she had taken a room. Not long afterward, they drove to Nijmegen to visit. But when they asked for Haweya at the student house, the other residents didn't seem to know who she was. The Louwés tracked her down, and she seemed out of sorts. They got the feeling she had kept to herself since their last visit. "She was very much alone."

Ayaan would say that it was as if her sister had nothing to live for now that she had the freedom to do as she liked. To Ayaan, it was almost as if Haweya missed the drama of quarreling with their mother in Nairobi. Holland was so gray and rainy; life could be so humdrum. One was constantly filling out papers, and the Dutch were always admonishing others to plan ahead, to save, to conserve. It brought Haweya down.

Ayaan had to struggle with the Dutch grind, too. She wanted to live for the day, whereas Marco always worried about saving for the future. Not long after they began seeing each other, he moved into his own apartment in Leiden. Ayaan applied to the city council for a flat with two bedrooms, and the council found her a nice one on the Langegracht, across from the police station. When she couldn't afford it on her own, she talked Marco into leaving his new apartment and sharing hers. He laughed about it later as the first of many expenses that he felt Ayaan manipulated him into. "Okay," Marco said, "I didn't really want to do it at the time, but it turned out fine." They moved in on January 1, 1997.

Haweya joined them for a New Year's celebration. She seemed to be feeling better. But one day Leo Louwé got a telephone call. Haweya had been taken to a psychiatric hospital in Nijmegen. She was suffering a severe psychotic disorder. Louwé and his wife rushed from their village to the clinic, but when they found Haweya sitting in the garden she cursed them and called them "dirty Christian dogs." "I didn't start crying, but I was very surprised," Louwé said. The staff at the clinic told him she had been sleeping with the Quran under her pillow.

Ayaan and Marco hurriedly drove two hours to Nijmegen, where they found Haweya in a kind of religious mania. She had been smashing her head against walls, shouting, "Allah Akbar! Allah Akbar!" She was also raving about Jesus. In Somalia, people would have assumed she was possessed. Marco, the science journalist, told Ayaan that in the West psychiatrists saw such religious outbursts as expressions of chemical imbalances in the brain. Either way, Haweya's behavior was terrifying to watch.

The prince of their subclan, Yassin Musse Boqor, who had visited Ayaan when she had first arrived in the Netherlands, also visited Haweya. His eyes misted over later as he recalled her illness: "Haweya, she is coming to be sick. She comes very sick, and she is in the psychiatric hospital in Nijmegen. Since I was living in Nijmegen, I cared for Haweya. Every day, she can't eat, I fed her. Ayaan comes one time per week because she is busy for university. Sometimes she comes with me and lives in my house to visit Haweya."

Yassin Musse Boqor often talked by phone with Ayaan's father about clan business. He told Hirsi that Ayaan was studying at university and taking good care of her sister. He urged Hirsi to get in touch with her. One night the phone rang at Ayaan and Marco's apartment. It was Ayaan's father calling her from Somalia. Despite all their differences, he was still her father and the man she most wanted to impress. Ayaan wrote that she wept and wept. "It was one of the most beautiful days in my life."

Twenty-seven

Aafia's parents talked her into getting a doctorate in neuroscience. Her mother said that even if Aafia became an Islamic preacher, having a "Dr." in front of her name would heighten her credibility. Aafia applied to Brandeis University to work toward a Ph.D. in cognitive neuroscience, and when Brandeis accepted her, she began studying there in the fall of 1995. She was seven months pregnant at the time and still disappointed that she and Amjad hadn't gone to Bosnia.

Brandeis seems a strange choice. The university could be described as a flagship of Enlightenment Judaism. Founded in 1948 by American Jews fed up with Ivy League quotas, it prided itself on not discriminating against students on the basis of religion. Yet it retained a strongly Jewish character—an odd fit for a devout Islamist like Aafia.

Amjad has said that his wife chose Brandeis for its convenient location in the Boston suburb of Waltham, for its excellent scientific reputation, and for its offer of generous financial aid. Around the same time, though, Aafia began reading books about the tactics of deception and about the Israeli spy agency, Mossad. Perhaps she saw herself as getting to know her enemy.

She must have been conspicuous when she showed up on campus, heavily pregnant and dressed in her Muslim head scarf and long dark gown or *jilbab*. It wasn't her clothes, though, that got her in trouble for the first time in her academic career, and it wasn't the anti-Semitism that she kept to herself. Instead it was a conflict she had with the university's commitment to secular, rational principles.

What puzzled Brandeis was that it hadn't happened earlier, when she was an undergraduate or even in high school.

Brain science was very much the family field, what with Aafia's father a neurosurgeon and her sister training to be a neurologist. For most scientists, however, the term "science" itself implies a commitment to a certain type of truth that can be determined only through reason, experiments, and careful observation. Aafia saw things differently: for her the scientific method was a tool in the service of religion.

When she started at Brandeis, she told people that her ambition was to open an Islamic women's university in Pakistan under the auspices of her mother's UIO. It would teach Western science from what she saw as the right perspective. She wrote on an MSA Web site that she wanted to create a "modern, well-equipped scientific institute" that would "serve to establish the supremacy of the Quran and Sunnah in the scientific world." The institute would teach "Western un-Islamic theories" but "with logical refutations and Islamic alternatives so that students are well-prepared to answer any objections raised against Islam."

Like other graduate students, Aafia had to prepare and deliver papers in front of classmates and professors at seminars. One early paper concerned the effects of fetal alcohol syndrome. She gave a fine summary of the latest research on how and why a pregnant woman could damage the future cognitive abilities of her unborn child by drinking alcohol. But then she concluded that this science showed why God had forbidden alcohol in the Quran.

Her professors were astonished and dismayed. Of course, scientists believe all sorts of things they can't prove. But most students learn in high school if not earlier that scientific knowledge needs to be based on testable hypotheses. That's close to the definition of science: it can be tested, proved, or shown to be false, whereas other forms of knowledge frequently cannot. Careful observation and measurement showed that a significant number of babies born to women who consumed alcohol during pregnancy suffered from brain damage. But no amount of measurement showed that God had forbidden everyone to drink.

Aafia's professors tried to explain that, but Aafia didn't agree. She told them that the Quran prefigured scientific knowledge and the scientist's job was to discover exactly how the laws in the Quran worked. "She saw science as a way of celebrating her religion," one faculty member recalled. "Many people were very disconcerted. A number of her teachers told her that it was inappropriate. She didn't like that. She didn't see a boundary there, and we did." Although Aafia was always "sweet and nice," in the words of another professor, she continued to bring up the Quran in her papers.

Aafia's professors could not imagine how she had graduated from MIT still holding on to this way of thinking.

Her undergraduate records offered no clue. One Brandeis teacher said later that Aafia had worked in various MIT labs but "there was no hint in her letters of recommendation" of any problem. Perhaps Aafia was becoming more confrontational about her faith, or perhaps no one at MIT had paid attention to her religious beliefs. Finally Brandeis gave her an order: "You can't turn in a paper that's all about the Quran. You have to learn to compartmentalize." Some of the same neuroscientists who criticized her said that apart from her religious absolutism, she performed well. "She was a very intelligent young woman. The only thing that was noticeable, that stood out, was that she wanted to bring fundamentalist Muslim tenets into our work."

She bitterly resented their criticism and complained of discrimination to the associate dean of graduate studies. Later she wrote that she had told the dean that "if they would let me graduate in peace, I would not go after Brandeis on any issues I had, but if not, I would be forced to open a can of worms." The dean apparently smoothed things over. But the tension between Aafia and her department persisted, and the episode seems to have reinforced her private belief that American Jews—or, as she often called them, "Israeli Americans"—were forever intriguing against Muslims.

Aafia and Amjad moved to Lexington, which was closer to her

classes. Amjad was deep in his residency, and they were both very busy. Their landlord in Lexington said they paid their rent on time and minded their own business. "At no time did she discuss anything about politics," said Gerald Ross. "I've got to tell you, if you're looking for an al-Qaeda person, I think you'd pick her, out of a hundred people, ninety-ninth or something."

Aafia's mother came over for the birth of Muhammad Ahmad on November 29, 1996. Ismat had managed to get a coveted residence permit or "green card" from the U.S. Immigration and Naturalization Services, and it allowed her to stay to help with the baby. For a while, Aafia's troubles seemed to vanish.

She finished her course work rapidly, earning a master's degree in a year. She made all As despite bearing her first child during the same period. After that she was allowed to focus on experiments for her thesis, and she began visiting the lab at night and on weekends. She told her supervisors that her family responsibilities made it hard for her to be at the university all day. But her colleagues felt she wanted to stay away. "She became a ghostly presence," one said.

It was perhaps unfortunate that Aafia eventually abandoned neuroscience. Just as she was entering the field, it began witnessing extraordinary discoveries. In the early 1990s, a team of Italian neuroscientists working with monkeys in Parma observed that the same brain cells that the monkeys used to send signals to their muscles to grasp food and then lift it to their mouths also fired when they watched another monkey or even a human being performing the same action. The Italians were identifying mirror neurons, special brain cells that allow human beings and other animals to understand the actions and emotions of others by instinctively and unconsciously simulating them. The eminent University of California cognitive neuroscientist Vilayanur Ramachandran later called this a breakthrough that would "do for psychology what DNA did for biology . . . provide a unifying framework and help explain a host of mental abilities that have hitherto remained mysterious and inaccessible to experiments."

The discovery of mirror neurons overturned a paradigm of learning that had dominated Western science ever since the Enlightenment. To be sure, it was still true that humans gained knowledge through deliberate reasoning. But experiments with mirror neurons showed that we learn more of what we know from unconscious and sometimes uncontrollable imitation.

Aafia's thesis adviser, Robert Sekuler, was already doing research on imitation. He and his colleagues at the university's Vision Laboratory were examining how people learn to do ordinary tasks such as drive a car, play the piano, and tie their shoelaces, all through unconscious imitation. Aafia developed her own hypotheses about how the brain accomplished this kind of learning, and she set up experiments to test them. She told her sister she wanted to use the new science to help disabled children learn.

In her dark, concealing clothes, Aafia must have cut a somber figure, and one professor recalled that Aafia, though pleasant, "was not known for her sense of humor." Her friend Imam Faaruuq said, "She was not a joke-teller." Her lawyer once put it this way: "Aafia was very serious about doing the will of Allah, and she irked some people with that." An Orthodox Jewish professor told the *Boston Globe* that she was always trying to convert him to Islam. "She was not hostile to me or anything but she kept telling me how I have to learn about Islam and see the light," the professor recalled. "She kept putting books in my mailbox." But by all accounts, Sekuler bent over backward to accommodate her and her schedule.

Aafia's own research could be tedious, as the scientific spadework of graduate students often is. But the discovery of mirror neurons *might* have reinforced her belief that science should illustrate the truth of Islam. Mirror neurons could help explain the tremendous emphasis that Islam places on imitation—an emphasis that can be hard to explain to Westerners who see morality as a more rational affair. If, as the new studies seemed to show, imitation is the basis of empathy as well as learning, generations of Islamic scholars might have been correct to believe that inward morality follows outward practice rather than the other way around. She might have found biological evidence to support the hadith that says, "Whoever imitates a people becomes one of them." But Aafia seems not to have made those conceptual leaps. Not long into her work on her dissertation, she seemed to lose her curiosity about neuroscience.

Twenty-eight

After Haweya left the hospital in June 1997, she went to live with Marco and Ayaan in their new apartment. It didn't work out. Ayaan wrote that Marco and Haweya quarreled. Haweya went to stay with Faduma Osman, the kinswoman who, with her son Mahad, had attended Ayaan's wedding in Nairobi; both were now living in the Netherlands.

Haweya was so religious by now that even her Somali relatives found it unnerving. To her cousin Mahad, she and Ayaan had practically exchanged roles. "If you compare the two, Haweya was more liberal when we were in Nairobi. In those days, Ayaan was a very fanatical Muslim. Here they changed. Ayaan became more liberal, and Haweya became very conservative."

Another relative, Guled Ahmed Yusef, was also shocked by Haweya's transformation when he visited her at Faduma's house. "Usually she was laughing and talking, but this time she was really low. She just sat in the corner with her head down."

She was taking medication. After a while it seemed to work, and she returned to university in Nijmegen. Faduma and Mahad thought she was getting back to normal. But to others she still talked about how Holland was making her ill. Her brother says she called him and her mother in Nairobi to complain that Ayaan was busy in Leiden and she had no one to talk to. She told Leo Louwé she needed a vacation.

The prince of their clan remembers, "Haweya got a little bit well. Then she started to say, 'I want to go back to Nairobi with my mom.'

Her mom was ill with psoriasis. She said, 'I want to go, Yassin, you must pay the ticket.' But I'm not agreeing with it. I said she's ill. Sometimes she's laughing and seeing something that is not there. I say, 'It's not good, you won't find medicine in Kenya, please stay here with me.' "

Ayaan said she didn't try to stop Haweya. She says her foster parents told her that if Haweya wanted to go home, Ayaan shouldn't prevent her.

And so, one day in July 1997, Haweya was gone. "I don't know who paid for the ticket," Yassin told me.

Twenty-nine

Aafia and Amjad moved yet again. This time, in the summer of 1997, they moved all the way to Worcester, almost forty miles west of Boston. Amjad began a new internship there at Saint Vincent Hospital. The town was also the home of several "Care brothers," as the couple called them. Care International's president, Emaddin Muntasser, owned the local Logan Furniture Store. The imam at the Worcester mosque was Muhammad Masood, a Boston University graduate and former MSA member whose brother was the leader of the Pakistani jihadi group Lashkar-e-Taiba. Aafia liked Worcester.

Aafia admired Lashkar for its strong women's wing, which held regular meetings and ran its own publications and girls' schools in Pakistan. The top woman of Lashkar, Umm Hammad, was a celebrated speaker. She edited the Lashkar magazine, as well as books such as *We Are the Women of Lashkar-e-Taiba*. Her troops wore the female jihadi uniform of black burkas, gloves, and socks. Yet Aafia disagreed on certain theological points with the Ahl-e-Hadith sect of Lashkar-e-Taiba and thus could not join Umm Hammad. She wished her own Deobandi sect would produce an equally strong women's group.

The Western world was just learning of the Deobandis' views on women, and it did not share Aafia's admiration. In 1995, with support from ISI and Saudi Arabia, an army of Taliban, or religious students, had wrested control of southern Afghanistan from the warlords who had ruled and terrorized the country since 1992. Deobandi madrassas all over Pakistan sent students to join the movement. The Taliban leader, Mullah Omar, was a mujahid who had lost an eye fighting the Soviets. He and his men were determined to stamp out any signs of female freedom left over from the days of the godless Soviets and their Afghan allies.

After seizing the Afghan capital, Kabul, in 1996, the Deobandi militiamen forbade women to leave their houses without a male relative. They banned women from working in any public occupation except medicine. Girls were banished from school. Women could not wear makeup, high heels, or "squeaky shoes." Bathhouses, beauty parlors, and home schools for girls were closed. The young zealots of the Taliban even whitewashed the first-floor windows of houses so that no one could see the women inside.

The United Nations and Western aid agencies objected, but the Taliban refused to repeal their edicts. "This is a big infidel policy which gives such obscene freedom to women which would lead to adultery and herald the destruction of Islam," the Taliban's attorney general told some UN officials. "In any Islamic country where adultery becomes common, that country is destroyed and enters the domination of infidels because their men become like women and women cannot defend themselves."

Other Muslims complained that the Taliban gave Islam a bad name, but the group's leaders told the Pakistani journalist Ahmed Rashid that the women's issue was too important to their own rank and file for them to compromise.

When the United Nations cut off development funds to Taliban areas in response to the measures against women, the Karachi fraternity of Deobandi divines formed a charity, the al-Rashid Trust, to funnel new money to the Taliban. Al-Rashid also started a newspaper, *Zarb-e-Momin* (Sword of the Believer) that Aafia read on the Internet. *Zarb-e-Momin*'s motto was simple: "News with a Lesson." Usually the lesson was about the evil designs of Jews, Crusaders, and Hindus on the Islamic paradise that the Taliban had created in Afghanistan. But the newspaper also focused on defending the

Islamic emirate's new gender regulations. Its writers attacked the United States for "ruthlessly exploiting women" by allowing thousands of unwed mothers to raise their children alone and for creating "government-sponsored Old Homes for aging parents." In a feature for children, the paper praised a boy who refused to let his mother go out fully veiled to buy him some shoes, since "it is better not to go outdoors" and "to leave the shopping" to men.

Aafia considered it far more important that the Taliban had made parts of Afghanistan safe for women and children than that females could no longer hold jobs and go to school. She trusted that they would be allowed to return when the war ended, but under properly Islamic conditions. About jihadi groups in general, says Amjad, "She thought the ones blowing up schools, throwing acid [into the faces of unveiled women], are a few misguided black sheep. Otherwise the movement is noble, i.e., to establish the law of God in the land, and end injustice by it."

She also agreed with another Taliban decision that the United States criticized: to play host to the multimillionaire Saudi militant Osama bin Laden.

U.S. investigators first became conscious of bin Laden during the trials of the Al-Kifah conspirators for the 1993 World Trade Center bombing. The FBI learned that he had contributed to Sayyid Nosair's defense fund after Nosair had assassinated Rabbi Meir Kahane. When Ramzi Yousef was captured, they found that Yousef had stayed in some guesthouses owned by bin Laden. The Americans had only the dimmest understanding of the network of banks and charities that the Islamists had established—in some cases right under their noses—and they began to suspect bin Laden of personally financing this jihadi movement. It was under strict secrecy that the U.S. attorney's office in New York empaneled a grand jury to begin investigating bin Laden in 1996. Equally secret was a special unit that the CIA set up that year to investigate the same man. It was the first unit the agency had ever created dedicated to collecting intelligence on a single person.

Aafia thought of bin Laden as a great Islamic hero, modeled after the Prophet Muhammad himself. TV interviews of him sitting on the ground in his camouflage jacket, eating with his hands, and sharing a tin cup with his fellow mujahideen moved her to tears. Here was a man who could be living like a prince. Instead, he had given it all up for Islam.

Thirty

In Kenya, Haweya stopped taking the medicine she had received in Holland. Her brother, Mahad, said she seemed okay for about three months. Then all of a sudden she became disturbed again. There were times when she lost control. "She would be talking the whole day complaining about hearing voices," Mahad said. She began raving about religion.

Ayaan wrote later that their mother summoned mullahs and an exorcist to drive out Haweya's psychoses. Their brother, Mahad, said that Haweya herself, in desperation, sought out faith healers—"but there was no change in status."

Ayaan talked with Haweya every ten days or so. By October, Haweya begged her sister to come to Nairobi and rescue her. She said their mother had taken her to an exorcist, who had beaten her with sticks. But Ayaan was behind in her studies, and she spent the Christmas break writing overdue papers.

On January 8, 1998, her father called to say that Haweya was dead. Again, Ayaan has described this event differently at different points. In *The Caged Virgin* she said she never found out exactly what happened. In *Infidel* she wrote that her sister ran outside in a lightning storm, suffered a miscarriage, and died a week later. Haweya had told her she was pregnant; Ayaan did not write by whom. Other Somalis in Nairobi say Haweya committed suicide. But they don't want to talk about it.

Ayaan later said that Haweya's death was the lowest point of her life. She flew to Nairobi but missed the burial. Ayaan found her mother alone, living in "utter squalor" in a small room with a cement floor and smoke-stained walls. Mahad had recently married a Somali girl from a respectable clan and fathered a baby. Their mother disapproved and was refusing to acknowledge either the wife or the child. When Ayaan went to see the baby, Mahad's new wife broke into a tirade about how selfish and ungrateful she was not to help her relatives in Africa. "You drive around in a fancy car; you make money from the misery of the refugees in Holland, translating for the infidels. And yet you did not bother to bring the little boy anything. You are rich and you don't share a penny."

In truth, Ayaan said, she had been sending her family money for almost six years—ever since she had arrived in Holland. She asked Mahad what had happened to it. He shrugged and said he had invested it with a man who had stolen it.

It was all unspeakably depressing. Ayaan decided she wouldn't be going back. Before leaving, she said, she gave her mother $1,000 so that she could finally return to Somalia and her own clan.

Thirty-one

Aafia had never given up on her causes, not even when she became a mother and a graduate student. When the war in Bosnia ended, she started raising money for Chechnya and Kosovo.

Her friend Imam Faaruuq at the Mosque for Praising Allah remembered a time when Aafia got up at a fund-raiser and asked how many men there owned two pairs of boots. If they had two pairs, she said, they could afford to donate money for boots to give to the mujahideen in Chechnya. "You don't need two pairs of boots in this country," she scoffed. "They're facing a cold winter there!" The imam said he took his own boots off and gave them to her.

She taught at several Boston-area mosques, and on Sundays she drove across town to teach the Quran to converts. "She used to go to all the places and to our center, too," said Imam Talal Eid of the Islamic Center of New England, in Quincy. "Whenever there is an event, she comes."

"She was a popular and well-liked member of the community," said Imam Faaruuq. Faaruuq's wife later told the *Boston Globe* that Aafia Siddiqui had given powerful speeches urging women, especially new converts to Islam, to start wearing the head scarf and to refuse to shake hands with men. "She shared with us that we should never make excuses for who we are," Faaruuq's wife recalled. "She said, 'Americans have no respect for people who are weak. Americans will respect us if we stand up and we are strong.'"

She was working incredibly hard. She attributed her discipline to a lifetime of fasting, getting up at 5 a.m. for prayers, and avoiding all frivolous entertainment. Yet having a baby, commuting to work, and pursuing two careers added to the usual strains of marriage. Her mother's long stay created one kind of friction. Then, after she returned to Pakistan, Amjad began complaining about the long hours that their son, Ahmad, was spending in day care. Finally Aafia found a suitable Bosnian "sister" to care for the boy at home. But the tension between them did not abate.

Both looked to Islam for guidance at such times. Unfortunately for Aafia, the Deobandi interpretation to which they both subscribed came down squarely on Amjad's side: her primary duty was to be a wife and mother, while his was to make money to support their family. The Quran said, "Men are the protectors and maintainers of women, because Allah has given the one more (strength) than the other, and because they support them from their means." Amjad quoted scholars who said that Allah had established this rule so that households would run smoothly. But Aafia became so offended when he suggested that she postpone her studies until Ahmad went to school that he stopped talking about it.

Her acquaintances in Boston were still puzzled that she had married a man who appeared not to share her zeal for jihad. Amjad struck them as "soft." He never wore "jihad attire." He wore Western clothes or, more often, a doctor's scrub suit. "He was just a busy doctor," said a Pakistani American. "I never heard him say anything about jihad."

The couple moved again, this time to be nearer to his residency at Brigham and Women's Hospital. Their new apartment was on the twentieth floor of Back Bay Manor, a redbrick apartment complex in Mission Hill that housed enough Muslims to have its own prayer room. Amjad also helped some of Aafia's friends from Roxbury start a group to deal with domestic violence. He seemed to be falling into the patterns of conventional American life.

By contrast, Aafia seemed increasingly anti-American. She would study their tax returns for hours, looking for ways to get a refund;

Amjad recalls her saying, "Every dollar I give to the U.S. government will be used to kill Muslims somewhere or other in the world." When one of his cousins argued that Muslims could do a lot of good living in the United States—for example, by being models of moral and professional excellence or by voting for candidates who saw the Muslims' point of view—Aafia flew into a rage. She said those were just excuses; the truth was that some Muslims would rather chase money than wage jihad. "Yet Allah said, 'Fighting is prescribed for you, even though you dislike it. It is possible that you dislike a thing which is good for you and that you love a thing which is bad for you. Allah knows and you do not.' "

Aafia's activism was beginning to grate on Amjad. After their second child was born in September 1998—a daughter they named Maryam bint Muhammad, in Arab style, or "Maryam, daughter of Muhammad"—Aafia returned to her commitments outside the home. "She was a very good speaker and she was very fond of giving speeches, but she sometimes neglected the children," one of Amjad's relatives told me. "He got upset. His idea was the priority of the children. She was not very interested in family. She was giving speeches, fund-raising, things like that. She used to go to jails—all of these things."

Her husband's tepidness toward jihad was becoming worse than embarrassing. Now that she was married, she couldn't attend mixed gatherings alone. But Amjad was always working at the hospital, and when he wasn't there he was writing papers at home. His adviser, Dr. Daniel Dedrick, was so impressed with his work that he let Amjad sign up for courses at Harvard's School of Public Health, leaving him even less time for rallies and conferences. Aafia wanted him to take the family camping with her "Care brothers," but as much as he liked camping, Amjad had to study on weekends. She argued that the "brothers" were doing important work and he should get to know them; he shot back that his and her first responsibility was to their own family.

Amjad remembers her getting so angry that she would clench her teeth and come after him, beating him with her fists and kicking if he tried to hold her down. She weighed so little that she couldn't hurt him, and he claims she liked him better after their fights. But two of Aafia's professors at Brandeis later told the FBI that "at various times" she had bruises on her face. The honeymoon was definitely over.

Thirty-two

Ayaan threw herself into her studies after she returned to Holland from Nairobi. As the only licensed Somali-Dutch translator in the country, she was also in demand at work. "She worked really, really hard," Marco said. "She would leave early in the morning and drive four hours to Groningen. She would come back at seven in the evening, and she would only have had one cup of tea all day." Marco told her that her employers were obliged to give her time to eat. She answered that they had usually waited so long for a translator and were so happy to see her that she didn't have the heart to ask them for a break.

Marco admired Ayaan in many ways. When her teenage cousin Magool ended up in a juvenile home after her parents paid a trafficker to take her to the Netherlands, Ayaan made room for Magool to share their Langegracht flat. But Marco also began to realize that some of the same characteristics that set his stunning African girlfriend apart from her Dutch counterparts made it hard for them to live together.

Marco worried about saving money, getting along with friends and family, and getting ahead in his career. "Here you have everything ready for you from the time you are born—a future, a house. Your only concern is your pension and to take care not to get hit by a bus." Ayaan didn't share such concerns at all. When she had money, she spent it. Even when she bought meat, she would insist (to the point of serious anger) that they eat all the meat the same day. She took risks that made Marco's head spin. If she didn't like a job, she would quit on the spot. If someone crossed her, she would instantly confront the person.

That didn't mean she was fearless. Quite the opposite, Marco felt. It meant she had been taught that the world was so dangerous that one *had* to react quickly to a challenge. "She is always on guard," he observed.

He could not convince her that she would not be robbed if she went alone to Leiden's Central Station. Once when she got lost in the car, he told her to follow the road signs back to Leiden. "She really didn't believe me," he recalled. He marveled that "her distrust of government and society is just so big." Sometimes he found it touching that Ayaan viewed the Dutch as absurdly trusting. But at other times her suspicions exhausted him.

He had come to believe that her assumptions about life being dangerous and uncertain—assumptions that may have been realistic in Africa—served in Holland to create some of the danger and uncertainty she sought to avoid. "She would spend money easily, so she was always short-cashed. But if you are short-cashed, tomorrow will always be uncertain. And so tomorrow *was* always uncertain. If you live each day as if it is your last day, and you never think ahead, it becomes a self-fulfilling prophecy."

On the other hand, he realized that what seemed to him reckless imprudence sometimes worked to Ayaan's advantage in a society like the Netherlands, where everyone else felt so constrained. "We are always worrying about what will happen if we do this or that," he said. "Ayaan doesn't worry about that, and she often ends up in very nice and unexpected situations because she is willing to take risks." But her appetite for drama and excitement was far greater than his.

He found it painful to follow her relationship with her family. Ayaan showed him the letter her father had written that called her a "Deceitful Fox" for backing out of her marriage to Osman Musse Quarre. She told Marco without bitterness that her father's honor had been at stake, and she could understand why he had written the letter.

Marco didn't agree at all. "It was such a stupid, childish letter that you couldn't even use it in a soap!" he said. Ayaan seemed to feel that all the obligations went one way, from children to parents. It was a common view in Africa and Asia, but it made Marco angry. "What about the obligations they had to her?" He couldn't imagine parents treating a child the way Ayaan said her parents treated her. But he was getting the idea that "it's unbelievably harsh how people treat each other in Africa."

Ayaan received a Dutch passport in 1997, and she began joining Marco on his shoestring travels. They visited China and the Middle East. Their trips afforded her another view of the world through Western eyes. Marco gave her a book about Egypt called *A Good Man Sometimes Beats His Wife*. The Dutch journalist Joris Luyendijk had written it about the circle of Egyptian friends he had made while studying for a year at the University of Cairo. Luyendijk had taken the title from an Egyptian woman who told him that a woman couldn't be sure a man loved her if he didn't beat her. The book was a Dutch bestseller, largely for the window it opened on the different views of sex held by Egyptian and Dutch young people. Ayaan has said that she read for the first time in Luyendijk's book about the Quranic texts that men used to justify beating their wives. She later told the Leiden student newspaper that the book had opened her eyes. She had never really thought before about the specific impact of Islam on women.

Luyendijk himself felt that his book's more important message was the enormous gap in wealth between him and his fellow students and the obstacle it presented to real friendship. "The cultural things, you can get past," he told me. "The poverty was more important. It's like me trying to be friends with a millionaire. I can't do it. I can't live in his neighborhood, I can't do the things he does. That's how it was for them to be friends with me." The difference between the life he could expect as a middle-class Dutchman and what they had to settle for as middle-class Egyptians was so painful and insoluble that they never talked about it explicitly. The book ends when Luyendijk learns that the brother of one of his friends has died because the family couldn't afford to take him to a hospital.

With her new Dutch passport, Ayaan had become one of those relative millionaires, and, as time passed, she found it easier to identify with the Dutch point of view.

Her fellow clansmen now saw her as a great success. "Everyone forgot about her marriage," said Faduma Osman. Somalis called her up to ask favors. Ayaan didn't mind giving them advice, but she got tired of their endless needs. The clan had set up something called the Kah Foundation (*kah* means "dawn" in Somali) to help its members in the Netherlands. The prince of her lineage, Yassin Musse Boqor, asked Ayaan to join the board. "I said, Ayaan, you are very clever, you are very intelligent, will you sit on the board and help us?" Ayaan told him she was too busy with her studies, but every now and then she gave him 5 or 10 guilders as a contribution.

She still considered herself a Muslim, but has written that she kept that part of her brain separate. When she read or heard something that conflicted with Islam as she understood it, "a little shutter in my brain clicked" and she mentally closed her faith against whatever she was hearing. But she grew tired of the way other Muslims—including total strangers—would approach her in a bar or on the street and tell her she was sinning. And when Marco lent her *The Atheist Manifesto* by Herman Philipse, a philosophy professor at Utrecht University, she didn't read it, she says, because she feared the book might convince her.

Thirty-three

The turn of the world's calendars from 1999 to 2000 excited as much superstitious hope and apprehension among jihadis as it did among other people. They speculated that the dawn of a new Christian millennium might presage the coming showdown between Muslims and the followers of the Dajjal.

The new year also brought the news that the husband of Aafia's friend Marlene—Bassam Kanj, a leader of Al-Kifah in Boston—had been martyred in his native Lebanon.

The newspapers said that Kanj, a Boston University graduate and sometime Boston taxi driver, had been trying to establish an Islamic state. But his friends at Care International said the shooting had started when Lebanese government troops tried to raid one of the training camps Kanj was trying to build for aspiring Lebanese jihadis. Some reports added that, before he was killed, the burly Kanj had threatened to behead two Lebanese soldiers whom his followers had taken hostage. Kanj's former comrades were sure he had gone to paradise. The "Care brothers" were recorded at the time talking about it at the office. One had recently visited Kanj in Lebanon. "I was very affected by the brother," he told the other members of the group while the FBI bugged their conversation.

Aafia visited Marlene, who had been shown a picture of her husband with a bullet through his head. She felt sorry for Marlene but also in awe of her friend. Marlene was now the widow of a *shahid*, whose passage to paradise was almost guaranteed. The "brothers" soon arranged for Marlene to marry a Saudi jihadi named Anwar al-Mirabi, who had fought in Afghanistan and attended a mosque in Arlington, Texas, that was run by an imam named Moataz al-Hallak. During the embassy-bombings trial in New York in 1999, prosecutors alleged that Hallak had been the Texas go-between for bin Laden and his followers in the United States, though Hallak was never charged with any crime. Marlene and her five children soon trooped off to Arlington with her new husband.

For the next year, Aafia was busy around the clock. She had a tiny baby and a toddler to care for, she had started teaching a new class at the mosque in Sharon, and she was writing her dissertation. She finished her thesis in February 2001. It was called "Separating the Components of Imitation." An article based on her master's thesis had been published the month before in a prestigious scientific journal. She had completed the requirements for both her master's and her Ph.D. in less than four years—record time, especially considering that she had meanwhile borne two children. In the dissertation's acknowledgments, she wrote that she "would like to thank my mother, Ismat Siddiqui, for my dissertation is a direct result of her motivation, strong encouragement and support. . . . Nothing in the universe can replace her!" One of her advisers asked about her career plans. She replied that for the time being her religion required her to concentrate on her family.

After so much work, the change was abrupt. Finally free to wear what she liked, she started pinning her black veil so that it covered everything except her eyes when she left the apartment.

As for Amjad's career, it was taking off. He graduated as the best in his class of residents in anesthesiology at Brigham and Women's Hospital. In February 2001, the American Association of Anesthesiologists named him editor of its national newsletter. Now that he understood how the U.S. medical system worked, he thought he could someday branch out into health care management. He applied to study for a master's degree in public health at Harvard, and Harvard accepted him. His adviser at Brigham and Women's, Dr. Daniel Dedrick, was proud of him—but Aafia seemed not to share

Dedrick's pride. She often quoted the Quranic verse that said, "Oh you who believe! Let not your riches and your children divert you from remembrance of Allah." Amjad tried to mollify her by finally growing a beard again.

With the millennium still hovering, many Muslims felt that something awesome and ordained would happen. After the leader of Israel's right-wing Likud Party sparked an already planned Palestinian uprising by visiting Jerusalem's Dome of the Rock in September 2000, groups affiliated with the Muslim Brotherhood began holding wildly emotional rallies in the United States. The Salafist scholar and spiritual adviser to Osama bin Laden, Safar al-Hawali, wrote a treatise called "Day of Wrath" predicting that the intifada could be the precursor to the final battle with the Dajjal.

Since finishing her Ph.D., Aafia had been translating *The Lovers of the Paradise Maidens* by Abdullah Azzam ("the Godfather of Jihad") from Arabic into English and posting the chapters on a jihadi Web site. The book consisted of short biographies of about 150 martyrs who had died in the Afghan jihad.

Aafia also participated in Islamic discussion groups on the Internet. The arguments she got into sometimes made her very angry. She thought Muslims who said Islam required them to live peacefully with unbelievers and confine themselves to *dawah* were probably U.S. agents.

She was also growing more rigid in her personal life. When Amjad's brother and his family visited Boston, they all went to see a science museum. One exhibit included background music. Aafia backed away. Music was *haram*—forbidden.

Thirty-four

Leiden's student magazine interviewed Ayaan in May 1998, five months after Haweya's death. The headline read, "Soon I Will Go into Politics."

She appears not to have had any special cause to fight at the time. But she was her father's daughter, and politics ran in her veins.

She had joined the Labor Party, which was ruling the country at the time in a so-called "purple coalition" with the more conservative parties. Yet her political party wasn't part of her identity the way it was for many others in Holland. In *Infidel* she wrote that she never really liked social work. She didn't want to save Africa. According to her boyfriend, Marco, she wasn't especially interested in women's rights.

In her last years at Leiden, however, she noticed a possible political niche for an immigrant like herself.

For much of the 1990s, many Dutch people felt that the Netherlands possessed a great secret of government in its devotion to consensual decision making. Under the country's unusual "pillar system," the population was divided according to religion and political affiliation. The government gave each of these "pillars" the money to run its own schools, television stations, newspapers, and even sports clubs, and by 1998 an astounding 80 percent of the country's citizens were satisfied with their government. The reigning attitude was a jaunty tolerance summed up in the Dutch phrase "Anything goes."

But beneath the surface, cracks were showing.

Muslims made up 5 percent of Holland's sixteen million people.

They were poorer and less educated than the native-born population, and there was an undercurrent of hostility toward them. In 1991, the chairman of the opposition Liberal Party, Frits Bolkestein, expressed his fears that the country was admitting more Muslim immigrants than it could absorb. He argued that the Dutch should set aside their traditional separate "pillars" and work toward integration instead. But he warned that integration would fail if Muslims refused to accept homosexuality and the equality of women.

The Left pilloried Bolkestein and accused him of pandering to racists. But the tensions that he noted were real.

A few years later a Rotterdam sociologist and columnist named Pim Fortuyn picked up the theme with more bite, railing against Islam as "a backward religion" that was hostile to women and gays. The title alone of his 1998 book, *Against the Islamicization of Our Culture*, suggested the alarm that more than a few Dutch citizens felt.

Fortuyn argued that sexual freedom was essential to Dutch culture and worth defending. He assailed what he called "the left church," or the politically correct establishment, that, he claimed, made it impossible in Holland to talk frankly about Muslims and immigration. He pointed out that Moroccan youths committed much of the crime that plagued immigrant neighborhoods. He called for a crackdown.

Fortuyn's arguments startled people. As a former Catholic and former Marxist who was also gay, he had benefited from the country's tolerance. But now he seemed to be saying that if the Netherlands wanted to keep its culture of "anything goes," it would first have to exclude entire ethnic and religious groups. He clearly struck a chord, and Fortuyn and Bolkestein together made it seem that the Dutch had to choose: either they could support the Muslims, or they could support women and gays.

Their arguments put the Labor Party in a bind. On the one hand, the party refused to descend to Muslim bashing. But it also worried that the conservatives (including Bolkestein's Liberal Party) might steal Labor's defense of liberal values. On January 29, 2000, the left-leaning

Dutch intellectual Paul Scheffer published an article called "The Multicultural Drama" in *NRC Handelsblad*. In it, he played on the Dutch fondness for Calvinist self-flagellation. It wasn't the Muslims who were to blame for Holland's predicament, he wrote, it was progressive Dutchmen like himself; they had turned a blind eye to the failures of multiculturalism and allowed an underclass to develop in the country's cities.

Either way, the message was the same: it was time to get tougher on Muslims.

Ayaan found the whole kerfuffle overdone. In her view, the Dutch tended to turn little problems into crises.

Nearing graduation, she took Marco to Germany to meet her father. Hirsi was in Düsseldorf to have an eye operation, and the two visitors spent a pleasant afternoon with him. Marco was touched to see how happy it made Ayaan to be with her father. "They were really cuddling all the time, and Ayaan was kissing him." But he also found the meeting painful to watch.

Ayaan had often told him how liberal and broad-minded her father was. To Marco, though, Hirsi seemed a real Muslim patriarch. Even Ayaan seemed surprised by what a stickler he had become regarding Islam. "He was always preaching," Marco said. It made the young Dutchman furious to see that, despite all Ayaan's accomplishments, Hirsi and her other male relatives still treated her like a child because she was a woman. "Some nephew came in," Marco recalled. "Without even saying a word to Ayaan, he started telling her father that she should wear a scarf. If you are a woman in their society, you are nobody, really nobody."

Marco didn't try to hide his irritation, but Ayaan kept it from her father that she and Marco were living together. She said they were just friends. Yassin, however, and other relatives knew about their relationship.

In any case, Hirsi tried to release his daughter from her marriage to the Canadian Osman Musse Quarre, who, Faduma Osman says, had, out of spite, refused Ayaan's requests for a divorce. Hirsi wrote a rather groveling general letter to the Osman Mahamud lineage in Europe and North America asking his fellow clansmen to help Ayaan free herself legally from the husband she had not seen in eight years.

"My dear fellows," Ayaan's father began, "I would like to inform you that eight years ago Mr. Osman Muse Qaare [*sic*], himself of our clan, married Ayan Hirsi [*sic*] under the auspices of the Osman Mahamud community in Nairobi." He admitted that although Osman had "met all the marriage expenses plus Ayan's travel expenses to Kanada [*sic*], she went to Europe, ignoring all her sacred obligations of the marriage. This was a wounding, heart-breaking betrayal of Osman and [an] indelible shame on our family. I expressed to Osman my outrage and tried to console him." Still, he appealed "to you, my brothers and sisters, to your grace and sympathy in an attempt to resolve this awkward problem."

Around the same time, Prince Yassin says, Ayaan also asked his help in persuading Osman to divorce her. "Ayaan says to me, 'Can we talk, can I tell you something?' And then she tells me, 'When I'm in Nairobi, my father, Hirsi, he gave me to one of my family. I don't want him, that guy.' . . . She said, 'I need help. You are our prince. Can you help me?' "

Yassin told her, "Just talk to him, and say you don't want him. If you still cannot find a solution, I can make an announcement. I can call all the men in my family, and we can have a meeting to decide what to do."

Yassin says he told the elders—including his brother, the prince of the Canadian branch of the clan—that they had to help Ayaan. Approached this way, Osman finally agreed to let Ayaan go. "After that," Yassin said, "Ayaan, she's not married. This is our culture."

Ayaan graduated from Leiden University with a master's degree in September 2000. A nephew and one other man were the only Somalis at her graduation party. Yassin says she called him later to tell him she had taken her degree. "I would have come," Yassin says, "but she didn't give me the invitation."

Thirty-five

It was spring 2001. Aafia Siddiqui e-mailed her friend Salma Kazmi, a Wellesley graduate and fellow MSA member, to say she would be running a children's playgroup that summer. Her sister, Fowzia, was moving to Boston to do a fellowship at Brigham and Women's in neurology. She rented an apartment two floors below Aafia's. Her two children would be in the group, Aafia's, too.

Fowzia and Amjad had never gotten along, and when Fowzia arrived in Boston she noticed something was wrong with her sister. "Aafia was not happy," she said later. "She had lost her contagious smile." Amjad says Fowzia aggravated the tensions already evident in their marriage.

Fowzia says her children spent a blissful summer in Aafia's care. "It was perfect for me," she said. "I couldn't get a better babysitter. She did games, songs, and different activities." Aafia's American neighbors found her and her charges rather glum. A man who lived on the same floor said the children played outside in the hall while Aafia worked on the computer. When he asked young Ahmad, in the elevator, what he was learning at his preschool, the four-year-old said, "The Quran." Another time Aafia quarreled with the building management when the fire sprinkler system caused a flood in her apartment. She accused the management of mistreating her because she was Muslim.

One night she got so excited at one of her fund-raisers that she tossed a ring—an expensive one that Amjad had given her—into the collection basket for the mujahideen. Amjad and the children were at the fund-raiser that night, and Amjad could tell that Aafia was tired. Then two-year-old Maryam began to cry that she was hungry. Amjad told Aafia it was time to go home and feed the baby, but Aafia insisted that she needed to stay. "She said, 'No, no, I still want to see how many people are giving funds,'" a relative of Amjad's told me later.

Taking both children, Amjad left the hall. Aafia followed, but in the car she complained that he failed to appreciate what she was doing for oppressed Muslims.

Their argument continued once they got home. According to Amjad, he was trying clumsily to feed the baby a bottle. Aafia shouted that he was doing it wrong. Furious, Amjad spun around, and, he says, the milk bottle slipped from his hands and struck her on the mouth. (Aafia told the FBI that he had thrown the bottle at her "out of frustration.")

Amjad took her to the emergency room and asked a friend there, a plastic surgeon, to stitch her up. Back home again, he apologized and made some chocolate milk for Aafia before they went to bed.

The next morning, after Amjad went to work, Fowzia stopped at the apartment to drop off her children. Seeing Aafia's face, she insisted that her sister take the children and stay in her apartment.

Amjad found his apartment empty when he got home. Realizing that Aafia must be at Fowzia's, he knocked on her door. But Fowzia wouldn't answer, and Aafia wouldn't come to the phone. Normally he brought home milk and food for breakfast at the end of his workday. The next morning he left the things outside Fowzia's door and left for work.

After four days, Aafia decided to return. But Amjad says that before she agreed to stay, she showed him a photograph that Fowzia had taken of her bruises and told him that if he ever laid a hand on her again, Fowzia would take the picture to the police.

Hoping a change of scenery might improve matters, he proposed yet another move, away from those unpleasant memories. He could afford a bigger apartment now. The Tufts New England Medical

Center at Tufts University had offered him a full-time position as an attending physician, and he wanted to move back to Malden, the northern suburb where they had been happy early in their marriage. In June 2001, he and Aafia signed a lease in a complex called Granada Heights, with a lake and a swimming pool, and after subletting their Back Bay apartment to a Saudi whom Amjad had met at the hospital, they moved to Malden on July 1.

Thirty-six

The pharmaceutical company GlaxoSmithKline offered Ayaan Hirsi Ali a job selling Imigran, an antimigraine drug, to doctors. Despite her political ambitions, she took the job. She couldn't resist the lure of a company car. And she wanted to leave the council flat on the Langegracht.

At thirty-one, she felt that she had lived like a student long enough and, now that she had a full-time job, she could afford to buy a house. She found a nice one near the train station in Leiden. When Marco said he didn't want to buy a house with her, she talked a girlfriend into joining her instead.

She and Marco were on the verge of breaking up. They were always arguing about money and other things. Ayaan says she got tired of it. They were still very fond of each other, but "in the end," she wrote later, "it did not work out because we are both strong-willed and neither of us are inclined to give in. That always led to arguments. Moreover, I am rather scattered, while he is meticulous and strict."

She called Prince Yassin and said she wanted to visit his mother, a grand old lady who was in the hospital in Groningen. "I said, 'Tell me—what's your life?' " Yassin remembered asking Ayaan. "She said, 'I've got the good job and new car and a petrol pass.' " Ayaan told Yassin she would visit him soon and they would go to the hospital together. "I am very happy at that time." But she didn't come. That was the last time they spoke.

The Glaxo job didn't work out. After two weeks, Ayaan quit. She took a job working for the small town of Oegstgeest, but she didn't like that, either.

The soaring popularity of Pim Fortuyn had turned the subject of Muslim integration into a hot topic in the press. Other Dutch politicians could no longer avoid taking a stand on what more and more people seemed to agree was the problem of too many Muslims in Holland.

Through her work as a translator for the immigration service, Ayaan appeared in a couple of television debates on immigration. The views she presented were middle of the road, but she showed a definite talent for the medium, sometimes stealing the show with a quick riposte. When, in March 2001, Marco read in the newspaper that the Labor Party was looking for a research assistant at its think tank, the Wiardi Beckman Institute in Amsterdam, he told her the job sounded perfect for her. It would start in the autumn and focus on immigration and integration. Ayaan decided to apply.

Several of her former professors at Leiden offered to vouch for her. She also impressed the institute by entering and winning a national debate competition in Utrecht. ("She comes from an oral culture," Marco commented, "and she is much better than the average Dutchman at thinking on her feet.") But with more than a hundred applicants, the competition for the job was stiff.

While the selection process inched along, another TV show about Muslim immigrants focused on gay teachers being harassed by Moroccan schoolchildren. A conservative imam from Rotterdam opined that homosexuality was "a contagious disease." Fortuyn seized on the man's words as proof that Muslims didn't respect Dutch values.

Later commentators noted that the Dutch acceptance of homosexuality was actually quite new and more tentative than most outsiders imagined. (Only a few weeks earlier, in fact, the new mayor of Amsterdam had officiated at Europe's first same-sex marriage.) Moreover, it wasn't exactly true that Dutch Muslims were untouched by Dutch attitudes. They were less approving of homosexuality than non-Muslim Dutch, but they also were less critical of gays than Muslims in other countries. At the time, though, the whole country seemed to agree with Fortuyn that, citizens or not, people who said they didn't want their children to be gay simply didn't belong in Holland.

Ayaan sat down and wrote an article for *NRC Handelsblad* blaming Islam for the imam's prejudice. "I wrote that this attitude was much larger than just one imam: It was systemic in Islam, because this was a religion that had never gone through the Enlightenment that would lead people to question its rigid approach to individual freedom." It was her first article, and it appeared in May 2001. It positioned her as a perfect defender of the Labor Party. Here was a Muslim woman who wasn't afraid to criticize Islam. Here was an immigrant who embraced the "Enlightenment," a term that neatly allowed a person to be Western without being Christian, and one that Fortuyn was making a totem of "Dutchness."

A few weeks later, Ayaan learned that she had landed the job at the Wiardi Beckman Institute, starting in September.

Thirty-seven

A few weeks after Aafia and Amjad moved into the Granada Heights complex, a professionally produced video began circulating on the Internet chat rooms Aafia frequented.

In the video, which was two hours long, Osama bin Laden, dressed in white robes, read a poem recalling the victory of the Muslim hero Saladin over the Crusaders in the Middle Ages. The film then showed familiar footage of Israeli soldiers beating Palestinian women and a young Palestinian boy being shot outside the Dome of the Rock in Jerusalem, a city that Muslims call al-Quds. "Jews are free in al-Quds to rape Muslim women and to imprison the young cubs who stand up to them," bin Laden said. "The blood of Muslims is the cheapest of all blood!" He ranted against the Jews who he said ran the U.S. government. "We speak of an American government, but it is in reality an Israeli government, because if we look at the most sensitive departments of the government, whether it is the Pentagon or the State Department or the CIA, you find that it is the Jews who have first word in the American government."

Peter Bergen, a CNN correspondent who had interviewed bin Laden in 1997 and had just finished writing a biography of him, saw the video and reacted with alarm. Bin Laden's statements clarified something that had puzzled Bergen: why had the jihadi leader, whose speeches condemned Jews and their supposed conspiracies, never attacked Jewish or Israeli targets? "I came to realize that for bin Laden, the Pentagon *was* a Jewish target," Bergen said later. He wrote to a friend at the *New York Times* on August 17 and urged him to look into the possibility that a plot was in the works.

The Al-Kifah circle also seems to have heard the message that something sensational was about to happen. Aafia's friend Marlene was heavily pregnant in Texas by her new Saudi husband, Mirabi, and in late August the couple piled her five children into a car and drove 1,500 miles from Arlington to Boston. Marlene said she wanted a friendly midwife there to deliver her baby. The FBI later suspected that she and Mirabi had some knowledge of what was coming and may have wanted to deliver the message to friends or even meet with the hijackers, who were already taking up positions along the East Coast. Marlene's Boston circle put on a reception for her that Aafia attended. Yet Aafia said nothing special to her husband about the occasion, and he noticed nothing different about her behavior afterward.

Marlene's baby—a boy she named Bassam after her martyred first husband—was born on August 29. She flew back to Texas with the infant a few days later. Her new husband and the rest of the children drove home via New York.

In Boston and up and down the East Coast, September 11, 2001, dawned crystalline blue. It was ten years to the day since Aafia had been a student in Houston and President George H. W. Bush had called for a "new world order" in the aftermath of the Gulf War. For those like Aafia who believed that this order was ranged against Islam, the superpower's comeuppance was about to begin.

At 8:46 a.m., American Airlines flight 11 crashed into the World Trade Center's North Tower. Seventeen minutes later, United Airlines flight 175 crashed into the South Tower. Both planes had taken off from Boston's Logan Airport. Two other scheduled airliners also crashed, one of them into the Pentagon. Within hours the *Boston Globe* reported that police were looking for Osama bin Laden's "cells and sympathizers" in Boston's jihadi network.

Amjad was scheduled to start classes that week at Harvard's School of Public Health. He didn't show up, according to a spokeswoman for the school. As soon as Aafia heard what had happened, she started crying and praying. All day long, they watched TV and talked on the phone with worried friends. By the end of the day, Aafia had decided that they had to leave immediately for Pakistan. "My life is in danger," she insisted, becoming hysterical; "my children's lives are in danger." Amjad was just a few months away from taking his anesthesiology board exams. He wanted to wait and see what happened. Aafia refused. "You stay here," she said, "but I must go."

If Aafia knew in advance about the 9/11 attacks, Amjad insists she never told him.

Police in Boston began raiding hotels that the hijackers had stayed in. They also hunted for Nabil al-Marabh, a Boston cabdriver who had worked with Bassam Kanj. They had learned that two of the hijackers who left from Boston were known to these sometime cabdrivers, and that al-Marabh had sent them money. Several other hijackers had spent their last weeks in Laurel, Maryland, living down the street from Moataz al-Hallak, the imam from Arlington, Texas, who had guided Marlene and her Saudi husband and who, prosecutors said, was bin Laden's U.S. go-between.

Marlene's new husband was arrested on September 13. And the FBI questioned Aafia's friends at Care International.

Amjad tried to calm her, but she wouldn't have it. Within hours of the attacks, prominent Deobandis in Pakistan, including General Hamid Gul, began claiming that Israel's Mossad must be to blame. Aafia told Amjad that a "sister" had warned her that Americans would soon be kidnapping Muslim children. When Amjad asked who this "sister" was, Aafia said she was someone he didn't know. He argued that they ought to wait and see what happened before abandoning everything he had worked for. But she refused.

Despite the chaos and the shutdown in air travel, Aafia managed to get tickets for herself and the children on the first day the airports reopened. Amjad drove them to New York, and she left for Karachi from JFK International Airport on September 19.

Thirty-eight

Ayaan had been working at the Wiardi Beckman Institute for little more than a week when she noticed several of her colleagues gathered around a television set. She could hear them talking about something in America.

She disliked American television and had written a paper at Leiden about what she considered to be the media hype over President Bill Clinton's relationship with Monica Lewinsky. She thought the Americans, like the Dutch, tended to get hysterical about trifles.

But as she joined her new colleagues, she saw first one plane and then another crash into the World Trade Center, and finally each gigantic tower crumble into rubble and smoke.

She felt terribly afraid. Unlike her coworkers, she understood what these falling Western symbols would mean to many Muslims. She knew it was meant to signal that Armageddon was at hand.

She assumed the United States would retaliate on a massive scale. Her Dutch friends told her not to get so upset, but for once she thought they were the ones who were underreacting.

The Dutch were shocked when television cameras captured young Muslims dancing for joy in the streets of Ede, the little town where Ayaan and Haweya had lived. And they were frightened as well as puzzled to learn that an Islamic school in the town of Almere had distributed a calendar, months earlier, that showed a burning plane zooming over the Manhattan skyline in September. But Ayaan knew that Islamist images of Western destruction were everywhere. The imaginary battle with the Dajjal had become a kind of Muslim kitsch.

A few days after the attacks, she called a television researcher she had been working with over the summer. As they talked about the attacks, Ayaan became very agitated. She told the researcher that she herself had once been a Muslim fundamentalist. "You don't understand," Ayaan kept saying. "That could have been me. I could have been one of those hijackers."

PART II

Acting

One

Ayaan was obsessed with the 9/11 attacks. She kept thinking about the lead hijacker, Mohamed Atta, and his cold, dead eyes. She and the Egyptian were the same age, and they had both arrived in Europe in the summer of 1992. "I felt that I knew him, and, in fact, I did know many people like him."

Later she wrote that she identified with Atta's rage. She felt she understood the hostility and hatred that he felt toward himself and others. She watched a television interview with Atta's father. The man was angry and despairing. He refused to believe that his son could have committed the attacks. When he insisted that the Jews or the CIA must have done it, Ayaan knew that Atta must have been taught the same hateful version of Islam that she had been taught.

"Did the 9/11 attacks stem from true belief in true Islam?" she asked herself. The "little shutter" in the back of her brain opened, and her thoughts came tumbling out. She remembered what she had learned about "love and hate for Allah" from her teacher Sister Aziza and the preacher Boqol Sawm in Eastleigh. She had believed what Atta believed, only she hadn't been given the chance to do anything about it. "This was not Islam," she decided. "This was the *core* of Islam." She felt "enormous fear."

She read bin Laden's statements. She looked at Atta's will. She heard the note of the Islam she had grown up with. "Every devout Muslim who aspired to practice genuine Islam—the Muslim Brotherhood Islam, the Islam of the Medina Quran schools—even if they didn't actively support the attacks, they must at least have approved of them." She asked herself questions: "Was innovation forbidden to Muslims? Were human rights, progress, women's rights, all foreign to Islam?"

The dissonance became excruciating. "I realized I could either go mad, join the Bin Ladenists, or step out of the religion."

It doesn't seem to have occurred to her that a murderous Islamism wasn't the only way to interpret Islam. For her, as for millions of other believers who had come of age during the oil-fueled "Islamic awakening" of the late twentieth century, Islamism *was* Islam. The Egyptian theorist of jihad, "Sayyid Qutb didn't invent anything, he just quoted the sayings of Muhammed," she later told a reporter. Many Islamic theologians would have disagreed strenuously, but she was no longer close enough to the Muslim community to know about the debates raging within it. Nor did she seem to realize that, even in the Netherlands, many Islamic scholars were still trying to reconcile reason and religion—scholars who believed that Islam was compatible with human rights, progress, and women's rights. Some of them worked only a few blocks from her house in Leiden, at the International Institute for the Study of Islam in the Modern World. Ayaan didn't mention them.

Ayaan has often said how close to madness she felt after September 11. Of course she wasn't alone. The attacks were *meant* to arouse great fears and apocalyptic rumors, and they succeeded awesomely. Psychological studies have shown that, several years later, the mere mention of "September 11" or "the World Trade Center" reminded Americans of death. But for Muslims who were raised as Ayaan was, believing that "if I was not a follower of God, I must be a follower of Satan," the attacks also conjured up the hellfire that awaited "hypocrites" who pretend to be Muslim but align themselves against the *ummah*.

Ayaan felt that bin Laden was forcing her to make a personal choice. Either everything that reality told her was wrong, or else she belonged to the party of the West, the party of Satan.

She chose Satan.

Two

Aafia Siddiqui had already made her decision. "See you in Paradise," she told her girlfriends in Boston as she left for Karachi on September 17. As far as Aafia was concerned, the clash of civilizations had begun.

She was surprised, therefore, and disappointed when she reached Pakistan and learned that most Pakistanis did not seem to understand that life as they had known it was over.

Amjad's family was mystified by her unexpected arrival. They had been asking their son for years to bring his wife and children home for a visit, but the young doctor had always refused to splurge on overseas travel while his father was still subsidizing his education. "We were surprised, but I was very happy," his mother, Zahera, said later. Amjad's father, Aga Naeem Khan, had never even met Aafia, and Amjad's parents knew their grandson Ahmad and granddaughter Maryam only from photographs. But custom decreed that their daughter-in-law and the children stay with her husband's family rather than her own.

Aga Naeem was proud of his son for working hard and saving money. Those were the virtues that had helped him rise to be director of a large pharmaceutical company after he and his brothers had arrived in Pakistan from India penniless at the time of Partition. He and Zahera still lived in the comfortable white stucco house with the red-tiled roof and neat lawn that he had built for them in the 1960s in a fashionable area of the KDA Housing Scheme. They had raised their three sons in the same house, sending two of them to the Karachi American School just down the street. Aga Naeem's hair had turned white since he had retired, but he was still slim and fit and still accustomed to giving orders. He and his wife considered themselves good Muslims; they prayed and fasted and gave to charity. But Aga Naeem disapproved of showiness in religion, as in other things.

Into this atmosphere of quiet restraint, Aafia arrived like an electrical storm. She couldn't stop talking about the 9/11 attacks, and she seemed quite fearful.

The Khans knew all about "the event," as they called the attacks. Like everyone else, they had watched the TV images again and again. They knew the United States was planning to invade Afghanistan to oust the Taliban, Pakistan's erstwhile ally. They had watched Pakistan's military dictator, President Pervez Musharraf, make a television statement promising Washington his support. It was a humiliating statement, many Pakistanis thought—and all very sad, especially for the poor Afghans, who had already suffered two decades of war and now faced the wrath of another superpower. What the parents could not understand was what any of this had to do with Aafia and Amjad. Why would Aafia be safer in Pakistan than at home with her husband?

The answers she gave them didn't make sense. "Amjad *must* come back to Pakistan," she said. "His life is in danger." But when they asked why, she refused to explain.

At first they put her behavior down to shock and jet lag. But rest failed to calm her. The United States had given the Taliban's one-eyed leader, Mullah Omar, the choice of handing over Osama bin Laden or facing a U.S. invasion of Afghanistan. The week after Aafia arrived, her family's spiritual adviser, Mufti Muhammad Taqi Usmani, joined a delegation of Deobandi luminaries who traveled to Kandahar to meet with Mullah Omar. When they returned, the mufti produced a fatwa blaming the United States for the crisis. On October 7, the United States dropped its first bombs on Afghanistan. Aafia followed every twist of the developments, swirling into and out of the house, wrapped in her black abaya and niqab face veil.

Her behavior puzzled and disturbed her in-laws. Because of her American education, the Khans still thought of Aafia as somehow modern, even though no one else in the family wore the face veil. Amjad's older brother had been hearing for years about how brilliant she was. He could not believe it when she confided that she had left Boston because she thought the Americans were going to start kidnapping Muslim children. He told her at the dinner table that what she was saying sounded irrational. Aafia's own nieces and nephews were still in the United States, along with thousands of other Pakistani children, and as far as anyone knew they were fine. No one had reported any missing children.

Aafia threw down her napkin and ran out of the room.

Amjad's mother, Zahera, suffered from osteoporosis and had to walk slowly, but she followed Aafia up to her bedroom that night as quickly as she could. She found her daughter-in-law sprawled on the bed, sobbing. "You people just want to blame me for everything!" she cried. Zahera felt confused and misunderstood. No one had blamed Aafia for anything. What was there to blame her for? The family just wanted to know what was wrong.

The next night, Aafia came down to dinner wearing her face veil. Amjad's father and brothers asked her to take it off, reminding her that she was among family, but she refused. They tried to reassure her that no one was blaming her for anything. Was Amjad in some kind of trouble? they asked. Aafia avoided their questions. Then she launched into a lecture about how certain Muslims were hypocrites.

Aga Naeem was outraged. How dare this young woman, who had been living off his largesse for the last six years, walk into his house and presume to instruct him about religion? That night he called Amjad in Boston and told him he needed to come home and deal with his wife.

Aafia had also been calling Amjad. She told him it was time for him to choose: would he side with the party of God or the party of Satan? Amjad saw his dream of going to Harvard slipping away, but he argued that he needed to stay in Boston at least until he got his board certification in anesthesiology. His exam was only five months away!

His wife replied that work wasn't everything, and she recited the hadith that says the *ummah* is like one body: "If one limb complains, the rest responds with wakefulness and fever." The extra money, Aafia said, that he could earn as a specialist after taking his board exams would only tempt him to stay in the United States and shirk his duty.

A few days earlier, their friend Imam Faaruuq had stopped by their apartment in Malden to pick up some furniture. Amjad described his dilemma. The imam had advised him to stay and take his exams. But the doctor missed his wife and children, and now even his father was telling him to come home. He finally asked the Tufts New England Medical Center for permission to take a month off.

It was November when he arrived in Pakistan. He found Aafia in a state of great excitement. Her friend Suleman Ahmer from Benevolence International had returned to Pakistan earlier and set up his own charity. Ahmer was now organizing aid to the Taliban, and Aafia told her husband that she had already arranged for him to join Ahmer's group. Amjad would travel to the border town of Quetta, in Baluchistan. Then he would proceed to Kalat, an Afghan town where an Islamic relief group that Ahmer recommended was running a field hospital. It would be jihad, the highest form of worship. She had already bought the tickets.

Amjad was deeply conflicted. Like his wife, he had grown up hearing heroic stories of the mujahideen. He believed, as she did, that armed combat on behalf of Allah (under the right circumstances) was the highest form of jihad and thus of worship. But he also knew that orthodox Islamic teaching required a Muslim to master nine other levels of jihad, starting with the struggle against one's own desires and leading up to the struggle against lies and falsehood, before he reached the state of purity sufficient to make war for Allah. Had he and Aafia done that? He wasn't so sure.

Men who made the mistake of engaging in what they thought was religiously sanctioned violence, when they didn't really know what they were doing, could end up *causing* corruption and injustice rather than ending it. Amjad found himself wondering—as he often had lately—whether Aafia knew as much about Islam as she claimed. Sometimes it seemed to him that she understood the surface teachings but missed the inner meaning.

The 9/11 attacks had made him realize something else, as well. For years he had regarded his wife's fascination with jihad as mostly fantasy, though one he knew better than to discuss with his American colleagues. Now it had become deadly earnest.

Of course he agreed with Aafia that Muslim life was far too cheap for the Americans. They were probably killing more innocent Afghans with their bombs, he felt, than had died in the World Trade Center. But he wasn't sure it was right for him as a Muslim to wage war against a country that had shown him nothing but hospitality. Moreover, Islam said a son should obey his parents. He would need their blessing before he could go to Afghanistan.

Aafia suggested he leave his parents in the dark. He could say he was going to Quetta, to treat the wounded.

But Amjad was unconvinced, and, the night before he was supposed to leave, he asked the advice of his oldest brother.

The brother reacted with alarm. In fact, neither of Amjad's brothers saw the war in Afghanistan as a legitimate jihad. They found the Taliban barbaric—an embarrassment rather than the world's only "truly" Islamic government. The brothers didn't think bin Laden was as innocent as Aafia claimed. And they blamed the Taliban who had harbored him for bringing disaster on Afghanistan *and* on Pakistan.

When Amjad showed his older brother the tickets that Aafia had bought, the brother went straight to their father, who exploded.

"What is this nonsense?" Aga Naeem roared. Like many Pakistanis, especially of the older generation, Amjad's father was deeply cynical about the jihadi movement. Having watched Pakistan's jihadi groups grow and develop since they had first appeared under the Zia regime, he considered them a Frankenstein's monster of the world's intelligence agencies. The spectacle of the so-called mujahideen cruising around town in their Pajero jeeps, showing off their Kalashnikovs while the police stood by, helpless to stop them, filled him with revulsion. Recently in Karachi those mujahideen had begun murdering Shiite doctors. Aga Naeem wasn't about to sacrifice his son to their deadly games, and he told Amjad so.

Amjad went upstairs with trepidation to give Aafia the news. He knew she would throw a tantrum. The family, downstairs, could hear her screaming. "Why do you listen to your father and your brothers rather than to me?" she yelled. "You should go!"

Aga Naeem couldn't believe his ears. Here was a privileged young woman who had everything most Pakistani women only dream of, yet she yearned to send her husband and the father of her children off to live in caves and be cluster-bombed. "I became very angry," he remembered. He shouted at Amjad to come back downstairs. "This is nonsense," he told his son. "If you go there, don't come here again."

To the family's collective astonishment, Aafia came flying down the stairs and into the living room, with its brocade curtains and green velvet settees. Grabbing Amjad by the shirt, she spun him around and started beating his chest with her fists. She demanded that he choose between her and his family. "So what will you do, divorce me?" she screamed. "Then divorce me! Divorce me! Did you hear me? I said *divorce me*."

Amjad's parents thought she was losing her mind. "Until then, we did not know there was any friction between them," his mother explained later. Such things happened in Bollywood movies, not in the deeply respectable interiors of the Khan household.

A servant finally broke the shocked silence by running upstairs to fetch the wife of Amjad's brother. "Please see about Aafia," he cried. "Something has happened to her!"

Amjad knew that if he and Aafia remained another day at his parents' house, the break between them and his wife would never be repaired. So he decided that he and Aafia should leave and drive north to Islamabad, where they would visit Aafia's uncle S. H. Faruqi.

Faruqi, an affable and distinguished geologist, lived in a house filled with rocks and geological records in the capital's exclusive F-7 Section of treelined streets and large white bungalows, populated mainly by top bureaucrats. Amjad took his degrees and certificates with him, thinking he might apply for a job at a hospital in Islamabad.

But over the next few days Aafia devised a new plan. She decided she and Amjad should take the children and go to live with a radical new group called Jaish-e-Muhammad, or "Army of the Prophet Muhammad," in the mountains between Kashmir and Afghanistan.

Jaish-e-Muhammad had been founded the year before, after some Deobandi jihadis had hijacked an Indian Airlines plane in order to exchange it and its passengers for a comrade, Maulana Masood Azhar, imprisoned in India. When Azhar returned triumphantly to Pakistan, he established Jaish-e-Muhammad. It was fully intertwined with Pakistan's Deobandi military-religious complex, being financed by the al-Rashid Trust and blessed by Pakistan's intelligence agencies. Few outsiders at the time realized how extreme Jaish-e-Muhammad was, but it was essentially the Pakistani arm of al-Qaeda.

Jaish-e-Muhammad had a women's wing—Banat-e-Ayesha, or "Daughters of Ayesha"—and Aafia wanted to join it. Banat published a monthly jihadi magazine in Karachi that claimed to have a circulation of 17,000. The November 2001 issue showed the Christian cross, the Jewish Star of David, and the Communist hammer and sickle, all destroyed and bathed in the light of the Holy Quran.

Like other militant groups, Jaish-e-Muhammad ran schools and clinics for the poor. Aafia now proposed that they live in the group's compound at Balakot, in Pakistan's North-West Frontier Province. The children could go to a Jaish-e-Muhammad madrassa. Amjad could work at one of the group's medical facilities. And Aafia could preach for the women's wing.

As a counterproposal, Amjad suggested they drive from Islamabad to the town of Abbottabad, a former colonial hill station about fifty miles west of Balakot, where Osama bin Laden would ultimately be found hiding and be killed in 2011. There was a teaching hospital there where he might land a job. Abbottabad was also the site of Army Burn Hall School and College, an excellent private school founded by Christian missionaries that several of his cousins had attended. If they lived in Abbottabad, the family could attend Jaish events on weekends, and the children could go to Burn Hall.

This compromise initially seemed to placate Aafia. They made the journey past the towering maple trees that led to Abbottabad, which had once been a gateway to the ancient Silk Road. They saw the streams, the chattering monkeys, and the glacier-topped mountains at Balakot. Yet the prospect of being close to jihad, while remaining outside its sacred precincts, frustrated Aafia.

And when it looked, a few days later, as if the hospital in Abbottabad might offer Amjad a position, she became furious again. Even with Americans killing Muslims across the border in Afghanistan, she said, Amjad still wanted to send his children to a school founded by Christian missionaries. He was afraid to break with the *dunya*, the everyday world of corruption and compromises with evil. He was just like his parents. All he cared about was a comfortable life.

Amjad decided there was no point in moving to Abbottabad. Aafia wouldn't be happy there or anywhere until he became a full-time jihadi, and he wasn't ready to do that. So they drove back to Islamabad and then continued south to Karachi.

Amjad's parents were angrier than ever when they heard about Aafia's latest scheme. Aga Naeem told his son he should go back to Boston right away and prepare for his board exams.

Aafia refused to fly back with him. It was late November. She and the children saw him off at the airport. Once he was gone, they left her in-laws' house and went to stay with her own parents on the other side of Karachi.

Three

One day in November 2001, Ayaan and some colleagues from the Wiardi Beckman Institute attended a debate at the De Balie cultural center, off the Leidseplein in Amsterdam. The Dutch intelligentsia liked to meet in the cavernous De Balie for coffee and beer and spar over political and cultural issues. The title of this particular debate was "The Enlightenment After September 11." Ayaan would later recall the topic as "The West or Islam: Who Needs a Voltaire?"

The ignorance of most Westerners about Islamism before 9/11 cannot be overstated. For example, the Egyptian ideologue of jihad, Sayyid Qutb, was virtually unknown to non-Muslims despite having been the bestselling and most influential Arab writer of the twentieth century. Even fewer Westerners knew how semipublic groups such as the Muslim Brotherhood and Jamaat-e-Islami operated, much less what was going on inside secretive jihadi outfits such as al-Qaeda and Jaish-e-Muhammad.

After the attacks, the administration of President George W. Bush added to the confusion. Instead of a clear campaign against a specific entity or ideology, Bush announced that the United States would fight a "war on terror." Vice President Dick Cheney proposed further that the war would be waged on "the dark side," in secrecy and using unconventional means. Even in Europe, people weren't sure what the plan was. Debates like the one at De Balie were one way they attempted to get their bearings.

Ayaan has said she listened to five or six speakers argue that it was the West, not Islam, that needed a Voltaire. "The West was arrogant, imperialist and cruel and took without giving," she recalled the speakers saying. "America was most evil of all, was under the control of the Jews, and was responsible for all the conflict in the world today." The only speaker who disagreed, she said, was an Iranian professor of law named Afshin Ellian, who argued that Islam needed a reformation. Ayaan got so frustrated that she stood up to support Ellian.

"We Muslims are truly living in the Dark Ages—just look at the situation of our women," she told the audience. "The West has had countless Voltaires. Allow us just one, please." Everyone present remembered the moment when the striking young African woman seized the floor. "She spoke Dutch with a light accent, and she was black," Jaffe Vink, the editor of *Trouw* newspaper, recalled, "and immediately the hall went as still as a mouse."

After the debate, Vink asked Ayaan if she would write down her thoughts in an article for his paper. Ayaan wasn't a polished writer, and Vink said later that the article had to be rewritten four times before he was satisfied. It was published on November 24, 2001. The title was "Don't Leave Us in the Dark—Give Us a Voltaire."

What Ayaan wrote after 9/11 resembled what Pim Fortuyn and other Dutch critics of Islam had been saying for years. But her personal experiences seemed to give her critique an authenticity that their words lacked.

For her, there was no distinction between Islam and Islamism. There was only Islam, and its influence was unrelentingly negative. It was "hierarchical," "a mind-set far removed from reason," and "in need of Enlightenment." Terrorists weren't holding Islam hostage, as Bush and British prime minister Tony Blair said; on the contrary, terrorists were implementing Islam.

Leon de Winter, a Dutch writer and strong advocate of Israel who was often criticized for writing scornfully about Muslims, was correct, Ayaan wrote, to make fun of Muslims for believing in "a row of saints, demons and ghosts." Very few Muslims were "actually capable of looking at their faith critically." They lived in a world of "colorful dreams and fantasies" and refused to "take responsibility for their own state and their own deeds." They tended "to be passive in life and guided by a sense of fatalism."

Ayaan lamented that Muslims weren't more like Westerners: "Unlike Islamic society, the West places much emphasis on the individual's independence and personal responsibility and on the necessity of investing in this life. Education and employment, rather than piety, are the measure of success." Above all, the West didn't share Islam's hang-ups about sex. "Homosexuality is not a sin to be punished with death, nor is it considered a threat to the survival of mankind, but is seen as a form of love, normal like that between heterosexuals. Moreover, love and sex are not restricted to marriage but can be enjoyed between two people by mutual consent."

She wrote that Muslims were so filled with hatred, especially against Jews, that they couldn't think straight, and she offered her younger self as an example. Westerners who felt that everything would turn out fine "didn't know what they were talking about." The Dutch needed to put more pressure on Muslims to integrate. They needed to let "the Muslim Voltaires of today work in a safe environment on the enlightenment of Islam."

In the years that followed, Ayaan's critics would fault her reasoning and her evidence on every point. In academic terms, she had proclaimed herself an "essentialist," or someone who believed that Islam and Muslims could be reduced to an essential set of characteristics. To those who knew something of the Islamic world, she had started out on shaky ground by claiming there was something like an "ideal" Islam. Didn't she see that Islam was whatever Muslims made of it and that it differed greatly across time and space? What about Muslims like Benazir Bhutto who had been fighting the fundamentalists all along?

Ayaan waved away such objections by saying that "moderate" Muslims were marginal figures, lacking the authority of the Quran. That led orthodox Muslim theologians to oppose her from a different position. One heresy they attributed to the Islamists was that they had introduced or revived *takfir,* the idea that any right-thinking

Muslim is authorized to decide who is and isn't a real Muslim. To Muslims familiar with the *takfiri* confusion, Ayaan seemed a kind of reverse jihadi: she, too, claimed that any Muslim who didn't agree with Osama bin Laden simply wasn't a Muslim.

Others, Muslim and non-Muslim, found her generalizations as shallow as they were insulting. For example, her former hatred of Jews and gays was no reason to say that *all* Muslims felt that way. And who was she to say that all Muslims were hierarchical or incapable of self-criticism?

The liberal South African Islamic theologian Farid Esack made some of those points in a TV debate with Ayaan and others that was broadcast on Holland's Muslim network. Esack protested that Ayaan reduced all the problems of the Muslim world to Islam. "To say that 'Islam is the problem' is just the reverse of the fundamentalist slogan 'Islam is the solution,'" Esack said. "Certain problems are related to Islam, but others are not. Just like the fundamentalists, you are leaving out all the other factors."

Ayaan struck such critics as too admiring of the West. What about the West's long power over the Middle East? What about the wars that the United States and its allies had backed in Iran, Iraq, and Afghanistan? And what about the Palestinians? Ayaan also seemed unaware that Islam *did* have its Voltaires and that Europe, and Holland in fact, had provided some of them with safe havens.

She appeared, for example, not to know about the teachings of Mahmoud Mohamed Taha, a Sudanese philosopher who argued that Islam should reform the sharia so that it reflected the ethical teachings of the Prophet Muhammed at Mecca, making women equal to men before the law. Sudan's Islamists saw the group that Taha founded, the Republican Brotherhood, as so threatening that they had him executed in 1985. Yet Taha's followers, such as Abdullahi An-Naim, have taught in Dutch and American universities about a vision of Islam compatible with modern human rights.

She also seemed not to know about an Egyptian theologian in Leiden, where she had lived for years. But Nasr Hamed Abu Zeid had fled to Leiden University in 1996. Egypt's courts and a group of Islamist scholars from El Azhar had declared him an apostate for saying that certain verses of the Quran should be treated as metaphors and that the Islamic courts should treat women as equal to men when apportioning inheritance and crediting testimony. They declared that Abu Zeid was no longer married to his wife, since according to sharia a Muslim woman cannot be married to a non-Muslim man. They also threatened him with death. But he continued to write from Leiden about how religious governments of any description were incompatible with universal values.

Human rights activists in every Muslim country risked their lives and the lives of their families to stand up to the Islamists, but Ayaan didn't acknowledge that fact. Nor did she acknowledge the work of Fatema Mernissi, the Moroccan feminist whose books questioned male interpretations of the Quran; of Khalida Messaoudi, the Algerian mathematics professor who was hunted by her country's radical Islamists because she opposed their power over schools; of the Iranian former judge Shirin Ebadi, who was imprisoned for investigating the murders of Iranian intellectuals; or of the Pakistani lawyers Asma Jahangir and her sister Hina Jilani, who continued to defend women under the Hudood laws even after an assassin burst into Jahangir's office and killed a client in front of her.

Obviously most of Ayaan's readers had never heard of those Muslim liberals, either. Nor did they note a possible contradiction in the idea of fighting a war for enlightenment on "the dark side." But what Ayaan said in her article and in subsequent TV appearances did coincide with what many Dutch and other Westerners suspected about Muslims. And they were delighted to hear a feisty and attractive Muslim woman endorse their suspicions.

Four

Amjad's mother, Zahera, felt terribly guilty. She had chosen Aafia for him, and now look what had happened: Amjad was back in Boston, while Aafia and their two precious children were holed up across town.

The more Zahera thought about it the more she attributed her daughter-in-law's behavior to stress. Finishing her Ph.D. in such a hurry, having two babies in quick succession, being far from home, the mysterious attacks on the United States, the turmoil in Pakistan, the U.S. invasion of Afghanistan—it was enough to upset anyone. And Aafia was a brilliant girl, sensitive and religious. Zahera urged her son to make up with her. She told him that such things sometimes happened to women.

Amjad wasn't so sure. He had seen this behavior in Aafia before. He knew her craving for jihad wasn't a passing whim. He had never quite understood why she had insisted on leaving Boston so suddenly after 9/11. He hadn't believed her when she said she feared that their children would be kidnapped.

Had her fund-raising for Care International and other jihadi charities made her a target for the FBI? Or had she used the attacks as an excuse to run away from a troubled marriage?

He was lonely by himself in the icy Boston December. Even a visit to the supermarket reminded him of how he and Aafia had used to push Ahmad and Maryam in the cart when they shopped together. He phoned Aafia and asked her to come back to him. Aafia's father told her that her duty as a Muslim was to try to save her marriage.

The anti-American jihad in Afghanistan, meanwhile, appeared to be sputtering. Within six weeks of the U.S. invasion, the Taliban collapsed. Osama bin Laden and his fighters began streaming back into Pakistan, and hundreds of militants regrouped in Karachi, where Ramzi Yousef's uncle, Khalid Sheikh Mohammed (KSM), was waiting to receive them.

Unfortunately for the Americans' war on terror, however, the U.S. government didn't yet understand how important KSM was. The CIA had mislabeled KSM and his nephew Ramzi Yousef as freelance Arab terrorists. Thus, in the summer of 2001, when the CIA received tips that the rumpled, round-faced KSM was planning a major terrorist operation, the tips weren't matched with concurrent warnings that al-Qaeda had an operation in the works. Two months after 9/11, Washington still didn't understand that the same al-Baluchi family that had planned the 1993 bombing of the World Trade Center was also behind the 2001 attacks. And the Bush administration's focus was moving away from Pakistan because plans were being made to attack Iraq.

As the various foreign jihadis from Afghanistan sought refuge in Pakistan during the autumn of 2001, the women of Jamaat-e-Islami were apparently enlisted in finding hiding places for al-Qaeda leaders. It may be that Aafia's mother, Ismat, was part of that network. She had been a speaker for Jamaat and, according to Aafia, would eventually rent part of her house to KSM's al-Baluchi family. KSM himself, meanwhile, was desperate to land another blow that would show Muslims that al-Qaeda was still in the fight, and he began looking for U.S. citizens and visa holders who might carry out a new round of attacks. Aafia later told the FBI that she hadn't met the al-Baluchi family until 2002 and that she had never met KSM at all; but several of the Americans he succeeded in recruiting had links with people whom Aafia did know and with whom she would later be accused of conspiring.

Jose Padilla, for instance, was a tattooed former gang member from Brooklyn who had converted to Islam in south Florida. He had been recruited for jihad in 1997 by Adham Hassoun, a representative of the Benevolence International Foundation. Hassoun knew Aafia's friend Suleman Ahmer and had worked closely with Aafia's friends the "Care brothers" in Boston. Another American resident, Adnan Shukrijumah, came out of the same south Florida Islamist milieu as Padilla. Shukrijumah was the Saudi-born son of a Trinidadian mosque leader who had been the blind sheikh Omar Abdel Rahman's translator in Brooklyn. Both men trained at al-Qaeda camps in Afghanistan, and both joined up with KSM in Karachi after 9/11.

Whether Aafia met any of those conspirators around that time, she did shift her focus back to the United States. She told Amjad by the end of 2001 that she might, under certain conditions, return to her home with him in Boston. One condition was that he buy her a new computer, plus some religious books she needed. Another was that he join her in Islamic activities. He agreed, and Aafia flew back to the United States on January 5, 2002.

Five

Ayaan's article about Voltaire led to an invitation to speak on the great Enlightenment philosopher Benedict Spinoza. Ayaan wrote in her autobiography that she had to go back to her books and read up on Spinoza, but she agreed to do it.

Then she gave a speech answering yes to the question "Should We Fear Islam?"—after which she drafted an article attacking various Dutch politicians. They included the mayor of Amsterdam, who had called on nonbelieving citizens to respect the unifying power of religion. Ayaan showed her piece to the editor of *Trouw.* He wanted to publish it, but her boss at the Wiardi Beckman Institute, Paul Kalma, was aghast. He made her take out material calling the popular mayor, Job Cohen—a fellow member of the Labor Party—"Ayatollah Cohen." Normally a disagreement between a junior researcher and her supervisor wouldn't qualify as news, but Ayaan rarely minded talking to the press, and a few days later *Trouw* published an article describing the dispute at the institute.

Cohen, whose mother had survived the Holocaust, was about as far from being an ayatollah as a man could get. If anything, the former law professor's fault during the immigration debate was his determination to hear every side, a policy he called "keeping it together." Personally very modest, he was devoted to his handicapped wife and shopped for their food (which he often cooked himself) at the little Albert Heijn supermarket around the corner from the mayor's official house on the Herengracht. Cohen could also be tough. He had written the restrictive new immigration bill that had passed in 2000. If Ayaan couldn't see the difference between him and an ayatollah, some of her colleagues later asked me, what could she see?

Ayaan wrote that she couldn't understand what the fuss was about. "I was learning that in these extremely civilized circles, conflict was dealt with in a very ornate and hypocritical manner."

Her institute held a meeting with Cohen to discuss the article. To Ayaan's surprise, he stood up for her right to publish it. "He blew me away with his open-mindedness," she later wrote. "I thought he was a hero." Nonetheless, she still called him "Ayatollah Cohen" in the version of her article that later appeared in her book *The Caged Virgin*.

Ayaan got more invitations to speak on radio and then television. Producers instantly recognized her as a media natural. As the British journalist Andrew Anthony later wrote, she "looks like a fashion model and talks like a public intellectual." Yet Ayaan had more than that. After years of double-talk from Islamists, and excuses from Dutch politicians and academics, her willingness to speak openly about aspects of Islam that bothered Westerners came as a huge relief to many people. "She is very pretty, but she has something extra," said Eveline van Dijk, a filmmaker with whom Ayaan had worked as a translator. "She has an aura that is really unusual."

With their Calvinist fondness for preaching, moreover, the Dutch were ready to hear her message that they needed to get over their fear of offending Muslims and confront them with the truth about their religion. The Dutch also approved of her view that Islam's biggest problem was its sexual morality.

Polls show that Muslims and Westerners disagree more about sex than about any other subject. Whereas Muslims see themselves as protecting women, Westerners see Muslims as oppressing women. Whereas Westerners feel they're liberating women, Muslims feel that Westerners exploit women for commercial gain. Ayaan was a Muslim who told the Dutch in no uncertain terms that they were right and the Muslims were wrong.

Ayaan's Dutch was now excellent, but there was something un-Dutch and exotic about the way she framed her ideas. Like her father, she used simple stories—almost like fables—to illustrate her meaning, and she told her stories with calm precision and a cadence that was almost hypnotic. She was cool, even analytical, yet she radiated passion. Her righteousness acted like a magnet, attracting as many people as it repelled. She talked tough, yet people sensed in her a mixture of bravery and barely repressed fear that reflected their own churning emotions.

More than one Dutch citizen would say later that a tingle ran up their spines when they first saw her on television or heard her on the radio. It was hard for them to explain why. No doubt the troubled times had something to do with it. As Naïma Azough, a young Muslim woman who had just been elected to Parliament, later said, "Without the attacks of September 11, the Hirsi Ali phenomenon would never have happened. She fit perfectly in the world of fear, war and doubt that unfolded."

Dutch intellectuals often sensed irritating barriers between themselves and Muslims. But they felt nothing of the kind with Ayaan. She wasn't defensive. It didn't seem to bother her when a Western admirer knew nothing about Islam. She didn't preface her statements with tirades about the Palestinians or invocations to God. She was warm and funny. Above all, she was ready to talk critically about the three subjects most Muslims seemed to want to avoid: Islam, sex, and anti-Semitism. She also attracted the attention of influential leftists who were criticizing multiculturalism, such as her former professors Paul Cliteur and Bart Tromp and the columnist Margo Trappenburg.

For some other people, however, who had made it their life's work to learn about the Islamic world, the debate unfolding in the media could be painful.

"It was stupid," said Annelies Moors of the University of Amsterdam. "They were trading in fear and gross generalizations." "Overnight," said the journalist Joris Luyendijk, "the Dutch went from saying there was no problem with Muslims to saying there was no solution."

Six

In Boston that January of 2002, Amjad tried to woo Aafia by putting the family up in a fancy hotel on the Charles River. They had never been able to afford a holiday like that before. Now that he was earning a good salary at Tufts, he wanted to treat her to it.

But Aafia scolded him for wasting money on luxuries when Muslims were dying in Afghanistan. So they returned to Back Bay Manor, and Aafia found herself pregnant again.

Her attention seemed to be elsewhere. She didn't resume her missionary activities at the Roxbury mosque, and she didn't put the children in kindergarten. Instead, she homeschooled them.

Sometimes she put on makeup and a pretty shalwar kameez and greeted Amjad with a smile and a hug at the door, as *The Muslim Marriage Guide* recommended. But at other times she grew morose and withdrawn, and she curled up with the children and watched videos of dead Muslims in Chechnya or Afghanistan. When Amjad complained that the children were too young for such gruesome films, she flew at him and accused him again of wallowing in Western comforts. Her bad moods often seemed related to discussions on the Internet of Muslim wars abroad.

The American mood meanwhile was triumphant, even vindictive. Secretary of State Colin Powell was in Kabul, and there were pictures everywhere of Afghan women flinging off their powder blue burkas. The first prisoners from Afghanistan were being locked up in the U.S. base at Guantánamo Bay, Cuba. In a frieze of humiliation, they appeared on television in orange jumpsuits, manacled and shuffling into open cages under twenty-four-hour halogen lights. Bush's government announced that the prisoners were covered neither by the Geneva conventions nor by ordinary criminal statutes. Aafia said that proved that such treaties and agreements on human rights were just a smoke screen for U.S. imperialism.

Most Americans didn't know yet that the U.S. government was already making plans to invade Iraq, but Aafia did. She studied right-wing blogs and publications, Israeli as well as American. Few Americans had reacted the way she predicted they would after 9/11 (they hadn't kidnapped Muslim children, for example), but the administration did seem to be acting according to the jihadi playbook. For one thing, she felt certain that Zionists in Israel and the United States planned to use the invasion of Iraq as a step toward a "Greater Israel" and Western control of Muslim oil.

According to Amjad, the only way to keep Aafia quiet while he got through his exams was to make her think the two of them were still training for jihad. She often recalled the U.S. Army manuals she had mailed to Pakistan after the FBI had come looking for her in 1995. She said they had never arrived, and she went to look for more at the used-book store near Harvard Square where she had bought the originals, but the store no longer sold such books. Amjad suggested they try the Internet. That spring, he ordered *The Anarchist Arsenal: Improvised Incendiary and Explosive Techniques* and *Homemade C-4: A Recipe for Survival*, together with other books on weapons and explosives from Paladin Press, a publisher specializing in survivalism and warfare.

Only a few days after Aafia returned to Boston, Daniel Pearl, an American reporter for the *Wall Street Journal*, was kidnapped from Karachi's Village Restaurant, across the street from the Sheraton Hotel, where Aafia's mother used to hold her conferences. Pearl's pregnant French wife, Mariane, went on television and begged her husband's kidnappers to return him. But a month later, the U.S. Consulate in Karachi received a video that showed Pearl being decapitated.

The film had a title: "The Slaughter of the Spy-Journalist, the Jew Daniel Pearl."

A few days before he was kidnapped, Pearl had written an article about the jihadi group that Aafia had wanted to join, Jaish-e-Muhammad. It soon emerged that Jaish-e-Muhammad was deeply involved in the murder. A former bodyguard for the Jaish leader, Maulana Masood Azhar, had set up the meeting between Pearl and those who turned out to be his kidnappers. Later, Pearl's body was found on some property owned by the al-Rashid Trust.

Soon the ghastly video of Pearl's murder appeared on a new Web site called www.ogrish.com. The aptly named site featured macabre images of dead bodies, mostly taken from footage of auto accidents and crime scenes, juxtaposed with slick ads for pornography. The FBI discovered that a Dutchman named Dan Klinker ran the Web site out of Amsterdam, although a U.S. company, Pro Hosters LLC, of Sterling, Virginia, hosted the Web site. The FBI asked Pro Hosters and Ogrish to remove the video, and initially the companies complied. But when they realized how much money they could make with 750,000 people a day watching Pearl's execution, they decided to fight back. Pro Hosters contacted the American Civil Liberties Union, won its support, and ten days later the beheading of Daniel Pearl was back online. The Web site ran a notice claiming that "all people out there have the RIGHT to see the Daniel Pearl video if they CHOOSE to. Banning this video would violate the 1st amendment: freedom of speech; do we want that? NO!" Thousands of people signed a petition imploring Klinker to take the video down, but he refused. The FBI backed down, too, after the ACLU said the government had no grounds for prosecution under U.S. obscenity laws because obscenity involved only sex.

Aafia usually followed all the news about Jaish-e-Muhammad, but Amjad says he doesn't recall them ever talking about the Pearl murder. Other news stories seemed to hit closer to home. While Aafia had been in Pakistan the previous autumn, the FBI in Massachusetts had interviewed her friend Suheil Laher and other volunteers at Care International. The "Care brothers" and Laher's employer, Ptech Inc., would become the focus of a wider investigation of several Boston companies that were later accused of having ties to terrorism. (Ptech's chief executive officer and chief financial officer were charged in 2009 with concealing the fact that one of their investors was on the U.S. terrorism watch list.)

Amjad and Aafia didn't know it, but they too had been the objects of official curiosity. Auditors at Fleet Bank filed a suspicious-activity report after Amjad, on December 21, 2001, transferred $8,000 to their joint account at the Habib Bank in Pakistan, a sum he says he used to settle the family's bills and pay for their tickets back to the United States.

The Americans finally captured an important al-Qaeda figure, Abu Zubaydah, in March 2002. Under questioning by an FBI interrogator, Abu Zubaydah revealed what the Bush administration had not known until then: that Ramzi Yousef's uncle, Khalid Sheikh Mohammed, had planned the 9/11 attacks.

Abu Zubaydah also told them that KSM had other plans. One was to send Jose Padilla, the American convert and former gang member, to the United States, either to set off a radioactive bomb or to spark natural gas explosions in high-rise apartment buildings. Abu Zubaydah named Adnan Shukrijumah as the person al-Qaeda was most likely to use as an operative in a future attack on the United States.

Within a few weeks of his arrest, FBI agents began quietly questioning Aafia's former professors and other associates at Brandeis and MIT.

Amjad passed his final board exams in April. He had the highest score in his cohort. He had also turned out to be so good at teaching that Tufts named him teacher of the year and promoted him to assistant professor.

He began taking Aafia and the children on weekend camping trips to Cape Cod and the New Hampshire mountains. Amjad says he saw the trips as a way to introduce the children to his family's passion for hunting. Aafia got the chance to practice the techniques of survival outlined in her books. They went to a Boston camping store to buy hunting gear and supplies. Amjad purchased survival guides, a global positioning system, a night-vision device for hunting, and a bulletproof vest. But he says he had no intention of going back to Pakistan anytime soon. He wanted to resume his original plan to earn a Harvard master's degree in public health and other qualifications in pain management and health care administration. He says he went along with Aafia's fantasies of jihad simply to keep her from bolting back to Pakistan.

Three or four weeks after the couple visited the camping store, the FBI appeared at their door. Aafia and Amjad assumed that their purchases had triggered the bureau's interest.

But possibly not. A few days before the FBI's visit, agents had arrested Jose Padilla when he landed in Chicago on May 8. Padilla was carrying the e-mail address of another nephew of KSM, Ali Abdul Aziz Ali. The FBI soon learned about Padilla's ties to the other Florida jihadi, Adnan Shukrijumah, and they accused Padilla of plotting to combine ordinary explosives with radiological matter in order to launch a dirty bomb attack on the United States. The FBI evidently learned, too, that Aafia was e-mailing one or more of the conspirators, and perhaps it suspected her of being involved in the same plot.

Aafia was at home in Back Bay Manor when the agents arrived. She heard them at the door but refused to open it. Then she telephoned Amjad at the hospital to tell him what she had done.

Amjad had barely hung up when two other FBI agents appeared at the hospital. When he sat down with them, they asked a disturbing question. Some of the 9/11 hijackers, they said, had been seen entering and leaving their apartment building the summer before. Did he or his wife know any of them?

Amjad said he didn't, and he didn't think his wife did, either. (Since the FBI never raised this point again, the agents may have been fishing.) They told him they would call later and make an appointment to talk with him and Aafia together.

When Amjad got home, he called Aafia's brother in Texas, as

well as some Boston friends from Care International whom the FBI had already questioned. They told him being questioned was no big deal. Even if the FBI knew about the anti-American speeches that Aafia had made before 9/11—and even if the bureau could prove that the hijackers had been in their building—she and Amjad hadn't committed any crimes.

Aafia balked. She didn't want to talk to the FBI. She wanted to go home again.

"Why?" Amjad asked. Her refusal made no sense. He didn't want to return to Pakistan.

All they had to do was to sit down and explain everything. The FBI would leave them alone after that. The FBI, Amjad argued, had questioned their friends the "Care brothers," who had done far more for jihad than Aafia or Amjad had, and the "Care brothers" hadn't been arrested.

But Aafia wouldn't budge. Amjad called a Boston lawyer, James Merberg, anyway and made an appointment to meet with the FBI at Merberg's office. Aafia's brother, after numerous phone calls, convinced her to join them.

The interview started slowly. The agents asked about the Saudi man who had been living in their apartment the summer before. Amjad explained that the man had briefly sublet their apartment after meeting Amjad at the hospital. The agents wanted to know about the camping equipment and the night-vision device Amjad had bought. He told them that his uncles had been champion hunters in Pakistan and he hoped to take up hunting in the United States. They asked about the books he had bought online. Amjad offered to return them, but the agents told him that wouldn't be necessary. "This is a free country," one said solemnly.

They wanted to know if Amjad or Aafia had ever met Osama bin Laden. The couple said they hadn't.

The talk grew more pointed. The agents noted that Aafia had made donations to the Benevolence International Foundation and the Global Relief Foundation. When she asked how they knew that, they showed the couple printouts of their bank statements. Aafia retorted that it was her duty as a Muslim to contribute to charity, and those seemed to be worthy charities.

The agents asked about their friends. Did they know Emadeddin Muntasser of Care International? Or the Global Relief founder, Mohammed Chehade? Or the Benevolence International fund-raiser Suleman Ahmer?

They said they did. Aafia had met them through the Muslim Students Association.

What about Adnan Shukrijumah? Was he a friend of theirs?

Amjad said no, he didn't know anyone named Shukrijumah. Aafia also shook her head.

The agent asked Aafia if she was sure she didn't know Shukrijumah.

She repeated that she didn't.

The agent gave her a long stare. In that case, he said, why had she e-mailed him?

Aafia was silent. "May I see this e-mail?" their lawyer interjected.

The agent just looked at them. The e-mails are classified, he said. But we have them and more like them. Then he asked about some other people that Amjad had never heard of.

They made an appointment to meet again in a few weeks.

Amjad thought the meeting had gone pretty well, but by the time they got home Aafia was in a state of agitation. The whole family had to leave for Pakistan, she said. Amjad tried to get her to tell him what she was so afraid of. Who was Shukrijumah? Aafia said she didn't know. She e-mailed lots of people in connection with her charities. She didn't know them all.

Then she had nothing to fear, Amjad told her. But she was already packing.

Amjad phoned the lawyer, Merberg, and said they couldn't keep their date with the FBI. Aafia's father had suffered two heart attacks in recent years, and she needed to be with him. She was also six months pregnant. If she waited much longer to travel, she wouldn't be allowed on a plane.

Merberg had been impressed with the young doctor and his scientist wife. He advised them, though, to postpone their departure long enough to attend the second meeting. Nothing the FBI had said made him think its interest was serious, but he told Amjad that if they left the country without answering all the government's questions, their case would remain open and that this might cause difficulties for them when they returned. It would be better to get it over with.

Aafia's brother said the same thing. He and Amjad begged Aafia to go to the meeting. But she told them she couldn't.

"Do you want to kill me?" she screamed at Amjad. "Do you want to kill the children? If you make me stay here, that is what you will be doing!"

Amjad couldn't understand why she was so frightened. It was true that her father had heart trouble, but there was nothing new in that. He had had the problem for years. Did she know something that Amjad didn't know? Was she just rejecting Boston again? Sometimes he felt she was determined to destroy his career.

He decided to return to Pakistan with her. The FBI agents had told them that they couldn't take their night-vision device out of the country, so Amjad gave it and the survivalist books to Merberg. The lawyer could show the FBI that the couple had left them behind.

Aafia agreed. But first she photocopied some pages of *The Anarchist Arsenal* and several other books.

The Tufts New England Medical Center granted him a one-year leave of absence, and the family left for Karachi on June 26, 2002.

Seven

A filmmaker named Karin Schagen asked Ayaan if she could make a short documentary about her. Ayaan dressed up for the film in a long red veil and played herself arriving at Amsterdam's Central Station in 1992. Schagen also wanted to interview Ayaan's father, who had left Somalia and was staying with her stepmother, Maryan Farah Warsame, in London.

But when the filmmaker phoned Hirsi Magan in August, he told her that Somalis had been calling him from all over Europe to complain about what his daughter had been saying.

Ayaan later wrote that they had told him, "Hirsi, if you don't do something fast to rein in your daughter, she's going to get killed."

The mood in Holland was growing ugly. Early in February, Pim Fortuyn, the sociologist turned politician, had called Islam a "backward religion." When members of his party had remonstrated with him, Fortuyn replied that Muslims were a "fifth column" who could destroy the country. His words had caused such controversy that the party had kicked him off its ticket.

Two days later he formed his own party, The Fortuyn List. The Labor Party dismissed its members as hysterical right-wingers. But his new party won the local Rotterdam elections by huge margins.

Ayaan went on TV the night after his victory. The occasion was International Women's Day, and the Dutch television host and columnist Theodor Holman wanted to ask her and Fatima Onasser, a Dutch judge of Moroccan background, about Fortuyn's claims that Muslim women were oppressed.

Onasser began with the argument that Islam called for equality between men and women. Ayaan broke in. She called it ridiculous to pretend that Islam had nothing to do with the condition of Muslim women. As a translator in shelters and abortion clinics, she herself had met abused women who believed that Islam gave their husbands the right to beat them. Moreover, Ayaan said, the oppression of Muslim women was the key to the problem of integrating Muslims into Dutch society.

She got her first hate mail the very next day. But the overall Dutch reaction was extremely positive. The country's bestselling historian, Geert Mak, a Labor Party stalwart, watched the program with his wife. "She was fantastic," Mak recalled. Noting proudly that she worked for the Labor Party's Wiardi Beckman Institute, Mak e-mailed her. "You are the woman we have been waiting for," he wrote. "You can make the change!"

Dutch feminists were even more enthusiastic. As the journalist Alies Pegtel later reported, Jolande Withuis, a columnist for *Opzij*, Holland's most influential women's magazine, had an epiphany: "Finally a Muslim woman saying what I have all these years thought."

Steffie Kouters of the newspaper *De Volkskrant* decided to write a profile of the striking young Somali. "Dare to Clash" appeared in *De Volkskrant* on April 11, 2002, and Kouters began by quoting Ayaan: "The majority of Islamic women here are oppressed." A few weeks earlier, fifteen Saudi Arabian schoolgirls had died in a fire in the holy city of Mecca when the country's religious police had stopped firemen from rescuing them because the girls inside might not be wearing their veils. Ayaan told Kouters there were women in the Netherlands who were kept indoors on the same principle.

"Take the Amsterdam neighborhood of Bos en Lommer," Ayaan said. "A group of women live there whom you never see on the street. According to the Quran, they must not go out of their houses unless veiled, chaperoned, and with a good reason. Is taking Dutch lessons a good reason? The husband determines that."

Ayaan admitted that not all Muslim women were forced to stay at home. She herself, she said, had escaped Islam's "mental cage." But many other women had internalized their oppression. "What does a bird that has grown up in a cage do when the door is opened? It holds itself captive."

Kouters asked Ayaan about her own background. It was the first time that anyone of the press had asked Ayaan how she had gotten to the Netherlands, and she seemed reluctant to talk about it. She said that she had been married off to a fundamentalist Muslim and an aunt in the Netherlands had helped her get away. "It's so personal, and people will think I am a frustrated woman and I'm projecting my own traumas, when in fact millions of Muslim women are oppressed." Her theme for the next twenty years, she said, would be to draw attention to the plight of Muslim women in the Netherlands.

Ayaan accused the Left of ignoring Muslim women. "The progressive parties and the media have always condemned the backwardness of women, but they are extremely careful not to blame immigrants for fear of awakening racism. Meanwhile, the discrimination against women by men in the Muslim community is much greater than the discrimination against immigrants by the Dutch."

She conceded the existence of modern, educated Muslim women in Holland. But she wanted to draw attention to the "much larger group" who remained oppressed. She said 753 Islamic organizations—most of them run by men—were subsidized by the Dutch government. She wished that Holland would shut the country's Islamic schools, though she admitted that such an action would be hard to square with freedom of religion. Her advice to the Dutch was "Dare to clash. It is unavoidable."

Fortuyn wasn't afraid to clash, and it didn't seem to be hurting him at all. By May, he was riding so high in the polls that he seemed likely to become the next prime minister. His rise panicked the established parties that had run the country since World War II, and their attacks, like those of their friends in the media, fed the hysteria of Fortuyn's supporters. Soon the entire political class seemed to be reaching what the Dutch saw as a deeply un-Dutch state of frenzy. Fortuyn was called a demagogue and compared to Mussolini and Hitler. Even the leader of the conservative Liberal Party, Gerrit Zalm, said, "Fortuyn is a dangerous man. He deceives the people."

On May 6, 2002, the editor in chief of the country's most respected newspaper, *NRC Handelsblad*, wrote of his fear that Fortuyn would be elected. It would be a "huge disgrace" for the Netherlands to have a prime minister who failed to understand the lesson of World War II that it simply wasn't permissible to fan the flames of hatred against a religious minority. That afternoon, Pim Fortuyn was shot dead while leaving a TV studio in Hilversum. Everyone feared the assassin would turn out to be a Muslim. Instead, he was a Dutch activist for animal rights named Volkert de Graaf—a loner, like so many assassins, who wanted to be a hero.

Fortuyn's stricken followers accused the Left of stirring up hatred against him, while those who had led the charge against the professor slunk away in guilty silence. Ever since the seventeenth century, the Left had been seen (or had at least seen itself) as the defender of Enlightenment values such as rationalism, secularism, and individual rights, while the Right had been linked with the Christian churches and traditional family roles. Now Fortuyn's vegan assassin appeared to turn three hundred years of Dutch politics upside down. The Left was blamed for the murder of a politician who was proudly gay and a defender of Muslim women. The Right, meanwhile, claimed to be defending the Enlightenment.

Ayaan continued to wrap her calls for the liberation of Muslims in the banner of the Enlightenment. But her supervisor at the Wiardi Beckman Institute wondered whether she understood the principles that underlay Holland's tolerance and freedom. Ayaan proposed shutting down the country's Islamic schools. Paul Kalma, her supervisor, said that doing so would violate Holland's freedom of religion and belief, as laid out, for example, in Article 23 of the Dutch Constitution, which guaranteed citizens the right to send their children to state-supported religious schools or other schools of their choice, as long as the schools met government standards.

If the government closed down Holland's Muslim schools, it would be discriminating against Muslims, Kalma argued. Ayaan's response was to suggest that Holland rid itself of Article 23.

Kalma tried to explain how strongly the average Dutch person felt about Article 23. But Ayaan brushed him aside, saying, "The arrival of migrants in this country is going to affect the heart of Dutch society, and it's time to face that."

Her former statistics professor at Leiden, Huib Pellikaan, shared Kalma's concerns. Ayaan had been assigned to work with Pellikaan on a book he was writing for the institute on multiculturalism, but she failed to produce any studies or other empirical evidence to support her contention that Islam was threatening the Dutch. "I told her, 'You can write your political manifesto someplace else, but my book is going to be a work of comparative analysis,' " he said.

She and her housemate went away to Greece that summer. Ayaan took the book that Marco had once given her, Herman Philipse's *The Atheist Manifesto*. After reading it, she realized that she had stopped believing in Allah years before. She had simply been afraid to admit it to herself.

When she got back, she began studying Enlightenment thinkers. She also decided to give up lying. "I would no longer lie to myself or to others. I had had enough of lying. I was no longer afraid of the Hereafter."

The *Trouw* editor Jaffe Vink had introduced Ayaan to Tilly Hermans, the head of the Dutch publishing house Augustus. Ayaan told Hermans that she wanted to write a book about her policy prescriptions for immigration. But Hermans wanted to hear her personal story. When Ayaan told it, Hermans said, "*That* is the book you are going to write," and she gave Ayaan the autobiographies of earlier feminists to read.

In the summer of 2002, she wrote her first piece for the Dutch women's magazine *Opzij*. The magazine's fashionable red-haired editor, Cisca Dresselhuys, was the Gloria Steinem of the Netherlands, an icon of 1960s Dutch feminism, and she would become one of Ayaan's most influential mentors. Dresselhuys remembered later that Ayaan had contacted her first. "She called and asked, 'Can I come and meet you?'" Dresselhuys believed that all religions were basically hostile to women's liberation. Well before 9/11, she had announced she wouldn't hire a female editor who wore a head scarf. Ayaan struck her as having the potential to lead the "third wave" of feminism, which would liberate African and Asian women. "She spoke in a free and open manner about Islam and the threatening side of Islam. We didn't know such a person in Holland."

Dresselhuys introduced her to the work of the American feminist Susan Moller Okin, who argued that multiculturalism placed the rights of cultures above the rights of women. Ayaan seemed to bring out the older woman's motherly side. "Sometimes," Dresselhuys said, "she is a very powerful woman, and sometimes she is a giggling little girl."

In early August, Ayaan appeared on another TV show about women and Islam. She told her audience again that Muslim women who claimed not to be oppressed were the victims of false consciousness. Again she used the simile of the imprisoned bird. The broadcast struck many Muslims as condescending. Her father called to say he was hearing complaints again.

Ayaan told him she was trying to expose the link between Islam and women's oppression. Her father disputed the relationship. "You can fight the oppression of women, Ayaan, but you must not link it with Islam."

She didn't have the courage, she wrote, to tell him that she no longer agreed.

Eight

When Aafia and Amjad reached Karachi at the end of June 2002, the Khans were furious with her. They felt she had wrecked their son's budding career. The younger couple took the children and went to stay at her family's house in Gulshan-e-Iqbal, but Amjad was anxious and unhappy. He still loved Aafia, but he felt she was forcing him to choose between her and his family. The meeting with the FBI had also shaken him. Either her judgment and reasoning were skewed, or she was hiding things from him. Who, for example, was Shukrijumah?

Aafia prayed all the time now and insisted on their duty to join the jihad. But Amjad's parents were more opposed to that than ever. At length Amjad decided that the only solution was to seek advice from a higher authority. Grand Mufti Muhammad Rafi Usmani was the highest Deobandi cleric in Pakistan. Amjad persuaded her that they should ask him what to do.

She went to the meeting, properly veiled and covered, at the grand mufti's house in the Darul Uloom seminary complex. After greeting the mufti's wife and daughter-in-law, she joined Ahmad and the cleric on the lawn. The mufti was a heavy man, with smooth olive skin and a fluffy white beard. He listened attentively as Amjad explained their problem: Aafia felt their duty was to fight the infidels, but Amjad's parents were against it and Amjad himself believed he could best serve Islam through his work as a doctor. Amjad agreed with Aafia that a Muslim's whole life should be an act of worship, but he did not believe that he had reached the level of self-mastery necessary to engage in the highest form of worship, holy combat.

The mufti thought about it before giving his opinion. It was commendable, he said, that Aafia's heart burned so brightly for the *ummah*, but he did not agree that jihad was now an obligation for her and Amjad. Given their circumstances, the mufti said, it was more important for the two of them to serve the *ummah* by sharing the knowledge they had gained in America.

Getting the grand mufti himself to consider their problem was a great honor in Pakistan, and a petitioner's normal reaction would be to thank him profusely and ask for a blessing. Instead, to the astonishment of both men, Aafia piped up from behind her niqab and began arguing in her high, sweet voice with the country's highest religious authority. What about the view of Sheikh Abdullah Azzam? she demanded. Hadn't he called jihad a community obligation incumbent on every Muslim?

The mufti repeated his advice and was visibly irritated. By the end of the meeting, his tone toward Aafia had cooled considerably. She said that one reason she wanted to go and live with the Jaish-e-Muhammad was to raise their children in a truly Islamic environment, but he corrected her again. It was quite possible to raise truly Muslim children in Karachi. The city now had excellent English-speaking schools that followed the strictest Deobandi interpretation of Islamic law. The mufti's own grandchildren attended one, called Nakhlah.

Aafia realized she had made a mistake and later telephoned the mufti to apologize. Considering the matter settled, Amjad began looking for a job in Karachi. But Aafia still seemed distracted. A few weeks after they returned, she came home late one afternoon with the children. Amjad asked where they had been; she replied that she had gone to the beauty parlor. But their driver later mentioned to Amjad that he had taken Aafia to the Habib Bank earlier in the day. Amjad visited the bank the following day. There he learned that Aafia had withdrawn $6,000.

That night he asked Aafia if she'd been to the bank. She said she had not. Later he searched her purse and found the money in her wallet. He decided to set a little trap to show her that he knew she was deceiving him.

The next morning he told her he wanted to take some money out of their Habib account to buy a car. Aafia was heavily pregnant, and in the mornings she usually had a ravenous appetite. But after he announced his intention to visit the bank, she said she didn't want to eat the omelette that her parents' cook had made her for breakfast.

At the bank she volunteered to go inside and cash his check while Amjad waited in the lobby. As he watched, she went up to the teller and said something while calmly opening her purse. What she didn't know was that he had removed the money she had in it. She frantically turned the purse upside down on the teller's desk. Amjad came up beside her and asked what was wrong.

"I knew I couldn't trust our servants!" she burst out. Only then did she admit that she had withdrawn the money the day before.

The couple later had a terrible fight in front of Amjad's mother. Aafia claimed she had taken the money out because she was afraid the United States would freeze their accounts. Amjad asked why, if that was true, she had left $2,000 in the account and why she had lied about it.

"I can't trust you," he told her. "You hide things from me! We can't live together."

So Aafia and the children went back to her parents' house while Amjad stayed with the Khans.

A few days later, both families organized another session with the mufti, and it was decided that Aafia and Amjad should live apart from both their families.

They rented an apartment and set it up, but within days they were fighting again and Amjad told Aafia he wanted a divorce. This time he went back to his parents' house, and Aafia's mother came to pick her up. His parents tried to call the Siddiquis to arrange another mediation, which is customary in Pakistan. But the Siddiquis now refused to answer the phone.

On his previous visit Amjad had tried to shield his parents from his marital troubles. But since his return they had pressed him to say more. His stories alarmed them. Aafia struck them as utterly headstrong and reckless. His parents feared that if he went back to her, the two might run off and join one of the militant groups. If he divorced her, on the other hand, his parents told him, they would find him another, better wife.

Amjad knew that if he left Aafia, the Siddiquis would never forgive him. He had heard Aafia's father say that anyone who divorced his daughters was committing adultery and had no right to see his children. (Dr. Siddiqui's view was inconsistent with sharia, which makes divorce easy for men, but he didn't seem to care.) Amjad's older brothers, however, told him they knew many divorced Pakistani couples who raised their children amicably.

Aafia recalled in talking with the FBI in 2008 that while her father had outwardly defended her against the Khans, he had been deeply distressed by what Amjad said about her. Her father had even wondered, in the FBI's telling of her story, "if it would have been better if she would have died before she was born." She told the agent that until he said this to her, she had considered her father "a kind and gentle man she was close to," and she began to cry.

The Islamic laws put in place by General Zia ul-Haq gave Amjad the right to initiate a divorce unilaterally by saying "I divorce you" three times. Since Aafia and her family had refused to see him or answer his calls, he sent her a letter by courier on August 17 saying precisely that.

He would need to wait three months before the divorce became final, unless he and Aafia reconciled before then.

Amjad did not know that only two days before he had sent his letter, Aafia's father had died of a heart attack. The Siddiquis blamed Amjad for his death, and they refused to have anything more to do with the Khans. "I liked her very much, but she was rigid and stubborn," Amjad's mother said sadly of Aafia. "Whatever she wanted to do, she was going to do. She was so crazy to help the world."

Nine

On the first anniversary of the 9/11 attacks, Ayaan was invited to appear on Holland's most popular nighttime talk show, *Barend & Van Dorp.* The show sent bodyguards to escort her to various panel discussions she attended earlier in the day. Ayaan noticed an unusually large number of Moroccans at some of the debates, and they booed when she entered.

The show's host that evening asked her if she had lied—"as everybody else did"—when she sought asylum in 1992. Ayaan replied that she had because she was fleeing an arranged marriage and she feared for her life if her family found her.

The host asked if she agreed with Pim Fortuyn that Islam was backward. It was the same question that had landed Fortuyn in trouble the year before, but Ayaan thought she had a clever way to get around it. "According to the Arab Human Development report of the UN," she answered, "if you measure by three things, political freedom, education, and the status of women—then what Pim Fortuyn said is not an opinion, it's a fact." As usual, both she and her Dutch interviewers failed to distinguish between Islam the religion and the sociopolitical environment of various majority-Muslim countries, and her answer failed to appease her critics. But many Dutch viewers saw it as a refreshingly blunt statement of the obvious.

The next day Ayaan and a Dutch-Pakistani lawyer named Naema Tahir faced off on another program (*Rondom 10*, or *Around 10*) against the Saudi-funded imam Mohammed Cheppih and the Moroccan youth activist Ali Eddaoudi. Like Ayaan, Naema Tahir had gone through a stage as a teenage Islamist. The men began shouting at the two women and cutting them off. Ayaan had said on an earlier radio show that she had lost her faith. "Then you are not a Muslim!" one of the men shouted. "You said Islam was backward! You are lying!"

Without losing her cool for a minute, Ayaan replied, "It's my religion, too, and if I want to call it backward, I will do so. Yes, Islam is backward." After the show, *Rondom 10* received more than two thousand e-mails, many of them threatening Ayaan and Tahir.

Her phone was ringing when she got home. Friends feared for her. Her foster father warned her not to get into a slanging match with Holland's Muslims. Her supervisor, Paul Kalma, advised her to stick to writing opinion pieces. Her housemate told her she had lost her mind. Four days after the broadcast, Ayaan's father warned the filmmaker Karin Schagen that Ayaan was in danger of being assassinated. Marco took her out for a drive. He begged her to be careful.

But while they were talking, her phone rang. It was Leon de Winter. Ayaan had never met the famous Jewish writer, but she knew about his books. She had mentioned his criticism of Islam in her first article, "Give Us a Voltaire." He told her how much he admired what she was doing, and he invited her to dinner with him and his wife, another well-known writer and television personality.

Schagen was still trailing Ayaan for her documentary, which was becoming more topical than anyone imagined. She filmed Ayaan going to the Leiden police to file a complaint. The police advised her not to stay at home, but they said they couldn't offer more than advice unless she wanted to file charges against a specific person. That day a reporter from *De Volkskrant* called. On September 18, the newspaper reported ominously that Ayaan was going into hiding.

Her former statistics professor Huib Pellikaan was incensed that the police had no plan to keep her safe. He lived in Amsterdam, around the corner from the Wiardi Beckman Institute, and he invited Ayaan to stay at his house. She accepted.

The news that Ayaan was going into hiding caused a commotion.

Commentators noted that Ayaan was the first person in Holland to go underground for a political opinion since World War II. Her photograph appeared on the covers of newspapers and glossy magazines. Some called her "the Dutch Salman Rushdie." Others preferred "the black Voltaire." All the talking heads whom Ayaan and Marco had watched for years on *Nova* suddenly wanted to meet her. But when she rang her father, he hung up on her.

The memory of Fortuyn's murder was still raw, and many Dutch were outraged to think that another citizen was being threatened for speaking out about Islam. "This was something new in Holland," said the filmmaker Eveline van Dijk. Tilly Hermans, the publisher who had tried to talk Ayaan into writing her autobiography, rushed to bring out a collection of Ayaan's articles and op-eds in book form. The historian Geert Mak and other writers organized a petition drive to support her. *Opzij* took out an ad in her defense. Kalma and de Winter raised 25,000 euros to pay for her protection.

Years later, Ayaan's host, Huib Pellikaan, shook his head in disbelief when he recalled the whirlwind that followed Ayaan into his house. She herself seemed unafraid, indeed ready to take the offensive. But being around her felt dangerous, and Pellikaan, a kindly middle-aged academic with a sizable belly, wasn't accustomed to feeling that way. Afterward, he could never explain quite why he had felt so threatened except to say that Ayaan "can be very intoxicating."

His biggest concern at first was to get his waifish guest to consume something more than gallons of coffee while she talked a mile a minute on the phone. Within a few days, however, he was smoking four packs of cigarettes a day, and he had decided to shave off his curly gray hair and start wearing a black leather jacket to intimidate anyone who might threaten her. "It seems crazy when I look back on it," Pellikaan said with a sheepish laugh. "I look more like a nutty professor than Bruce Willis in *Die Hard*. My friends took one look and said, 'Nobody is going to be afraid of that.'"

Paul Kalma at the Wiardi Beckman Institute asked the government to provide bodyguards for Ayaan. He was told she wasn't entitled to government bodyguards because she wasn't a government official. So Kalma decided to hire some privately. He called the TV station that had briefly provided her with guards and hired two from the same company the station had used for 50 euros an hour each. At that rate, it would cost the Labor Party five times as much to protect Ayaan as to pay her, but Kalma saw no alternative.

Meanwhile, a good deal of related politicking was under way in Holland. After Pim Fortuyn's murder, the new political party he had formed got enough votes to join the governing coalition. But the coalition was so unstable that everyone expected a call for new elections. The threats against Ayaan frightened Labor not only because its members liked and esteemed her but also because they did not want to be branded as soft on terrorism. And people across the political spectrum feared what might happen if another public figure died after criticizing Islam.

Marco arrived to stay with Ayaan in Pellikaan's house. He and Pellikaan urged her to lie low. "This is supposed to be your *hiding* place," Pellikaan pleaded, but she paid them no mind. Reporters kept phoning and ringing the doorbell. "Within three weeks, she had turned the whole place into some kind of press conference center," Pellikaan recalled. Every conversation was about Ayaan's future. Pellikaan felt the drama was going to her head.

The three of them sometimes sat up late drinking wine. Ayaan would give her opinions. She thought religion was the root of all evil and should be abolished. "She has absolutely extremist ideas about how to solve problems," said Pellikaan. "She hates consensus politics. We Dutch are all wishy-washy idealists in her view. She's the toughest girl I have ever seen."

Her former professor was fascinated to learn how ambitious—and how radical—she was. He told her only half jokingly that she thought like a member of the Baader-Meinhof gang. She had never heard of the left-wing German terrorist group of the 1970s, so she wasn't offended. But she did get cross when Pellikaan and Marco told her she was dreaming if she thought that she—a junior researcher with a year's experience working for the Labor Party—might be elected head of the party in time for the coming elections. "She had even selected the leaders of the fraction," Pellikaan remembered. "We talked about it for about three hours. Finally I told her, 'Ayaan, this is never going to work.'" She and Marco went downstairs, but Pellikaan could hear them still arguing late at night about whether she could lead the Labor Party.

Cisca Dresselhuys, the editor of *Opzij* magazine, invited Ayaan to her house in Hilversum, and Ayaan arrived with the two bodyguards that Labor had hired. Privately, she told Dresselhuys they were "amateurish." "Please, Cisca, do you know how I can get better guards?"

Dresselhuys decided to speak about Ayaan's plight to some politicians she knew. One of them was Gerrit Zalm, the leader of the opposition Liberal Party.

The Liberals were planning to use the issue of immigration to take a serious chunk out of the Labor Party vote in the next elections. Rescuing this threatened Somali beauty became part of their strategy.

Labor itself had invited its researcher to speak before Parliament on October 2. A few days beforehand, the *Opzij* columnist Pauline Sinnema stopped by Pellikaan's house and offered to help Ayaan write the speech. Pellikaan let her use his computer. But the speech that Sinnema helped Ayaan write surprised him as much as it would other Labor Party members.

Ayaan rounded on her own party in the speech for treating Muslim women as second-class citizens. A day after she gave the speech, it appeared as an op-ed piece in *NRC Handelsblad* under the headline "Labor Party Underestimates Suffering of Muslim Women." By the following week, leading Liberal Party women such as Cisca Dresselhuys's friend Neelie Kroes, a businesswoman and former cabinet member, were calling on the government to protect Ayaan.

Not everyone in the Labor Party disagreed with Ayaan's criticism. Many thought the party had turned a blind eye to the rift between Holland's natives and immigrants. Huib Pellikaan told Ayaan she had the gifts to become a political leader but needed to learn more. He began trying to get her into graduate school at Harvard. Leon de Winter proposed she go stay at a writer's retreat in California. De Winter also wanted to get her together with friends in the United States about the possibility of her studying under Bernard Lewis, the famous historian of Islam who had inspired Samuel Huntington's thesis about the clash of civilizations. Some Labor Party members helped set up a foundation to raise the needed cash, and in October the foundation flew Ayaan to the United States. It was her first trip there.

Soon after she left, an article in the magazine *Vrij Nederland* suggested that the threats against her were exaggerated. The author, an investigative journalist named Elma Verhey, had interviewed not only a high-ranking police officer but also some of Ayaan's Somali relatives in Nijmegen, who had claimed she wasn't in any special danger. Verhey tried to reach Ayaan's father, but the former Somali rebel leader was avoiding reporters. Relatives said later that he had washed his hands of Ayaan. Yet he may have had another reason to stay out of the public eye. He was applying for asylum in Great Britain and using another name—possibly to conceal the fact that he already had refugee status in Kenya.

VARA Television had a program called *De Leugen Regeert* (*The Lie Prevails*) on which journalists and the people they criticized were invited to duke it out on the air. The show's producers asked Verhey to defend her article. Verhey expected to face Ayaan herself or perhaps one of Ayaan's media friends. She planned to say that it made journalistic sense to check and see if the police and other Somalis took the threats against Ayaan as seriously as she did.

To Verhey's astonishment, it wasn't Ayaan or another journalist who showed up but Neelie Kroes, the highest-ranking woman in the Liberal Party. Kroes proceeded to accuse Verhey on national TV of selling out not just Ayaan, a vulnerable and threatened young Somali, but Muslim women generally. Kroes didn't call Verhey a

"Muslim hugger"—as Fortuyn's followers called those they accused of weakly handing Holland to the Muslims—but plenty of Web sites soon did.

On October 16, the Dutch government fell. By that point, Ayaan had been talking quietly with the Liberal Party for more than a month. *NRC Handelsblad* reported the result of its wooing two weeks later: Ayaan planned to leave Labor and join the conservative Liberal Party.

The Liberal Party was often called the "party of businessmen," and it tended to avoid social issues, calling instead for less government regulation of the free-market economy. But Pim Fortuyn's example had presented conservatives such as the Liberals with an irresistible temptation. By appealing to the government to liberate Muslim women and gays, he had shown that it was possible to appeal to the Dutch xenophobic vote in a socially acceptable way, while at the same time drawing feminists and homosexuals away from the Labor Party. Fortuyn's rise had also revealed that the anti-Muslim vote was much bigger than anyone had realized: between 5 and 15 percent of the population, or as much as three times the size of the entire Muslim vote.

As Ayaan herself later wrote, she became the face of the Liberals' new electoral strategy.

She had said nothing to the Wiardi Beckman Institute about her plan to join Labor's opponents. Harry van den Bergh—who had headed Labor's fund-raising effort to protect her—couldn't believe the news of her switch. He called Ayaan in the United States to ask if the report was true. When she said it was, van den Bergh told her he saw no reason why the Wiardi Beckman Institute and his foundation should continue financing her stay in California. Ayaan answered with the "historic words," as van den Bergh later told the magazine *HP/De Tijd*, "Okay, I will come back, but first I'm going on vacation to Hawaii."

"And then Ayaan, at our cost, went to Hawaii." Van den Bergh said he never heard from her again. "Ever since then, I have found her to be a terribly clever opportunist."

Ayaan's former professor and host, Huib Pellikaan, also read about her plans. Pellikaan had been pulling strings to get Ayaan into Harvard. He had even booked a ticket to New York, where the two of them planned to meet before going on to Cambridge. She never called him, and she never apologized.

Pellikaan came to believe that she had already decided to join the Liberals by the time she gave the speech that Pauline Sinnema had helped write in his house. "She's very brave on a macro level but not very brave on a micro, individual level," he said. "She doesn't like confrontation."

A Dutch reporter phoned her in California to ask if she wasn't betraying her party. Ayaan responded, "Looking at it from here, all 150 members of the Dutch Parliament may as well be in one party. The Netherlands is a small, emotional country. You can't run politics on the basis of feelings. . . . I belong to no one, only to myself."

Ten

Aafia's father was the parent she had written to about her scientific studies in America. He had tried to mediate between Aafia and her in-laws. Now he was dead, and the family said the stress of Aafia's breakup had killed him. They blamed Amjad, but Aafia knew that her father had been angry with her, too.

She had few friends in Pakistan, having been away for twelve years. She had a six-year-old and a four-year-old to care for, and she was eight months pregnant. About two weeks after her father died and she received Amjad's letter declaring their divorce, she came down with chicken pox.

When a woman catches chicken pox in the third trimester of pregnancy, she risks a virus that can damage the baby's brain and even kill both mother and child. Aafia's due date was a month away, but her doctor rushed her to the hospital on September 3, 2002, for an emergency C-section. Afterward, she and the baby boy, whom she named Suleman Fateh, were put on antiviral treatments. They stayed in the hospital for more than a week.

Neither she nor her family called Amjad or his parents to let them know about the new baby. Amjad had not seen Ahmad and Maryam since the day in July when he had told Aafia he wanted to separate. The Khans phoned the Siddiquis, but Aafia refused to take their calls. She also refused to talk to the local official who came around asking her to sign a certificate confirming that she was divorced.

This time Amjad asked his parents to find him a bride "we have known for a long time," meaning a girl from within their extended family. His mother took him to meet a selection of cousins. The father of the one he liked best accepted his proposal immediately. His impending divorce was no problem: he was a handsome young doctor with the potential to become a wealthy man after he resumed his American career.

Amjad was now working at a Karachi hospital. He was there on the day that had been set for his wedding dinner when a nurse informed him that he had a visitor. In the waiting room he found Aafia. She was dressed up in a mauve silk cloak and head scarf with matching lipstick. It was just the sort of fashionable but conservative outfit he loved, but she had rarely worn such clothes since she adopted the black abaya and niqab. Amjad had not known that Aafia had given birth—yet here she was, looking so alluring that the nurse who announced her assumed she must be the new bride. Aafia suggested brightly that they go out for lunch at the Sheraton Hotel.

Dining at one of Karachi's most expensive restaurants was the sort of extravagance that Aafia usually chided Amjad for, but this time she seemed to enjoy the meal. She told him about Suleman's difficult delivery, and she said she hadn't lost her feelings for him. At the end of the meal, she invited him to Gulshan-e-Iqbal that evening to meet his new baby son and to play with the two children he had not seen for almost two months.

Amjad realized she was offering him the chance to reconcile rather than marry his pretty young cousin. Her behavior reminded him of their happy days, before they had begun to fight about jihad and before their families had gotten involved. He missed Ahmad and Maryam. He missed Aafia, too.

He barely knew the cousin he was marrying. He had been so depressed by his split with Aafia that he'd lacked the energy to learn much. He was going into this marriage on faith—the faith, this time, that strong family ties and a shared understanding of Islam would carry him through. Now Aafia was testing that faith.

But he could not go with her, despite the guilt and confusion he felt. They couldn't possibly live together now. If they tried, he knew, it would only be temporary. And he had given his word to his cousin's father. Her mother and sisters were already decorating her hands and feet for that night's wedding.

So he refused to go to Aafia's house. He offered instead to visit the children first thing in the morning.

Aafia backed off at that point, saying her mother and sister might not let him in the house. And she suggested that they go see her lawyer right away.

The lawyer wrote up a divorce settlement. Aafia agreed to give Amjad access to the children, while he agreed to pay for the children's maintenance in addition to her recent hospital bills.

Amjad's uncle hurried over to act as a witness. After they signed, Amjad and Aafia went out for tea at the Avari Towers, another expensive hotel near the Sheraton. At about 6:30 in the evening, Amjad left the hotel to get married again. His second wedding day was the last time he ever spoke with Aafia.

She signed a statement confirming the divorce on October 21, 2002. Amjad sent her his first monthly maintenance check the following month. Aafia cashed it but refused to let him see the children.

When his parents asked Aafia's mother to intervene, Ismat told them that Amjad was an abusive husband and father who did not deserve to see his children. Then she stopped talking to the Khans, and they never did see the children.

Amjad attempted to press his case before the town union council, but the Siddiquis and their allies outmaneuvered him. The Jamaat-e-Islami had a majority on the council, and at an angry council meeting packed with party activists, Ismat produced Fowzia's photographs of Aafia with her split lip as evidence of why Amjad shouldn't see his children. The council sided with the Siddiquis. Amjad stalked out of the meeting, and Aafia was awarded sole custody.

The Khan family's lawyers told the family that the council had no authority to decide matters of custody. Amjad and his father therefore filed a lawsuit claiming his right, under Islamic law, to visit his children and to pay for their maintenance. Fowzia later said that Aafia saw the Khans' demands as harassment.

Eleven

Ayaan's switch to the Liberal Party was a major political event in Holland that autumn. The election turned on the question of whether Muslims could or should be integrated into Dutch society, and Ayaan was at the center of it. She wrote in a newspaper piece announcing her decision that there were three things she wanted to achieve in Parliament: "I wanted Holland to wake up and stop tolerating the oppression of Muslim women in its midst. . . . Second, I wanted to spark a debate among Muslims about reforming aspects of Islam so that people could begin to question and criticize their own beliefs. . . . Third, I wanted Muslim women to become aware of just how bad and how unacceptable their suffering was."

Her old friends from Leiden and Ede were stunned by her turnaround. But Neelie Kroes and other Liberals pointed out that they were offering Holland and Ayaan benefits that Labor had failed to offer: not just a place on their ticket that could send Ayaan to Parliament but also a chance to get the police protection as an elected official she needed to continue her work of liberating Muslim women. By contrast, they suggested, Labor wanted to send her off to the United States and avoid the question of the oppressed Muslim woman.

Karin Schagen's sympathetic portrait of Ayaan, "The Fear in the Back of My Head," appeared on television on November 1, the day after Ayaan's article appeared announcing her decision. Solomon Burke's mournful rendition of the American blues song "Don't Give Up on Me" was the sound track. But even as her friends were adjusting to her sudden national prominence, Ayaan was taking her first steps onto an even wider stage.

On November 9, the *New York Times* published a flattering full-length "Saturday Profile" of the woman it quoted others as calling "the Dutch Salman Rushdie." Fortunately for Ayaan, the reporter who wrote the piece was Marlise Simons, a Dutchwoman of the same generation as Cisca Dresselhuys and Neelie Kroes. Although Simons was based in Paris, she had been covering the Dutch debate over integration and was struck by the impact Ayaan was having.

Her article told essentially the same story about Ayaan's life and views that Steffie Kouters had told in *De Volkskrant* a month earlier. But whereas Kouters had helped turn Ayaan into the darling of the Dutch intelligentsia, Simons's article introduced her as a heroine to a worldwide elite. From Washington to London, readers took note. Simons also took a personal liking to Ayaan, and when Ayaan confided that she was overwhelmed with foreign media requests and needed a literary agent, Simons recommended that she contact the Paris-based agent Susanna Lea.

Lea was making a name for herself in Paris by introducing American-style marketing techniques to the relatively dowdy European publishing industry. One specialty she was developing was packaging books about women from the Third World for Western audiences. She had sold *My Forbidden Face*, one of the first books written by an Afghan woman about life under the Taliban, in November 2001. She had followed it up with the memoir of Osama bin Laden's former sister-in-law Carmen bin Ladin, which had become a bestseller. She agreed to represent Ayaan.

Holland's political and intellectual celebrities were already clamoring to meet her. Most came away charmed. In the hothouse world of Dutch journalism and politics, it was refreshing to meet someone new, especially a beautiful African woman with such a dramatic background. Ayaan's imperious style could be an asset in Dutch eyes during this early phase. "You know she comes from nobility," Neelie Kroes's husband, the Labor Party politician Bram Peper, often said.

Ayaan often mentioned the Enlightenment, but she didn't seem to exhibit the typically Dutch need to qualify every statement and cite studies and statistics. As the left-wing journalist Stan van Houcke said, "She acts by impulse and instinct, and that makes her stronger than an intellectual."

She often bonded with other women by suggesting that they shop for clothes together. When she went to meet Neelie Kroes in San Francisco, Ayaan bought a burgundy sweater that Kroes said suited her. Kroes was smitten with her young Somali protégée; later she proudly told reporters that Ayaan "had lived through five civil wars." In truth, Ayaan could claim to have seen one, briefly, during her 1990 stint in Somalia. Within a month of the meeting, the Dutch newspaper *Het Parool* was comparing Kroes and Ayaan to mother and daughter.

Kroes paid for Ayaan to visit an expensive hairdresser in the chic Hague suburb of Wassenaar. The Dutch hairdresser straightened Ayaan's hair and encouraged her to pull it back in a sleek chignon. When out campaigning, Kroes suggested, Ayaan should wear the kinds of professional suits favored by the Dutch bourgeoisie. It was the Wassenaar look, but Ayaan managed to turn it into her own style. She preferred bold solids to prints and crisp fabrics to soft ones. Even when she had held a job, Ayaan couldn't have afforded the boutiques that Kroes favored, and soon she was spending more money than she had. Bram Peper said his wife loaned Ayaan the extra money.

Before the Liberals officially named her their candidate, Ayaan had to make her case to the rest of the party. Not everyone was enthusiastic. Other Liberals who for years had been working their way up the lists to run for Parliament were angry that Kroes and another party leader, Gerrit Zalm, wanted to exalt a newcomer with practically no political experience. The party's few young Muslim members were especially dismayed.

In 1998, Fadime Örgü had been one of the first two Dutch citizens of Turkish descent ever elected to Parliament. Now thirty-four, Örgü had entered public life when she was fifteen years old because she wanted to help immigrant women. Attractive, with shoulder-length brown hair, Örgü considered herself a true Liberal. She believed in the absolute separation of religion and state. Her goal was to emancipate Muslim women and make them economically independent. She didn't think that bringing Ayaan into the party was the way to achieve that. "If you want to represent people, you have to listen to them, and you have to have support among your target group," Örgü said. "I didn't see Ayaan doing that."

Several Somali refugees approached the Liberals with another complaint. They told party leader Bas Eenhoorn that Ayaan had lied on her application for asylum.

The Somali complaint presented a ticklish problem for the Liberals. They had adopted Pim Fortuyn's anti-immigration platform. One of the party's campaign promises was to kick out the bogus asylum seekers, who the Liberals claimed were making a mockery of Holland's laws and borders. For the same party to nominate a bogus asylum seeker for Parliament could be disastrous. Gerrit Zalm and other party officials called Ayaan in to ask if she had lied.

Ayaan has never made it quite clear what she told the Liberals, except that she admitted to having changed her name and birthday and not telling "the whole truth" (as she put it in her autobiography). But she probably said something similar to what she was telling journalists at the time.

A few days earlier, Marlise Simons had reported in the *New York Times* that Ayaan, at the age of twenty-two, had narrowly escaped being forced to marry "a distant cousin, a man she had never seen." Simons had gone on to say that "a friend helped her to escape and she finally obtained political asylum in the Netherlands."

The implication was that even if Ayaan did not fit the definition of a refugee under the 1954 Refugee Convention, she had been fleeing danger of another sort when she had come to the Netherlands, just as she was menaced by danger now.

Whatever Ayaan told them, the Liberals decided that her statements to the immigration authorities should not impede her candidacy.

No one, it seems, not even Fadime Örgü, asked in public whether Ayaan might be lying about having had to marry a fundamentalist cousin she had never met. Everyone knew that honor killings were a serious problem in the Turkish community, who made up much of Holland's Muslims, and the Dutch could easily assume that other Muslims lived under the same threat. The country's Turkish and Moroccan communities, moreover, may have made a similar assumption about Somalis, especially after learning about their startling custom of female genital mutilation. And in general, it was becoming risky if not taboo to question Ayaan. Those who did so could be accused, as the journalist Elma Verhey had been, of siding with Islamic fascists, who, the Dutch were frequently reminded, in addition to trying to silence Ayaan, wanted to limit free speech and turn the Netherlands into a sharia state.

Zalm ranked Ayaan as such a positive addition to the Liberal Party that he listed her on the ballot as number 16, well ahead of dozens of long-standing party members. Kroes's husband, Bram Peper, helped Ayaan write her maiden speech to the party. Peper also edited a slender collection of articles and papers that Ayaan had written that Tilly Hermans was rushing out in time for the election. The book was called *The Son Factory*—that's what Ayaan said Islam expected the proper Muslim woman to be.

Now that she was running for office, the Royal and Diplomatic Protection Service supplied her with armed bodyguards. Ayaan traveled with them everywhere, sometimes in a convoy of bulletproof cars. She had no apartment of her own but stayed with new friends, such as Nellie Kroes and her husband. The filmmaker Eveline van Dijk decided to take up where Karin Schagen had left off and began following Ayaan with a camera.

One night before the election, van Dijk accompanied Ayaan to a dinner party at the Amsterdam apartment of the talk show host and newspaper columnist Theodor Holman. Marco and Ayaan were still close, so Marco came, too.

Holman lived on Willemsparkweg, a wide treelined street in the

Oud Zuid neighborhood near the Rijksmuseum and the Concertgebouw. As Ayaan's caravan arrived and her bodyguards took up positions outside Holman's brick town house, the middle-aged columnist stood outside and narrated for van Dijk's camera, in a hushed voice, how strange it felt for him to feel threatened in his own home. Holland was so small and safe that even semicelebrities like him rode their bicycles to work.

But the dinner was a jolly one in Holman's book-lined living room, with plenty of candles, wine, and Ayaan's favorite rare beef.

The half-submerged topic that dominated the conversation was fear: what Ayaan feared, and who feared her, and the fear that others felt around her. Ayaan is apparently scared of cats, and Holman had tried to lock up his old white cat for the night. But the cat had gotten loose and prowled around Ayaan, whom the camera recorded looking very fetching as she quivered in a red blouse and black sweater and trousers. In her film, van Dijk made the irony unmistakable: this delicate woman, so personally unthreatening that even a cat could frighten her, had somehow aroused the fury of millions. Holman asked Marco whether Ayaan should be afraid of entering a snake pit such as Parliament, and Marco quipped that, more likely, Parliament should be afraid of her. The party laughed loudly. She was brave, yes, but it seemed absurd to think of Ayaan as scary.

As the evening wore on, Ayaan brought up the Somalis who had told the Liberal Party's leaders about the story she had told the immigration authorities. Ayaan was laughing, but she admitted that she was concerned. She said the problem was mainly her safety. "If they keep me out of Parliament, then nobody will protect me," she said earnestly. "There will be no place for me. If I don't go to Parliament, then I am outlawed."

She didn't ask (and perhaps it never crossed her mind) whether anyone at the table disapproved of her lying. Back at Lunteren, the social workers hadn't seemed to care. Ayaan may have thought that since, on the *Barend & Dorp* show, she had already admitted to lying about being a civil war refugee and no one had seemed to mind, no one ever would.

But that program was the one where she had called Islam a backward religion. And amid the uproar and the threats that had followed the program, few people had focused on what she said about obtaining asylum. Holman, a professional political commentator, clearly hadn't, and he was surprised now, and more than a little dismayed, to learn at his dinner that she had lied to the government.

After Ayaan and Marco left, Holman gave a little speech to van Dijk's camera about how conflicted he felt. On the one hand, he considered it news that this candidate had not told the truth on her asylum application. On the other hand, he was afraid that if Ayaan lost the election, she would lose her bodyguards, which allowed her to keep speaking out against Islam. Finally he decided that his duty was to keep silent. "It is a duty that she goes to the Chamber, that she gets protection for her situation," he said. "For me to endanger this would be the beginning of the end. It would be to give up free speech, to submit to this diplomatic terror. For me, it would be to say that the Netherlands is no longer tolerant."

The leaders of the Liberal Party evidently agreed. Frits Bolkestein, the former Liberal Party leader, who had first sounded the alarm in 1991 about Islam's threat to Dutch values, gave a speech making Ayaan's themes those of the party. "Those who fail to see the discrimination against Muslim women that is going on are simply refusing to face facts," he said. "Why should we not be allowed to criticize Islam and the Koran? Do we live in a free country or not? Let us not mince our words."

Twelve

Ever since Aafia had been a little girl, she had excelled at practically everything. But in the fall of 2002, at the age of thirty-one, she was reeling in the face of failure.

While she and Amjad were still married, her mother had told him over and over that he would never find another woman on Earth like Aafia. But he had divorced her anyway, and now he was married to some stranger from his own extended family. Aafia could tell herself he was a weakling and a hypocrite, but that didn't change the fact that she was now that scorned and lonely creature, a divorced woman in Pakistan.

Was she already entangled with al-Qaeda at that point? She later told the FBI that she was not. If she wasn't, she certainly became so within months of her divorce.

She told agents that she had come under the influence of Mufti Abu Lubaba Shah Mansoor, a fanatical Karachi cleric who was the ideologue of the al-Rashid Trust.

The al-Rashid Trust was founded by Mufti Rashid Ahmad, one of Karachi's original fire-breathing preachers of jihad, to support the Taliban. Abu Lubaba Shah Mansoor was Rashid Ahmad's deputy. Prior to the U.S. invasion of Afghanistan, *Asia Times* reported that, among Karachi's divines, only Abu Lubaba and Mufti Rashid had direct access to Osama bin Laden.

Aafia told the FBI that when Mufti Abu Lubaba had learned of her scientific background, he had given her a fatwa ordering her to conduct research on germ warfare and other unconventional weapons against the United States. Yet in the fall of 2002, she seems to have concentrated on furthering Abu Lubaba's cause in another way: by working with KSM's al-Baluchi clan.

She said her involvement began late in 2002 when her mother decided to divide her house into two apartments and rent one out. The al-Baluchi family answered Ismat's advertisement and became her tenants for a few months. Who and how many of the al-Baluchi came to stay is unknown. Aafia herself admitted that the family had houses of their own in the Karachi area. Assuming that Ismat and Aafia had joined the network of women providing shelter for jihadis on the run, it seems likely that only *some* of the al-Baluchi stayed with Ismat.

Whether some or many, Aafia became friendly with the grown daughters of KSM's older sister Maryam, and these daughters introduced her to their twenty-five-year-old brother, Ali Abdul Aziz Ali, who also went by the name Ammar al-Baluchi.

Despite his youth, this handsome young man was one of his uncle KSM's agents even before 9/11. It's also possible that Aafia had known him before fall 2002. Ali had been in touch with Jose Padilla and Adnan Shukrijumah the previous spring, when Aafia had been questioned about e-mailing Shukrijumah. U.S. deputy attorney general James Comey later testified that it was Ali who had given Jose Padilla $10,000, a cell phone, and his e-mail address before he left Karachi for Chicago.

Clean-shaven, with close-cropped dark hair, Ali had the same wiry build and heavy-lidded gray eyes as his cousin Ramzi Yousef. He was born in Kuwait in 1977 and spent most of his teenage years in the Iranian part of Baluchistan. Somewhere along the way, probably in English-language schools, he picked up an easy fluency in English. He wore slick Western clothes and introduced himself as a businessman, though in fact his uncles and cousins had groomed him since boyhood to join their clandestine war. Ali felt comfortable enough with Western ways that KSM assigned him to teach some of the 9/11 hijackers how they should buy clothes and food in America.

Starting in the spring of 2000, Ali helped at least nine of the 9/11 hijackers prepare for their mission. He sent for a Boeing 727 flight simulator program to train Marwan al-Shehhi, the twenty-three-year-old suicide pilot from the United Arab Emirates who would crash United Airlines flight 175 into the South Tower of the World Trade Center. Between June 29 and September 17, 2000, Ali wired a total of $114,500 to Shehhi and the lead hijacker, Mohamed Atta. Later, Ali organized hotel reservations and travel documents for eight other hijackers who passed through the United Arab Emirates en route to the United States. Eventually he admitted having helped Shehhi and others, but he claimed he'd had no idea they were planning a terrorist operation.

According to the 9/11 Commission, Ali asked his uncle KSM for permission to join the hijackers on their mission. U.S. immigration records show that on August 27, 2001, he applied in Dubai for a visa to the United States. His application was turned down, and on September 10, he left Dubai for Karachi, where he was reunited with KSM.

After the 9/11 attacks, Ali helped KSM find safe houses in Pakistan for al-Qaeda operatives and their families. His uncle also put him in charge of communicating with men who were about to undertake missions in the United States, such as Padilla and the "shoe bombers" Richard Reid and his friend Saajid Badat. Ali's e-mail exchanges with Badat, revealed at Badat's trial, give a sense of the jaunty tone Ali maintained. "Hey, what's up, where are you?" he wrote when Badat seemed to be avoiding him.

One of the operatives Ali ran for KSM in the fall of 2002 was a young Pakistani computer programmer named Majid Khan. Khan was twenty-one and chubby. His family lived in Baltimore. It was a favor Ali asked Aafia to do for Majid Khan that put her on the FBI's Most Wanted list.

Khan had moved to Baltimore from Karachi at the age of fifteen after the United States had given his family political asylum in 1996. (His mother had claimed they were being persecuted because she belonged to a political party of Mohajirs, or Pakistanis who had migrated from India.) The family owned and operated several gas stations in the Baltimore area.

As a teenager Khan liked hip-hop music and baggy jeans, but his aunt says he became more religious after his mother died. Early in 2002, he and his brother returned to Pakistan to find brides.

As with Aafia and the al-Baluchi clan, there was a Deobandi connection in Majid Khan's family. His grandfather had been a Deobandi religious scholar in the Sindh town of Tando Allahyar. His aunt Khadija Arshad still ran a madrassa for girls there. She told me that Khan asked her to find him a wife. "Majid's insistence was that he wanted to marry with a woman who was a religious scholar," Arshad said, sitting on a floor cushion in her nearly bare Karachi apartment. So Arshad arranged a marriage in February 2002 between her nephew and one of her students, eighteen-year-old Rabia Yaqoob. A month later, Khan returned to Baltimore and his job. But he returned to Pakistan later in the year; his family says he wanted to be with his wife while he waited for his U.S. citizenship to come through. (The U.S. government claims he returned to work for KSM, whom they say he met on his previous trip through his aunt's husband and son.)

KSM has told his U.S. interrogators that, for him, the most important quality in a recruit is his willingness to carry out a suicide operation. According to a secret assessment of Khan prepared at Guantánamo in 2008, KSM tested Khan by asking him to strap on a vest he believed to be filled with explosives and go to a mosque where he said Pakistani president Pervez Musharraf would be visiting with the intention of detonating the vest. Khan passed, and then KSM asked the programmer to travel to Singapore in the fall of 2002 to deliver $50,000 to an associate of his old comrade Riduan Isamuddin, aka Hambali, the head of Jemaah Islamiah, al-Qaeda's Indonesian affiliate. Hambali had orchestrated the killing of 202 people in the suicide bombings of two Bali nightclubs. The money that Khan delivered was used to bomb Jakarta's Marriott Hotel, killing 12 and injuring 150. KSM said Khan had also given him the names of other potential operatives in the United States, such as Iyman Faris, an Ohio truck driver who had fought the Soviets in Afghanistan and would later be sentenced to twenty years in prison for helping Khan and KSM.

By late 2002, KSM seems to have settled on a scheme to send Khan back to the United States to begin preparing the ground for a spectacular new attack.

But Khan had made a mistake when he left the United States that was hampering his return. He had failed to obtain a travel document from the U.S. Immigration and Naturalization Service (INS) that he needed before he would be allowed to reenter the country. According to U.S. military prosecutors—and to Aafia's statements to the FBI—that was how Aafia entered the plot.

She told the FBI that Ali had described Khan to her as a friend who needed her help to get back into the United States. KSM's nephew evidently knew that Aafia would have no difficulty entering the United States because she still had a U.S. visa that Amjad had obtained for her the year before. Ali therefore arranged several meetings among Aafia, Khan, and Khan's wife and sister. Since Khan was an unrelated man, Aafia sat behind a partition at the meetings while Khan's female relatives did the talking.

Khan explained that he needed an address in the United States from which to mail his application for the travel document. He offered to pay for her to fly to the United States and open a post office box for him in the suburban Maryland town of Gaithersburg; then he needed her to collect the refugee travel document from the same box when the INS mailed it to him and carry it back to him in Pakistan.

Aafia told the FBI that she had agreed to do part of this job because Khan was "a family friend." She agreed to open the box but not to wait around to collect his papers. Khan supposedly agreed.

Thus she left her three-month-old, Suleman, and two other children in Karachi with her mother, and on Christmas Day she flew to the United States, the country she had been desperate to leave only a few months earlier.

Her sister, Fowzia, says she made the trip to interview for jobs at Johns Hopkins University and the State University of New York. "She was all set to go back to the U.S. because Pakistan was too traumatizing for her," Fowzia wrote me in an e-mail. But both universities were closed that week for the winter holiday, and university spokespeople could not verify that she had had any interviews. Aafia testified at her trial that she had gone looking for work but then returned to Pakistan early because her mother was ill.

Given Aafia's intense fear of the FBI, the journey must have been stressful. In fact, though she didn't know it, the FBI had placed her on an airline watch list after she and Amjad had left the United States without attending their second FBI interview. Now the FBI was alerted as soon as she entered the country. Yet she moved about freely, and on December 30 she entered the Gaithersburg post office and asked to rent a box.

Michael O'Hora, a twenty-seven-year veteran of the U.S. Postal Service, was the clerk on duty that day. He later testified that Aafia was "well dressed" in a woolen scarf and coat. (There's no mention of a head scarf.) When O'Hora asked her for identification, she showed him her Massachusetts driver's license and the Tufts University health insurance card that she had been given under Amjad's plan with the Tufts New England Medical Center.

She told O'Hora that the post office box was for her and her husband, whose name was Majid Khan, and that Khan would stop by later to show his identification. She said she was staying with friends in Gaithersburg, and she gave her telephone number as 301-529-9363 and her address as 18529 Reliance Drive. After signing the application and paying 29 dollars, she left with a receipt and two keys to P.O. box 8642.

At about 3 p.m., Aafia entered a second Gaithersburg post office about a mile and a half away. There she purchased a money order payable to the INS for 110 dollars and a large envelope. She placed the money order in the envelope with an application for a refugee travel document that Majid Khan had signed and dated December 20, 2002, and mailed it to the INS in Lincoln, Nebraska. She listed Khan's return address as the post office box she had rented.

Three days later, on January 2, 2003, she returned to Karachi.

Thirteen

Holland's elections took place on January 22. The front-runners for prime minister were Jan Peter Balkenende of the Christian Democrats and Job Cohen, the Labor mayor of Amsterdam whom Ayaan had called an ayatollah. Labor came in second behind the Christian Democrats, but together with the conservative Liberals and the small left-leaning D-66 party, the Christian Democrats won enough seats to form the first governing coalition in a decade that excluded Labor.

It was a tremendous setback for the Left, and Ayaan, number 16 on the Liberals' ballot, got the sixth largest number of votes in her party. She wasn't just in; she was a power in the land.

Ayaan and her new colleagues exulted. But even in the photos taken on election night, there's something incongruous about the spectacle of this gorgeous young Somali woman popping champagne corks amid so many pale Dutchmen in dark suits. Ayaan stands out like a beautiful leopard in a herd of cattle. And the Liberals were about to learn that she had claws.

The newspaper *Trouw* had an unusual feature. One of its reporters, Arjan Visser, regularly asked politicians and other public figures to discuss what the biblical Ten Commandments meant to them. In the United States such a question would probably elicit solemn homilies, but Holland is different. Pim Fortuyn, for example, when asked about the commandment "Thou shalt not commit adultery," had talked about the pleasures of having sex with men in the back rooms of Rotterdam's gay bars. On January 25—only three days after the election—*Trouw* published Visser's interview with Ayaan on its front page. The headline said, "Hirsi Ali: Muhammad Is a Perverse Tyrant."

She had been asked to comment on the commandment "Thou shalt not take the name of the Lord thy God in vain." Among other things she asserted that in Islam criticism of the Prophet Muhammad was a capital offense. She went on to describe how the Prophet had married Aisha, the daughter of his friend Abu Bakr, when she was nine years old. Ayaan added, "In other words, Muhammad teaches us that it is fine to take away your best friend's child. By our Western standards, Muhammad is a perverse man. A tyrant. He is against freedom of expression. If you don't do what he says, you will end up in hell. That reminds me of those megalomaniacal rulers in the Middle East: bin Laden, Khomeini, and Saddam. Are you surprised to find a Saddam Hussein? Muhammad is his example. Muhammad is an example to all Muslim men. Why do you think so many Islamic men use violence?"

The words Ayaan used in this interview have probably sparked more resentment against her than anything else she has done. As she has noted many times, devout Muslims consider Muhammad to be the most perfect human being ever, and they use the Sunna, or stories about his life, as a guide to how to live today. Because Salafists, for instance, in Saudi Arabia believe the Prophet wore an ankle-length gown rather than a longer one, they wear ankle-length gowns today. Because Ayatollah Khomeini believed the Prophet married Aisha when she was nine, he reduced the legal age of marriage for girls in Iran from sixteen to nine. Saudi Arabia executes some criminals by chopping off their heads: that is what the Prophet is supposed to have ordered. The point Ayaan wanted to raise—and she has raised it many times since—was a serious and important one: is the exact way the Prophet led his life the best guide to behavior in the twenty-first century? But the way she said it ensured that no believer would listen.

The Dutch tend to treat religious sensitivities far less seriously than Americans do, and, in general, the Liberals were remarkably careless when it came to Muslims' feelings. But even that party's leaders realized when they read her interview that, by inviting Ayaan to represent their party, they had gotten more than they bargained for.

The article appeared on a Saturday. The Netherlands had a law banning hate speech, a law usually used to prosecute anti-Semites. By midday, hundreds of Muslims were heading for police stations to demand that she be punished for insulting Muslims.

Someone phoned the house she had shared in Leiden and threatened to blow up the building. More restrained critics spoke out about how Ayaan was smearing Muslim men, that her statements about the Prophet's life and marriage were incorrect, and that she had failed to mention his modesty, kindness, and generosity. What made Muslims especially angry was that Ayaan wasn't just a private citizen but an elected member of Parliament.

She went on in the same interview to offend a good many Christians, saying she doubted that most intelligent people who claimed to be religious really believed in God. She didn't believe, for example, that the new prime minister, Balkenende—a Christian Democrat and the leader of her own party's coalition—was himself truly a Christian. "He is an academic, a man who has learned to use well-reasoned arguments to find certain truths. Can he believe that the world was created in six days? That Eve was created from Adam's rib? That simply cannot be true. Scientists are unbelieving."

She failed to note that many Christians do not believe in the literal truth of the Bible, yet they remain Christians, or that many scientists accept various religious ideas yet remain scientists. For her, it seemed, Christians who not did accept every word of the Bible were not Christians, and religious scientists were not real scientists.

Gerrit Zalm and his Liberal colleagues, as the Dutch journalist Alies Pegtel later wrote, were "not amused."

They called a meeting to tell Ayaan that it wasn't their party's role to take positions on theological controversies. They tried to explain that she was a member of the governing party now, and that the Liberal creed—and the idea behind the Dutch state—was that government should deal with the *actions* of citizens, not their beliefs. As one party member said, "It is not liberal to take a stand on religious beliefs. In this country we have separation of religion and state."

Ayaan would not accept it. Eyes blazing, she insisted that what she had said was true and that she had the right and duty to say so. The Prophet had married Aisha when she was nine. A man who did that in Holland today would be considered a pervert, would he not? Therefore the Prophet was a pervert, and anyone who said he wasn't was either a fool or a coward.

One of her mentors approached her afterward and asked why she had talked back to the Liberal leaders when he'd told her not to. "Because it's true," she retorted. "I'm not going to apologize for the truth." She would not concede that even if it was historically true that the Prophet married a nine-year-old, which some scholars doubt, the society of seventh-century Arabia was different from ours and calling him a pedophile was her opinion, not "the truth."

It's unlikely that Ayaan's fellow Liberals knew a peculiarity of the Somali language—that (except for foreign borrowings) its range of words for colors is extremely limited. But the *Trouw* affair gave them their first inkling that shades of meaning they considered vital to politics were practically invisible to their Somali comrade. "She spoke Dutch well, but the nuances escaped her," observed Frank de Grave, a Liberal member assigned to coach her in political etiquette. Yet she took her oath of office in the Binnenhof fortress, which houses the Dutch government, and, at the age of thirty-three, became a member of Parliament.

In February, the Organization of the Islamic Conference, which represents fifty-seven Islamic countries, sent four ambassadors to the Liberal Party leader, asking him to remove Ayaan from Parliament for her remarks about the Prophet. Theodor Holman held one of his dinner parties not long afterward. Ayaan and Holman were discussing a newspaper article about the complaints of the Muslim ambassadors when she first met the filmmaker Theo van Gogh.

Van Gogh, a heavy man with curly yellow hair whose great-great-grandfather was the brother of the great artist Vincent van Gogh, was Holman's best friend. A columnist and TV host as well as a filmmaker, van Gogh was notorious for his coarse verbal attacks on anyone who claimed that religion deserved special respect. He accused Ayaan's new friend Leon de Winter, who often wrote about the Holocaust, of wrapping barbed wire around his penis and shouting, "Auschwitz! Auschwitz!" when he made love to his wife. He called Muslims "goatfuckers." And when he climbed the narrow staircase to Holman's apartment, Eveline van Dijk happened to be filming the party.

Van Gogh seems to have been rather subdued that night. Perhaps he was intimidated by Ayaan's reputation for being fearsomely intelligent. He arrived late, wearing his usual suspenders, sat down heavily in an armchair, and started reading the newspaper article. "I think we still have free speech in the Netherlands," he said, creasing the paper thoughtfully back and forth in his hands. He was clearly mulling it over in his mind: Ayaan and her comments, which were so like his own, and then the ambassadors' attempt to punish her. Knowing, as we do, van Gogh's fate, it was a poignant moment.

Later in the evening Ayaan told the party that her goal in life was to knock the Quran off its pedestal. She got so wound up about the need to stop Muslims from revering their holy book that she started going on about being prepared to die—yes, die!—if necessary.

The film shows Holman, van Gogh, and their friends clucking a bit and looking patronizing as they pat Ayaan on the shoulder and try to calm her. "Now, now, Ayaan," one says. Clearly the Dutchmen wanted to protect and encourage her, but they didn't think death would be required.

For them the issue was free speech. They wanted to argue that, as Dutch citizens, they had the right to criticize Islam.

Holland's equal willingness to allow the same freedom to a very different type of expression escaped their attention. The country was also a platform for violent and murderous snuff movies that can be described as jihadi pornography—such as the video of Daniel Pearl's beheading.

Pearl's family continued to speak of their anguish over the film. But none of the men at the party knew that the Ogrish Web site that carried it and other jihadi snuff films was registered on Amsterdam's busiest shopping street, the Kalverstraat, a short distance from Holman's house. Ogrish's German Web distributor had recently yanked its registration at the request of Germany's public prosecutor, who had charged Ogrish with the crime of "glamorizing brutal force." But hardly anyone in the Netherlands knew that the owner was Dutch, and there was no debate in Holland about Germany's decision to shut the Web site down.

Ogrish used atrocity pictures to sell pornography. "Gore and porn is a good combination," Dan Klinker, Ogrish's owner, said in one interview. The complex psychological and neurological factors that made such a combination lucrative were forces that Theo van Gogh might have enjoyed exploring. But Holman says that neither he nor van Gogh had ever heard of the site.

That night, at Holman's flat on Willemsparkweg, the lovely Ayaan and her talk of violence and death were exciting enough. "She's incredibly hot," van Gogh exclaimed to Holman after she had left. "I wish I could fuck her. Can a circumcised woman come?"

Fourteen

After her quick trip to Maryland, it becomes harder to say what Aafia was doing and why. In 2008, U.S. prosecutors filed a formal letter in federal court holding out the possibility that they might charge her in connection with opening the post office box for Majid Khan. But as of 2011, they have not done so.

It is possible, however, from evidence presented in court and at the military tribunals of her alleged coconspirators, as well as from a trove of secret documents about Guantánamo leaked to the press in 2011, to piece together what U.S. prosecutors believe was the scheme involving the two of them.

The plot also involved a Karachi businessman and his family, whom Aafia seems not to have known. Like Aafia, this businessman, Saifullah Paracha, was a successful Pakistani who had studied in the United States but retained his strong Deobandi faith. But unlike Aafia, Paracha in his outward life did not seem even slightly anti-Western.

His links with the plotters still appear contradictory. He may have been pulled in by the same undertow of religious guilt that caused Amjad, for years, to go along with Aafia's yearning for jihad. Or perhaps he just wanted to do business with some "mujahideen" who had the money to invest in his various businesses.

In any case, at fifty-five, Paracha was a large balding man with a warm smile. He had studied physics in Karachi and won a scholarship in 1972 to attend the New York Institute of Technology. He had met his wife, Farhat, while he was running a travel agency and she was studying sociology at New York University. After the Paracha family returned to Pakistan in the 1980s, he formed an export-import business selling Pakistani textiles to U.S. retailers such as Kmart. The company had an office and a partner in New York, Charles Anteby, and the fact that Anteby was Jewish never presented a problem. "We had friendly talks on religion," Anteby wrote in an e-mail released by the Paracha family, "and he never showed any animosity to the Jewish people or to America." Farhat says the whole Paracha family loved America.

The Parachas had three children, all of whom attended select English-language schools in Karachi. And they lived in a luxurious villa, complete with gilded furniture, in the Defense Housing Authority neighborhood.

Paracha later told U.S. military investigators that he had met Osama bin Laden in 1999 and again on a 2000 visit to Afghanistan as head of a delegation from the Rice Exporters Association of Pakistan. He said another member of the group, Maulana Mazhar, whom Paracha described as "a well-known religious leader in Karachi," offered to introduce him to the al-Qaeda leader. Paracha testified that he had given bin Laden his business card and invited him to contribute to a television program about Islam that another enterprise of his, Universal Broadcasting, was developing. Bin Laden, in Paracha's words, "said he would think about it."

After 9/11, a man appeared at Paracha's business office in Karachi and showed him the card that Paracha had given bin Laden. The man called himself "Mir," but actually he was Khalid Sheikh Mohammed. KSM wanted more information about the studios and equipment at Universal Broadcasting. He also asked for Paracha's help in opening a bank account and finding rental houses. Over the summer of 2002, the U.S. government claims, Paracha laundered more than $500,000 of al-Qaeda money for KSM. KSM subsequently introduced Paracha to an "agriculturalist from Baluchistan" named "Mustafa." This "Mustafa" was really KSM's nephew Ali.

Later that year, Paracha allegedly agreed to perform an even more valuable service for al-Qaeda.

U.S. military prosecutors claim that he agreed to let KSM ship C-4 plastic explosives and other chemicals to New York in the containers Paracha used to ship women's and children's clothing to the United States. Once Majid Khan returned to the United States, using the refugee document Aafia had obtained for him, Paracha was supposed to help the young programmer set up a dummy import-export company to receive the shipments. Aafia was supposed to return to the United States, too, and rent houses and handle administrative tasks for the company. Eventually, Khan was supposed to attack American gas stations and underground fuel storage tanks in the Baltimore area with the explosives shipped in the containers. KSM and Paracha allegedly also discussed a plan to either poison or destroy the pumps to U.S. water reservoirs.

Paracha's oldest son was supposed to have been another member of the plot. Uzair Paracha was twenty-two and had recently graduated from Karachi's top business school. Now he was selling some Karachi condominiums for his father and was about to visit New York in search of well-heeled Pakistani buyers.

Uzair would testify later that, two weeks before he was due to leave, his father introduced him to a young man who he eventually learned was KSM's nephew Ali. Ali told Uzair, at the Parachas' business office, that he had a friend who needed help with a U.S. immigration problem.

A few days later, Ali showed up at the office again—this time with a Pakistani American about his own age who Uzair learned later was Majid Khan, the former resident of Baltimore. Khan told the Parachas he needed a certain travel document to return to the United States to earn enough money to support his new baby.

Uzair's father asked him to help Khan. All four men met less than a week later at Snoopy Ice Cream Parlor, across from the glittering shops on Zamzama, Karachi's most fashionable shopping street.

Majid Khan and Uzair sat with their ice cream at one of the little tables while Uzair's father, Saifullah, sat with Ali at another. Majid Khan had brought an envelope filled with documents and identification. He explained that a person had to be in the United States to apply for the travel document he needed, and he wanted Uzair to pretend to be him and to telephone the INS from an American pay phone, so that the INS would think he was still in the United States. He also wanted Uzair to use his credit cards and to deposit money in his bank account. Majid Khan gave Uzair the key to his new post office box in Gaithersburg, Maryland, where the INS was supposed to mail the document.

"A good sister who wanted to help us out" had rented the box, Khan told Uzair.

Once the INS sent the document, Majid Khan wanted Uzair to pick it up. He should pretend to be Khan, open the box, collect the mail, close the box, and give the postal service a new forwarding address. Khan said that if anyone asked where the woman was who had rented the box, Uzair should say they had broken up.

Uzair seems to have been wary from the start about doing such a favor. He told the FBI later that, the summer before, his father had confided that members of al-Qaeda had come to him asking for money to buy weapons to fight in Afghanistan. His father had shown him a bag of money that he said he was holding for al-Qaeda. Around the time Paracha had introduced Uzair to Ali, Uzair said, he had also introduced him to a Pakistani scientist and chemistry professor who he said had been recruited to develop chemical weapons for the group.

Now, at Snoopy, Uzair asked uneasily what using Majid Khan's credit cards and putting money into Khan's bank account had to do with the INS. He became so nervous that he rose from the table and said he had to pick up some passport photos. But Majid Khan and Ali weren't about to let him go.

Khan offered Uzair a lift to the photo studio on his motorbike. En route, Uzair recalled, Majid Khan confided that he did not want

Uzair to know too much in case he was captured and tortured. "We need brothers like you," Khan told Uzair. As Uzair recalled, that was when he came to suspect that Khan belonged to al-Qaeda.

Khan's words made Uzair so uncomfortable that he gave Khan's envelope to his father when he got home, saying he didn't want to carry it to New York. But his father persisted. As Uzair later described it to the FBI, Paracha told his son that they needed to help Khan and his colleagues, who were "supporters of Osama bin Laden" and who planned to invest at least $180,000 in the Parachas' condos.

Uzair left the envelope behind when he flew to the United States on February 19. But his father gave the envelope to another relative traveling to New York. This relative took it to Uzair at his father's office in Manhattan's Garment District, and Uzair did eventually phone the INS and pretend to be Majid Khan.

Aafia—the "good sister" in this costly and time-consuming scheme to get one operative, Khan, into the United States—never met either of the Parachas. But about a week before Uzair was scheduled to leave for the United States, on February 11, she sent an e-mail from Pakistan to her former dissertation adviser at Brandeis, the neuroscientist Robert Sekuler. She told Sekuler she wanted to return to the United States and asked him to help her find a job. She added that she didn't know whether her children would be coming with her.

Fifteen

During the first few months of 2003, while Ayaan was in Parliament, the United States made its case for invading Iraq. The planned U.S. attack was deeply unpopular in the Netherlands, and the Dutch who opposed the military action held huge demonstrations in Amsterdam and other cities.

The Dutch had taken pride ever since the Enlightenment in their commitment to international law. Erasmus of Rotterdam and Hugo Grotius, both Dutchmen, established the idea centuries ago that laws should govern even wars between states. Much later, the seat of the Dutch government, The Hague, became the home of the International Court of Justice and the International Criminal Court. Like Immanuel Kant, who coined the Enlightenment slogan "Dare to know," the Dutch professed to believe that only justice—dispensed freely, openly, and according to international law—could bring about lasting peace.

Once it was clear, however, that the UN Security Council would not approve the U.S. plan to invade Iraq, the Bush administration abandoned all pretense of obeying international law, and the Dutch government, over warnings from its own lawyers, went along with Bush.

Reports were already seeping out that Bush's military and intelligence agents were torturing prisoners at Guantánamo and elsewhere. Torture had been illegal in the Netherlands since the eighteenth century; stamping it out had been one of the Enlightenment's most celebrated achievements. In theory, anyway, the illegality of torture under international law (as well as U.S. law) could expose high U.S. officials to prosecution at The Hague's International Criminal Court.

The previous Dutch government had protested Washington's announcement that the Geneva conventions did not apply at Guantánamo. In April 2003, the Dutch Foreign Ministry's lawyers warned the newly elected governing coalition that if the government supported the U.S. invasion, "the Netherlands would likely lose any case brought before the International Court of Justice" in The Hague. Yet the government agreed to support the U.S. plan "politically but not militarily." And they kept silent about Washington's violations of international law.

Ayaan's former professor Huib Pellikaan had forgiven her for not telling him that she wouldn't be going to Harvard. He joined her for a meal in The Hague around the time U.S. troops occupied Baghdad. Ayaan was excited that night. She supported the U.S. invasion. She told Pellikaan she hoped the United States would attack Iran, too.

She told him that the Shiites of Iran and Iraq had a theory, as the Sunnis did, about the ordained "end times." But whereas the Sunnis believed that Jesus would come to Jerusalem to save the Muslims, the Shiites believed the savior would appear at the holy Iranian city of Qom in the form of a mahdi or messiah. The Americans had only to bomb the mosques of Qom, Ayaan cried, and the Iranians would lose their morale and the war would be over!

Pellikaan insists that Ayaan was serious. She was more circumspect with reporters. But, rather like her father, Hirsi, when he had imagined in the 1960s that Somalia might quickly become a superpower, she did not seem to grasp the monumental social and political changes that would be required for the Middle East to replicate the Enlightenment. In her interview with *Trouw* about the Ten Commandments, she revealed a similar naïveté when she said that the U.S. invasion would demonstrate how much worse things had to get in the Islamic world before "Islam as we know it" came to an end. She didn't seem to think the turnaround would take very long.

The United States was right, she said later, to try to make Iraq a democratic country, but Bush's government underestimated how long and violent the task would be. When a Belgian newspaper asked whether she saw the invasion as "an enlargement of her own life," in which the West brought freedom to caged Muslims, she answered that she did.

From the day she was elected, meanwhile, Ayaan had been setting her own parliamentary agenda. She still had friends in the Labor Party, and she relied on some of them to formulate policies that contradicted Liberal Party dogma. She favored an amnesty for asylum seekers, for example, and independent residence permits for immigrant brides.

Other Liberals complained that she refused to submit to the apprenticeship and party discipline that everyone else observed. She also paid little attention to other members' bills on meat-and-potatoes issues such as education and social security. She had her own media contacts, besides. "She became a kind of one-man party within the party," said Fadime Örgü.

One of Ayaan's new Liberal friends was an outspoken member of Parliament with a helmetlike bleached-blond hairdo named Geert Wilders. Wilders had been elected in 1998. Before that he had been an assistant to Bolkestein, the former party leader. He had always been fascinated with the Middle East, and he often spoke of his admiration for Israel, which he had visited several times as a young man. From the moment he arrived in Parliament, he began pounding on Islam.

On April 12, 2003, a day after U.S. secretary of defense Donald Rumsfeld waved away televised reports of looting and disorder in Baghdad by remarking, "Stuff happens," Ayaan and Wilders published an article in the *NRC Handelsblad* titled "It Is Time for a Liberal Jihad."

In it she and Wilders argued that the radicalization of Dutch and European Muslims demanded a more punitive reply. Once again, they jeered at the "naive and cowardly" policy associated with Amsterdam's popular mayor, Job Cohen, and his Moroccan-born deputy, Ahmed Aboutaleb, of "holding it together." The way Cohen and Aboutaleb went around meeting with Muslims "exudes weakness," they said, and would only make Muslims regard the Dutch with "scorn." Calling on the government to shut down two notoriously intolerant mosques and an Islamic school, they warned that, in order to protect freedom of religion in the long term, Holland must limit it in the short term.

"To maintain a tolerant and liberal Netherlands," Ayaan and Wilders argued, "we must put aside basic rights and laws to address people who abuse them and who then want to remove them as the foundation of our society."

The article affirmed basically what Bush and his people were saying to justify their handling of the "war on terror." But the sheer speed with which two supposed Dutch champions of Enlightenment were ready to dump "basic rights and law," which they themselves conceded were the "foundation of our society," was breathtaking. The United States had been under attack by the jihadis since 1993. But not a single act of Islamist terrorism had yet taken place in Holland.

The left-wing opponents of Ayaan and Wilders naturally criticized their willingness to deny Muslims equal protection. But the Dutch intelligence service, the AIVD, worried about the article for a different reason.

Only a few dozen Dutch Muslims were preparing for jihad, according to the AIVD's estimates; two-thirds of the country's one million Muslims were not religiously observant, and only about 5 percent of those who were observant felt drawn to radical Islamist ideologies. The intelligence agency believed that Ayaan and Wilders were playing into the hands of the jihadis when they whipped up fear and anger against the Muslim community as a whole.

With its surveillance power, the AIVD knew just how paranoid and isolated Holland's very few jihadis really were. They knew that al-Qaeda and its supporters sought to stage symbolic confrontations identical to those that Ayaan was proposing—confrontations that would polarize society and alienate Muslims from the West. The intelligence agency's 2002 report concluded, in fact, that one reason the 9/11 attacks had furthered the interests of radical Islam was that Western governments "were successfully provoked to make generalizing statements or even generalizing acts toward Muslims and 'Islam.'" They worried that remarks like Ayaan's made the moderate majority of Muslims less likely to cooperate with the government in tracking down the jihadis.

In any case, liberal Muslims noticed the fear and suspicion hanging over the whole Muslim community. It seemed, especially to young Muslims of both sexes, to vindicate the radicals' claims that the West *talked* about universal values but would never accept Muslims as equals.

Karima Belhaj, a counselor at Amsterdam's largest center for Muslim women, noticed that the women her center dealt with were starting to wear veils and head scarves as a symbol of defiance against Ayaan and her allies. "Because she attacks Islam," Belhaj said, "they are becoming more fundamentalist. She attacks their values. We are losing women over her. They are wearing more and more veils. This frightens me."

Belhaj despised the jihadis. "These crazy dangerous people—we are the biggest victims of them." But she insisted that what was turning some young Dutch Muslims against their country wasn't so much Islamism as Islamophobia. "The problem is that hatred against Arabs and Muslims is shown in the Netherlands without any shame." She didn't know Ayaan, but she wanted to tell her, "Don't create hate. When you are teasing people, you create monsters."

The AIVD had recently spotted a clique of "these crazy dangerous people." Mohammed Bouyeri was the twenty-five-year-old son of a Moroccan man who had washed dishes for thirty years at Schiphol Airport before retiring. Shy, short, and with a scraggly beard, young Bouyeri was a loner frustrated by the world's failure to recognize his importance.

The police were first called to his house in 2000, after he locked his sister in her room. He had accused her of fouling the family's honor by having a secret affair with a local boy. His sister managed to phone the police, and the incident was resolved without charges being filed.

A few months later, Bouyeri pulled a knife on his sister's boyfriend. That time he ended up in prison, where he got interested in religion.

When he was free again, he began attending the El Tawheed Mosque in Amsterdam West. The 9/11 hijacker Mohamed Atta and other members of KSM's Hamburg cell had visited El Tawheed before embarking on their attacks.

Bouyeri shaved his head, grew a beard, and began wearing a long cotton caftan and knit skullcap. His new costume got him attention. So did the articles and religious treatises he started writing for a local newsletter. At the neighborhood center where he worked, he refused to shake hands with women or allow mixed gatherings.

In early 2003, he wrote in the center's newsletter that "the Netherlands is our enemy because they support the invasion of Iraq." He threatened a female staff member who disagreed with his interpretation of the Quran. The staff reported him to the police, and the police reported him to Dutch intelligence. His own sister and father began to avoid him.

Possibly at El Tawheed, Bouyeri met a Syrian preacher who called himself Abu Khaled. This preacher had appeared in Europe claiming political asylum in 1994, and he had a certain sinister charisma. Abu Khaled claimed to be an Islamic scholar. At the refugee centers where he lived, he laid down fatwas that his followers enforced down to the smallest detail. Men stopped shaking hands with women. People stopped drinking alcohol.

It was under the influence of this cult figure that Bouyeri decided in 2003 that even the El Tawheed mosque was too liberal for him. He began downloading jihadi videos from Dan Klinker's Web site, www.ogrish.com. The beheading of Daniel Pearl became a special favorite.

He and other followers of the strange Abu Khaled would gather in Bouyeri's neat two-story semidetached house outside Amsterdam to listen to their guru and watch the Pearl film and similar fare. Abu Khaled's Surinamese wife, her grown daughter, and other women followers attended, sitting behind a curtain at the meetings. Bouyeri's elderly Dutch neighbors would pull back their lace curtains to stare when the women arrived in their long black veils, niqabs, and gloves.

A childhood friend of Bouyeri, Abdellatif el-Morabet, went to some of the meetings and was terrified. Abu Khaled talked about occult Quranic meanings based on numerals and prophecies, and he claimed that murder and bloodshed were forms of prayer. "I saw the Devil in him," Morabet said. Morabet also told police that Abu Khaled and his followers "enjoyed" videos of infidels being tortured and beheaded. "Mohammed Bouyeri was even aroused by them," Morabet said.

Much later some women from the group gave two Dutch reporters, Janny Groen and Annieke Kranenberg, a CD that they said Bouyeri had made. In a file called "Slaughter of Allah's Enemies" it contained twenty-three films of Westerners and Iraqis being murdered by jihadis. As Groen and Kranenberg wrote in their book *Women Warriors for Allah*, "no fewer than twenty-eight men's throats are cut or chopped with a machete and more than ten victims are executed in other ways. . . . All the beheadings appear to follow the same pattern. The throat is cut while the perpetrators shout 'Allahu Akbar' ('Allah is great')."

The women told the reporters that the first few beheadings were terrifying to watch, but they got used to them.

Abu Khaled's circle claimed to abhor pornography. The murder films, however, appeared on a porno site. And just as mirror neurons stir many people watching pornography to share the sensation of having sex, so they seem to have stimulated this group to discover pleasure in murder.

Sixteen

Aafia didn't know it, but she was under surveillance well before Uzair Paracha arrived in New York on February 19, 2003, with instructions to collect Majid Khan's mail. Because the FBI had put Aafia's name on its aviation watch list when she failed to show up for her meeting with them in 2002, Pakistan's Federal Investigation Agency informed the bureau as soon as she boarded her flight to the United States in December, according to the Pakistani newspaper *Daily Times*. FBI agents visited the Gaithersburg post office the day after she left the United States for Pakistan and questioned postal clerk Michael O'Hora about her. Within a few months of her return, moreover, U.S. and Pakistani officials announced the arrest of the 9/11 mastermind, Khalid Sheikh Mohammed, and everyone else allegedly involved in his plot to blow up American gas stations—except for Aafia.

The arrests began on March 1, when Pakistan announced that it had captured KSM and another 9/11 planner, Mustafa al-Hawsawi, in a 3 a.m. raid in Westridge, a suburb of Rawalpindi, the army garrison town near Islamabad. U.S. officials later said that an informant had been paid $25 million to finger the al-Qaeda operations chief.

Within hours, newspapers and broadcasters around the world were reporting the capture of the man the White House now admitted was the mastermind of the September 11 attacks. A photo showing the previously dapper KSM looking fat and disheveled in a wrinkled undershirt was splashed across the front page of every newspaper in Pakistan. Ali took one of those papers to Saifullah Paracha's office and showed Paracha the photo of the man he knew only as "Mir."

Paracha was alarmed; he later told military investigators that he'd had no idea how important KSM had been to the global jihad. Worried, he called his son in New York to ask if he'd seen the news and to warn him to be careful with Majid Khan's documents.

Aafia, for the time being, seemed quite calm. That very morning she sent another e-mail to her former adviser at Brandeis, looking for a job. "I prefer to work in the United States," she wrote, adding that Pakistan had no positions in her field.

Perhaps she hadn't heard about KSM's arrest when she wrote to Sekuler. Or maybe, as she told the FBI, she had never met him and did not understand the implications of the news for her. Certainly it would have frightened her if she had. The Pakistani police said they had found KSM at the home of Malaqah Khanum, a middle-aged leader of Jamaat-e-Islami's women's wing.

The Siddiquis may have known Khanum's family. Her husband, Abdul Qadoos, was a bacteriologist who had worked for the UN Food and Agriculture Organization in Zambia at the same time Aafia's father was a doctor there. Ismat Siddiqui and Malaqah Khanum were both among Pakistan's early female Islamist activists. Police would later accuse one of Khanum's sons, a Pakistani army major serving in the border town of Kohat, near the tribal areas where many al-Qaeda fighters were hiding, of having concealed KSM and helped Arab jihadis find Jamaat-e-Islami's underground trail to safety in Pakistan.

The CIA found handwritten documents in the Qadoos household, plus files on a computer, that made them think al-Qaeda's biological weapons program was further along than they had believed—and that KSM himself had been plotting to use it. With the help of Pakistani scientists the group had made plans and obtained materials to manufacture two biological toxins, botulinum and salmonella, and the chemical poison cyanide. They also found a document directing operatives to purchase *Bacillus anthracis*, the bacterium that causes anthrax disease, and other evidence suggesting that al-Qaeda could produce a form of inhalable anthrax that would kill three-quarters of the people exposed to it even if they received treatment.

Investigators soon followed up on what they had learned at the Qadoos house and from KSM's interrogation.

Majid Khan was arrested on March 5. He was allowed to see his brother on March 13, and Khan "looked terrible and seemed very, very tired," as his father later testified. Khan told his brother that the Americans had beat him, tied him painfully to a chair for eight hours at a time, and deprived him of sleep. When he wasn't being questioned, Khan said, he was held in a coffinlike cell so small that he couldn't lie down.

On March 10, the FBI appeared at the door of Aafia's sister, Fowzia, in Baltimore. She phoned her brother in Houston later that day and told him that the FBI was looking for Aafia. The brother called Annette Lamoreaux, a lawyer for the American Civil Liberties Union then based in Texas, for advice and Lamoreaux agreed to represent him if the authorities contacted him.

The news that the FBI was looking for her evidently sent Aafia into a panic. Against Ismat's wishes, she announced that she was leaving the house. Ismat cried and screamed for her to stay, but Aafia left anyway, in a minicab. Ismat later said that her daughter had taken all three children with her.

Aafia told Ismat that she and the children were going to Islamabad to stay with her uncle S. H. Faruqi. They planned to stop on the way and visit friends in Rawalpindi whom Ismat didn't know. She said Aafia had called her from what she believed was the Karachi train station—but then she had never arrived at Faruqi's house. Aafia's uncle said she had gone underground after learning she was wanted by the FBI.

It seems that rather than going to her uncle's house Aafia went into hiding with the al-Baluchi clan. That, at least, is what she told the FBI, and what members of the al-Baluchi family confirmed to Pakistani reporters. (Aafia's lawyers, however, later said that she repudiated all the statements the FBI attributed to her. They also pointed out that she had been recovering from surgery and under sedation when FBI agents questioned her.)

Her intimacy with KSM's family did not end there. Aafia told the FBI that because she could not live in the same house with an unmarried male—namely Ali, KSM's handsome young nephew and protégé—Ali, through his sister, proposed that they marry and she accepted.

She said she and Ali were married in the inner courtyard of his family's house. "His female family members were present for the wedding, and provided her with some nice clothes," notes the FBI's report of her interrogation in 2008. Members of the al-Baluchi family have said the ceremony took place in Hub Chowki, a grimy industrial area outside Karachi on the main road to Baluchistan.

It was a far cry from her first marriage, yet Aafia may actually have loved Ali. She told the FBI that she had spent the next few weeks in the house, partly because she was hiding "but also because her husband was a very strict Muslim and wanted it that way." She said she had not minded because he was very kind to her. As an example of his kindness, she said, once, when they had been praying, a baby had started crying. Ali, she said, hadn't gotten angry but instead had picked up the baby to soothe it and continued with his prayer.

She also said she didn't believe Ali belonged to al-Qaeda: "He is a good man who is wrongly accused." But Ali himself later told U.S. investigators that he told Aafia that al-Qaeda had set up a biological weapons lab. He had asked her advice on how long it would take to develop such weapons and whether the man in charge was capable of it. He said she had been willing to participate but that he had never asked or considered allowing her to work in the laboratory.

While Aafia was enjoying her surprise honeymoon, the FBI was tracking down her friends and relatives in the United States. On March 17, agents showed up at her brother's house in Houston. The agents rudely demanded that he answer their questions immediately. When Ali phoned his lawyer and she asked to speak to the agents, they shouted into the cell phone that Ali had no right to legal counsel.

The FBI posted pictures of Aafia and her ex-husband, Amjad, on its Web site the next day, in a new "Wanted" category it had set up for people associated with terrorism but not facing criminal charges. The Web site said the FBI was merely seeking information about the couple and had no information connecting them to "specific terrorist activities." But with her black hair pulled severely back and her mouth set in an uncompromising line (the photo was a retouched version of the one on her Massachusetts driver's license), the diminutive Aafia looked distinctly menacing.

Majid Khan's friend the truck driver and former mujahid Iyman Faris was arrested in Ohio on March 19, and on March 20 the FBI announced a global manhunt for Adnan Shukrijumah, the Saudi man about whom Aafia had been questioned the previous May. Five days later, the bureau's Baltimore office put out a worldwide alert for Aafia and Amjad, and on March 26 the U.S. District Court for Eastern Virginia issued a warrant for Shukrijumah's arrest. The *Washington Post* quoted unnamed FBI authorities in the Baltimore office as claiming that Aafia and Amjad were both suspected of having ties to Shukrijumah. The article quoted the same FBI sources as saying without elaboration that Aafia had visited the Baltimore area in late December or January.

Amjad and his parents read about the FBI's hunt in the newspapers. Frightened, they sought advice from a family friend who had worked in Pakistani military intelligence. The friend arranged for Amjad to meet with the ISI. The intelligence officers asked him what he knew about Aafia's activities. Did she have contacts with the Taliban? With Osama bin Laden? Amjad told them that he and Aafia were divorced and that he knew nothing about her contacts. The ISI let him go.

On March 28, FBI agents went to see Uzair Paracha at the office Uzair's father shared with his business partner in Manhattan. When Uzair agreed to let them search the bags he had left where he was staying in Brooklyn, agents found Majid Khan's Maryland driver's license, Social Security card, and bank card and the receipts that Aafia had signed for the rental of the Gaithersburg post office box. As for the key to the box, they found that on Uzair's own key ring.

After two days of round-the-clock questioning, Uzair admitted that he had agreed to help Majid Khan and Aafia's new husband, Ali, even though he had suspected they belonged to al-Qaeda and were planning a chemical attack on the United States. Uzair said he had never met Aafia Siddiqui. But when the agents asked him if he thought she was the kind of person who would agree to receive anthrax through the mail, he told them he thought she was.

His admissions seemed to shock the agents. He was arrested and taken to New York's Metropolitan Detention Center.

The very next day, March 29, 2003, Pakistani and U.S. news media began airing a confusing series of on-again, off-again reports that Aafia had also been arrested—reports that to this day have led some people to believe that she was captured during that period, handed over to the Americans, and then held in a secret prison for the next five years. Others (and I count myself in this group) believe that she may have been arrested but was probably released soon afterward.

The mysterious Aafia reports began on March 29 when the Pakistani newspaper *Dawn* wrote that police had picked her up the day before at the Karachi airport. Unnamed FBI officials in Washington were quoted as saying she was the first woman suspected of being an al-Qaeda operative in the United States. Other news reports claimed that she had been captured and was being interrogated by the FBI.

On March 31, Pakistani and Indian newspapers again reported that Pakistan's intelligence agencies had detained her in Karachi. But the following day, Pakistan's interior minister denied having her in custody. "You will be astonished to know about the activities of Dr. Aafia," the minister told a press conference, adding to the haze.

(In 2011, lawyers from the International Justice Network, representing the Siddiqui family, released what they said was a transcript of a secretly recorded conversation in which Imran Shaukat, the superintendent of police of Sindh Province, told an unnamed witness that he had been present at Aafia's arrest in 2003. According to the transcript, Shaukat said Aafia had been on her way to Islamabad when she was arrested wearing a veil and gloves. He described her as a "minor facilitator" for al-Qaeda who had been "hobnobbing with clerics." He said the police had turned her over to the ISI.)

For months after that, Aafia's mother gave contradictory statements about her daughter's whereabouts. But in later years she would single out March 30, 2003, as the day that Aafia and her children had supposedly disappeared into the hands of Pakistani intelligence agents. (Aafia herself, of course, eventually told the FBI that she had gone into hiding with the al-Baluchi family then.)

In the United States, the FBI gave every indication that it was still looking for her. The *Washington Times* reported that the bureau had intensified its search and thought she might be linked to Jose Padilla and Adnan Shukrijumah.

Yet the Pakistanis continued to view Aafia's whereabouts as more complicated. On April 9, for example, the Pakistani newspaper the *News* reported that Ismat said her "missing" daughter—the newspaper itself put the word in quotes—had left her house in Karachi during the last week of March and was now being held either by the FBI or the Pakistani government. "The matter of Aafia's 'arrest,'" the newspaper said, "became a mystery as no one, including the U.S. Federal Bureau of Investigation (FBI), has claimed responsibility for holding Aafia at any forum."

Ismat also told the *News* that the government had denied her daughter's arrest and that "recently an unknown man came to her house and informed her that her daughter was safe and sound. He told her not to make a fuss about her daughter's disappearance, if she wants safe recovery of her daughter. He also threatened that if she made the matter public, her daughter would meet the same fate as Asif Bhuja met." The article went on to say that sources in Pakistan's intelligence agencies suggested that "militants" had taken her away to prevent "information being provided by her."

Asif Bhuja was a suspect in the Daniel Pearl murder case who was found dead when police arrived to question him. To an American reader, the reference was almost incomprehensible. But sophisticated Pakistanis were used to reading between the lines. They read the *News* as suggesting that the same nexus of Pakistani and Arab jihadis who had killed Pearl had also hidden Aafia and that both they and the ISI had warned Aafia's mother not to talk about it.

The next mention of Aafia suggested that U.S. officials were still pressing Pakistan to arrest her. The Indian newspaper the *Hindu* quoted Pakistan's interior minister as saying, after a meeting of the U.S.-Pakistan Joint Working Group on Terrorism and Law Enforcement, that Pakistan would extradite Aafia to the United States if she were arrested, despite its rule against extraditing its own nationals, because she had become a U.S. citizen.

Ismat quickly called reporters to correct the minister, telling them that Aafia had never become a U.S. citizen. She also denied reports that Aafia was a fanatic. Ismat claimed that it was Aafia's ex-husband, Amjad, not Aafia, who had wanted to send their children to Islamic schools and that Ismat had their custody agreement to prove it. The Siddiqui family also told *U.S. News & World Report* that Amjad had abused Aafia and the children and that he might have kidnapped them.

In Boston, the FBI interviewed her friends the "Care brothers." In New York, they found the Saudi man who had once sublet Amjad and Aafia's apartment, yanking the man from an airport line and showing him pictures of Aafia. But he didn't know where she was, either.

On April 21, the *NBC Nightly News* reported that Aafia had been detained in Pakistan. "Senior U.S. officials say Siddiqui definitely has ties to very radical individuals in Pakistan and may be working as a fixer for al-Qaeda," NBC's investigative reporter Lisa Myers said.

Ismat told reporters in Pakistan who called her about the NBC report that Aafia had disappeared from her "hiding place in Karachi" about ten days earlier. She seemed frantic with worry. Yet the following day, U.S. officials backed off, saying they were "doubtful" that Aafia was in custody. They offered no explanation for the bizarre and continuing confusion. Aafia's picture remained on the FBI's Web site, and on April 24 the bureau issued another warning that al-Qaeda might start using women in its attacks.

Amjad read about Aafia's serial "arrests"—and about the Siddiquis' added accusation that he had beaten her before their divorce—with growing alarm. Aafia's mother still refused to take his calls about the children. In April, an FBI agent from the Baltimore office interviewed him. The agent asked about Aafia's trip to Gaithersburg in December. To Amjad's relief, he could honestly say he knew nothing about it. The agent wondered if Aafia knew anyone who could give her a false identity. Amjad replied he had no idea. He asked the agent if the FBI knew where his children were. The answer was no. The agent gave him a card and told him to get in touch if he ever wanted to come back to the United States. He never heard from the man again.

That FBI agent wasn't the only person present at Amjad's interview. Agents from Pakistan's ISI were also there, and they took Amjad aside afterward. They suggested he contact Aafia and tell her she needn't fear talking to the FBI; the Pakistanis would guarantee her security if she would just sit down with the Americans for a meeting.

But Amjad replied that he had told the FBI the truth. He didn't know where she was.

After the FBI arrested Majid Khan's friend the truck driver Iyman Faris in Ohio, he was taken to a Virginia safe house and told to stay in touch with his Pakistani contacts. Perhaps it was through Faris that the FBI managed to close in on Aafia's new husband, Ali Abdul Aziz Ali. On April 29, Ali was arrested in Karachi along with Khalad al-Attash, a Yemeni accused of plotting al-Qaeda's 2000 attack on the USS *Cole.* Two days later, on May 1, Faris pleaded guilty to scouting out the Brooklyn Bridge and other potential sites for al-Qaeda terrorist attacks. He was sentenced to twenty years in prison.

In the seven weeks since his uncle's arrest, young Ali had been busy. He had married Aafia, and U.S. officials say he had taken charge of a series of new attacks that were still being planned. One was a scheme to hijack airliners and crash them into London's Heathrow Airport. But apparently Ali had put off that plot in order to plan the bombing of multiple Western targets in Karachi, including the U.S. Consulate.

U.S. military officers later testified at Ali's combatant-status review in Guantánamo that he and Attash had been captured in a Karachi apartment while awaiting delivery of the explosives they needed to blow up the consulate. Pakistani newspapers reported that the truck Ali was waiting for contained three hundred pounds of fertilizer—the kind that Ali's cousin Ramzi Yousef had used to build the first World Trade Center bomb. The truck also reportedly contained sulfur, gunpowder, ammunition, pistols, submachine guns, and AK-47 rifles. Ali's own possessions were said to have included a letter to Osama bin Laden from some scholars in Saudi Arabia, a computer disk containing a draft of a letter to bin Laden, and a container of perfume spray containing a small dose of cyanide.

But since Ali was unknown to the public, the news that another nephew of KSM had been arrested was lost in the jubilation over the capture of Attash, a militant long on the FBI's Wanted list.

Years later, Amjad heard that a woman had been in the apartment where Ali and Attash had been caught. A retired Pakistani federal investigator told Aafia's ex-husband that when the police had arrived at the apartment, in the early morning of April 29, the militants inside had begun firing at them immediately. But after half an hour they had asked for a cease-fire so that a woman could get out. The police agreed. Soon a woman had come downstairs, completely veiled, and had been taken into FIA custody.

The woman said her name was Zainab. She refused to remove her veil and began shrieking at the officers that if they dared to touch her she would have them arrested and beaten. Then she asked to call her mother.

According to the officer who placed the call, the person who answered the phone at the number the veiled woman gave the police said her name was Ismat Siddiqui. Soon after that, the police began getting calls from headquarters ordering them not to harm the woman or question her. Within an hour, ISI agents appeared and took the woman away. The FIA agents were told they would be fired if they mentioned the incident to anyone.

I have no way of verifying this account of Aafia's presence at her husband, Ali's, last shoot-out. But if it's true that Aafia left the al-Baluchi family compound with Ali and proceeded to a Karachi apartment, that might explain why Ismat told reporters that her daughter had left her "hiding place." Moreover, Aafia's special relationship in the story with the ISI sounds a theme that often reappeared in the rumors that swirled around her subsequent disappearance. Of course, some elements of the ISI have been tight with Deobandi militants and even with al-Qaeda for decades.

One of KSM's uncles, Mohammed Hussein, offered what may be a reason for the newlyweds' departure from their hiding place. According to him, despite the conspirators' intense activity and despite the added drama that the authorities were closing in on their secret world, Aafia found time to quarrel with Ali's family and perhaps even with Ali himself.

Hussein said the short marriage was on the verge of breaking up before Ali was arrested. He claimed that Aafia's "liberal way of life" had put Ali off.

Aafia described the family's tensions differently. She told the FBI that Ali's relatives had been "very upset" when he was arrested and that she had left their house. She also said the family had told her that Ali had divorced her while he was detained. Perhaps Ali was as startled as Aafia's first husband was to learn how willful this pious young woman could be. Or perhaps the inbred family of terrorists simply didn't trust her.

Whatever the facts, at the end of April, the reports of Aafia's arrest ceased. Both the Pakistani and U.S. authorities now said that she was still at large. But almost everyone else involved in KSM's Baltimore plot had been captured.

Seventeen

The Liberal Party asked Ayaan to write a policy statement summarizing her specific proposals on the integration and emancipation of Muslim women. With the help of two University of Amsterdam sociologists, Paul Scheffer and Abram de Swaan, she came up with a twelve-page statement. She proposed abolishing Article 23 of the Dutch Constitution, closing down existing Muslim schools, and refusing to finance new ones. She wanted to reduce unemployment benefits—dramatically—and abolish the minimum wage.

She got a pilot project under way that required police in two of the country's sixteen districts to register suspected honor killings. The results shocked the country: in a six-month period, eleven Muslim girls were killed in the two regions.

Ayaan's supporters were thrilled by the way she was forcing Holland to pay attention to the suffering of Muslim women. "She has an un-Dutch way of making policy, but in more than twenty years, she is the only one who has succeeded in putting this pretty sharply on the agenda," said Margreet Fogteloo, an editor of the left-wing magazine *De Groene Amsterdammer*, who was frustrated and mystified by the increasing number of veiled women in The Hague. "We tried to help them, but in the end their position was getting worse."

Ayaan argued in speeches and articles that the country's Islamic schools isolated Muslim children from the rest of society and were breeding grounds for radicalism. But the ruling Christian Democrats weren't about to stop funding religious schools, and their coalition partners in Ayaan's Liberal Party weren't prepared to make it an issue.

To show how wrong they were, Ayaan took a camera crew from the TV program *Nova* to an Islamic school in Amersfoort. "What is higher to you, Allah or the Constitution?" she asked a classroom full of twelve-year-olds sitting on mats, boys separated from girls. "Allah," the children answered. "So Allah is higher than the Constitution," Ayaan repeated in a voice heavy with meaning.

The school's principal protested that it wasn't fair to single out Muslim children and ask them to choose between God and the Constitution. "The children at any strong Christian or Jewish school would answer the same way," he told *Nova*.

Some of Ayaan's Liberal colleagues agreed. Surely one great lesson of two world wars, not to mention the Holocaust, was that citizens have to remember that there is a higher morality than a government's orders. Nor was the Constitution quite as sacred to the Dutch as Ayaan seemed to think. The latest version had been written only twenty years earlier, in 1983. As one of her party colleagues put it, "Ayaan did not really understand the Dutch sensibility." Muslims, meanwhile, were furious that Ayaan, as one Moroccan woman told *Nova*, had "humiliated small children on national television just to further her own agenda."

Ayaan admitted she had never been inside an Islamic school in Holland before she visited the one for the TV show. Yet she refused to consider the studies that Dutch experts had done showing that the country's Muslim schools varied widely. There were liberal ones and conservative ones. Students at some scored highly on national exams, while others had dismal records. The fact that a school was Islamic didn't tell much about whether it provided a good education.

She seemed to regard it as appeasement when Dutch politicians and intellectuals sympathized with Muslims' unwillingness to reject their religion and families as harshly as she had rejected hers. "All this talk about respect for the identity of immigrants and their culture," she said, is "nothing but thoughtlessness, laziness and fear of openly addressing human rights violations." But many Dutch people, when they stopped to think about it, realized that they could never cut themselves off from their culture as fully as she had done.

Ayaan initially asked the government to cut funding for every Muslim organization in the country, including Muslim women's shelters and Muslim gay and feminist groups. Muslim feminists protested. They charged that despite her claim to be an advocate for Muslim women, Ayaan had never belonged to any Muslim women's organization in the country. Now she wanted to shut down neighborhood groups that actually did the work she claimed to support, such as rescuing girls threatened by their families. Ayaan changed her mind—but not before she had alienated many progressive Muslim women.

Holland had a substantial number of Muslim women in politics. In addition to Fadime Örgü in Ayaan's own party, Khadija Arib was a power in the Labor Party and Fatima Elatik was an up-and-coming young Amsterdam city councilwoman. Karima Belhaj was one of those running shelters and women's centers. Many of these capable Muslims were the first in their family to attend university. (Often their mothers had been illiterate.) Some had spoken out about the battles they had waged with their families to gain the right to make their own decisions. Most felt that Ayaan, by telling the world that women had to choose either Islam or liberation, was forcing them into a false and impossible choice.

Ayaan dismissed such colleagues as "proxies put forward to get subsidies from the government." She brushed their reservations aside by saying she would be gone by the time they were assertive enough for her to bother working with them. Nor did she want to hear from Dutch teachers, social workers, and police officers who worked in the Muslim community. Instead she accused them, too, of dismissing the rights of Muslim girls. "I called it the paradox of the left," she said. "On the one hand they support ideals of equality and emancipation, but in this case they do nothing about it; they even facilitate the oppression."

Ayaan's accusatory style put off those who might have been her natural allies in fighting for women's liberation. "Hirsi Ali has the idea that the liberation or the support of women's rights of Muslim women should be forced by public means, and in doing so, she neglects the processes going on inside the women's movements in the Muslim community," said Gijs von der Fuhr, a spokesman for the Amsterdam Migrant Center, who advised several liberal Muslim groups. "We support totally the goals she sets, but her confrontational way of talking and acting alienates exactly that kind of woman she wants to influence."

The Somali immigrant novelist and television personality Yasmine Allas knew and liked Ayaan and had demonstrated on her behalf when Ayaan first went into hiding. But as people grew polarized over Ayaan's provocative statements, Allas found the atmosphere in Holland "more and more suffocating." She was Somali *and* Dutch, and she felt like a child whose parents were divorcing. "How can someone be forced to choose between a mother and a father?" she asked.

Eighteen

After Aafia's second husband, Ali, vanished into a secret CIA prison in April 2003, Aafia seemed to vanish, too.

Her family claimed that the United States had imprisoned her. Her mother told Aafia's American lawyer that she had read in the Urdu press that Aafia had been taken away in a Gulfstream jet like the ones the CIA used for "high-value" prisoners. "My daughter is lost in the U.S.," Ismat sobbed to Hamid Mir, a talk show host for the Geo Television network and the biographer of Osama bin Laden.

Aafia's sister, Fowzia, in Baltimore, had been subpoenaed. Family lawyers later claimed that in a closed hearing related to her case, an FBI official had assured her that Aafia was alive and well.

With her green card, Ismat could travel to the United States, and in May she flew to New York. Landing at JFK, she was surrounded by agents from the Department of Homeland Security and the Joint Terrorism Task Force. The tiny grandmother rounded on the men and demanded, shrieking, that they tell her what the United States had done with her daughter. The Americans insisted that they didn't know where Aafia was. For nearly four hours they questioned Ismat, who was now "crying and breaking down . . . hysterically weeping," according to Elaine Whitfield Sharp, the Siddiquis' American lawyer.

Fowzia was outside the terminal waiting to meet her mother. Eventually she drove Ismat to Baltimore. But "after about two or three days, the FBI was banging on Fowzia's door again," Sharp said. "They were very aggressively serving a subpoena for Ismat Siddiqui to appear before a grand jury here in Boston." That was when a friend of the family suggested to Aafia's brother in Houston that they hire Sharp, a trial attorney from the pretty Massachusetts seaside town of Marblehead.

Sharp wears horn-rimmed glasses and has a comforting manner that puts clients at ease. She works out of a home office in a house decorated with cat knickknacks and needlepoint pillows. Ismat, Fowzia, and Ali drove up to Marblehead from Baltimore and checked into a bed-and-breakfast down the street.

Ismat was distraught by the time they met Sharp, and the lawyer got her excused from testifying before the grand jury in Boston by finding a psychiatrist to attest that she was mentally incompetent. But Sharp did agree to let the FBI and Michael Riciutti from the U.S. Attorney's Office talk with Ismat.

"You've got my daughter!" Ismat told the men at the meeting. The men said it wasn't so.

Her son took her to his house in Houston. There they met again with their lawyers, the FBI, and an Urdu translator the agents brought along. The agents asked Ismat about KSM and Ali Abdul Aziz Ali. Sharp said later that Aafia's mother strenuously denied that Aafia knew either man.

The FBI also asked about Aafia's mood at the time of her disappearance. They wanted to know about her trip to Gaithersburg and the post office box she had opened for Majid Khan. They inquired about her donations to Benevolence International and Global Relief and about her ex-husband, Amjad's, purchase of night-vision goggles and manuals for working with C-4 explosives.

Ismat just kept telling them that her daughter had been a straight-A student who loved America and could not possibly have broken the law. "We think she has another life that you don't know anything about," an FBI agent replied, according to a lawyer who was present. Ismat told them they were wrong.

Pakistan's ISI also acted as if Aafia was still at large. In the middle of May, intelligence agents made Amjad go with them to the Karachi airport, saying they had heard a report that she might be arriving by plane and they needed him to identify her. Amjad saw a woman who looked like Aafia, except that her nose seemed thinner and her hips looked unusually heavy. She was with a boy who looked like their seven-year-old son, Ahmad. Amjad recalled Aafia telling him that she had read in one of her books, *The Fugitive*, that putting a small pillow around the hips was a good disguise. He decided to pretend he hadn't seen her. He wasn't certain it was Aafia, and anyway he didn't want to hand her over to intelligence agents.

Ismat was still in the United States that June when *Newsweek* published a sensational cover story about KSM that for the first time laid out parts of the plot into which U.S. officials said the al-Qaeda operations chief had drawn Aafia and Majid Khan. Alarmed by the publicity, Aafia's uncle S. H. Faruqi sought help from the famous Pakistani politician and ex–cricket player Imran Khan, who had publicly defended Amir Aziz, an orthopedic surgeon from Lahore whom the CIA had accused of supplying al-Qaeda with anthrax. (After Khan's intervention, Aziz was released by Pakistani authorities without charge.) Faruqi told Khan that Aafia had said in March that she was taking a train to see him but then had never shown up.

On Hamid Mir's TV program, *Capital Talk*, Imran Khan confronted Pakistan's interior minister with various reports about Aafia. He demanded that the minister tell the public where she was. But the minister, Faisal Saleh Hayat, insisted he didn't know.

The grand jury in Boston subpoenaed Ismat again in July. Elaine Sharp, the lawyer, got the subpoena quashed on the grounds that Ismat was ill, and Ismat and Fowzia decided to return to Pakistan. Fowzia told Sharp that the FBI had harassed her so much at the hospital where she worked in Baltimore that she had lost her job, and that two other hospitals had withdrawn their job offers.

For months, meanwhile, the FBI had been investigating young Uzair Paracha's statements. His father's bank records showed deposits of hundreds of thousands of dollars that matched the dates when Uzair said his father had been holding money for al-Qaeda. The

U.S. government concluded that Saifullah Paracha was an al-Qaeda financier.

By the summer of 2003, Washington had apparently decided it couldn't trust President Musharraf's government to arrest prominent Pakistanis whom the U.S. government suspected of terrorism. Earlier the Americans had relied on Pakistan to arrest KSM, Ali, and Majid Khan—all of whom appeared to be involved in plotting a second big attack on the United States. But Aafia and some others whom the CIA wanted had managed to escape, and now the CIA seems to have feared that if it asked the Pakistanis to take Paracha into custody they might help him get away. So the Americans concocted an elaborate plot to lure the businessman to Bangkok.

Paracha's American business partner, Charles Anteby, asked him to come to a meeting in Thailand, and the CIA kidnapped him as soon as he stepped off the plane. They took him first to a secret prison in Thailand, then to Afghanistan, and later to Guantánamo. It was more than a year before the International Committee of the Red Cross told his wife, Farhat, where her husband was—a year in which she was often beside herself with fear and grief.

The U.S. silence, however, which was standard procedure during its secret war, may have provided Aafia's family with an opportunity. Since the CIA refused to admit that it *was* holding kidnapped men like Paracha and the others, no one believed the agency when it said it *wasn't* holding Aafia.

Ismat stopped circling the country asking for help. Both women stopped talking to journalists. They telephoned Imran Khan, the politician whom Aafia's uncle S. H. Faruqi had approached for help. Weeping, they asked him not to publicize Aafia's case. "They told me, 'We've had phone calls, and they say if we speak out, the same thing that happened to Aafia will happen to us,' " Khan told me later. "These poor women are afraid."

Pakistanis across the political spectrum accepted the Islamist line that Musharraf and his government would sell their own mothers in exchange for American dollars. "To stay in power, these people are jumping at every order from D.C.," Khan told me. He assumed that the CIA or the ISI was holding Aafia prisoner.

Amjad and his parents did not believe that Aafia had been arrested, nor did they want her to be. Amjad felt that wherever his children were, they needed their mother. But they needed their father, too, and he thought the Siddiquis, if they wanted to make a reunion possible, could have arranged it.

They pressed ahead with their custody suit. When their lawyer deposed Ismat on August 1, 2003, she claimed under oath that FBI and Justice Department officials in Boston had verbally informed her American lawyer "that the minors are with the mother and are in safe condition."

Ismat's testimony was the opposite of what her American lawyer had said of the FBI's and Justice Department's comments to her in May. As Sharp later told me, U.S. officials had said they had no idea where Aafia and the children were.

But the judge in the Pakistani custody case ruled that since the children had disappeared, there was nothing he could do.

The Khans sought help from government ministers and an ISI officer they knew. They said they were told that a government decision had been made. Through her family, Aafia had assured the government that she simply wanted to live quietly and raise her children. The government, for its part, had agreed not to reveal her location to the Americans. "The gist of what they said was 'We know Aafia is around,'" Amjad said. "'The only reason we are not exposing her and continuing to let her be "lost" is that she is after all a woman and a mother.'"

One day late in 2003, the same uncle who had witnessed Aafia and Amjad's divorce decree saw a woman he recognized as Aafia outside Karachi's English-language Nakhlah school. He caught the woman's eye; she drew her veil over her face and turned away. It was the same school that Grand Mufti Muhammad Rafi Usmani had recommended when Aafia and Amjad had visited him the year before. As soon as the Khans heard about the uncle's sighting, Amjad and his father rushed to the school to see if Ahmad and Maryam were enrolled there. But they were told that the school had no children by those names.

Amjad felt he had reached a dead end.

He decided he had to get away. With his photograph still up on the FBI's Web site—though by now it was marked "Located"—he knew he could not work in the United States. So he took a job at a hospital in Saudi Arabia and moved there with his new wife and their baby daughter.

Nineteen

Ayaan often spoke of how much she missed her father. She had shown the filmmaker Karin Schagen the little picture she carried in her wallet of Hirsi in the 1960s, looking so young and optimistic. She told *Trouw* that her father was the one person she wished could have been with her when she was sworn in to Parliament. "To him I was an apostate," she wrote later, "but still, I was following in his footsteps, committed to working for the well-being of others."

Hirsi Magan now lived in London with his first wife, Maryan Farah Warsame. The last time Ayaan had seen any of her relatives was in 2002, at a celebration in Rotterdam of her older half sister, Arro's, marriage. Arro was still very stylish and beautiful. (Ayaan would later tell a reporter that Arro never left the house without her hair done.) Now a gynecologist, she had married a fellow doctor and was practicing medicine in England. Ayaan and Faduma Osman rode together to the party, which was strictly for women. Ayaan seemed to enjoy the dancing. But, that fall, the controversy erupted over the threats against her, and her half sisters never heard from Ayaan again.

Arro, like Ayaan, declined to be interviewed for this book. Other relatives told me that Arro didn't want to be associated with Ayaan in any way. Like her mother, Arro had dedicated herself to trying to eradicate the Somali custom of female genital mutilation. She worked with women all over Europe, including Zahra Siad Naleie, the director of the Dutch government's program to combat FGM. Naleie had initially welcomed Ayaan's campaign promise to make eradication one of her top priorities in office. But eventually she decided that Ayaan was making her job harder rather than easier.

Ayaan sometimes seemed to share the impatience that many Somali women felt with what they felt was a creepy Western curiosity about the practice. "That's just the way it is in Somalia," she told one journalist who asked her for the umpteenth time about what it was like to have her genitals cut. But she said that Cisca Dresselhuys and other Dutch feminists had talked her into speaking out about her personal experiences. They had told Ayaan it was her duty to expose the subject.

FGM had been illegal in the Netherlands since 1993, but Ayaan, Naleie, and others argued that it had merely gone underground. "During school holidays," Ayaan said, "children are taken to their countries of origin, where female genital mutilation is not forbidden, and then children are operated on without anesthetics. It's done with scissors; it's done with razor blades; it's done with broken glass, and that's really very inhumane."

In 2003, under pressure from Ayaan, the Dutch government commissioned two researchers from Amsterdam's Free University to study the issue. They found that anywhere from ten to a hundred girls with Dutch citizenship were being circumcised every year, most of them from within Holland's Somali community. Based on their findings, Justice Minister Piet Hein Donner proposed making it a crime for parents to have their daughters circumcised in any country, overseas as well as in the Netherlands.

But when Ayaan unveiled her party's plan in February 2004, she went a step further. Rather than wait for doctors or the girls themselves to report their circumcision, Ayaan proposed that the government require annual vaginal examinations for girls from high-risk countries such as Somalia until they turned eighteen. If a doctor discovered that a girl had been mutilated, he or she would be required to report it to the authorities for prosecution.

Naleie and other Somalis who had campaigned for years against FGM were aghast. They felt the law would invade the Somalis' privacy and stigmatize them besides. Naleie thought the plan could set her work back for years. She recalled, "We were very, very angry with Ayaan. The parents said, 'We don't want doctors examining our girls' vaginas.' If it were everybody [being examined], it would have been okay. But Ayaan said that would be too expensive. It was just Somalis, and we don't agree with that."

The national doctors' association also opposed the bill. Doctors argued that the measure would turn them into policemen, destroying the trust between them and their African patients.

For several years, Somalis had been leaving the Netherlands for the United Kingdom. Some had hoped all along to settle in an English-speaking country. Once they gained Dutch passports, they often exercised their right under European Union regulations to move to the United Kingdom.

But other Somalis said they had left because they disliked the way they were treated in Holland, especially in the years after 9/11. They chafed at bureaucratic restrictions that dictated where they could live and made it hard for them to start businesses. They resented the hostility they felt toward immigrants, and they resented the social workers and teachers who they believed disapproved of them and discriminated against their children.

By 2003, a third of Holland's 29,000 Somali residents had left—often for the growing Somali enclave in the city of Leicester, in the English Midlands. By 2005, an additional 10,000 Somalis joined the exodus.

Somalis told Dutch researchers that they could never "be themselves" in Holland. They often cited Ayaan as a factor in their departure.

The Dutch thought of Ayaan as a model immigrant. To Somalis, however, this woman, who insulted the Prophet and was written about proudly drinking alcohol and taking lovers, was a nightmare vision of what their children might become if they stayed.

For some Somalis, Ayaan's media campaign against female genital mutilation came to symbolize the deterioration of their dealings with the Dutch. "When I first came to Holland in 1994, I was seventeen, and I took a train to Amsterdam from Hoek van Holland," a Somali friend who later moved to the United States and married a British academic once said to me. "The conductor told me, 'You are a beautiful girl.' I was truly excited.

"In May 2005, I took the same train to the ferry. This time the conductor looked at me and said, 'They are barbaric where you come from.' I said, 'What are you saying?' He said, 'You cut your women's vaginas.' I was so angry. I was thinking, It's our culture. What has it got to do with you? There are a lot of things I don't like about Dutch culture, but I don't talk about them."

My Somali friend had two sisters with Dutch citizenship. One had already moved to England—"she just can't bear it here." The other was planning to move to England soon. Unlike Ayaan, my friend's sisters were already married and had children when they arrived in the Netherlands, and they found it hard to gain acceptance. In the fourteen years that one sister lived in Leiden, she was never invited into a Dutch person's house. Peering at her from behind their lace curtains, her neighbors spied a lot of Somalis entering and leaving her place. Soon a tax inspector came around to see if she was running an unauthorized day care center. It was a common suspicion. Dutch small-business men often accused immigrants who started small businesses of competing unfairly by failing to pay taxes and ignoring Holland's numerous rules.

Somalis, for their part, regarded Holland's large pornographic industry as utterly exploitive of women. Nothing could make them believe that the naked prostitutes standing in the windows of Amsterdam's red-light district really wanted to be there. (In fact, Amsterdam's deputy mayor, Lodewijk Asscher, who campaigned to control and roll back the district, argued that most of the prostitutes came from poor countries and were in bondage to their pimps because they were either drug addicts or illegal aliens.) The Somalis and many other Muslims found it hypocritical of the Dutch, who allowed women to be rented openly, to preach to them about mistreating women. And then there was the habit many Dutch people had of letting their dogs defecate on public sidewalks. "The Somalis," according to my friend, "say there are two reasons to leave this country—*han* and *harag*, gossip and dog shit."

Ayaan had argued that though female circumcision predated Islam, Islam reinforced it because of the religion's emphasis on virginity. Yet Somali activists like Ayaan's own stepmother had discovered decades earlier that the most effective way to persuade Somalis to give up circumcision was not to link the practice to Islam but rather to sever that link. Naleie, for example, said that the single most effective educational device she knew was a video in which a Somali imam explained that Islam did not mandate FGM.

Ayaan's friend Yassin, the prince of the Osman Mahmoud clan, had been proud that one of the clan was the first Somali elected to the Dutch Parliament. But after Ayaan made her comments about the Prophet being a tyrant and a pervert, other Somalis called him to protest. As for Holland's Turks and Moroccans, they were furious at Ayaan for ascribing to Islam what they considered a barbaric custom from Somalia, and they demanded that the Somali community do something about her.

Yassin described the growing anger: "A woman called, and she said, 'Ayaan is your family. She has joined the Liberal Party and she has gone to Parliament, and now she is talking about Islam the wrong way.'" A man called to say that Yassin should tell Ayaan other Muslims were talking about killing her. "So I called Ayaan several times on her mobile, and I left messages, messages. But she didn't call me back. I know the problem. She didn't want to talk to me.

"She is one of my family," Yassin told me, "and I would like to tell her, 'Ayaan, why are you saying the wrong things about the Muslims?'" He agreed with her that too many Muslim men mistreated their wives, but he thought *they* deserved the blame, not Islam. "If someone does wrong, that's his responsibility, not the religion.

"But she didn't pick up the telephone," he said. "I tried, I tried, I tried, but I can't get Ayaan."

Theo van Gogh, the Dutch filmmaker who made "Submission" with Ayaan and was murdered as he bicycled to work on November 2, 2004, by the would-be jihadi Mohammed Bouyeri. *(AP Photo/Willem ten Veldhuys/Dijkstra b.v.)*

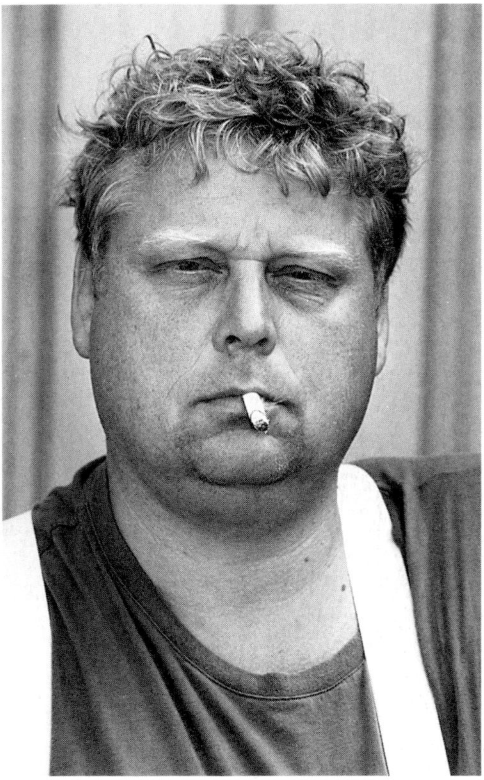

Mohammed Bouyeri, the twenty-six-year-old Dutch-Moroccan murderer of Theo van Gogh. *(AP Photo/Justice Ministry via Dutch television)*

Ayaan returns to Parliament on January 18, 2005. She spent more than ten weeks in hiding in the United States after the murder of Theo van Gogh. *(AP Photo/Fred Ernst)*

Ayaan chats with U.S. secretary of state Condoleezza Rice at *Time* magazine's 100 Most Influential People in the World Gala on May 8, 2006. Ayaan was named one of *Time*'s one hundred most influential people in 2005. *(Getty Images Entertainment/Evan Agostini)*

A tearful Ayaan announces her resignation from Parliament on May 16, 2006, after Dutch immigration authorities ruled that her Dutch citizenship was no longer valid, because she had changed her name and date of birth on her asylum application in 1992. *(AP Photo/Rob Keeris)*

Ayaan and the British historian Niall Ferguson at *Time* magazine's 100 Most Influential People in the World Gala on May 5, 2009. The two were married on September 10, 2011. *(Getty Images Entertainment/Jemal Countess)*

SEEKING
INFORMATION

Aafia Siddiqui

DESCRIPTION

Date of Birth Used: March 2, 1972
Place of Birth: Pakistan
Sex: Female
Remarks: Although Aafia Siddiqui's current whereabouts are unknown, the FBI believes she is currently in Pakistan.

DETAILS

Although the FBI has no information indicating this individual is connected to specific terrorist activities, the FBI would like to locate and question this individual.

IF YOU HAVE ANY INFORMATION CONCERNING THIS PERSON, PLEASE CONTACT THE LOCAL FBI OFFICE OR THE NEAREST AMERICAN EMBASSY OR CONSULATE.

Robert S. Mueller III

ROBERT S. MUELLER, III
DIRECTOR
FEDERAL BUREAU OF INVESTIGATION
UNITED STATES DEPARTMENT OF JUSTICE
WASHINGTON, D.C. 20535
TELEPHONE: (202) 324-3000

The Seeking Information bulletin issued for Aafia by the FBI after the arrests of Khalid Sheikh Mohammed and Majid Khan in March 2003. Seeking Information was a new type of bulletin created by the FBI in 2002 to acquire information from the public about terrorist suspects who had not been indicted by an American grand jury.

SEEKING
INFORMATION

Dr. Mohammed Khan

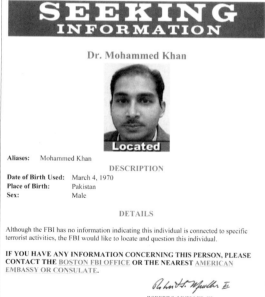

Aliases: Mohammed Khan

DESCRIPTION

Date of Birth Used: March 4, 1970
Place of Birth: Pakistan
Sex: Male

DETAILS

Although the FBI has no information indicating this individual is connected to specific terrorist activities, the FBI would like to locate and question this individual.

IF YOU HAVE ANY INFORMATION CONCERNING THIS PERSON, PLEASE CONTACT THE BOSTON FBI OFFICE OR THE NEAREST AMERICAN EMBASSY OR CONSULATE.

Robert S. Mueller III

ROBERT S. MUELLER, III
DIRECTOR
FEDERAL BUREAU OF INVESTIGATION
UNITED STATES DEPARTMENT OF JUSTICE
WASHINGTON, D.C. 20535
TELEPHONE: (202) 324-3000

The Seeking Information bulletin issued for Aafia's first husband, Mohammed Amjad Khan, in March 2003. After Amjad met with the FBI in Karachi, his bulletin was marked Located.

Elaine Whitfield Sharp, the lawyer Aafia's family hired, stands before a picture of Aafia at her 1995 graduation from the Massachusetts Institute of Technology. Sharp was speaking at a press conference held after U.S. attorney general John Ashcroft called upon Americans on May 26, 2004, to be on the lookout for Aafia and six other suspected terrorists. *(AP Photo/Chitose Suzuki)*

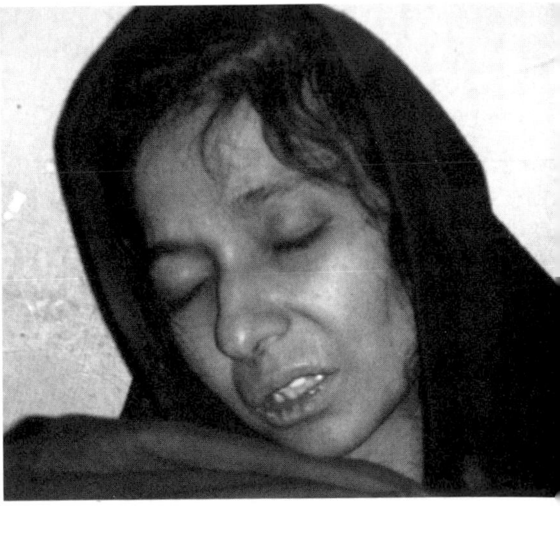

The iconic photograph of Aafia in the Ghazni police station in Afghanistan after she was captured and beaten by Afghan police on July 17, 2008. Many Pakistanis mistakenly believed the photograph had been taken after Aafia was tortured by the CIA in one of its secret prisons. *(AP Photo/File)*

Aafia *(right)* and her eleven-year-old son, Ahmad, cover their faces at a press conference that was held by the Ghazni governor's office on July 18, 2008, to announce their capture. Aafia told the police that her name was Saliha and the boy's name was Ali Hasan. She claimed he was an orphan she had adopted after the 2005 earthquake in Pakistan. *(AP Photo)*

Aafia's mother, Ismat Siddiqui, gestures despairingly as she and Aafia's sister, Fowzia Siddiqui, watch a February 4, 2010, news report on Aafia's conviction in a U.S. federal court on attempted murder charges. *(AP Photo/Fareed Khan)*

Aafia's son Ahmad shortly before he was returned from Afghanistan to Aafia's mother and sister in Pakistan in October 2008. *(AP Photo/Rafiq Maqbool)*

Aafia's daughter, Maryam, with her aunt Fowzia. Maryam had been missing for seven years when Aafia's mother and sister claimed that the twelve-year-old mysteriously appeared on their doorstep in April 2010 with a placard around her neck bearing their address. Aafia's youngest child, Suleman, remains missing. *(AP Photo/Fareed Khan)*

One of hundreds of rallies held in Pakistan to protest Aafia's imprisonment in the United States. After Aafia's 2010 conviction on attempted murder and assault charges, U.S. judge Richard Berman sentenced her to eighty-six years in prison. *(AP Photo/Fareed Khan)*

Ayaan's father called his daughter in May and asked her again to stop criticizing Islam. But Ayaan refused, and they didn't speak again for four tumultuous years. The prince of their clan tried to mediate between them. "After she came in Parliament," Yassin said, "I called her father, Hirsi Magan. I said, 'You have relations with Ayaan?' He said, 'I don't want relations with Ayaan.'" Yassin persisted: "You are a sheikh, and you are a very important man. You must have contact with your daughter. The Prophet Mohammed, peace be upon him, he had good relations with his family even when they were not Muslims."

The old lion Hirsi did not reply.

"Is that true or isn't it?" Yassin asked him. "If our Prophet could do it, why can't you? You must concern yourself with your daughter."

But Hirsi told Yassin, "I don't want to see Ayaan. I don't want to see her!" And then, more softly, he added, "I don't want to see Ayaan, because, if I see Ayaan, I'll kill her and go straight to Paradise."

At this, the prince could only shake his head. "I told him, 'Uncle, I am very sorry. All I can do now is to pray.'"

"Forget it, forget it," Hirsi said. "Ayaan is a hard problem."

Twenty

For six months, after Ismat and Fowzia returned to Pakistan in the spring of 2003, nothing was heard of Aafia. The two women lived very quietly in the old family bungalow with the bougainvillea-covered wall in Gulshan-e-Iqbal. Aafia's picture was still posted on the FBI's Web site, and the FBI continued to investigate her. The Pakistani authorities knew, as the Americans did, about Aafia's hasty marriage to KSM's nephew Ali Abdul Aziz Ali. But the general Pakistani public had no idea why the United States wanted her, and President Musharraf, who preferred to veil all his dealings with the United States in maximum secrecy, was happy to keep it that way.

The Bush administration knew by now that al-Qaeda was regrouping in Pakistan's tribal territory of Waziristan with the help of elements within Pakistan's own intelligence agencies. The Americans also knew that people on wanted lists, such as Aafia, were moving about Pakistan's cities quite freely and without hindrance. They suspected, in fact, that Osama bin Laden and Mullah Omar might be among them.

But they didn't know what they could do about it.

For one thing, the United States had become totally ensnared in Iraq, where al-Qaeda was seeking to lead a Sunni insurgency against it. For another, administration officials from President Bush on down had basically decided that Musharraf's cooperation—halfhearted and flickering though it was—was the best they could get out of Pakistan. Privately, Musharraf didn't deny his government's continuing links with the jihadi movement, a senior administration official told me, but he felt that jihadi groups were so interwoven with the Pakistani state that it would be suicidal for a Pakistani leader to confront them head-on. The official said that Musharraf told the Americans many times, "If we do that, they will tear this country apart." And since Musharraf was cooperating on other important issues, the U.S. government lived with his refusal to arrest such notorious jihadis as the Jaish-e-Muhammad leader, Maulana Masood Azhar.

More than once Musharraf nearly fell off the tightrope he was walking between the jihadis and the Americans. On December 14, 2003, militants from Jaish-e-Muhammad and another, even more violent group, Lashkar-e-Jhangvi, came close to assassinating him not far from his home in Rawalpindi, detonating a huge bomb under a bridge seconds after his motorcade crossed it. On December 25, two suicide bombers got even closer.

Investigators discovered that a young Jaish leader named Amjad Hussain Farooqi, who had ties to both the ISI and the Taliban, had orchestrated both attempts. Farooqi's funding, moreover, came from al-Qaeda, and he had coconspirators in Pakistan's armed forces.

Farooqi had taken part in the 1999 Indian Airlines hijacking that had freed the Jaish leader, Maulana Masood Azhar; he was an intimate of both Azhar and KSM. A former Jamaat-e-Islami student leader at the University of Karachi, Farooqi had been arrested in connection with the Daniel Pearl murder—but then mysteriously released. It was almost certain that some of Aafia's new husband's relatives were also involved in trying to kill Musharraf and that they had the support of some military officers.

Aafia's uncle S. H. Faruqi later wrote in a letter to the newspaper *Dawn* that days after the attempts on the president's life, Aafia's sister, Fowzia, went with their old family friend Ijaz ul-Haq (the banker son of Pakistan's former dictator Zia ul-Haq, who would soon be named minister of religious affairs) to see Interior Minister Faisel Saleh Hayat. Faruqi said that Fowzia wanted to ask the minister to help find her sister.

Faruqi wrote that Hayat had told Fowzia to go home and wait to hear from Aafia. But if Fowzia later heard from her sister, she didn't inform Faruqi. Finally, in March, he wrote his letter to *Dawn* complaining about the government's failure to produce Aafia. After that, Fowzia and Ismat stopped answering his calls.

Faruqi was afraid that his letter had landed them in trouble with the government. Ismat often said she had been warned not to talk about Aafia's case. He traveled to Karachi, and on April 22, 2004, he went to their house in Gulshan-e-Iqbal. There was a big lock on the gate. He stayed in Karachi for another three days but never managed to see Fowzia and Ismat. On May 2, he published another letter in *Dawn*, claiming that Ismat and Fowzia were under house arrest.

The next day Ismat and Fowzia called the newspaper to say that Faruqi was wrong about that. They were not being confined in any way. They just didn't want to speak to him.

(Like so many pieces of Aafia's story, it's not entirely clear what to make of this episode. My best guess is that Faruqi is telling the truth when he says that Ismat and Fowzia told him they had met with the interior minister and that they stopped talking to him after he wrote his letter to the newspaper because they had been warned to keep their dealings with the government over Aafia out of the press. But the Siddiquis' lawyer later said that Faruqi had written it out of spite, there had never been a meeting, and the women had never been under house arrest.)

The Siddiquis may have hoped that the United States' interest in Aafia would fade. If so, they were in for a shock.

On May 26, 2004, U.S. attorney general John Ashcroft held a press conference in Washington, D.C. Standing against a backdrop of enormous mug shots, he asked every American to be on the lookout for seven "armed and dangerous" terrorists who, he said, were plotting attacks against the United States. Ashcroft's "Deadly Seven" included one woman: Aafia Siddiqui. At the press conference, Ashcroft and Robert Mueller, the director of the FBI, described Aafia as an al-Qaeda "facilitator" who helped other operatives in the United States. But *Newsweek* soon reported that she might be "the most immediately threatening suspect in the group" because KSM himself had said she might facilitate al-Qaeda's next attack. Among the others named were Adnan Shukrijumah, the Saudi-born jihadi from Florida whose name had been repeatedly associated with Aafia's. Now officials said they believed that Shukrijumah could become another Mohamed Atta and lead a second great wave of terrorist attacks.

Pakistani officials, meanwhile, continued to issue contradictory statements about Aafia. In response to Ashcroft's press conference, officials told journalists that they had tried and failed to arrest Aafia in 2003, and that since then she had been underground. The following day, however, a spokesman for Pakistan's interior ministry denied that, saying that Aafia *had* been arrested in 2003 and handed over to the Americans. The U.S. government continued to maintain that it didn't have her and never had.

Then, on June 1, Elaine Whitfield Sharp held a press conference in Boston on behalf of the Siddiquis. She described Aafia as a battered wife and victim of terrorism, not a terrorist. She appealed to Americans to share any information they might have on her whereabouts. When reporters asked Sharp about Faruqi's letters to *Dawn*, which were available on the Internet, Sharp denied that Aafia's family was being intimidated or under house arrest.

The fog of rumors and announcements did not let up. The *Wall Street Journal* reported later that month that UN prosecutors thought al-Qaeda might have sent Aafia to Liberia on a secret mission in the summer of 2001 to trade diamonds. The story was an exciting one. But Sharp had evidence that Aafia had been in Boston when others claimed to have seen her in Liberia, and U.S. officials (while maintaining that they considered Aafia dangerous) quietly told reporters they didn't believe the Liberian witnesses, either.

Aafia's ex-husband, Amjad, followed all the reports from his new home in Saudi Arabia. He had a quiet chuckle over the charge of diamond trading in Liberia. Whatever else Aafia might have done, he knew she hadn't been in Liberia in the summer of 2001. Yet her legend seemed to grow and grow.

Twenty-one

Ayaan's political party made good on its promise to crack down on asylum seekers. Parliament voted in February 2004 to expel about 26,000 people whose applications for asylum had been denied, including some who had lived in the Netherlands for years. Immigration Minister Rita Verdonk, a member of Ayaan's Liberals, was placed in charge of implementing the policy.

Verdonk was a former prison warden who wore her dark hair in a square-cut bob; her simple slogan was "Rules are rules," and she prided herself on her tough-mindedness.

She set to work right away, marking the first three thousand people to be sent back to Iran, Afghanistan, Congo, and other countries before the start of summer.

The expulsions were the most sweeping in Europe since the 1940s. They caused bitter controversy in the Netherlands. Some were reminded of the deportations during World War II of Jewish refugees from Germany who had sought safety in Holland. For the first time ever, the United Nations, the European Commission, and several human rights organizations cited the Netherlands for human rights abuses.

Other Dutch voters regarded the decision as an overdue step toward regaining control of Holland's borders, and Verdonk, with her plain speech and plain shoes, became for them a symbol of Dutch common sense in the face of a sentimental political correctness that still minimized the dangers that immigrants posed to the Dutch welfare state.

Ayaan opposed the decision to expel the asylum seekers, but she did not make a big issue of it. She remained focused instead on Islam.

She wanted artists to join her in challenging her former religion. She often said that when a movie like Monty Python's spoof of Jesus Christ, *The Life of Brian*, came out about the Prophet Muhammad, it would be a leap forward for the Muslim world. She had told her friend Abigail Esman, an American journalist and art critic living in Amsterdam, about an idea she had for an art exhibit. Ayaan wanted to illustrate one of the Quran's pernicious effects by copying the Quranic verses that were used to justify the abuse of women onto life-size female dolls. Esman invited her to New York and introduced her to people she knew in the art world, but nothing came of the idea.

Ayaan found it frustrating to hear well-meaning Westerners tell her that Islam wasn't to blame for the oppression of Muslim women. "In reality," she said, "these Westerners are the ones who misunderstand Islam. The Quran mandates these punishments. It gives a legitimate basis for abuse so the perpetrators feel no shame and are not hounded by their conscience or their community."

Her battles in Parliament continued. The newspaper *Algemeen Dagblad* asked her to write a weekly column. One of her first, in April 2004, accused Mirjam Sterk, a member of Parliament from the Christian Democratic Party, of promoting "apartheid" by opposing her plan to drop Article 23 guaranteeing public funds for religious schools.

Once again, Ayaan's own party leaders were incensed. They told her she had to treat other members of Parliament, especially other members of their coalition, with respect. Ayaan finally agreed to apologize to Sterk, but she refused to take back the word "apartheid."

One day Ayaan was invited to lunch with Ebru Umar, a feisty young female columnist of Turkish descent and a friend of the filmmaker Theo van Gogh. Umar later wrote that she had taken an instant dislike to Ayaan, who struck her as needlessly combative and suspicious. Umar said Ayaan had asked her to write an article denouncing

Sterk, but she had refused. She says she told Ayaan that Sterk had promoted integration for a long time and Ayaan ought to work with her, but Ayaan disagreed. "Fighting is good," Umar quoted Ayaan as saying. "That's the way to score points in The Hague."

Theo van Gogh, for his part, had written a recent column calling the Prophet Muhammad a "rapist" and a "dirty uncle." Hundreds of Muslims signed an online petition against him. "Something like this breeds hatred and ultimately leads to violence," the organizers of the petition wrote. "That's why we have to bring this to an end soon." Ayaan asked Umar for van Gogh's telephone number.

A bit later she flew to New York on a holiday. *NRC Handelsblad* had assigned their star reporter Jutta Chorus to follow Ayaan for six months and write about her life, so Chorus went along. Ayaan was sitting in a New York taxi when van Gogh called her on her mobile phone from Amsterdam.

The filmmaker had just left a debate with Dyab Abou Jahjah, a former asylum seeker from Lebanon who had settled in Belgium and formed a political party there called the Arab European League, which was spreading into the Netherlands. Abou Jahjah's political model was Malcolm X. He traveled with a retinue of bodyguards, and the head of the Dutch branch of his party was Mohammed Cheppih, the Saudi-educated son of an imam whose televised debate with Ayaan had sparked the first death threats against her a year and a half earlier. Van Gogh told Ayaan that after he and Abou Jahjah had traded insults, several young Moroccans had threatened him outside the theater.

When Ayaan got back to Amsterdam, she went to see van Gogh at his apartment on Pythagorasstraat and told him about her idea for an art exhibit. He volunteered to turn it into a movie. She agreed and proposed making the film in English; she wanted it to reach an international audience.

She was seeing a new man. Herman Philipse was the debonair professor of philosophy at Utrecht University who had written the book she credited with changing her life, *The Atheist Manifesto*. In a country where professors often went to work in blue jeans, Philipse was famous for his Savile Row suits and bow ties. Ayaan first met him at a public lecture he gave in The Hague. She caused a stir when she got there and her bodyguards fanned out around the lecture hall. Afterward, Philipse introduced himself. By the summer of 2003, the two of them were an item.

Philipse lived in an elegant Amsterdam apartment almost across the street from van Gogh's friend Theodor Holman. When Ayaan arrived in her black car to spend the night, her guards would get out and stop traffic until she got inside. They did the same when she left in the morning. Philipse found the lack of privacy oppressive and embarrassing, and he didn't see how Ayaan could stand living the way she did. The only time the two of them really felt free together was when Ayaan left her bodyguards behind to go on vacation in New York with Philipse. Ayaan adored New York and told him she might want to live there.

Their relationship ended in July 2004, but they remained good friends. Ayaan told Philipse she thought the film that she and van Gogh were making could help her break into the U.S. market. Philipse agreed that moving to New York might be good for her, but he thought making a movie with van Gogh was the wrong way to go about it. For one thing, he doubted Ayaan's theory that she could wean Muslims from Islam by what he called "desacralizing" the Quran. "You might even call it childish," he said later of the idea. But mainly he advised against making the film because he thought it would defeat what he saw as the purpose of her moving to the United States—which in his view was to escape her notoriety in Holland. "I warned her against it because I thought it was high risk," he recalled. "She was trampling on their holy book. I predicted that she would no longer have to be protected just in the Netherlands but all over the world."

Ayaan knew the film would infuriate people. "The whole Muslim world will fall on top of me," she told Jutta Chorus almost gleefully. "They will be very angry." But she decided to make the film anyway. "She was just very passionate, and she felt she had to do it," Philipse said.

She was invited to appear in August on the popular Dutch television show *Zomergasten* (*Summer Guests*). The program usually profiled Dutch celebrities, who shared bits of their favorite childhood movies or TV shows. Only a few politicians had received such invitations, and Ayaan's friends urged her to accept. Ayaan asked the show's producers if she could show the film that she and van Gogh were planning, and they agreed.

While still working on the project and before appearing on *Summer Guests*, Ayaan got into another quarrel. She suggested in an interview on the TV program *Buitenhof* that potential employers should question Dutch Muslims about their religious beliefs. Why question Muslims and not Catholics? asked the host. "The threat of terrorism comes from Muslims," Ayaan replied.

Many Muslims—who as a group were poorer than non-Muslims and more often unemployed—felt that Ayaan's comments would make the Dutch even more suspicious of them.

Terrorism hadn't yet struck Holland, but the nation's mood kept getting uglier. Around the time of the March bombings in Madrid that killed 191 people, the Dutch intelligence service warned again that "a growing number of Muslims feel that opinion makers and opinion leaders are treating them rudely." A *De Volkskrant* poll taken a few days after Ayaan's television interview found that 68 percent of respondents felt threatened by "migrant or Muslim youths," that 53 percent feared a terrorist attack by Muslims, and that nearly half feared the Netherlands would someday fall under Islamic rule.

Considering that Muslims still constituted only 5 percent of the population, these fears might seem exaggerated or even bizarre. But many of the Dutch shared them.

Now when Ayaan and her bodyguards appeared in the streets, Muslim men hissed, "Whore," and spat at her. In June, she wrote in her column that a young Dutchman had tapped her on the shoulder in a bar in The Hague and told her "very politely" that he hoped the mujahideen would kill her. Ayaan gave the man a butter knife and asked why he didn't do the job himself if he thought killing her was such a good idea.

It was the kind of bravado that Ayaan's admirers loved, but it masked the serious dangers building.

A rap song about her appeared on the Internet. Called "Hirsi Ali Dis," by the Muslim rap group The Hague Connection, it attacked her viciously and threatened her with death, calling her a "cancer whore" and a "shit stain."

Police arrested the rappers and charged them under an obscure provision that made it illegal to hinder elected politicians in their work. But the song was a sign of the growing Muslim fury.

In Amsterdam West, the disciples of the Syrian cult leader Abu Khaled itched worse than ever to do violence against the enemies of Allah. The Dutch intelligence agency AIVD had already named them "the Hofstad network" after police, in 2003, arrested Abu Khaled, a young follower named Jason Walters, Samir Azzouz, and two others based in The Hague on suspicion of planning some kind of attack. (*Hofstad* means "capital city," in this case The Hague.) They were soon released. But then in June two more of Abu Khaled's acolytes were arrested in Portugal for plotting an assault on the UEFA European football championships. Meanwhile in Rotterdam, police who searched the house of Samir Azzouz and his wife, Abida Kabbaj, found a gun, two ammunition clips, night-vision goggles, a bulletproof vest, and chemicals commonly used in making bombs.

The AIVD also knew about Mohammed Bouyeri, in Amsterdam, but they didn't consider him as dangerous as some of Abu Khaled's other disciples. It was a feeling Bouyeri may have shared—and resented.

The videos that the group continued to download were themselves becoming increasingly ghoulish as jihadis in Chechnya and Iraq seemed to torture and butcher their prisoners in increasingly cruel ways.

KSM's former comrade and the leader of al-Qaeda in Iraq, Abu

Musab al-Zarqawi, brought different jihadi groups together to kidnap a twenty-six-year-old American named Nicholas Berg. In an imitation of the murder of Daniel Pearl, he sawed off Berg's head in front of a camera. The film was posted on www.ogrish.com, and Mohammed Bouyeri copied it onto a CD to pass around to his friends.

By the summer of 2004, Bouyeri was determined to show that he was as tough as his bloodthirsty heroes. So he looked around for suitable targets and was fascinated by the prospect of tearing out a living heart.

He wrote tract after tract on the Internet denouncing Jews and other enemies and raving about how the "knights of Allah" would soon march into the Binnenhof, the castle that served as the seat of Holland's government; they would rename Parliament "the court of sharia" and hoist the flag of *tawheed*, or the oneness of Allah. In May, Bouyeri grew so angry at some sluggish bureaucrats in a welfare office that he threw a trash can at a security guard and threatened to kill him, screaming, "I'll tear your heart out!" (The Dutch authorities merely banished him from the office.)

In the jihadi chat rooms Bouyeri frequented, he adopted a new pseudonym, Abu Zubair, and began threatening leaders from the king of Morocco to Queen Beatrix of the Netherlands. To the Moroccan king he wrote that "my greatest wish is to see how your chest is torn open, to see how your beating heart is wrenched out of your body, and then watch how death seizes your rotten soul to drag it to the dungeons of Hell while you are screaming and struggling."

Bouyeri narrowed his options down to local enemies, and on August 17 he began drafting letters on his computer threatening the deputy mayor of Amsterdam, Ahmed Aboutaleb, and also Ayaan Hirsi Ali.

Ayaan and the Moroccan-born Aboutaleb opposed each other politically. The deputy mayor thought the Dutch ought to make Muslims feel included as long as they obeyed the law. His solution to the problems of integration was to offer immigrants language training and other classes that would help them find jobs and fit in. But he and Ayaan were both prominent secular Muslims, and Bouyeri seems to have considered one as bad as the other.

All the members of Abu Khaled's little sect hated Ayaan with a passion. Jason Walters included her on a list of Dutch politicians he wanted to kill as early as 2003. The girls in the group shared his sentiment.

The gang was beginning to pair up in secret "marriages" performed by "the sheikh," as Abu Khaled's followers called him, or by Bouyeri himself, who had lately been functioning as Abu Khaled's deputy. Such marriages had no validity under Dutch or classical Islamic law, but members of the group argued that it was their Islamic duty to marry and procreate. "We do this for the *ummah*," a girl who called herself Fatima later told the newspaper *Trouw*. "If a man conceives children with several wives, he creates more Muslims." One girl blushed as she told the Dutch journalists Janny Groen and Annieke Kranenberg how she and her "husband" had used to lie in bed thinking up "battle names" for the children they were making.

Bouyeri had fallen for a neighborhood girl whom reporters later identified by the pseudonym "Fatima." She attended some of Abu Khaled's lessons. In August, Bouyeri asked "Fatima" to marry him, but she turned him down. "I didn't get on with such a quiet boy," she said. Instead she became the second wife of another member, Mohammed al-Morabit.

Clearly, Bouyeri needed to show that he was every bit the warrior his friends were.

Dutch Muslim chat rooms were already hurling threats at Theo van Gogh for his remarks against Muslims and the Prophet and because of a satirical book he had written called *Allah Knows Best*. That summer the filmmaker noticed men in long gowns and prayer caps watching his house.

Police suspect that one of Bouyeri's friends, who worked for a construction firm on the same street as van Gogh's apartment, let the rest of the group know that the filmmaker cycled back and forth to work each day at regular times. One night, as van Gogh left a restaurant, a man called from the darkness that he would kill him and his family.

Ayaan has said that she called their movie "Submission: Part I" because she intended it to be the first of a series exposing several kinds of suffering caused by Islam. The film was ten minutes long. Van Gogh's friends said his company spent 18,000 euros to produce it. Ayaan finished writing the script at the end of July. They shot it at an Amsterdam studio a few days later.

The film opens with a woman praying. She wears a transparent veil. (Ayaan has said she wanted to show the woman's naked body in order to challenge Allah metaphorically—and to challenge viewers, too, presumably—to recognize that a real woman lived beneath the veil. She may also have been inspired by an incident two years earlier in which some Muslims had smashed advertisements for a play called *The Veil Monologues*, which featured a woman in a similar see-through veil.) Inscribed on the woman's back are the opening verses of the Quran, which every Muslim recites at the start of a prayer. At the end of the prayer, she raises her head.

The camera turns to face the first woman of four in the story. She tells Allah that she has obeyed all of his injunctions, yet she has been flogged for falling in love. The next woman says that she was forced to marry her husband, and now she is forced to submit to him sexually. A third woman's husband beats her. The fourth is a girl who has become pregnant after being raped by her uncle. The last line contains the message "I may no longer submit."

None of Ayaan's friends liked the movie. "When I saw it for the first time, I said, 'It's a horrible film,'" Theodor Holman recalled. "There's no drama, no action. It's not a movie." He says van Gogh felt the same way but made the movie anyway because he was committed to helping Ayaan. "We all completely underestimated the effect."

Cisca Dresselhuys saw it and was worried. She asked Ayaan if she really wanted it shown on television. Not that Dresselhuys imagined that anyone might be killed. "No one thought about murder. If we had, we would have said, 'No!'"

Ayaan showed it to the leaders of the Liberal Party. She has written that her party mentor, Gerrit Zalm, was undisturbed. "He simply asked if all this stuff was really in the Quran; because it was, he concluded that there was no reason I shouldn't use it, although he thought it unfortunate that our actress was half naked." The minister of the interior, Johan Remkes, also seemed to think Ayaan was exaggerating the impact her little film would have.

But the press was excited. A few days before Ayaan was scheduled to appear on *Summer Guests*, the respected *NRC Handelsblad* published an article headlined "Hirsi Ali's Latest Provocation." The next day, Jutta Chorus's long feature on the past six months of Ayaan's life appeared. In still another article, "Uncrowned Queens of the Netherlands," Ayaan was listed as the sixth most influential woman in Holland.

"Submission" aired on August 29, 2004.

At first, nothing much happened. Then, in September, someone calling himself Abu Nawaar el Hosaymi published the unlisted address of the new apartment that the Dutch secret service had found for "the devilish apostate Ayaan Hirsi Ali" next to the Israeli Embassy in The Hague. Police concluded that militant Muslims were watching her movements. In a second message, "Abu Nawaar" threatened "the disbelieving diabolical mocker" van Gogh. The police transferred Ayaan to another house, but they appear not to have taken the threats against van Gogh as seriously.

When they tracked down "Abu Nawaar," he turned out to be a twenty-two-year-old Moroccan who had been posting jihadi comments for months.

Ayaan told van Gogh he needed bodyguards, but he resisted. The Dutch secret service saw the threats intensifying, but it protected royals, diplomats, and members of Parliament—not ordinary citizens like van Gogh.

Twenty-two

Relentless police work and international intelligence resulted in the roundup of more and more people in KSM's network and related groups.

In June, the police arrested Ramzi Yousef's brother, Abdul Karim Mehmood, and his sister's husband, the Lashkar-e-Jhangvi militant Dawood Badani, in connection with an attempted assassination of Karachi's corps commander. Abdul Karim—who also went by the name Musab Aruchi—had a U.S. bounty of $1 million on his head, and Pakistani intelligence agents told the *Washington Post* that he was in touch with people planning attacks on financial institutions in New York and Washington. "It seems that this family," one agent said about the al-Baluchi, "has something in their genes against the icons of financial power in the U.S."

The interrogation of Abdul Karim led to the arrest on July 13 of twenty-five-year-old Mohammed Naeem Noor Khan, a computer expert from Karachi who manned an al-Qaeda communications center. Police found files in Khan's computer containing the detailed surveillance of financial buildings in New York, New Jersey, and Washington, including the Prudential Building and the International Monetary Fund.

Pakistani intelligence decided to use the young computer whiz in a sting. Over the weekend of July 24–25, they had him send e-mails to all his contacts. When the replies came in, they helped the authorities track down dozens of his accomplices.

In Pakistan, Khan led the CIA and Pakistani police to the hideout, in Gujarat, of Ahmed Khalfan Gailani. Gailani was the Tanzanian who had helped plot the 1998 bombings of the U.S. embassies in Nairobi and Dar es Salaam and the man whom Aafia was alleged to have supervised buying diamonds in Liberia. He had a $10 million U.S. reward on his head, and he was captured with his Uzbek wife after a fourteen-hour gunfight.

In Britain, the e-mails Khan received prompted police to arrest twelve men of mainly Pakistani descent on suspicion of planning to attack Heathrow Airport—the operation that Aafia's husband, Ali, had taken over from the imprisoned KSM before Ali, too, was arrested. The e-mails led to the capture of Dhiren Barot, a British former airline agent and Hindu convert to Islam who had become one of KSM's top secret operatives, and of Babar Ahmad, the webmaster of the jihadi Web sites www.azzam.com and www.qoqaz.com, both of which Aafia had frequented before 9/11.

Aafia almost certainly knew the webmaster, Babar Ahmad—at least by e-mail. She frequently read www.azzam.com, and in the summer of 2001 she was probably translating Abdullah Azzam's book *The Maidens of Paradise* for the Web site. Babar Ahmad was about Aafia's age, and he worked closely with pro-jihadi activists in the United States, including some of Aafia's friends at Benevolence International. The name of the Florida jihadi Adnan Shukrijumah appeared in official comments on the wave of arrests, and credit card and telephone records indicated that Shukrijumah might have scouted out the Prudential Building and other sites and might have written the surveillance reports found in Khan's computer.

Some close observers of the roundup speculated that Aafia might be arrested next.

Noting that the Pakistani government "almost magically" managed to uncover high-level al-Qaeda figures whenever important Americans visited, *Asia Times* suggested that the ISI knew where most al-Qaeda figures were hiding and produced them "when and as needed" to stave off U.S. pressure. The magazine expected the pressure to heat up as the U.S. presidential elections neared.

As for Aafia, the reporter for *Asia Times* wrote, his sources claimed that she was in ISI custody but the ISI wasn't ready to hand her over. "Acquaintances of Aafia say she was an ISI contact and played an active role as a 'relief worker' in Chechnya and Bosnia—a role the government now does not want to reveal. She has also been connected with different Arab nongovernmental organizations in the United States, through which she also helped to supply aid and funds to Chechens."

British intelligence wanted to follow the victims of Khan's sting a bit longer to see where they led. It suspected that the Bush administration had leaked the news of his arrest in the hope of winning credit not long before the 2004 election. But it turned out to have been Pakistani officials who had leaked Khan's name to the press—possibly to halt the sting and prevent British and U.S. agents from penetrating deeper into al-Qaeda's Pakistani cells.

And Aafia's arrest did not occur. According to U.S. officials, she had become the most wanted woman in the world.

Twenty-three

Ayaan went to see her literary agent in Paris that October. She told Susanna Lea about all the press coverage that she and "Submission" were getting. Her agent agreed that she had a wonderful story. But if Ayaan wanted to produce a book, she would have to stop talking to journalists and start writing it. Lea could guarantee that if Ayaan wrote it, the book would be noticed.

Back in Holland, Ayaan got together with the television program *Nova* to show "Submission" to four Muslims in a shelter for battered women. The idea was to see how victimized women like the ones in the film would react to its message. As the cameras rolled, it became clear that the women didn't like the movie at all.

Ayaan tried to explain that she meant to help; but as the discussion continued the women from the shelter became increasingly emotional. "You're just insulting us," one woman cried. "My faith is what strengthened me. That's how I came to realize that my situation at home was wrong."

"I simply want this to stop," said another woman, whose face was disguised for the camera.

"But I am not going to stop," Ayaan said. She remained very calm.

"Then I stop," one woman cried. Another of the sheltered women sounded as if she was choking back tears. "If you can't see that you are hurting me, I will not continue this discussion with you any further. There is no use in talking with you."

Ayaan stood up. "Then, see you later," she said with a flick of her hand.

It was a very Somali gesture, and Ayaan probably meant no offense. But as the journalist Ian Buruma later wrote, "It may have been this wave, this gentle gesture of disdain, this almost aristocratic dismissal of a noisome inferior, that upset her critics most."

On the Internet, Moroccan chat rooms exploded with rage. Albert Benschop, a University of Amsterdam sociologist who has studied how the Internet fueled tensions between Muslims and non-Muslims in the period, said that very few of those railing against Ayaan had actually seen "Submission." But they had heard that it was blasphemous, and they had heard that she had put down the women at the shelter.

Meanwhile, Islamists were free to stoke the hatred, since the Dutch police and intelligence agencies hadn't yet discovered how to stop the radicals from flooding Internet chat rooms with their propaganda. "They could publish anything," Benschop said of the tech-savvy jihad sympathizers. "They could penetrate any site. They penetrated these websites where thousands of people would come."

"In the summer months preceding the murder, on any Islamic forum, there was heated debate: what are we going to do about this insult?" Benschop recalled. "There wasn't any discussion about the feminist intentions of the film. It was rejected on a massive scale. There was just the hatred and the feeling that van Gogh and Hirsi Ali had deliberately insulted them again. The wish to do something about this was very great and very broad."

In this violent atmosphere, the cult leader Abu Khaled and his disciples must have sensed their time had come.

They began writing to one another that they did not need to go to Iraq or Afghanistan to join the jihad. They could fight the unbelievers in Holland. In "Submission" they saw the opportunity to put their bloody fantasies into action.

In September, Bouyeri got into trouble again by screaming and spitting at an officer who caught him riding on a tram without a ticket. Again he went free.

He was reading a book about Zarqawi, and the films he watched on his laptop were getting more macabre and nihilistic. Along with videos of hangings, executions, beheadings, amputations, and tortures, police later discovered images on his computer of a penis being cut off and of a man having sex with a dead woman.

Bouyeri made up his mind. Presumably on the authority of Abu Khaled, he decided to act. He obtained a Croatian semiautomatic pistol and began practicing with it.

It isn't certain that Bouyeri ever saw "Submission." It wasn't among the films on his laptop. And he began writing his "Open Letter to Hirshi [*sic*] Ali" before the movie came out.

In it he says nothing about the movie—or even about women. He specifically condemns Ayaan for two television interviews. The first was the one in December, when she had asked Muslim schoolchildren to choose between the Quran and the Dutch Constitution, and the second had taken place in June, when she had proposed screening Muslim job applicants on the basis of their religious beliefs. But Benschop thinks that the furor over "Submission" gave Bouyeri the confidence to act. "My hypothesis is that Mohammed Bouyeri saw that there was a climate in which it was possible to kill Ayaan or a substitute and that he must have thought that almost all Muslims would applaud the action."

Bouyeri wrote a farewell letter to his family. "By the time you receive this, I will already be a martyr," he said. He expressed regret that he had never been able to persuade them to see things his way. "I have often searched for ways to point out the truth to you, but somehow it seemed as if there was a wall between us all the time."

In a letter to his comrades, he enclosed a memory stick and asked "all the brothers and sisters" to disseminate his religious and political texts.

The cult leader Abu Khaled made a quiet getaway at that point. On October 27, a fellow Syrian living in a small Dutch town booked a passage for him to Turkey via Greece. The date of his departure was set for November 2. From Turkey, this deeply mysterious man who had been seeking asylum in Europe since 1994 would make his way home to Syria. (He was later reported to have been arrested there.)

The last days of October also led up to the U.S. presidential election. On October 29, Osama bin Laden released a rambling videotape in which he told Americans that, by invading Iraq, Bush had pushed them into disaster. Many Western experts on terrorism agreed with bin Laden when he said that even he found it hard to believe how often "the White House seems to be playing on our team" by alienating Muslims and seeming to vindicate al-Qaeda's view that the war against terror was really a war to dominate the Muslim world. Most Americans, however, didn't like hearing that, and this first message in a year from the al-Qaeda chief probably helped a majority rally around their president.

On the night of November 1, Mohammed Bouyeri's friends gathered at his apartment to break the fast of Ramadan. They ate soup and reminisced about the crazy things they used to do, such as smoking marijuana and drinking alcohol, before they'd discovered "true Islam." Around midnight, Bouyeri took a walk around a park in his neighborhood, listening through headphones to texts from the Quran. Around 2 a.m., everyone went to bed. At 5 a.m., they got up again to eat breakfast and to say their morning prayers. Then Bouyeri left the house.

November 2, a Tuesday, was election day in America, but most Americans were still asleep when Theo van Gogh set off on his bicycle to work in Amsterdam. At about 8:30, he stopped to buy a newspaper and cigarettes. Although he had named his Web site "The Healthy Smoker," the overweight filmmaker told the tobacconist he wanted to try a new nicotine medicine to quit. Back on his bike again, he was cycling along the bike path of busy Linnaeusstraat when a bearded stranger in a caftan cycled up beside him.

Pulling out a gun, Bouyeri shot van Gogh in the stomach, then fired several more times. The filmmaker managed to crawl to the other side of the street. He begged his assassin for mercy, pleading, "Can't we talk about this?"

Bouyeri made no reply. Instead, he kicked the filmmaker twice and pulled two knives from the folds of his gown. With the larger knife he proceeded to saw van Gogh's head nearly off his neck. Blood spewed everywhere. With the smaller knife he stuck a five-page letter to the filmmaker's chest. Then he calmly reloaded his gun and began walking in the direction of a nearby city park.

"You can't do that!" screamed one of the dozens of eyewitnesses.

"Oh, yes, I can," Bouyeri replied. "He asked for it. Now you know what to expect."

A policeman wearing a bulletproof vest chased him into the park, and a shoot-out began. Bouyeri was shot in the leg and arrested.

Ayaan was in Parliament when she heard the news. Her bodyguards hustled her out of the building and into hiding.

She didn't learn until later that a woman, who has never been identified, arrived later that morning carrying a copy of one of Bouyeri's tracts, "The True Muslim." The woman told Ayaan's office staff that she wanted to meet personally with Ayaan. She left Bouyeri's book and a mobile phone number. When Ayaan called a few days later, the woman said she had wanted to warn her about Bouyeri. But then the mobile phone went dead, and apparently the police never tracked her down. Later, when two women in Bouyeri's group told *De Volkskrant* that it would be better for a woman to kill her, Ayaan wondered whether that was what her visitor had planned.

Job Cohen, the mayor of Amsterdam, called for a public demonstration in front of the Dam, the main square outside the royal palace. Ayaan wanted to attend it, but her security detail said the risks were too great. Although the public didn't know it at the time, the Jewish mayor and his Muslim deputy had also been on the list of politicians Bouyeri had threatened. (In a strange echo of Ayaan's technique of quoting the Quran in "Submission," Bouyeri's letter listed various quotations from the Talmud, concluding that "a mayor is leading Amsterdam who subscribes to an ideology that Jews can lie to non-Jews.") Cohen and his deputy, Aboutaleb, refused to go into hiding. They insisted on going out and trying to calm the public's fears. While Cohen attended the demonstration, Aboutaleb visited a mosque and warned Muslims that they had to stop segregating themselves and join Dutch society. "Anyone who doesn't share these values," the deputy said, "would be wise to draw their conclusions and leave."

But Bouyeri reserved his most terrifying curses for Ayaan. He promised in his letter that she would be destroyed, that the Netherlands would be destroyed, that Europe would be destroyed, and finally that the United States would fall. "AYAAN HIRSI ALI YOU WILL BREAK YOURSELF TO PIECES ON ISLAM," the letter said. "The death you are trying to prevent will only find you out, . . . Oh Hirsi Ali, you too will go down."

In the days after the killing, the Netherlands seemed to erupt. Dutch nationalists took their revenge by setting fire to four mosques. On November 8, the day van Gogh was to be buried, a powerful bomb exploded outside the school attached to the Eindhoven mosque, where the 9/11 hijackers had attended seminars. On November 10, an Islamic school in the town of Uden was burned to the ground. Altogether, seven schools were subjected to destructive attacks. The Anne Frank Foundation, which had noticed a big increase in arson and racist incidents since 9/11, reported more than 174 threats in the month of November. Only in Amsterdam, where Cohen and Aboutaleb continued to meet with community leaders, were no such threats reported.

A few miles from Parliament, police surrounded Bouyeri's friends Jason Walters and his brother Jermaine at their house in The Hague. The AIVD had learned that Walters had issued a communiqué taking credit for van Gogh's murder and promising to kill Cohen, Aboutaleb, and Wilders. Walters threw hand grenades at the police who surrounded him and threatened to blow up the building. After a fourteen-hour siege, during which Walters shot and wounded a policeman, he and his brother were captured, stripped to their underwear, blindfolded, and taken to jail.

Ayaan was told she needed to leave the country for her own

safety. A week after van Gogh's murder, she was flown secretly across the Atlantic to Massachusetts and installed in an anonymous high-way hotel north of Boston. She wasn't allowed to communicate by telephone or e-mail with anyone.

She became as invisible, at this moment of eclipse, as her opposite in Pakistan.

PART III

Being Regarded

One

The Islamabad Marriott was strangely quiet when I arrived in November 2004 to write my first article about Aafia. It was Ramadan, and the hotel would normally have been full of prosperous guests breaking the fast at nightly *iftar* banquets, the ladies dressed in a rainbow of silken shalwar kameezes. But there had been an explosion the week before in the Marriott's lobby that had injured a U.S. diplomat and several Italian tourists. The Pakistani government had blamed the blast on an electrical failure, but everybody knew that a bomb had gone off. I found myself wandering the red-carpeted halls with only the TV chatter of newscasters for company. They were talking about President Bush's reelection and the murder of Theo van Gogh.

I hadn't meant to stay in Islamabad longer than a day. I wanted to go straight to Aafia's hometown of Karachi and interview her family and friends. Instead, I was sent to the Interior Ministry to see a bureaucrat who kept slicking back his thinning hair as he nervously informed me that I needed an internal travel permit to go to Karachi.

It was my first inkling that something about Aafia's story seemed to rattle Pakistan.

Big, brash Karachi wasn't a secret installation, after all. As Aafia herself once said, it was "the New York City of Pakistan." It was the country's largest city, its main port, its economic heart. It was also the most populous Muslim city in the world, with more than twice as many people as New York. I had visited Karachi several times without any permit, most recently on an assignment for *Vogue* to write about al-Qaeda's female supporters.

I had tried earlier, by telephone, to arrange an interview with the Siddiquis through their lawyer in Massachusetts, Elaine Whitfield Sharp. Sharp was pleasant about it, but she warned me that the Siddiquis would not see me. That seemed strange, too. Sharp had emphasized how respectable the family was. She said that the Siddiquis were Westernized professionals and that Aafia's disappearance and the allegations against her had come as a terrible shock. In my own experience, even in Pakistan, such sophisticated people were usually the first to contact the media if they felt they had been wronged. And what was true of educated people in general was often doubly true of Islamists, though I wasn't sure yet whether Aafia's family shared her political beliefs.

I was happy to follow the evidence wherever it led. Whether Aafia was in hiding, as the U.S. government said, or she was being held by the CIA, as some human rights groups were speculating, her story was still a good one for *Vogue* because *Vogue* is a women's magazine and Aafia was the only woman the FBI had named as wanted in the war on terror. For all I knew (and I knew far less in 2004 than I've learned since), Annette Lamoreaux, the lawyer whom Aafia's brother had hired, might have been absolutely right when she scoffed at the idea that a Volvo-driving mother of two could be involved with al-Qaeda. "Is that where al-Qaeda is recruiting now, on playgrounds?" Lamoreaux had asked.

All I wanted to do was go to Karachi and try to persuade the Siddiquis to tell me their side of the story. But the Interior Ministry told me I needed permission from the head of Pakistan's terrorism and crisis management unit, Brigadier Javed Iqbal Cheema, before I could leave for Karachi. I called Cheema's office and learned that he had gone home for Ramadan. I called him at home and was told he could not come to the phone. So, with little else to do, I sat in my room at the Marriott, studying the few fragments of information about Aafia that had come to light since the FBI had put her name on its Most Wanted list in 2003.

As Sharp observed, the U.S. government had never spelled out why it wanted Aafia so badly. From the earliest press reports, anonymous officials had linked her to 9/11's mastermind, Khalid Sheikh Mohammed, but they had never explained the link. She had never been charged with anything, much less indicted. And no reward was promised for her capture, as it was for the others on the U.S. attorney general's list of the "Deadly Seven."

In New York, prosecutors had accused young Uzair Paracha of possessing the key to a Maryland post office box that Aafia had allegedly rented on behalf of Majid Khan in 2002. Yet Paracha's indictment didn't explain why possessing the key was a crime or how the prosecutors knew that Aafia had opened it. Sharp disputed that she had. "A simple fingerprint comparison would tell us whether Aafia is one and the same as the so-called 'good sister' who opened the post office box," Sharp said. "Has this been done? If it has, then why hasn't Aafia been indicted? Either they have the proof or they don't. They should put up or shut up."

But in the secretive world of the terror war, nothing was simple. Rumors, lies, and mysteries proliferated.

Sharp told me she felt that the Justice Department's people who had questioned Aafia's mother, Ismat (in Boston and again in Houston in 2003), had been telling the truth when they said they were still looking for Aafia. Still, Sharp thought, the CIA or Pakistan's ISI might be holding her without telling the FBI. But when I called the CIA to ask, its spokeswoman laughed. "Let me give you an off-the-record steer," she said. "If you say we have her, you'll be wrong."

I visited the U.S. Embassy in Islamabad to ask about her case and was told that no one knew anything. The embassy press officer also advised me not to go to Karachi. "The last reporter who went to Karachi to write a story they didn't want him to write," he reminded me, "was Daniel Pearl, and he got chopped up into little bitty pieces."

Pearl's horrible murder had been playing in my mind. Recently, the French intellectual Bernard-Henri Lévy had produced a book accusing the ISI of orchestrating Pearl's "state murder" in order to stop him from exposing its collusion with al-Qaeda. Levy noted that not long before Pearl was kidnapped, he had written several articles for the *Journal* exploring the links among the ISI, al-Qaeda, and Pakistan's jihadi groups.

Lévy finished his book before the State Department, in October 2004, announced that KSM had confessed to having personally cut off Pearl's head. I had also read an article by Pearl's friend Asra Nomani pointing out that some of the Jaish militants who had helped kidnap Pearl had told the Pakistani police that not one but a team of three "Yemeni-Balochi" men had carried out the slaughter and filmed themselves doing it.

If KSM, however, really was the man who had cut Pearl's throat, the many ties that Lévy and others had documented between the ISI and the Deobandi jihadis who had kidnapped him became even more sinister. They suggested that the Pakistani establishment was somehow associated not just with jihadi groups but also with KSM, the planner of the deadliest foreign attack on U.S. soil in history. Could a mother with a Ph.D. from Brandeis have been mixed up with conspirators like that? I found it hard to believe. Yet there was evidence that Aafia moved in similar circles.

I had obtained e-mails showing that Aafia, as a student in 1993, had volunteered to distribute videos from Mercy International, the charity whose office in Pakistan was being run at the time by KSM's older brother Zahid. Moreover, according to several books about Ramzi Yousef and KSM, police had found photos of Zahid with Zia's son Ijaz ul-Haq when they had raided Zahid's house in Peshawar searching for Ramzi Yousef. Ijaz ul-Haq was the man Aafia's sister, Fowzia, had gone to for help when Aafia had disappeared ten years later, according to their uncle's letter to *Dawn*. And in Islamabad I had learned from a columnist for an Urdu newspaper, Imtiaz Siddiqui, that Aafia had interviewed Haq, who was now Pakistan's minister for religious affairs, for the MIT paper she had written on Islamization and its effects on women.

I called Haq and asked him for an interview. He said he would be glad to see me. I put on a long tunic over my trousers, draped a scarf around my neck, and took a taxi to his office.

I recognized Haq's heavy-lidded eyes from old photos of his father, the military dictator, though with his square jaw and clean-shaven face, he looked less like an Islamist than like the captain of an American college football team. He welcomed me into his large office dressed in a spotless brown vest and long white shirt. The photographs lining the walls, of him shaking hands with presidents, princes, clerics, and such, showed him looking equally comfortable in a Western business suit or a Saudi gown. Haq had studied at Southern Illinois University. His son had attended Boston University, where either Aafia or Fowzia—he couldn't remember which Siddiqui sister—had made homemade curries for his son so he wouldn't feel homesick. If I hadn't read about it in a Pakistani weekly, *The Friday Times*, I never could have guessed that only a few months earlier this smooth and seemingly Westernized man had become so enthusiastic at the launch of a pro-Taliban cleric's book that he offered himself up (rhetorically, I presume) as a suicide bomber, exclaiming, "Anyone who does not believe in jihad is neither a Muslim nor a Pakistani!"

Instead I listened as he told me how terribly sorry he felt for the Siddiquis. He said that Aafia's disappearance had devastated the family. "It is a very humble family that has no political background or political inclinations," he said. "This was a very unfortunate incident."

The minister told me he had tried his best to help Ismat and Fowzia find her, but he hadn't succeeded. He personally suspected that her ex-husband might have had a hand in her disappearance. "I've told Mrs. Siddiqui to keep an eye on the father," he said in a confidential tone.

He asked if I was planning to see the Siddiquis. I told him I wanted to. He offered to call them for me. And while I sat in front of his wide desk, he telephoned Ismat and Fowzia.

After speaking to them in Urdu for a few minutes, he hung up with a long face. "They say that they have no clue where she is. She is probably not in the United States, probably not in Guantánamo, but in some third place. The mother was crying so much that she had to put down the phone. I spoke to Aafia's sister. She says her mother is very ill. They said they know about you, but their lawyer has advised them not to talk to you."

Sharp had told me she had wanted the Siddiquis to see me but they had refused. But I supposed that what he said could be true.

He wished me good luck.

I went to see Khalid Khawaja, a former Pakistani Air Force officer and ISI member who had once served as Osama bin Laden's pilot and had now joined the celebrity cricketer and politician Imran Khan in a campaign on behalf of "missing persons" in the war on terror such as Aafia.

Khalid Khawaja was a wiry, fidgety man with a frizzy gray beard, and when he got excited his knee jumped up and down. He had a round, mobile face that was almost comically expressive. One minute he'd scowl, railing against the United States and the Pakistani "puppets and slaves" who did Washington's bidding. Then he'd break into the sunniest of grins and describe bin Laden as "an angel of a man."

Khawaja spoke perfect English and knew everybody who was anybody in the jihadi firmament. (His wife, Shamama, a former lawyer, told me stories about bin Laden's wives. "So humble, yet so organized! They put on tea parties in a cave.") In the late 1990s, Khawaja had become a conduit for Western journalists seeking to meet jihadis. The CBS reporter George Crile, for instance, had relied on Khawaja while researching his book *Charlie Wilson's War*. But Western journalists had become wary of Khawaja after he was implicated in the Daniel Pearl kidnapping.

In the days after the attacks on the World Trade Center and the Pentagon, Pearl's friend Asra Nomani had met Khawaja through an aunt of hers who belonged to a group of devout middle-class Deobandi women that Nomani jokingly called "the ladies' auxiliary of the Taliban." Later, Pearl, who also knew Khawaja, asked him for help to meet Sheik Mubarak Gilani, a Deobandi cleric who Pearl suspected had acted as mentor to the shoe bomber Richard Reid. When Pearl went missing after leaving for what he thought was an interview with Gilani, the police took Khawaja in for questioning. The police had cleared him of any involvement. But Pearl's widow, Mariane, had written that she still suspected the former spy and confidant of bin Laden of being involved in the kidnapping.

I had read all this before I met Khawaja at the nearly empty office in Islamabad that he and Imran Khan called the headquarters of their organization. Khawaja had agreed to meet me, but he told me he didn't know Aafia or anything about her. At first he was unfriendly. "Ask your own cruel government where she is!" he said. "Maybe they have killed her three children in front of her. They are capable of anything. I should know."

The interview seemed to be going nowhere. Then, out of the blue, he looked at me and asked if I knew how to reach Mariane Pearl.

I didn't, but *Vogue* had featured Mariane in a recent issue, and I was sure my editor did. This information seemed to soften him. He told me he wanted to let Pearl's widow know that he had had nothing to do with her husband's murder. Then he said I should drop the Aafia story. Instead, I should come to his house for the post-Ramadan Eid celebration and meet some *real* jihadi women. "Come see how terrorists celebrate Eid," he joked.

Khawaja and his family lived in a three-bedroom flat in Islamabad's F-8 Sector, a neighborhood of large white bungalows with red-tiled roofs and well-tended gardens populated mainly by diplomats and retired military offers. I arrived dressed in a shalwar kameez and accompanied by a Pakistani journalist, and Khawaja introduced me to a woman I had read about. Her name was Zaynab Khadr, and she was the twenty-four-year-old daughter of Canada's most notorious jihadi. Her father, Ahmad Khadr, an Egyptian immigrant to Canada, had been a member of al-Qaeda's inner circle before Pakistani commandos killed him in a firefight in Waziristan in October 2003.

I also met Khawaja's wife, Shamama, that day. She looked very dignified in a white head scarf. "Does she look oppressed to you?" Khawaja asked me in his needling way. His son, Osama—named after bin Laden—and his daughter, Rubina, were also on hand. We ate dates and a plate of spiced chickpeas and yogurt.

Zaynab, the young Canadian, was wearing a black niqab, a long gray overdress, and black stockings. She related the story of her life in a flat Canadian accent that seemed not to match her clothes and story. Her father had moved the family from Toronto to Peshawar when she was five. She had then grown up with the children of the world's most militant jihadis and had later spent her youth in Taliban-controlled Afghanistan, a period she described as "the best five years of my life."

Alas for Zaynab, this Islamist Arcadia had ended with the U.S. invasion of Afghanistan. A younger brother had been captured and was now the youngest prisoner at Guantánamo. She and the rest of the family had dodged bombardment to escape across the mountains into Waziristan. Then her father had been killed and another brother had been paralyzed in a firefight with Pakistani forces, and Zaynab and her mother had left Waziristan. "We no longer had any men to protect us," she told me. Her mother had returned to Canada to get medical help for her paralyzed son, while Zaynab stayed in Islamabad with a third brother, twenty-three-year-old Abdullah. A few weeks earlier, however, Abdullah had joined the ranks of "the missing." The ISI, she said, had picked him up with some Pakistani friends, and no one knew where they were.

Khawaja told me he had been trying to find places for Zaynab and other al-Qaeda women and children to live but that even Pakistan's generals, admirals, and religious party leaders were too cowardly to help. They told him they wished they could, but they were too scared. This, said Khawaja, after men like Zaynab's father had dedicated their lives to ridding Afghanistan of communism! "They say, 'Our hearts are with you.' I tell them, 'We need more than your heart. We need a house.' But they are chickens."

As we talked, I realized that Khawaja knew the families of just about everyone I had seen mentioned in connection with Aafia's case. For example, he was helping the Paracha family. He was also in touch with Malaqah Khanum, the activist and wife of Abdul Qadoos, the Rawalpindi microbiologist in whose house KSM had supposedly had been found. (Khawaja said that KSM had not really been found there and that the Qadooses were being punished because their son, an army major serving in the border town of Kohat, which I had visited the year before, was friendly with the mujahideen.) Then there was Majid Khan, the Baltimore man for whom Aafia was accused of renting the post office box in Maryland: Khawaja knew his wife. He said she was only a slip of a girl but was stoutly supporting her husband.

The only family Khawaja *didn't* seem to know was Aafia's. "We haven't found any information about her," he said. His knee bounced nervously.

Khawaja wanted to know why I was so interested. After all, I could meet any number of women who supported al-Qaeda by visiting the female seminary next to the Lal Mosque in downtown Islamabad. He casually added that the most recent attempt to assassinate Musharraf had been planned at the Lal Mosque. Quite recently, he told me, three thousand women at the seminary had demonstrated against Musharraf's decision to send troops to Waziristan. The head of the mosque, Mufti Abdul Rashid Ghazi, was a good friend of his. Khawaja gave me the mufti's phone numbers. He also called Malaqah Khanum and asked her to see me. (I phoned Khanum later to set up an appointment, but she hung up on me.) As for Aafia, he advised me to quit looking for her.

Zaynab had been sitting on a bed, listening. "I pity Americans," she interrupted, her small black eyes glittering above her niqab. "Most of them don't understand why they are hated. They don't even know that they are the agents of Satan. You just have to read the Protocols of the Jews to know that America is hostage to a handful of Jews. But most Americans don't even know it. There should be ten more 9/11s if that's what it takes to wake Americans up to what their government is doing."

She said it with so little affect that I had to remind myself that she and Khawaja were friends of Osama bin Laden and that Daniel Pearl, as Khawaja kept reminding me, had been kidnapped and murdered not long after he had visited this very apartment. I began to notice that every time I steered the conversation back to Aafia, Khawaja returned to Pearl's kidnapping.

He said he had felt from the start that the shoe bomber Richard Reid had been a plant. "You can't blow up an airplane with some little stuff in your shoes," Khawaja said, as if he knew what he was talking about. He had become convinced he was being set up when American reporters such as Pearl had started calling him to ask about some link between Reid and Khawaja's friend Sheik Mubarak Gilani. "We could smell it—they are tightening the noose," he said. He warned Pearl to leave Gilani alone, but the journalist—did I know Pearl was a Jew?—wouldn't listen. Khawaja spread out his hands, helplessly. Zaynab looked on, eyes glittering.

I protested that I wasn't writing about Pearl; I was writing about Aafia Siddiqui.

But Zaynab broke in again. "This is an area where they don't want people to probe," she said. "When they keep it so quiet, they want it to stay that way." Zaynab didn't say who "they" were.

"Aafia is like Richard Reid," Khawaja chimed in from his armchair. "You are following a wild goose."

"We suggest to you not to put yourself in trouble," Zaynab added. "No one will talk to an American. They will think you are a spy."

Her tone sounded vaguely menacing, but when I thought about it later at the Marriott, I wondered if perhaps she was pulling my leg. "Come and see how terrorists celebrate Eid," Khawaja had said. Maybe he and Zaynab were having a laugh right now over scaring the gullible American reporter. Or perhaps everything was just as they said. Perhaps they were working for Osama bin Laden and wanted me to stop writing about Aafia, just as they had wanted Pearl to stop writing about Richard Reid and his friends. And perhaps they wanted to stop us both for the same reason: because the "wild goose" in each case led to the same hidden forces that had protected KSM and were still protecting Aafia and al-Qaeda. I really didn't know.

I had little time to ponder the question. The new U.S. ambassador to Pakistan was an old friend of my husband, and I had asked for his help in securing a permit to visit Karachi. The day after my troubling visit to Khawaja's house, the embassy called to say that the permit was waiting for me at the Interior Ministry.

After so many warnings, I wasn't about to go to my interviews in Karachi alone, so I hired a local Pakistani journalist to come along. We decided to drive over to the Siddiqui house in Gulshan-e-Iqbal and ring the doorbell. It was late November but still sweltering in Karachi. As we stopped and started through innumerable honking traffic jams, with candy-colored buses decked out in baroque decor and beggars in blue Afghan burkas sticking their hands up to our window, I thought about how antiseptic Islamabad was. Sand-colored Karachi was the real Pakistan.

We turned down Aafia's street, and the noise of traffic died. We were in a zone of large houses shaded by palms and mango trees, as quietly respectable as any in Islamabad. "This is the E Section," my Pakistani colleague breathed, audibly envious. We parked and approached a faded white stucco wall covered in pink bougainvillea. The gate appeared to have had an intercom once, but it had been pulled out of the wall. Through the bars we saw men in beige tunics sitting on the porch. My colleague thought they looked like intelligence men. After a while a servant woman dressed in a ragged black skirt came out with a baby on her hip. She said no one was home except Fowzia's son. We left a note for Fowzia and said good-bye.

I tried telephoning the house from my hotel. That time a woman who spoke English with an American accent answered. But when I asked for Ismat or Fowzia, she told me I had the wrong number.

Were they prisoners, or were they being protected? I asked the journalist I had hired. He spread his hands helplessly. He couldn't say.

I had read the Siddiquis' claim that Aafia's former in-laws, the Khans, lived behind high walls in a mysterious compound. I was therefore surprised when I visited the Khans the next day to see that their wall was no taller than the one that shielded the Siddiquis. We rang the bell, and Aafia's former father-in-law, Aga Naeem, emerged. He was silver-haired and wore faded gray trousers and a short-sleeved white shirt buttoned up to the neck. He called to his wife, Zahera, to come downstairs, and he invited us onto the porch for a cup of tea.

As we sat around a wicker table, I noticed how apprehensive this frail old couple seemed in the presence of strangers. She was bent with osteoporosis. His hand trembled slightly as he brought out a collection of newspaper clippings and court documents. Yet compared with most of the other people I'd met on this trip, they seemed amazingly straightforward. When I asked them about the Siddiquis' allegations that Amjad had beat Aafia, they didn't deny it—although they said the only incident they knew about was the one in Boston when he had thrown the baby bottle. They laughed when I asked if their son had gone into hiding. They said he worked at a hospital and didn't care to talk to the press. What made them despondent, and very angry, was the subject of their missing grandchildren.

"I was the one who arranged this marriage," Zahera told me sadly. "I liked her very much. But she was rigid. Stubborn. Whatever she wanted, she would do. More or less, she was an extremist. Now we are very sad. Where are the children? We don't know where they are. All we know is that they are with Aafia and Aafia is with them. We don't know if Mrs. Siddiqui knows where they are or not. She says they are with the FBI."

I broke in. "When did she say that?"

Aga Naeem pulled out a copy of the statement Ismat had given to the family court in August 2003. Ismat claimed she had contacted both the FBI and the U.S. Justice Department in Boston and that they had "verbally told the lawyer that the minors are with the mother in safe condition." I copied Ismat's words down by hand and returned the paper to them. When I looked up, I saw them gazing at an old photograph of little Ahmad and Maryam, smiling and dressed up for Eid in shiny green and yellow costumes. Zahera took off her glasses and wiped her eyes.

I asked if they believed that the FBI had Aafia and the children.

Aga Naeem slowly shook his head. "I think not," he said. "Mrs. Siddiqui hasn't filed any missing persons case. She doesn't meet us. She keeps very close. She doesn't answer phones. She doesn't answer the door. This gives us the impression that Aafia and the children are underground here."

Zahera spoke up with difficulty. "We don't want our names in a magazine. We don't want any trouble. We just want to find the children."

I promised I would let them know if I learned anything.

My stringer was impassive. I sensed that he either didn't believe the Khans or disapproved of them for talking to me, for some reason. But I felt as if I had just had my first honest exchange since arriving in Pakistan.

The Siddiquis, on the other hand, still refused to see me. In desperation, I phoned their lawyer in Massachusetts again. Sharp told me she had tried to persuade Fowzia to agree to an interview, but Fowzia's baby was sick and she couldn't manage it. As a last resort, I wrote down a few questions for my stringer to ask her. Then I sat in the room with him while he phoned.

My questions didn't even include asking where Aafia was. I felt sure that Fowzia wouldn't answer. But since many people had told me about her mother's charity, the United Islamic Organisation, and I had copies of e-mails from Aafia listing Fowzia's address in Chicago as one of the charity's locations, I thought it might be innocuous to ask about that. I also wanted to let her respond to the contradiction between her mother's claim that the FBI was holding Aafia and Sharp's statement to me that the FBI had denied holding her. So I asked him to pose those two questions to Fowzia.

With the call coming from my stringer's phone, Fowzia answered on the first ring. But she grew frosty when the journalist told her he was calling on my behalf. He asked about the UIO. "I've never heard of that organization," she answered curtly. He asked about Ismat's statement to the family court that the FBI was holding Aafia. She cut him off, saying there was no such court case.

Having seen the e-mails and court documents, I believed that Fowzia was lying. For all I knew, she had good reason. But I was surprised that a neurologist who Sharp claimed had been given a "genius visa" to stay in the United States would say things that could be so easily shown to be false.

I had one more interview before I left—with Hamid Mir, the famous Geo TV broadcaster and authorized biographer of Osama bin Laden. When it came to the shadowy world of intelligence and jihad, no civilian was said to be better informed than Mir. He was also the man who, in two TV shows, had confronted Pakistan's interior minister with the conflicting stories about Aafia's disappearance.

Mir was a big, raw-boned man with curly black hair and a broad pale face. We met in his large office off Geo's main television studio in Islamabad. Since his last program about Aafia, he had heard from Pakistanis who had known her in the United States. "They are whispering," he said, "that she fled from the FBI with the help of some of her friends and that she is living somewhere underground with her kids." Mir speculated that, with Aafia's education, she might even be teaching in a school under a false name. He said that underneath the official silence, the Pakistani public was enormously curious about Aafia. "Aafia Siddiqui is a heroine in Pakistan among educated women," Mir said. He found nothing strange in that. "Our women are more extremist than our men."

I still had no idea where Aafia was. But by the time I boarded my plane for the United States, I no longer felt she was a Volvo-driving mother who had gotten swept up in the war on terror by mistake. There were just too many people who didn't want to talk about her. I didn't know what the Siddiquis were hiding, but they certainly seemed to be hiding something. Whatever it was, I suspected that the Pakistani government and Khalid Khawaja were in on it, too.

Two

For about two weeks that November, after the Dutch government hustled her into a waiting airplane, Ayaan Hirsi Ali seemed to have vanished. Justice Minister Piet Hein Donner declared her hiding place a state secret, and he didn't conceal the fact that he was hiding Ayaan as much to protect Holland as to protect her.

With mosques and churches going up in flames and newspaper headlines saying things such as "Hatred Is Spreading Across Our Country like Wildfire," Donner and others in the government feared that an attack on Ayaan might push the country over the edge. The government put Ayaan's fellow Liberal parliamentarian Geert Wilders into a high-security prison cell—for his own safety, the government said. Even cabinet members weren't told where Ayaan was.

Donner and his colleagues would probably have been happy to keep the two "Islam critics" out of sight indefinitely. But Ayaan's powerful friends complained that they could not contact her, and rumors began to circulate that the government was holding her prisoner to prevent her supporters from taking revenge against the Muslims. So on November 27, Donner flew her back to the Netherlands to show everyone that she was alive and well.

She stayed long enough to share a bottle of champagne with her friend Herman Philipse, give an interview to *NRC Handelsblad*, and deliver an open letter to the Liberal Party. In her letter she declared that van Gogh's murder had made her "stronger and more combative" than ever. She promised that, even without the director, she would make a sequel to "Submission."

Donner sent her back to Massachusetts, but he couldn't keep her away much longer. When she finally returned to Parliament in an armored black Mercedes on January 18, 2005, she was greeted like a queen returning from exile.

Bystanders cheered, and a wall of photographers recorded the moment that she stepped from the car. Ayaan rewarded them with a dazzling smile as she walked across the cobblestoned yard into the walled brick Binnenhof. She seemed so small and fragile that, for the first time in centuries, it felt right that the seat of the Dutch government should also be a fortress.

Every member of Parliament stood up to applaud her as she took her seat in the ultramodern Second Chamber, the Dutch House of Representatives. She had become a living symbol of everything the Dutch held dear and felt now was at risk: the right to free speech, to safety, to love, to "anything goes." As she later wrote, "All the envy and bad feelings seemed to have melted away."

At first everyone vied to show support. Cisca Dresselhuys's magazine, *Opzij*, gave her a prize. The Dutch newspaper *De Volkskrant* named her Person of the Year. The newsweekly *Elsevier* had no such award, so it invented one and gave it to Ayaan. The rest of Europe showered her with recognition. The liberal European think tank Nova Civitas awarded her its prestigious Prize of Liberty. In Denmark, the Liberal Party awarded her its Liberal Prize. In Sweden she won the Democracy Prize. In Norway, Human Rights Service gave her its Bellwether of the Year Award. In Spain, she received the Tolerance Prize of Madrid. A Norwegian parliamentarian nominated her for the Nobel Peace Prize.

But the unadulterated good feelings didn't last long. I realized that when I arrived in Holland at the end of February 2005, in time for one last winter snowstorm to whiten Amsterdam's lacy bridges and gabled canal houses.

Some members of the governing coalition had made it clear even while Ayaan was still in hiding that they had had enough of her provocative style. Justice Minister Donner had used a TV interview to call her "an Enlightenment fundamentalist." The minister for economic affairs compared her decision to make the film "Submission" to "lighting a cigarette in a room full of munitions."

Ayaan's mentor, Gerrit Zalm, and the rest of the Liberal Party rushed to Ayaan's rescue, accusing Donner and the others of blaming the victim and appeasing terrorists. But in the subtly ponderous Dutch way, a message went out to the body politic: things had gone too far. It was time to pull back, to cool down. It was time to reflect on the next step.

But Ayaan seemed to believe that stepping back meant giving in, and she was having none of it. She announced plans to start work immediately both on "Submission II" and also on a book, *Shortcut to Enlightenment*. When a group of Muslims tried to block her from filming the sequel, she fought back in court and won.

She demanded on TV that the Dutch intelligence agency investigate honor killings of Muslim girls. She resumed her fight to abolish Islamic schools. And she complained to the UN Human Rights Commission that the Netherlands and other European countries were not protecting female Muslim citizens.

She became a looming presence in the public eye, like a dark avenging angel. And to a quietly growing number of worried Dutch, her ubiquity and harsh accusations began to feel like a guarantee of further conflict.

In a series of open letters to her, later published as a book, Dutch intellectuals debated her role in bringing Holland to what felt to some like the brink of civil war. The Flemish writer Tom Lanoye accused her of being fixated on Islam. "Your flaming hate I don't understand," he wrote. Bouchra Zouine, a second-generation Moroccan immigrant, said she was disappointed by Ayaan's failure to do anything concrete to help immigrant Muslim women. Referring to a magazine interview in which Ayaan had called herself a Somali warlord declaring war on "the Muslims," Zouine warned that warlords bring unrest and misery wherever they go.

Herman Philipse was so infuriated by those criticisms and by

Donner's jibe about Ayaan being an "Enlightenment fundamentalist" that he published a forty-page booklet attacking the justice minister. He declared that the term "Enlightenment fundamentalist" was itself a contradiction in terms and that in using it Donner was belittling the Enlightenment and apologizing for fundamentalism. Some of Ayaan's detractors had mocked her supporters for holding her up as a Dutch Joan of Arc. Philipse wrote that Ayaan was nobler than Joan of Arc: the French saint had led men into battle, but Ayaan "fights only with words." Joan had considered herself divinely inspired; Ayaan was sustained only by her faith in herself. All that Ayaan had in common with Joan was her bravery—a bravery that, as in Joan's case, was not shared by the men around her.

Holland's best-loved historian, Geert Mak, completed a pamphlet at the end of 2004 that would shock the country by taking a radically different stance. Mak had been one of the first prominent Dutch intellectuals to support Ayaan when she was first threatened in 2002. But in the course of writing a book about twentieth-century European history, Mak had become increasingly uneasy at the parallels he saw between the tone of the current Dutch debate over Muslim integration and the European debate over Jewish integration a hundred years earlier. His pamphlet was called "Doomed to Vulnerability," and it warned the Dutch that European politicians had been down the road of appealing to religious and ethnic hatreds before and that everyone knew where such appeals led.

Mak's argument was complex and politically sensitive. If the Dutch, and Europe, had achieved one moral consensus since World War II, it was that the demons that had led to the Holocaust should never be let loose again. That was why people were so disturbed by the anti-Semitism they saw taking root in Europe's Muslim communities. As the French philosopher Alain Finkielkraut and others wrote, when Muslims accused Israel of racism, it was as if the system of antiracism that had been erected as a barrier against the return of the Holocaust had been turned inside out and was being used as a way to reinject anti-Jewish hatred into European society.

But Mak wrote that Ayaan and her fellow critics of Islam, by stoking the hatred of Islam, seemed to be turning the language of feminism and the Enlightenment inside out. There was, first of all, "the tone, the new tone that was suddenly in vogue." It was belligerent and hostile, Mak wrote; it was "a dirty tone" that reduced complex issues to a simple common denominator: Islam and Muslims. Suddenly it had become acceptable to express hatreds and prejudices that would previously have been considered out of bounds. This time the Dutch were talking about Muslims, but the way they were doing it recalled the language that European newspapers of the early twentieth century had used in talking about Jews. For Mak, it was like hearing a song whose words had changed but whose tune remained the same.

There was also the constant evocation of cultural doom, the insistence that a Muslim fifth column was turning decadent Europe into "Eurabia." There was the sexual innuendo, too, the harping on perverts and "goatfuckers" and the semipornographic fascination with the sex lives of Muslims—or, as one titillating headline on a Dutch magazine cover put it, "How Muslims Do It." There were the calls for Dutch manliness and pride and tough leaders who weren't afraid to have a "straight back" and take ruthless measures. None of it matched the reality of a Europe that was richer, stronger, and more united than it had ever been—but then, as Mak pointed out, Germany's descent into self-pity and paranoia in the 1930s hadn't been rational, either.

Even the evocation of Joan of Arc was eerily reminiscent of the anti-Dreyfusards who had called on the French to rally around the saint against Jewish traitors, while Ayaan's attacks on "multiculturalists" such as Job Cohen brought to mind earlier anti-Semitic tirades against "cosmopolitans." Not that Mak thought that Ayaan intended any such effect; he didn't think so at all. But he had come to believe that, consciously or not, her rhetoric had sharpened a dangerous mood.

Mak wrote that after initially sympathizing with Ayaan and her friends, he had come to feel they were more interested in deriding

Islam than in emancipating women. He compared the way she had used the Quranic verses in "Submission" to the way the infamous Nazi propaganda film *The Eternal Jew* had used verses from the Talmud to show how Jews were supposedly driven by hatred of Gentiles. Mak reminded readers that films such as *The Eternal Jew* had drawn on unconscious religious archetypes and ancient fears to convince Germans that they were threatened by their tiny Jewish minority rather than the other way around. He warned that it could happen again. "Feelings of angst can be blown up into a permanent mental attitude and exploited for political ends," Mak wrote in his pamphlet. "In this way, we sober Dutch can end up in a closed-off, xenophobic fantasy land in which our coarseness and our ignorance of past and present become the norm, in which those who do not go along with this fear psychosis are denounced as weaklings and traitors, and discrimination and racism become the new ground rules."

Mak's pamphlet dismayed the many prominent Dutch feminists who still counted themselves among Ayaan's greatest admirers. Margreet Fogteloo, the young editor of the left-wing weekly *De Groene Amsterdammer,* told me flatly that the historian was crazy. "People like him feel guilty because they were closing their eyes for such a long time to what was going on," she said, taking a furious drag on her cigarette. Fogteloo said that politicians who claimed to support Ayaan's goals but not her methods were mostly just making excuses. "What have they done to put Muslim women on the agenda?"

Feelings ran so high that some guests walked out of dinner parties when Ayaan's name was mentioned, and old friends stopped speaking to each other over Mak's pamphlet.

Donner, the minister of justice, who had called Ayaan an "Enlightenment fundamentalist," was also responsible for her security. The Liberal MP Geert Wilders had accepted Donner's argument that his hiding place should remain a secret, but Ayaan and her friends defied Donner and went public with the news that Wilders was being held in a prison and that she spent her nights at a naval base. Ayaan complained that she and Wilders were being forced to live like fugitives while those who threatened them went free. "They are keeping me alive, but I cannot concentrate on my work," she told the press. "I need a place where I have my desk, my books, my papers, a home where I can meet with people." She demanded that the government provide her with normal housing.

Donner accused Ayaan of ingratitude for the protection she had received. But his government quickly bought a $1.1 million apartment in The Hague, added bulletproof glass, alarms, and metal detectors, and rented it to her for $1,500 a month. The building's previous residents didn't learn her name until Ayaan arrived in April and her bodyguards began checking visitors to the building. The other residents promptly sued the government for disrupting their lives and devaluing their property.

In Amsterdam, a group of left-wing Muslim women launched a campaign called "Stop the Witch Hunt!" Its stickers, featuring a veiled woman putting her hand up, appeared all over town. Pointing out that Spain hadn't seen one act of violence after the Madrid bombings that killed 191 people, organizers accused Ayaan of fostering feelings in Holland that led the police to brutalize Muslims and inspired others to burn Muslim schools. "The cover for racism today is feminism," an organizer named Miriyam Aouragh told me. "It's a cover for a racist agenda, and they are not embarrassed to do that."

Van Gogh's friend the journalist Ebru Umar wrote an open letter to Ayaan in which she bitterly congratulated her for turning a private war into a national one. "I have always found it strange that I haven't yet come across a Muslim woman who welcomed your concern for their emancipation," Umar wrote. "Recently I have heard many say that they were happy with the ritual murder of Theo. You have done a service for radical Islam, Ayaan, you can be proud of it."

Ayaan accused her critics of failing to understand the "tribal principle" driving the country's Muslims. But Umar and others charged her with injecting such a principle into Dutch politics. "You are a foreigner with a foreigner's mentality," Umar wrote. "You always think that a trap is being set for you everywhere by everybody, especially by other women, especially by other foreigners."

Ayaan's friends angrily reminded her detractors that the woman they were criticizing remained in mortal danger. The police continued to arrest members of the Hofstad group, and in January 2005 two of the group's women made their malevolent prediction to *De Volkskrant* that a woman would kill Ayaan. In June, Mohammed Bouyeri's former roommate Noureddine al-Fatmi was arrested at the busy Amsterdam Lelylaan commuter train station, along with Soumaya Sahla, another girl he had convinced to "marry" him. Al-Fatmi was carrying a fully loaded Agram 2000 submachine gun. Shortly after his arrest, it was reported that Soumaya had tried to persuade her sister, who worked in a Hague pharmacy where Ayaan shopped, to give her the MP's secret home address.

The public heard many lurid tales of the Hofstad group's brutality, fanaticism, and fascination with violence and pornography. But the members' appearances in court—chewing gum, dressed in skullcaps and abayas, hurling abuse at officials—also dramatized how different these Muslims were from the friendly Turkish grocers and even the unruly Moroccan street kids that most Dutch people knew. They seemed less like a disciplined branch of al-Qaeda than like some sick teenage cult. Commentators began saying that Mak had a point in accusing Holland of overreacting to van Gogh's murder.

Some Dutch spoke of "the Ayaan effect," a spirit of fear and rancor that seemed to have bewitched the country. To outsiders, the Dutch seemed to be having a collective nervous breakdown.

Ayaan's own Liberal Party shifted with the public mood. A poll revealed that Liberal voters disliked Ayaan more than any other politician except the rival Labor Party's leader. At one contentious party meeting, a Moroccan-born member told Ayaan he had talked to hundreds of Muslim women and hadn't found one who supported her. "They could drink your blood," he said. Jozias van Aartsen, a Liberal Party leader who still backed her in public, called her a "Somali clan fighter" in private. Some members suggested that

Ayaan could not do her duties as a representative and should quit. Hans Wiegel, a popular former Liberal leader who wanted to lead the party again, proposed expelling her. "Mrs. Hirsi Ali encourages polarization and emphasizes contrasts," Wiegel said. "She does not look for bridges but paints ethnic minorities and Muslims in a corner and tars them with the same brush."

Ayaan fought back. Calling Wiegel "a reactionary conservative," she threatened to form her own party if the Liberals expelled her. "He is just like one of those Turkish or Moroccan fathers who instinctively resist modernity, and when they can't hold it back, retreat into their neighborhood where they are safe," she told reporters. She later compared belonging to the Liberal Party to being part of a Somali clan. "And within the clan, you have to be extremely cautious, you have to take into account all kinds of unspoken mores. They told me I had to develop a feeling for this and a feeling for that. I hated those codes." She also said she didn't know how much longer she could go on living like this.

In public she never lost her composure. But she said she often dreamed of being chased. "In the dream I feel that they are getting close to me and I want to jump from the balcony. I run to the balcony and there are so many men there with beards and wearing galabiyas, like Mohammed Bouyeri. I feel that in another moment I will die, in another moment it will all be over. But then I wake up."

Three

A few weeks after my article about Aafia Siddiqui appeared in the March 2005 issue of *Vogue*, I received an e-mail from the Pakistani journalist I had hired in Karachi. He had received a tip that "Aafia Siddiqui, the associate of Adnan Shukrijumah," had been arrested the week before in Baluchistan and handed over to the CIA. According to his source, Aafia had first been arrested in Karachi two years earlier. But a former governor of Sindh and a retired lieutenant general had intervened to have her released. The same source claimed that Aafia's children were safe with her mother, Ismat. My journalist friend asked me to see if I could confirm the tip with my U.S. sources.

I called the CIA and the FBI, but, as usual, they had no comment. Finally I forwarded the journalist's e-mail to the Siddiquis' lawyer in Marblehead, Elaine Whitfield Sharp, to see if she knew anything about it. Sharp e-mailed me back a couple of days later. She said the Siddiquis had heard nothing of the sort. I wrote my Pakistani colleague that unfortunately, I hadn't been able to confirm that Aafia had been arrested. He replied that he hadn't found any confirmation, either.

A few days later he e-mailed me again. This note was labeled "MOST URGENT." "U have committed a big blunder by forwarding my mail regarding aafia's alleged arrest to her lawyer in Boston," the journalist wrote. "The lady lawyer forwarded my message to fauzia siddiqui who today called me and had a half-an-hour chat coupled with threats and grudge. i could not expect such unprofessional thing from a journalist who never reveals his/her source. u have no idea that u have risked my life."

The journalist went on to say that Fowzia and Ismat had charged him with "hatching a conspiracy against them" and spreading false information in order to get money from Aafia's former in-laws, the Khans. He complained that the two women had kept calling him for a whole day, until he finally had to switch off his phone. "Fauzia and Ismat insist that they have been given written assurance by state department that wherever aafia and children are they are safe and sound," he wrote. He also said that when he had told Fowzia what Sharp had told me—namely, that the State Department had given no such written statement—Fowzia had accused him of lying. My Pakistani colleague concluded despairingly that he was "screwed up."

I felt terrible. In retrospect, of course, I wished that I had just asked Sharp about the report of Aafia's arrest, rather than forwarding the e-mail with the journalist's name on it. But he hadn't asked me to keep the e-mail a secret, and it never crossed my mind that I might be putting him in danger. I had thought Aafia's family would *want* to know if she had been found.

I phoned the journalist and apologized for my mistake. He sounded quite shaken. But when I tried to inquire further about what the Siddiquis had said and how they had threatened him, he didn't want to talk about it.

Years later, Aafia's ex-husband, Amjad, heard from a Pakistani official that Aafia had been caught in Baluchistan around that time—early 2005—at the border crossing of Chaman, trying to enter Afghanistan without a passport. He was told that the ISI had quietly stepped in and had her released. If the incident really happened, it was never made public—like so much else in the war on terror.

Four

Ayaan had at least one consolation in the squall of bad feelings that descended upon the Netherlands. Foreign journalists were discovering what the Dutch media already knew: that this gorgeous young Somali and her story made irresistible copy. The earlier threats against her, in 2002, had lifted her from provincial obscurity to national fame. Now the international coverage of van Gogh's murder swept her into worldwide celebrity.

Marlise Simons of the *New York Times* had hurried to Amsterdam as soon as she learned of van Gogh's death. Simons had been the first to bring Ayaan to U.S. attention in 2002, and it was her front-page article about the 2004 murder that I had read while standing in line at the Atlanta airport. Soon her newspaper's Sunday magazine assigned the freelance writer Christopher Caldwell to write a full-length profile of this extraordinary African feminist.

Caldwell was a balding commentator who wore thick glasses and wrote more frequently for the neoconservative *Weekly Standard* than for the *Times*. He had an abiding fear of Muslim immigration. (In 2009, he would come out with a book warning that Europe was in danger of being overrun with Muslims.) In an early article for the *Standard* about the van Gogh murder, titled "Holland Daze," Caldwell sounded as though he had a reservation or two about Ayaan; he dismissed "Submission" as a "violent, semi-pornographic movie," and he wrote that one reason the Dutch regarded an African refugee as "something like Joan of Arc" was that "her outsider status makes her a natural leader for a society that fears it will die if it does not change, but would rather die than be accused of racism, gay-bashing, or Islamophobia." But by the time he was finished with his article for *The New York Times Magazine*, his skepticism had apparently melted.

"Hirsi Ali had been dealt a full house of the royal virtues: courage, intelligence, compassion," he proclaimed in the cover story that appeared on April 3, 2005, under the title "Daughter of the Enlightenment." He characterized Ayaan's life under twenty-four-hour guard as "an inseparable mix of the terrifying and the tender." "Hers is a big, heroic life that moves her fellow citizens but now gets lived mostly in locked rooms and bulletproof cars. She leads that life partly above other Dutch people, as a national symbol—and partly below them, as a prisoner."

Caldwell even suspended his habitual cynicism about Third World migration to give the most dramatic and detailed account until then of Ayaan's upbringing in Kenya and how she had fled Germany to escape marriage to "a Somali-Canadian cousin she didn't know." If Caldwell ever asked the question of how a runaway bride from Kenya had managed to qualify for political asylum in the Netherlands, the answer didn't figure in his published piece.

"Daughter of the Enlightenment" was a rapturous endorsement, and more than any other single factor it smoothed Ayaan's passage into the upper reaches of America's media and political elite. Within days of the article's appearance, *Time* magazine announced that the hitherto little-known Somali-Dutch politician had landed on its annual list of the hundred most influential people in the world. Soon Ayaan was flying across the Atlantic again, this time not to be bundled off to a suburban hotel but to be honored at a *Time* gala along with other "leaders and revolutionaries," including President George W. Bush, U.S. secretary of state Condoleezza Rice, Israeli prime minister Ariel Sharon, and an up-and-coming U.S. senator named Barack Obama. (Presumably not every "leader and revolutionary" got an invitation. Abu Musab al-Zarqawi was on the list but failed to show.)

Like Cinderella, Ayaan borrowed a gown for the ball. This one was a strapless silver frock designed by the Dutch duo Viktor and Rolf, and it showed off her slim figure and creamy brown skin to spectacular advantage. As she posed for the cameras outside Lincoln Center, the Dutch reporters filming every minute described her performance as "brilliant."

Ayaan's literary agent, Susanna Lea, was in the process of selling the worldwide rights to Ayaan's collection of essays, *The Caged Virgin*, as well as her proposed autobiography. Lea had finally convinced Ayaan that she should give up trying to actually write her book and do what other famous people did: hire a ghostwriter. Armed with this new plan and with the sensational acclaim Ayaan was getting, Lea managed to sell the U.S. rights to both books for a reported $125,000.

Mohammed Bouyeri's trial was still going forward in the Netherlands, and that kept Ayaan in the news. When four Muslim suicide bombers killed fifty-two people on July 7, 2005, in a series of explosions on the London Underground, Ayaan's warnings about the dangers of Europe's Muslim minority seemed—to many people, anyway—vindicated.

Less than a week later, Bouyeri himself boosted her profile even higher. Through most of his trial the young Dutch Moroccan had sat silently in his prayer cap and caftan, rocking back in his chair, the picture of sullen defiance. But when the time came for him to be sentenced, he stood up to announce that he did not regret killing van Gogh and would do it again if given the chance. "I don't feel your pain," Bouyeri coldly told van Gogh's mother. "I don't have any sympathy for you. I can't feel for you because I think you're a non-believer."

That day, even Ayaan's most vociferous Dutch critics had to ask themselves if she might have been right—that there were some aspects of Islam the Dutch Left just didn't want to see.

As the year wore on, and another crisis blew up in Europe, she threw herself onto the frontlines again.

In Denmark the editors of the conservative newspaper *Jyllands-*

Posten decided to test the limits of what they regarded as Danish self-censorship in regard to Islam by publishing a series of cartoons about the Prophet Muhammad. Some of the cartoons appeared to mock the Prophet. And in a familiar pattern, the Muslim Brotherhood and Jamaat-e-Islami seized the chance to energize their base and polarize millions.

After adding a few fake and even more inflammatory cartoons, imams who were linked to the Brotherhood began waving them around the Middle East as proof of Europe's lack of respect for Islam and of the weakness of corrupt Muslim leaders in the face of insults. The ambassadors of Egypt, Saudi Arabia, and other Muslim countries went to the Danish prime minister to complain. The Danish prime minister refused to see them, saying he had no responsibility for the Danish press. Islamist groups began rallying supporters around the Middle East and attacking Danish embassies, businesses, and citizens. The circle of violence widened, and much of it was televised.

Many European intellectuals were torn between seeing the cartoons as a provocation and condemning the attacks on them as stifling free speech. The Netherlands, Great Britain, and other European countries with troops already under attack in Iraq hastened to denounce them as tasteless. Ayaan, however, had no doubt where she stood.

In February 2006, she joined Salman Rushdie and ten other prominent writers in a manifesto condemning Europe for failing to stand up for the Danish cartoonists. Calling an international press conference in Berlin, she declared that freedom of speech must include "the right to offend." She accused her own government, and everyone else who had criticized the cartoons and the Danish government, of being cowards who hid behind excuses involving fairness and responsibility. The truth, she said, was that they were afraid to stand up to Islam. "I wish my prime minister had the Danish prime minister's guts."

David Harris, the executive director of the American Jewish Committee (AJC), was one of many in Washington who were impressed. The AJC was approaching its one hundredth anniversary, and President Bush and other dignitaries would be attending the centennial event. Harris proposed giving Ayaan the group's Moral Courage Award and thus the chance to address this influential convocation.

For months, various think tanks and other groups—including the AJC, the conservative Hudson Institute (where Ayaan's friend Leon de Winter was a fellow), and the American Enterprise Institute—had been promoting the idea that the United States needed to expand its war in Iraq to Iran in order to stop Iran's new president, Mahmoud Ahmadinejad, from developing nuclear weapons. Ayaan had never been to Iran. She had no way of knowing whether it could build such bombs or not. She did know that the growing threats to bomb Iran were already exciting Islamist fantasies about Jewish and American plots to eradicate Islam and oppress the *ummah*. Nevertheless, she decided to use her keynote address to pick up the neoconservative theme and urge the United States to take preemptive military action against a third Muslim country.

Five

To the outside world, Aafia seemed forgotten. Many wondered by the end of 2005 if she was locked in a secret CIA prison. But the silver-haired former head of the weapons of mass destruction unit at the Counterterrorist Center at the CIA, Rolf Mowatt-Larssen, told me after he retired that, far from being under arrest, Aafia remained for him the stuff of nightmares.

Mowatt-Larssen had a special deck of fifty-two playing cards made up. Each carried the face of a suspected terrorist he feared might be planning the next big attack. Aafia was the queen of spades, the only woman in the deck. Mowatt-Larssen wouldn't have put her at the top of his list of potential mass murderers, but he couldn't rule her out. She was his wild card.

As an intelligence officer, Mowatt-Larssen tried to put himself in the place of al-Qaeda's leaders and to think as they would. He believed that they had been close, several times, to obtaining weapons that could have caused huge casualties. In 2003, for example, the CIA heard that al-Qaeda had devised a small handheld weapon that could disperse hydrogen cyanide throughout an enclosed area, killing dozens or even hundreds of people. Al-Qaeda called it the *mubtakkar*, Arabic for "invention." Around the time KSM was captured and Aafia went missing, the United States received information that an al-Qaeda cell in Bahrain had been ready to mount a *mubtakkar* attack on New York City's subways but that Zawahiri had canceled the plan. Why did he cancel? Mowatt-Larssen feared that al-Qaeda's number two had pulled back to work on a more spectacular strike.

The group's biological and chemical weapons expert, an Egyptian named Abu Khabab al-Masri, was still at large.

Mowatt-Larssen believed that if al-Qaeda used Aafia properly, she could be of huge value. His hope was that, whether because she was a woman or because her bossy manner got on the nerves of its male leaders, al-Qaeda wouldn't be able to exploit her full potential.

It wasn't Aafia's prowess as a scientist that worried Mowatt-Larssen the most. The FBI had gone through her records from MIT and Brandeis. She had not taken any notably advanced biology and chemistry courses, and there was no obvious application to jihad in her neuroscience Ph.D. What set her apart in his eyes was her combination of high intelligence (including general scientific know-how), religious zeal, and years of experience in the United States. "So far they have had very few people who have been able to come to the U.S. and thrive," he said. "Aafia is different. She knows about U.S. immigration procedures and visas. She knows how to enroll in American educational institutions. She can open bank accounts and transfer money. She knows how things work here. She could have been very useful to them simply for her understanding of the U.S."

Mowatt-Larssen and his team had not forgotten the documents found in the Qadoos house at the time of KSM's arrest. They had shown that Abu Khabab al-Masri, the Egyptian weapons expert, was ready to produce botulinum, salmonella, and cyanide, and was close to producing anthrax. They believed Aafia had a connection both to the Qadoos family and to Amir Aziz, the Lahore orthopedic surgeon who had been accused of helping al-Qaeda obtain anthrax. They also thought she was better equipped than any of them to be creative in using such poisons against the United States. "She had the imagination to come up with the next 9/11," Mowatt-Larssen said. "The question was whether they would listen to her."

He felt they might take some of her suggestions but might leave her out of the loop when it came to operational planning. He had heard what detainees such as Aafia's second husband, Ali, had said about her. (Alas, the reports of these interrogations are still deeply secret.) Even with the hardest core of al-Qaeda operatives, she had a reputation for being headstrong. "I remember thinking at the time, 'She must drive them crazy,'" Mowatt-Larsson told me. But he couldn't be sure. The CIA had never pinned down her exact role. They just knew that "she was always in the picture. Connections between her and other people the FBI was looking at surfaced in just about every al-Qaeda investigation with a U.S. angle. She was always on our radar."

At the U.S. Embassy in Islamabad, Aafia's name was prominent on a different list, another former official in the Bush administration told me. This was a list of suspected al-Qaeda terrorists whom the U.S. government had authorized the CIA to "kill or capture" on sight. Once again, Aafia wasn't at the top of the list. But she was on it and she stayed there.

Unfortunately from the U.S. point of view, the CIA could not easily operate by itself in Pakistan. Thus, when it came to finding Aafia or anyone else on the list, it usually had to rely on the ISI. And most of the time the ISI gave the Americans nothing. Despite the millions of dollars in rewards that Washington was offering, the ISI seldom, on its own initiative, arrested even foreign al-Qaeda suspects, much less Pakistanis.

So the CIA wasn't surprised that its Pakistani counterparts showed little interest in finding a fellow Pakistani who was also a woman. "Everyone has patrons and protectors," Mowatt-Larssen said. And Aafia, as a female and a member of a respected Deobandi family, was even more sheltered than most from the prying of U.S. investigators.

The Americans tried to escape their dependence on Pakistani intelligence by playing from an American strength: technology. The phones and e-mails of Pakistanis suspected of links to people on the target list were tapped by the National Security Agency. Ismat and Fowzia no doubt fell into that suspect category, as did some senior politicians and generals who the United States believed were shielding militants. The former official in the Bush administration said that if the Americans happened to overhear the whereabouts of one of their targets, they would go to President Musharraf with the information. They would ask him for permission to capture the person and take "lethal action" if they failed to capture him.

But Musharraf didn't always agree. If he didn't want to go along, he might say, and in some cases he might be telling the truth, that the targeted person was actually an ISI asset whom the Pakistanis were using to infiltrate al-Qaeda. (Later it would be widely rumored that the ISI used Aafia to gather information on militant circles.) In that case, the United States refrained from action. In the years before the Americans began using drones to attack suspected militants (and eventually a Navy SEAL team to kill Osama bin Laden) in Pakistan, there was nothing else they could do.

But I have yet to find a source who recalls any such discussion of Aafia. She seemed to have disappeared into thin air.

Six

A Dutch television correspondent named Jos van Dongen read Christopher Caldwell's profile of Ayaan in *The New York Times Magazine* with interest. Van Dongen didn't normally cover Dutch politics, but he had won several awards for his investigative reports on the VARA TV network's *Zembla* program. What caught the lanky Dutchman's attention about "Daughter of Enlightenment" wasn't its laudatory tone—he had no particular opinion about Ayaan—but rather Ayaan's account of having changed her name and birth date on her application for asylum.

Holland's minister of immigration and integration, Rita Verdonk of the Liberal Party, was still directing a government drive to expel 26,000 asylum seekers whose claims had been rejected by the courts. "Iron Rita," as the former prison warden seemed to enjoy being called, had such a strong following with some (mostly working-class) Dutch voters that she was considering a run for party leader.

But her push to expel so many people had already resulted in tragic incidents, such as the deaths of eleven asylum seekers who had been caught in a fire inside an overcrowded detention center at Schiphol Airport. And by early 2006, the case of a Kosovar refugee girl named Taida Pasic had come to symbolize, for many people, its cruelty.

Taida Pasic's family had fled the civil war in Kosovo for the Netherlands when she was nine years old. Years later, she had been on the verge of taking her Dutch high school exams when her family's application for asylum was finally rejected on the grounds that the Kosovo war had ended. Her parents agreed to accept a 7,000-euro settlement and be deported. But, once in Kosovo, young Pasic learned that she would have to start all over again to take a high school diploma. Friends in the Netherlands agreed to let her live with them while she returned to complete her exams at her old school. After trying twice, she failed to get a Dutch visa, so she decided to reenter Holland by other means. She got a tourist visa to France and slipped back into the Netherlands in the fall of 2005.

In January 2006, Pasic was discovered. Dutch immigration police entered the classroom where she and her fellow students were taking their exams and ordered her to accompany them to a detention center. Pasic's schoolmates mounted massive protests, and more than 75,000 people signed a petition asking the government to let her stay long enough to take her exams. But Verdonk branded the girl a fraud and insisted that she be deported for lying on her visa application.

The TV journalist van Dongen had been following Pasic's case. When he read that Ayaan Hirsi Ali, a member of Parliament from Verdonk's own Liberal Party, had lied about her name and her age on her own application for asylum, he saw it as a piece of news.

Van Dongen didn't realize that Ayaan had referred in earlier interviews to lying on her application, nor did he know that many Dutch political insiders knew about her lies but had decided not to make them an issue. What struck him was the hypocrisy of Verdonk and the other Liberals rounding up asylum seekers who had lied to the authorities, when a well-known member of their own party had done the same. So he asked his young producer Sinan Can to look into how Ayaan came to the Netherlands.

Can had his own reasons to be curious about Ayaan's past. His parents were secular Turks who had moved to the Netherlands in the 1970s. Like van Dongen, Can lived in Nijmegen, the same ancient town near the German border where Ayaan's sister, Haweya, had gone to university and descended into madness. Can's parents ran a shop. He had been born in the Netherlands and was the first in his family to go to university. With his burly chest and warm personality, Can was popular with his Dutch neighbors, many of whom had known him since he was a little boy helping out in his parents' store. In the eyes of many Dutch, he was still a Turk, but what the Dutch called a *knuffel* Turk, a "huggable" Turk. Until 9/11 he had felt completely at home in Holland, certainly more so than in Turkey, which he hardly knew. But even for a "new Dutchman" as assimilated as Can, the atmosphere had changed since the rise of Pim Fortuyn, Ayaan, Geert Wilders, and Rita Verdonk.

Can would now sit down on a train, and the Dutch person next to him would take one look at his dark features and move away. He would turn on the television and see someone hammering away about Islam. Whether they were for it or against it, most of what they said struck him as ignorant and shallow, and he was shocked to think that the Dutch would believe such drivel about people like him and his parents.

Apart from Geert Wilders, Can thought Ayaan was the most simplistic of all, and he blamed her more than Wilders because he thought that Ayaan, as an educated Muslim, ought to know better. Her rigid insistence, for example, that Islam virtually required men to oppress women was completely at odds with what his own family's Alevi sect taught. (Turkish Alevis are monogamous; men and women pray together; and women are encouraged to go to school, work, and wear what they like.) Turkey's Sunni fundamentalists persecuted the Alevis for their beliefs, which was one reason the Alevis strongly supported Turkey's secular government. But he felt all this complexity was lost on Ayaan. According to her logic, he supposed, he wasn't even a Muslim. Of course, that wasn't what Dutch employers thought when he went looking for a job, and it wasn't what landlords thought when he wanted to rent an apartment. After listening to politicians such as Ayaan, they might take one look at Can and wonder if he was a terrorist honor killer.

Can's mother had spent decades as a volunteer with their Turkish community organization helping other Muslim families, especially other women, make the transition from Turkey to the Netherlands.

His family had taken girls into their house many times when the girls' families had wanted to control their lives in ways that weren't permissible in the West. His mother would spend hours, sometimes days, shuttling back and forth between the parties to a family quarrel, explaining Dutch mores to the parents and Turkish mores to the daughters.

Now the Dutch seemed to assume, because of what they were hearing from people like Ayaan, that honor was the only thing Muslim parents cared about. Sometimes that was true, but it wasn't *always* true and it probably wasn't true in most cases. Nor was the gritty underside of Dutch society, which the immigrants knew, quite the paradise it seemed to Holland's middle-class commentators. Quite often immigrant parents had good reason to be scared of what might happen to their daughters on the streets of Amsterdam or Rotterdam. Those cities were rife with pimps and drug dealers looking for young girls who didn't know anyone and didn't speak Dutch properly. Yet the quiet and effective work of Muslim women like Can's mother went unrecognized, he felt, while the Dutch listened to loudmouths like Ayaan.

She claimed that she understood the plight of Muslim women because she herself had been the victim of a forced marriage. But when Can began speaking with members of Nijmegen's sizable Somali community, including members of Ayaan's clan and others who had known Haweya, he heard that the story of her marriage that Ayaan told on television was no more factual than the story she had told the government about being a refugee from Somalia's civil war. Those Somalis claimed to have heard that instead Ayaan had tricked a Canadian stranger into marrying her, used his money to pay her way to Europe, and then dumped him when she had received asylum in Holland.

Can knew better than to believe everything such gossips said. They had an ax to grind against Ayaan. But as he began to dig, he found other problems with Ayaan's account of running away from a forced marriage to a stranger.

She had claimed that she had changed her name and age because she feared her family would track her down. But when Can looked into it, neither the social workers at Lunteren nor her Dutch foster family remembered her saying anything while she was there about being afraid of her family. They remembered her getting letters from her father and visits from other relatives. One person recalled her being interviewed by the Dutch Muslim television network. Can went through the network's archives and found the footage of Ayaan giving the reporter a tour of the refugee center. If she had been hiding from her family, he wondered, would she have gone on TV?

When Can examined the timing and circumstances of her asylum application, he noticed another possible reason for her to change her name and birthday. Only a few weeks before Ayaan first arrived in the Netherlands, Dutch newspapers reported that the government had started sending back Somali applicants who already had refugee status in Kenya. Can wondered if Ayaan had altered her name not to hide from her family but to conceal her real identity from the Dutch authorities, who would have deported her.

Another puzzle in her story, Can felt, was the way Ayaan had gone straight to her aunt's house as soon as she arrived. Would she have done that if she had feared her family? That wasn't the way Turkish girls behaved when they felt at risk of being hurt or killed to preserve their family's honor. Ayaan's story didn't add up.

Can talked it over with van Dongen. To get to the bottom of things, the two journalists agreed, van Dongen would have to go to Africa and find Ayaan's mother and brother.

Seven

In the shadows that enveloped Aafia's case, one little ray of light gleamed. Everyone else who was said to have been involved in KSM's plot to turn American gas stations into giant torches had vanished into "the dark side," but young Uzair Paracha had been in the United States when the authorities tracked him down. The hapless twenty-three-year-old Pakistani thus became the only overseas resident charged with furthering the plot, and in the fall of 2005, actually tried in a court of law. I flew to New York beforehand to see what I could learn about why the United States wanted Aafia so badly.

The Justice Department had attempted to avoid a trial. Defendants in a U.S. courtroom have the right to face their accusers and other witnesses. That meant that Uzair's lawyers wanted to put Majid Khan, Ali Abdul Aziz Ali, KSM, and Uzair's father, Saifullah Paracha, on the witness stand to testify that when Uzair had met them, he'd had no idea who they were or what they were plotting—and that he had agreed to mislead the INS simply because his father had asked him to. But the United States at that point still refused to admit it was holding KSM, Ali, and Majid Khan, and it later emerged that all three men claimed to have confessed to the plot only after being tortured. Such extralegal oddities put prosecutors into a bind.

Uzair's lawyers advised him to seize the opportunity and plead guilty. If convicted of all the charges against him, he faced seventy-five years in prison. His lawyer thought a guilty plea might reduce the sentence to ten years, less time already served.

But the lawyer couldn't persuade Uzair to take his advice. Having never been in legal trouble before, the young Pakistani evidently couldn't believe he might be locked away forever because he had lied in a single phone call to the INS. "He is a bright, handsome young man, but he has no real-life experience and no experience of the criminal justice system," his lawyer told me. "He doesn't really understand what he's up against." Finally a judge ruled that the government must provide Uzair's defense with witness statements from Majid Khan and Ali. It did not allow for the face-to-face cross-examination before a jury that Uzair's lawyers believed the U.S. Constitution required, but it was the first time a U.S. court was allowed to hear testimony from prisoners in the bowels of the CIA's secret prisons.

Once in court, Uzair recanted everything he had told the FBI. Majid Khan and Ali backed him up in their witness statements, saying they had never told him they belonged to al-Qaeda and hadn't tried to recruit him because they weren't sure of his sympathies. But the New York jury didn't believe them. And one piece of evidence it held against Uzair was his association with Aafia.

Witnesses testified that he had been found with the key and the receipt to the post office box that she had opened in Maryland. And an FBI agent testified that Uzair had told them he believed Aafia was the kind of person who might help launch an anthrax attack.

The jury didn't care that Uzair had never laid eyes on Aafia. In the end, it convicted him of providing material support to terrorism, and, on July 20, 2006, he was sentenced to thirty years in federal prison.

Eight

In the last week of April 2006, Jos van Dongen phoned Ayaan in The Hague with the news that *Zembla* was making a documentary about her. Van Dongen told her that he had just been to Kenya and Somalia, where he had interviewed members of her family. He asked if he could show her his footage and ask her about her early life.

Ayaan didn't know van Dongen, but she sounded surprised and pleased. She chided him for not having called her before he left for Africa; she would have put him into touch with more people. They agreed to meet at her parliamentary office on April 27.

She was in for an unpleasant surprise. Ever since Neelie Kroes, the doyenne of the Liberal Party, had given Elma Verhey of *Vrij Nederland* her televised dressing-down in 2002 for reporting that a police official and some Somalis thought Ayaan had exaggerated the threats against her, few journalists had interviewed any Somalis about Ayaan. Even fewer had inquired into how she had arrived in the Netherlands. Meanwhile, Ayaan had avoided reporters who might conceivably be skeptical.

For example, soon after I committed to write this book, in 2005, I wrote Ayaan's agent, Susanna Lea, an enthusiastic letter asking for an interview. I attached my book proposal and mentioned that I also had an assignment to write an article about Ayaan for *Vogue*. Thinking my serious interest would impress Ayaan favorably, I added that I'd be glad to go to Africa to interview her family, having spent time in Somalia during the civil war there and having written another book about Africa. But I never got a reply to my letter. Perhaps my interest in Africa wasn't the reason. Ayaan may have disliked two short articles I had written about her for other magazines. In any case, something made her stay away. Even after I moved to Amsterdam at the end of 2005, Ayaan adamantly refused to be interviewed by me.

A Somali-born reporter for the BBC, Rageh Omaar, also wanted to interview her. Omaar was a polished product of Cheltenham College and Oxford University, and he came from a family known to Ayaan as political liberals. His feminist sister Rakiya Omaar had helped found the original Africa desk at Human Rights Watch. But on a flying visit by Ayaan to England the previous November, when at least four other national British radio and TV programs had interviewed her, Ayaan had refused to see Rageh Omaar.

By the spring of 2006, Ayaan seemed to have grown so comfortable with the tale of her escape from a forced marriage that she may have forgotten that other people remembered the same events differently.

For months she had been spinning out the story of her life for the British ghostwriter who was weaving it into an inspiring account of female liberation, thanks to the West. (In one interview in New York, which was filmed, Ayaan sat on a couch while the ghostwriter questioned her about how her grandmother had seen the world. "Was the world flat for your grandmother? Was that how she saw the cosmos?") Thinking the ghostwriter might want to see van Dongen's footage of people and places in Africa that the two of them had talked about, Ayaan brought the writer along to the meeting with him.

Van Dongen began by telling Ayaan that he had found her brother, Mahad, and even traveled to the remote desert town in Somalia where her mother lived. He said he had asked them and other relatives about the circumstances of her marriage and arrival in the Netherlands. Ayaan seemed touched by his film from her primary school, but as he began to confront her with the statements of her family members, her expression turned worried and her answers became hesitant and evasive.

She had told several previous interviewers that she had refused to attend her own wedding. Van Dongen asked her why, if so, her brother, Mahad, said she had been there, and her aunt Faduma Osman had said the same thing. Ayaan answered that they were lying.

Next van Dongen asked her why she had told other interviewers that she feared her family. He showed Ayaan some film of her brother saying that he was proud of her for being elected to Parliament and he still hoped she might get him a visa to the West. Then the film showed Ayaan's mother refusing to talk to the Dutch reporter and producer on the grounds that she didn't want to take the chance of saying anything that might harm Ayaan's political career. Her relatives appeared to be proud and protective of her.

Ayaan said none of that mattered. She maintained that she had been afraid of her family and that the reason she had changed her name and birthday was to hide from them—rather than to conceal the fact that she already had refugee status in Kenya. But, possibly for the first time since she had arrived in the Netherlands, Ayaan faced an interviewer who was clearly dubious about what she had to say.

"You believed you were at *physical risk* of getting killed by your family?" van Dongen asked.

"I don't know. You are putting words in my mouth," Ayaan snapped.

"No, I'm asking a question," van Dongen snapped back. "Let's get down to it. What were you afraid of when you ran away from your family?"

"I never said I was afraid of honor killing."

"What were you afraid of, then?"

"Look, I could go to this man and do what my father wants me to do. Or I could run away and start a new life for myself. I knew I was paying a price for this. My family would be very angry at me."

Van Dongen looked at her. "But that's totally different," he said slowly, "from being physically threatened."

"But just think, my father would be very, very angry . . . " Ayaan insisted.

Then van Dongen informed her that he had tracked down not only her brother and her aunt but also her Canadian ex-husband.

The ex-husband, Osman Musse Quarre, had refused to go on camera. (Perhaps he, too, feared being charged with immigration fraud if he admitted he had tried to bring a woman into Canada illegally.) Off camera, however, he not only said that Ayaan had been at the wedding but that they had known each other for about five weeks before they were married. Osman also said that he had thought Ayaan liked him very much and wanted to marry him. Van Dongen said to Ayaan about his conversation with Osman, "He told me, 'Why would I want to marry a woman who didn't want me?'"

Ayaan denied it, her eyes blazing. "He—how can he say I have known him for five weeks?" she burst out. "He went to a man who has five daughters and said, 'I want one of your daughters,' and my father said, 'You get this one.'" But she went quiet again when the Dutchman told her that Osman also said she had written to him after she arrived in the Netherlands and had telephoned him and that he had visited her there before they finally broke up. None of that had featured in her story as she had told it before.

"Yes, I did that," she said.

The scuffle over Ayaan's marriage ended in a bit of a draw. She had been forced to concede she had known Osman before she married him, and she had admitted she had been in no physical danger from her family or anyone else when she sought asylum in the Netherlands. Yet she continued to insist that her father had forced her to marry the Canadian and that she had taken a terrible risk in running away.

From Ayaan's point of view, she was probably telling the emotional truth when she said that gaining asylum had saved her life. There's no doubt that if she had failed to seize the chance to escape the bonds of family and clan, she could never have become the individual she became. Yet she was too intelligent not to realize that the emotionally and factually muddy account that van Dongen had extracted from her was a far cry from the romantic tale she had told Christopher Caldwell and many other Westerners about narrowly escaping clan minders to avoid a lifetime of servitude to a man she had never met.

Then van Dongen asked another hard question: The Kosovar high school girl Taida Pasic was due to be deported the very next day for lying on her visa application. Wasn't there something wrong with the fact that the Liberals were trying to expel Pasic while Ayaan herself was allowed to stay?

Ayaan stammered that she hadn't supported Pasic's deportation and that she opposed the whole Liberal expulsion program. In fact, Ayaan said, she had phoned Verdonk and asked her to reverse her decision on Pasic. "But Rita," Ayaan recalled pleading, "almost all asylum seekers lie. That's how the system is. I lied, too." But Ayaan told van Dongen that Verdonk had replied, "If I had been the minister when you applied for asylum, I would have deported you, too." (Verdonk later said she had had no such conversation with Ayaan.)

Ayaan knew, after the interview, that the *Zembla* program wouldn't look good.

Later that same day, she received another piece of bad news. In an unexpected ruling, an appeals court had decided that the Dutch government had been wrong to move her and her security detail into her Hague apartment building without first consulting the other residents. She was now being given until the end of August to leave the premises.

Those nasty developments couldn't be coming at a worse time. Ayaan was leaving for New York the next day. The English translation of her book *The Caged Virgin* was being published in the United States. She was scheduled to give her big speech at the American Jewish Committee in a week's time, and her publisher, like much of the neoconservative establishment, was counting on her to make a good impression.

She was already talking quietly with the American Enterprise Institute about becoming one of its fellows. She was planning to meet with the institute's selection committee in Washington. It was no time for her to stumble.

Nine

Where was Aafia? Only later did court documents reveal parts of what she told the FBI about how she spent those missing years.

She said that in 2004 or 2005, she had secured a small apartment in Karachi's wealthiest area, the Defense/Clifton neighborhood. "It was a safe building and she was on the third floor," an FBI agent noted in an investigation report. She had supported herself, she said, by working as a lab technician at the Karachi Institute of Technology. (It's not clear what this institute was, but that is the name she gave the FBI.)

She also said she had met with Mufti Abu Lubaba Shah Mansoor—whom she called Abu Lubaba—and with an imam named Abdus Sattar at a nearby mosque. Aafia didn't name the mosque, but during that period Abu Lubaba served as an imam at Jamia Islamia Clifton, a seminary in the same neighborhood.

Abu Lubaba was then writing a column, as he still does, for the al-Rashid newspaper, *Zarb-e-Momin*. Every week he fills its pages with fevered warnings about the diabolical international conspiracy subverting Islam and bringing the religion to its knees. He writes of Jews, Hindus, Freemasons, the Illuminati, and the United Nations—some of whom use "brain transmitters" to send "Satanic whispers" to believers. He attacks Sufi "grave-worshipers" and clerics who interpret Islam more liberally than he does. His articles are often illustrated with weird symbols: evil eyes and blood-drenched American eagles pecking open the globe to extract dollars; Masonic pyramids and space weapons. But Abu Lubaba is known best for his popular apocalyptic books about the ongoing confrontation between the forces of good and those of the Dajjal, and the coming reign of the Mahdi. The title of one of those Internet bestsellers is *Dajjal: Who, What, When, Where.*

Aafia described Abu Lubaba as "a fat man," and in a single fuzzy photo on the Internet he does look pale and obese—rather like his protégé the Jaish-e-Muhammad leader, Maulana Masood Azhar—with small brown eyes and a patchy brown beard beneath a white turban.

He comes across in his writings as a paranoid figure whose nearly incoherent accusations about secret plots give fresh meaning to the concept of psychological projection. He accuses an array of enemies—Zionists, Crusaders, India, Russia, Israel, the United States, and the "deviant" Muslim sects to which most Muslims belong—of pursuing schemes to bring about the apocalypse. Yet the reverent accolades of his former students, who have translated *Dajjal* and posted it on the Internet, make it clear that many Pakistanis at home and abroad greatly respect Mufti Abu Lubaba Shah Mansoor. On one Internet forum a former student described him as "a nice down to earth guy. A mufti you can chill with." "His books go down like a box of popcorn," wrote another admirer.

Aafia told the FBI that Abu Lubaba had convinced her that Pakistan was about to come under attack from the United States and she had a religious duty to help him develop defenses. He wanted her to make "a biological agent for him to keep them safe from the enemies of Islam," according to an FBI note from a 2008 conversation with Aafia. He also promised to arrange for her to get the means to make it.

At Abu Lubaba's request, she said, she had collected materials on viruses and provided Abu Lubaba and Abdus Sattar with the results. One of her projects involved finding a way to infect America's poultry supplies with an antibody that would allow chickens to pass salmonella on to humans more easily. Another was to alter viruses so they would kill only members of "certain ethnic groups" or only adults and not children. She also said she provided them with a small amount of a mysterious substance "which would be used to scare people."

Perhaps the coconspirators' paranoia had fed on itself, for Aafia told the FBI that she had come to suspect Abu Lubaba and Abdus Sattar of luring her into the research "so that they could inform the United States that she was involved in bad things for a large monetary reward." She said she had demanded that Abdus Sattar return the papers and other research materials she had given them. At first he refused, but after a few days, he gave them back. Aafia said she had burned most of the documents, as well as the laptop computer she had used to store them. She kept just a few papers and a thumb drive that she carried with her.

She said that to get away from Abu Lubaba she eventually left the apartment in Clifton and went to live in the servants' quarters of a small house in Karachi's Nazimabad district. "She lied to the occupants of the house," the FBI report notes, "telling them that she was hiding from family members that were giving her a hard time due to her divorce."

But court documents and her statements to the FBI suggest that Pakistan's intelligence agents knew where she was. Among the papers found on her in 2008 was an undated letter, apparently to a well-known Pakistani personality whose name was omitted from the translation provided to the court, in which she volunteered to help "think of ways to rid our nation of the 'superpower' bent on destroying us." She described herself as "a Western-raised and educated Pakistani (NOT American) doctor/scientist who is wanted by our enemies for the crime of wanting to serve Pakistan and protect its innocent citizens' lives, properties, and cherished values." She also wrote, "Since my whereabouts are known and activities are closely monitored by various agencies, I guess if Pakistan really needs any cooperation from me, they can contact me—that is, if they still left me around to be of help and not arrested me or handed me over—(Allah forbid!)."

For the time being, however, no one seems to have bothered her.

Ten

Ayaan's first Sunday in New York got off to what seemed a promising start. Philip Gourevitch of *The New Yorker* interviewed her for the PEN World Voices Festival of International Literature. The event was a bit of a lovefest. Ayaan used the occasion, at the New York Public Library, to apologize to Salman Rushdie, who was in the audience, for having wanted to kill him when she was a teenager. Gourevitch seemed quite charmed.

But in a tactic that would become all too familiar among Ayaan's most aggressive supporters, the *New York Sun*, a right-wing newspaper partly owned by Bruce Kovner, the chairman of the American Enterprise Institute, used a May 3 profile of Ayaan to launch a surprise attack on Gourevitch and U.S. liberals in general.

Using a tone that echoed Ayaan's Dutch followers who had charged "multiculturalists" with failing to honor and protect her, the *Sun*'s Brendan Bernhard accused the polite Gourevitch and the head of the PEN American Center, Ron Chernow, of being "ungracious." Ayaan, Bernhard claimed, represented a "problem for liberal intellectuals" because she "refused to have a 'victim' label pinned to her lapel." (The truth was surely the other way around: if Ayaan had *not* become famous as a victim of radical Islam, her book *The Caged Virgin*, a thin patchwork of heavily edited opinion pieces written for Dutch newspapers and magazines, would never have been published in the U.S., nor would Ayaan have been invited to speak at the festival.) Bernhard also criticized Gourevitch for having insufficient admiration for Ayaan, complaining that Gourevitch "didn't put her in the dock, exactly, but he didn't put her on the pedestal either."

This profile set the partisan and combative mood in which Ayaan received the Moral Courage Award at the American Jewish Committee's hundredth anniversary gala. On hand to hear her acceptance speech were President Bush, UN secretary-general Kofi Annan, German chancellor Angela Merkel, most of the U.S. Congress, and many other notables. Merkel had made her trip partly to confer with Bush about a common strategy for dealing with Iran's newly elected president, Mahmoud Ahmadinejad. Ayaan's speech seemed calculated to reach exactly the right audience.

With their playful slogan "Anyone can go to Baghdad. Real men go to Tehran," some of AEI's conservative ideologues made no secret of their desire to force a regime change in Iran. In the weeks leading up to the dinner, the AJC and other pro-Israeli groups ran full-page ads in American newspapers warning that Ahmadinejad's efforts to build nuclear weapons posed an intolerable threat. "Suppose Iran one day gives nuclear devices to terrorists," the AJC ad said. "Could anyone anywhere feel safe?"

Ayaan began her speech in her usual dramatic fashion: "Ladies and gentlemen, I have a confession to make if you are Jewish. It is a testimony from my dark past, when I lived in ignorance." She paused, then said, "I used to hate you."

Without ever mentioning Israel, she confessed to having believed a frightening litany of anti-Semitic canards before she learned better. "I didn't need proof," Ayaan told the audience. "You are by nature evil and you had evil powers and you used them to evil ends." She went on to warn that "thousands and perhaps millions are learning to blame you and to want to destroy you."

Finally, she asserted that the West had two choices: a war against Iran while it still lacked nuclear weapons or a war against a nuclear-armed Iran. She predicted that if the West failed to go to war against Iranian president Amadinejad before he got the bomb, he would launch a new Holocaust.

Evoking the memory of World War II, she said, "For me the lesson of that war is 'Never appease evil.' May our elected leaders have the courage to make the right choice."

Bush and the rest of the crowd gave her a thunderous ovation.

Five days before that anniversary dinner, Ayaan had shared a podium with Vice President Dick Cheney. The occasion was a conference in Philadelphia in honor of Professor Bernard Lewis's ninetieth birthday, and the room was full of notables from the AEI. Cheney was reported to be highly impressed by this brave young Somali, who was almost the same age as his daughter Liz, then deputy secretary of state for Near Eastern affairs. Ayaan also impressed Cheney's friend, the AEI chairman, Bruce Kovner. *Forbes* magazine listed Kovner as the ninety-third richest man in the world. In his quiet way, he played a significant role in shaping the neoconservative agenda.

Ayaan later said that she had told AEI's selection committee that she was an atheist with "a big mouth" and planned to make a sequel to "Submission" focusing on Islam's condemnation of homosexuality. "No problem," she quoted AEI's president, Christopher DeMuth, as saying—though some of the anti-gay Islamic attitudes she planned to criticize weren't very different from those of some conservative Republicans. As her AJC speech indicated, Ayaan had already joined the AEI choir on matters of more importance to the organization.

DeMuth invited her to become an AEI fellow in the fall.

Much as she enjoyed the accolades, she had to have been slightly worried. She knew the *Zembla* program was going to air soon. Perhaps to prepare the ground, she began suggesting to American interviewers that the Dutch were trying to get rid of her because they were too spineless to protect her from her enemies.

The British-born writer Christopher Hitchens was the first to advance this line of attack. In an article headlined "The Caged Virgin: Holland's Shameful Treatment of Ayaan Hirsi Ali," which appeared on May 8 in *Slate*, Hitchens noted Ayaan's "arresting and hypnotizing beauty" and gave a capsule account of how she had fled to Holland "after being nearly handed over as a bargain to a stranger." He then announced the "grave and sad news" that Ayaan was thinking of resigning from Parliament and leaving the Netherlands. Hinting that the Dutch were closet racists, Hitchens wrote that "after being forced into hiding by fascist killers, Ayaan found out the Dutch government and people were slightly embarrassed to have such a prominent 'Third World' spokeswoman in their midst." He said that the Dutch court's decision to evict her from her apartment had convinced her to think about leaving.

Zembla's documentary, "The Holy Ayaan," aired three days later.

Ayaan's brother, aunt, and ex-husband Osman Musse Quarre, all said on the program that far from being forced to marry, Ayaan had seemed happy to do it. Osman had thought that Ayaan loved him. But once he had paid for her tickets and "papers" to get to Europe, she had failed to continue on to Canada. He had gone to Holland, looking for her. When she'd told him that she didn't want to go to Canada with him, he had left peaceably. "Without me, Ayaan wouldn't have reached the Netherlands," Osman said. "She used me. But I'm not angry. It's something between her and her God."

The program suggested that Ayaan had lied not because she feared her family but because she feared the Dutch authorities might discover she already had refugee status in Kenya. But why, asked the *Zembla* team—if the lies of eighteen-year-old Taida Pasic had resulted in her deportation—had those of Ayaan been accepted?

Minutes after the broadcast ended, viewers began venting on the Internet.

"Just watched an interesting report on the *Zembla* news show about everyone's favourite asylum seeker Ayaan Hirsi Ali," wrote a blogger who started a thread on the Expatica Web site that drew hundreds of comments. "A journalist investigated her story about why she sought asylum in the Netherlands in 1992 and found she made up a lot of it. . . . Now she's MP of a party that is turning back asylum seekers. Nice. Looking at Hirsi Ali try to answer the questions she reminded me of a bold child caught out in one lie after the next."

"The asylum process in the rich countries actively encourages people to take a shot at lying to get in," another blogger countered. "How else are they going to get in? If you were a third worlder desperate to have a better life in the first world, wouldn't you take a shot at it?"

"I can't see how she can look herself in the mirror knowing that she supports policies that reject people with more claim to be here than she does," a woman wrote next. "What an incredible sense of entitlement this woman has. I can walk all over everybody and lie to get what I want, but don't you dare try the same thing."

"Iron Rita" Verdonk was in the middle of her fight to take over the Liberal Party, and she hoped to become prime minister in the country's next elections. At first the immigration minister said she didn't expect the *Zembla* broadcast to have any legal consequences. But the day after the documentary aired, an attorney from the Dutch Association for Asylum Lawyers told reporters that Verdonk was mistaken. Under the naturalization law the Liberals had helped pass in 2003, he said, asylum seekers who were found to have lied on their applications were being stripped of their citizenship. The lawyer's group planned to use Ayaan's case as evidence that "two different standards were being applied" to the MP and to other former asylum seekers.

The following day, Verdonk announced that she was ordering an investigation. But before it could start, another immigration lawyer stepped forward. He said that an investigation was superfluous. If Ayaan admitted she had lied on her application for asylum, the asylum status that she had been granted in 1992 was simply invalid. Without that status, her citizenship was also invalid. Ayaan was not Dutch, the lawyer claimed, and never had been.

To the astonishment and consternation of the whole country, Verdonk came back with a verdict almost instantly. The lawyer was correct. Pending further notice, Ayaan, who had returned to Holland from the United States a few days earlier, must surrender her Dutch passport.

Ayaan gave a tearful press conference the next day at the Binnenhof, which I attended. She was dressed in black and white with her hair pulled back severely, and she looked exhausted. Announcing that she was moving to the United States, she resigned from Parliament.

Many intellectuals and politicians found the spectacle of her being hounded out of the country by her own party shockingly like a witch hunt. And in one of the amazing reversals that have marked Ayaan's career, some of the same people who had been her fiercest critics joined forces with her friends to decry the way she was being treated.

Five million television viewers, nearly a third of the country, tuned in to a parliamentary debate that began that night and lasted almost until morning. From Ayaan's own political party, Verdonk paced the floor while opposition politicians such as the Green Left leader, Femke Halsema, subjected her to a withering assault. Where exactly was Verdonk planning to send Hirsi Ali now that she had taken away her passport? Back to Kenya? If she hadn't been in danger from Muslims there in 1992, she certainly was now. Didn't the Dutch state have a responsibility to protect her?

Verdonk was forced to relent. Ayaan got her citizenship back, and later in the summer the whole government fell after one of the smaller parties quit the ruling coalition in protest over Ayaan's treatment.

Yet Ayaan refused the calls of those who urged her to stay and help overturn the naturalization law that now threatened the citizenship of thousands of former asylum seekers who had also lied, including most of the Somalis still left in the country. "We begged her friends and her," the historian Geert Mak recalled with some bitterness: "help to save the others, the poor Iraqis and Afghans who don't have the benefit of her celebrity. She wouldn't. As usual, it was only about Ayaan."

Instead, she made plans to move to Washington, where Christopher DeMuth had written her in an open letter that he looked forward to welcoming her to "AEI and America."

Ayaan could see the writing on the wall even if she hadn't wanted to leave Holland. Many of the same politicians now making speeches about how sad her departure would be had been text-messaging one another congratulations since they'd heard the news. They wanted her gone. Polls showed that most of the Dutch public agreed.

What caused such fury at the woman they had lauded a year earlier as Holland's Joan of Arc?

Ayaan's supporters, especially overseas, tried to argue that the timorous, penny-pinching, lily-white Dutch taxpayers had gotten tired of protecting a troublemaking black woman.

It was true that she had made trouble; even her own party had never fully accepted her. But I came to think, and I was living in Holland then, that the real problem was the unflattering mirror the *Zembla* program held up to the Dutch themselves. Ayaan's story had previously struck the country as a fairy tale in which the Netherlands played the knight in shining armor. But *Zembla*'s "Holy Ayaan" cast them very differently. According to *Zembla*, the Dutch hadn't rescued a princess—they had been played for suckers. As a widely reprinted cartoon put it, Ayaan had used Holland as a stepping-stone to the United States, just as she'd used Osman Musse Quarre to get to Holland. She had been laughing all the way to *Time* magazine's gala.

But there was also something darker about the way they cast her out.

"The Netherlands is under the spell of Ayaan," were the ominous first words of "The Holy Ayaan." To many of the Dutch, bewildered and even frightened by what seemed a national personality change, the word "spell" had the ring of truth. Ayaan hadn't said anything about Islam that the country's other "Islam critics" hadn't also said. But amid the drama of van Gogh's murder she had an uncanny ability to conjure up the public's fears and anxieties. Of course, that changed rapidly when the Dutch began to see her as a clever foreigner on the make. Once she no longer seemed a victim, the embarrassed Dutch felt like pushing her out.

What's more, the sun really *did* seem to shine again after the passage of "Hurricane Ayaan," as a Dutch book called the crisis. For a while, a sullen mood lingered like a hangover. But before long the country's divided intellectuals began speaking to one another again, and the pages of newspapers that for months had been filled with arguments for, against, and about Muslims slowly gave way to articles about art exhibits, problems in the pension system, and whatever the royal family was doing. For at least a little while, it seemed as though "the fever had broken," as Geert Mak said.

Or, as a Somali might have put it, the cows had rid themselves of the leopard.

Eleven

Yvonne Ridley was another ambiguous figure thrown up by the war on terror. A former reporter for the *Sunday Express* in London, Ridley had converted to Islam after the Taliban took her prisoner in 2001. Once freed, she went on to become a star presenter for Britain's Islam Channel. I wanted to meet her because of a program she had made about Aafia Siddiqui a few months earlier. And so, on the first anniversary of the 7/7 bombings, I went to London to hear her talk at the IslamExpo about how she had become a Muslim.

Even in her previous incarnation as a left-wing journalist, Ridley had been a strident critic of Israel, the United States, and Great Britain. One thing that seemed to attract her to Islamism was its stance against the West. "How can anyone be proud to be British?" she asked in a 2006 article. "Britain is the third most hated country in the world." Now she traveled the world decrying the war on terror and extolling the "Islamic resistance."

Ridley wrapped herself in turbans and long skirts and punctuated her sentences with invocations to Allah. She still described herself as a feminist, saying that the difference between Muslim and secular feminists was that "Muslim feminists are more radical." But she had no time for Iranian women who complained about the Iranian regime's treatment of females. "I know the hijab is a pain for them, but they will get no sympathy from me. It is clear that hijab is an obligation, not a choice." Her speeches attracted thousands. IslamOnline, a Web site linked to the Muslim Brotherhood, had voted her the world's most recognizable Muslim woman.

Ridley was also a patron of Cageprisoners, a slick British advocacy group, founded in 2003, for Muslim prisoners in the war on terror. Although Cageprisoners claimed to be a human rights organization, it seemed to regard any jihadi imprisoned in the West as unjustly imprisoned, and some of its volunteers claimed that the Universal Declaration of Human Rights was part of a Zionist plot. Since the Bush administration, however, still maintained that the war on terror existed in its own law-free universe, Cageprisoners' demands for justice struck many observers as relatively reasonable. Western officials accused Ridley of being more of a propagandist than an investigator, but, thanks to her Islamist sources, she often scooped the Western media when it came to reporting on the war.

The show that Ridley had produced on Aafia for the Islam Channel was in honor of "Torture Week." Making much of the repetitive reports in the Pakistani press that Aafia had been arrested in 2003, the show suggested that a bungling FBI had mistaken her for a terrorist and that either the U.S. or Pakistani government could be holding her and her children. Cageprisoners had sent a researcher named Asim Qureshi to Karachi to interview her family, but the family had refused to come to the door. Qureshi said on Ridley's program that he had found a guard outside the gate. He concluded that Aafia's mother was under house arrest, and he thought it likely that Aafia had died in "ghost detention." "To be honest," he told me when I called him later, "if the ISI pick you up, after this length of time, there's not much chance of coming back."

The star of "Torture Week" was Moazzam Begg, a British prisoner released from Guantánamo the year before and now the author, with a former editor of the *Guardian*, of a bestselling memoir, *Enemy Combatant*. Begg had written in his book that while he was a prisoner at Bagram, he had heard the screams of a woman he thought at first was his wife. He said his interrogators later suggested that the screams came from a tape recording designed to terrify him. But Ridley said the screams might be evidence that the CIA was holding women in its prisons.

Pale and freckled, she appeared at IslamExpo in a dark green suit with a long skirt and a pink blouse, a fashionably tied scarf on her head. She warmed up the mostly female crowd for her talk "A Woman's Journey to Islam" by insisting that it was wrong for the British media to focus on such issues as honor killings and female genital mutilation. "These are issues that are not specific to Islam, that have nothing to do with Islam." For her, as for many other Western women, the biggest obstacle to accepting Islam had been the "mantra" she'd heard all her life that the religion oppressed women. But as a Taliban prisoner she had promised her captors that, if they would only let her go, she would read the Quran and study Islam—and when she did, "I realized I had been lied to." After that, Ridley said, "I embraced what I consider to be the biggest and the best family in the world." Her audience liked it.

I went up afterward and introduced myself. Ridley brightened when she heard I was writing a book about Aafia. She said she had never had such a lively response to a program as the one she had gotten to her show on Aafia. Viewers had flooded her with calls and e-mails asking to know more. Clearly the story of the missing scientist and her three children had struck a chord that the stories of seemingly hardened male jihadis did not. Ridley wanted to do another program about Aafia. But with Aafia's family refusing to talk and no new information available, she seemed as stymied as I was. She asked if I wanted to go on the show and talk about what I knew. I told her I doubted that there was much that I could add, but we agreed to stay in touch.

Twelve

America's neocons turned out in force to welcome Ayaan to Washington in the fall of 2006. Her steely optimism reminded some of another conservative icon, Great Britain's Margaret Thatcher. It wasn't the best of times for Republicans; many were beginning to worry that their war on terror was being lost, first on the streets of Iraq and second in the U.S. courts. Ayaan's fighting spirit felt like a tonic. And the fact she had nearly lost her Dutch citizenship didn't bother them at all.

One of the favorite neoconservative maxims, as Robert Kagan wrote in his bestselling book *Of Paradise and Power,* was "Americans are from Mars and Europeans are from Venus." In other words, Americans were manly and martial while Europeans were timid and effete. Viewing Dutch politics through this lens, the neocons were ready to interpret Ayaan's disgrace as another case of the weak-kneed, left-leaning Europeans bowing to Muslim pressure. They accepted her explanation that left-wing Dutch political enemies had concocted the *Zembla* documentary as a way to get rid of her. It didn't surprise them that this beautiful, threatened woman had turned to them for safety.

Actually, Ayaan was still being protected by Dutch diplomatic security, a situation that heightened her aura of danger and importance. American and British interviewers often wrote of the cloak-and-dagger security measures involved in meeting her: the coded telephone messages from Dutch security informing them, "I have a person to deliver to you"; the squealing tires of the bulletproof convoy that delivered her to restaurants and clubs; the hulking bodyguards who fanned out around her.

Just as in Holland, correspondents who did manage to talk with Ayaan were struck by the contrast between her vulnerable femininity and the ferocity she aroused and sometimes displayed. Numerous articles commented on how soft her voice was; how she liked to take off her shoes and tuck her feet up under her legs; how she would suddenly look away and then wrap herself closely in the shawls she often wore, as if startled by a chill premonition. She often told interviewers about the book she planned to write at AEI, *Shortcut to Enlightenment*. It was to feature the Prophet Muhammad waking up at the New York Public Library and debating three of her favorite Western philosophers, Friedrich Hayek, John Stuart Mill, and Karl Popper. White, conservative men were especially taken by the idea.

George Will dined with her in a Georgetown restaurant while her security detail prowled outside. She ate steak tartare. Bowled over by what he saw as Ayaan's courage and the breadth of her intellectual ambitions, Will could not condemn the Dutch strongly enough. He wrote in a column that "the recoil of many Dutch people from Hirsi Ali suggests that the tolerance about which Holland preens is a compound of intellectual sloth and moral timidity." Ayaan told Will that the problem with the Europeans was that, after two generations without war, they had become prissy invertebrates who "have no idea what an enemy is." "I can hardly tell it without laughing," she said of the belief that some Dutch held that, with patience and understanding, their government would eventually bring their Muslim population into the mainstream.

Ayaan's most influential American fans, the neoconservatives, probably acted more like a Somali clan than the Dutch Liberal Party she had once criticized for its clannishness. Many neoconservatives were Jewish intellectuals who had shifted rightward after an earlier background in Marxism or mainstream American liberalism. Some of their leading families had married and socialized with one another in the Washington suburbs, and they had raised their children to assume important positions in their own small but distinctive political movement. Prominent neocons were often literally related, and they made it their fiercely partisan duty to defend one another, whether on the op-ed pages or in backroom politics.

They combined internationalism and a fascination with military power, and they considered the United States a global force for good. They wanted it to act unilaterally if need be. They had no patience for international law or the United Nations, and they despised "multiculturalism," which they saw as anti-Western, shallow, hypocritical, and worse. While the Cold War lasted, many neocons still belonged to the Democratic Party. Yet even then they felt deeply at odds with various Democratic currents and politicians, and they exhorted their fellows to support President Ronald Reagan's military buildup against the Soviet Union. When the Cold War ended, many prominent neocons switched to the Republicans.

They saw a powerful new threat in the Middle East, arguing tirelessly that the United States needed to dominate the region to protect Israel, Western oil supplies, democracy, and even Western civilization. In the late 1990s William Kristol and Robert Kagan established the Project for the New American Century—again at the American Enterprise Institute—to champion a second war against Saddam Hussein's Iraq. The neocons developed strong ties to the Israeli Right, as well as to evangelical Christians in the Republican Party, both of which factions saw modern Israel as the fulfillment of biblical prophecy. Some neocons also took pleasure in their image as the inner circle of Republican power, at least on foreign policy.

Many of Ayaan's old friends couldn't imagine her in this new environment. How would their atheist fit into an American party that made the defense of religious values one of its planks? How could she cozy up to Christian and Jewish defenders of beliefs that could be as patriarchal and millenarian as the Muslim doctrines she denounced? Ayaan was determined, though, to make it work. She told *De Volkskrant* that she had learned from her mistakes in the Netherlands. She said she planned to be more restrained and "careful about what I say. I will have to be smarter, more strategic, more tactical."

Thirteen

Five years had passed since Vice President Dick Cheney had proposed conducting a war against al-Qaeda on "the dark side." But the Bush administration was learning how costly this darkness could be. In the summer of 2006, the U.S. Supreme Court halted the administration's effort to remove its war on terror from the reach of law and public scrutiny when it ruled in *Hamdan v. Rumsfeld* that both the U.S. prison at Guantánamo and the U.S. president remained subject to domestic and international law. Never sure of the legality of various practices that Bush's team had authorized, the CIA informed the administration that it would no longer be responsible for Washington's system of "black sites" for holding prisoners.

The CIA hurriedly released dozens of kidnapped and secretly held prisoners into the custody of their own governments. Only in the cases of a few prisoners deemed most culpable for 9/11 and other attacks on the United States were Bush officials willing, reluctantly, to account for their own actions.

President Bush announced on September 6, 2006, that he had moved KSM and thirteen other "high-value detainees" from CIA custody to Guantánamo Bay. In the same White House speech he also admitted what human rights groups (and al-Qaeda) had been saying for years: that the United States had been holding prisoners without being charged and beyond any proper authority and subjecting them to "an alternative set of procedures." For the representatives of the International Red Cross and other human rights groups in the audience, Bush's admission of what everyone already knew was a watershed. But for me, the most intriguing aspect of his speech was that for the first time in years it led to important government revelations about Aafia Siddiqui.

Among the fourteen hard cases Bush referred to were several people who had been linked with Aafia. These included not only KSM but also his nephew Ali Abdul Aziz Ali and Majid Khan. Until Bush's speech, no one outside the secret world of antiterror warriors knew what the connection was between them and Aafia or between her and KSM, apart from the obscure allegation that she had opened a post office box for Majid Khan.

But the White House that day released a series of CIA biographies of the detainees. And among other nuggets was a revelation about Ali, whom the CIA called by his alias Ammar al-Baluchi: "In 2002, Ammar directed Aafia Siddiqui—a U.S.-educated neuroscientist and al-Qaeda facilitator—to prepare paperwork to ease Majid Khan's deployment to the United States. Ammar married Siddiqui shortly before his detention."

Fourteen

The first five printings of Ayaan's autobiography sold out in the Netherlands within a week. In the United States and the United Kingdom it was also a quick bestseller. Eventually it would become a number one bestseller in Europe and a long-running bestseller in the United States, Canada, and Australia. It would also be published in more than thirty languages.

Starting in January 2007, Ayaan embarked on a worldwide promotional tour that took her all over Europe and the English-speaking world. The tour was expected to end in March, but, as Ayaan later told the journalist Clive Crook at the Aspen Ideas Festival, spring arrived and she and her publisher were getting more invitations than ever, so she kept on traveling and making speeches. "I spend my time in airports, in airplanes, in hotels and in places like this," she said. "My initial plan when I came to the U.S. was 'I'm going to get a rest, I'm going to get a normal life, I'm going to have free evenings and free weekends, I'm going to discover the American way of life.' . . . But some of my capitalist friends in the United States said, 'You can't miss this opportunity—you have to do this!' " So she left her things in storage and kept moving, accompanied by bodyguards who were still being paid by the Dutch government.

With very few exceptions, *Infidel* got glowing praise from English-speaking reviewers across the political spectrum. "She delivers a powerful feminist critique of Islam informed by a genuine understanding of the religion," said *Publishers Weekly.* "In the tradition of Frederick Douglass or even John Stuart Mill," wrote Anne

Applebaum at the *Washington Post*, "*Infidel* describes a unique intellectual journey, from the tribal customs of Hirsi Ali's Somali childhood, through the harsh fundamentalism of Saudi Arabia and into the contemporary West." The *New York Times* called the book "a brave, inspiring and beautifully written memoir." In Britain, the *Daily Telegraph* said, "If there is one book that really addresses the existential issues of our civilization, then Ali's autobiography is it."

Ayaan's ghostwriter wasn't named in the book, and many reviewers apparently thought that Ayaan herself had written it. For example, Natasha Walter wrote in the *Guardian*, "She proves herself here a true writer, able to sum up a scene that may be completely foreign to the reader in a way that makes it a living, breathing experience, unforgettably raw and immediate." At the *Jerusalem Post*, Caroline Glick said simply, "Ayaan Hirsi Ali is arguably the bravest and most remarkable woman of our times."

Only a handful of non-Muslims voiced any dissent. Among them were Ian Buruma in the *New York Times Book Review* and Timothy Garton Ash in *The New York Review of Books*. Buruma praised *Infidel*'s virtues but doubted Ayaan's methods of combating Islamism: "much though I respect her courage, I'm not convinced that Ayaan Hirsi Ali's absolutist view of a perfectly enlightened West at war with the demonic world of Islam offers the best perspective from which to get this done." In a review of Ayaan's first book, *The Caged Virgin*, Ash described her as "a brave, outspoken, slightly simplistic Enlightenment fundamentalist." I, too, reviewed *Infidel*; the piece appeared in *The Economist* (unsigned, like all its reviews) and pointed out certain disparities between the facts as she had described them in her autobiography and the stories she had told in the Netherlands, for instance, about what she maintained was her forced marriage.

The few Muslims who reviewed Ayaan's book in the Western press, all liberal opponents of Islamism, were far more critical. In *Newsweek*, for example, the music critic Lorraine Ali noted that *Infidel* told only one side of Ayaan's story. "Hirsi Ali is more a hero among Islamaphobes than among Islamic women," she wrote. "This would-be 'infidel' often sounds as reactionary and single-minded as the zealots she's worked so hard to oppose."

In the *New Matilda*, Irfan Yusuf worried that *Infidel* could have the same impact on gullible Western readers that the autobiography of Maryam Jameelah had on Pakistani readers in the 1980s. The former Margaret Marcus, Maryam Jameelah was a Jewish woman from New York who had joined Pakistan's Jamaat-e-Islami party and became an anti-Semitic Islamist ideologue after converting to Islam in the 1960s. "Sadly, for many Pakistani Muslims, Marcus's views on Judaism are all they will ever get to read," Yusuf wrote. "Pakistanis assume this Muslim convert Maryam Jameelah must be telling the truth. She must know what many Jews try to hide. She has 'insider' knowledge. In this sense, Jameelah and Hirsi Ali are similar—both 'insiders' of their ancestral faiths (which they now reject), both writing critically about their upbringing and the communities and cultures they were nurtured in."

Even Taslima Nasreen, a Bangladeshi feminist writer who also lived under the threat of death from Islamist fanatics, felt that Ayaan had gone too far in *Infidel*. "For her, Islam is responsible for child marriage, incest, purdah, the insistence on chastity, female foeticide, genital mutilation, honor killing and everything else. This, even according to a rabid anti-Islamist like me, is too much."

But in the tide of adulation surrounding the book, those skeptics seemed just a few carping fish. In the United States, Amazon.com customers named the book among their hundred top choices for 2007. Hundreds of readers posted comments on the Web site testifying to *Infidel*'s readability and its heroine's courage and honesty. Laura Bush read it. The leader of the New Democratic Party of Canada mentioned it on her Facebook profile. In Hollywood, movie producers called meetings about it. Ayaan—who said she saw the Somali model Iman in the role of herself—added modestly that she didn't know what all the excitement was about. "The issue of freedom of women, the right to criticize Islam and the content of my criticism has all been there since the 1700s," she told *Variety.* Then she noted, "I've taken a different path and of course, I've taken on the jihadists."

Ayaan's family obviously had a very different take on some of the tales that Ayaan and her ghostwriter told in *Infidel.* But under orders from Ayaan's father not to talk to the press, they sat very quietly lest another "Hurricane Ayaan" jeopardize their right to remain in Europe and Canada.

Some members of the clan may have taken added steps to protect themselves from exposure. For example, on February 21, 2007, the woman who had been calling herself "Ayan Hersi Magan" was granted a divorce in Finland's Vantaa District Court from Mohamud Mohamed Artan on the grounds that the two had not lived together for at least three years. Whoever she was, this other Ayaan, who had entered Finland as a student in 1993 and lived there as a refugee until 2001, vanished as noiselessly as she had arrived. According to court documents, she returned to Somalia. When I asked Mohamud about her in 2009, he said he thought she was living in England.

The real Ayaan returned to Washington after months of travel, saying she felt at home. "I am a happy individual now," she told a reporter. Once again her luck had held.

Fifteen

I called Elaine Whitfield Sharp about the White House dossier on KSM's nephew Ali that mentioned that he had married Aafia. Sharp told me the Siddiquis knew nothing about it.

But the same grudging dawn of lawfulness in Washington, which had prompted the disclosures about the United States' secret prisoners, seemed to be affecting Islamabad as well.

A few days after Bush announced the existence of the CIA's extralegal program, the relatives of some missing Pakistanis told a news conference of the Human Rights Commission of Pakistan that they were going on a hunger strike. Pakistan's chief justice, Iftikhar Chaudhry, promptly agreed to accept the commission's petition asking the government to reveal what it knew about forty-one missing persons. Squirming under the unaccustomed light of publicity, President Musharraf's government reported back that it had traced twenty of them.

No one knew how many Pakistanis had been imprisoned in the terror war: the U.S. and Pakistani governments had refused to say, and those they released were often told they'd be rearrested if they discussed where they had been. The Human Rights Commission guessed that the number could range from hundreds to thousands. It also questioned their guilt. As the commission's general secretary, Syed Iqbal Haider, stated, the government's refusal to press charges or say where the prisoners were "gives rise to the suspicion that these allegations are unsubstantiated and there are no charges and no crimes committed by the people picked up." Indeed it was widely believed that Pakistan had detained the prisoners simply because the Americans had paid them to.

In Karachi the families of some other missing persons began a hunger strike beneath a dusty tree across from the elegant old sandstone building that housed the Karachi Press Club. More and more of the families had begun flouting orders from the intelligence agencies to keep quiet about their vanished relatives. Even KSM's sister Maryam filed a suit in the Sindh High Court demanding that the government explain where KSM, her son, and her nephews had been taken. "Every male member of the family has been detained or tortured by the state agencies," her lawyer told reporters.

Aafia was often mentioned as one of the better-known Pakistanis whom the intelligence agencies had supposedly kidnapped. Yet her mother and sister failed to join the protests. Amjad's father, Aga Naeem, contacted the Human Rights Commission to ask whether Aafia and the children were on the list that the commission had presented to the court. The commission responded that the Siddiquis had not asked the group to include them.

Amjad, who had recently returned from Saudi Arabia, wrote to the secretary-general, I. A. Rehman, in December 2006, "Kindly can you let me know if Aafia Siddiqui is among those twenty persons whose whereabouts were reported or is she still missing? I am more interested in my children. Please let me know if you have any information that will help me in contacting or locating my children and their mother." Amjad had meant his e-mail to be private, but Rehman showed it to a reporter as evidence of the need to investigate the disappearances. A few days later, it showed up in *Dawn*. After that, the group included Aafia and her children's names on the lists of missing persons it was compiling for the court.

The CIA was still thought to be holding some "ghost prisoners" in places such as Bagram. Human Rights Watch, Amnesty International, and several other groups listed Aafia as one of twenty-two people who might be among them. I called Joanne Mariner of Human Rights Watch to ask if her group had any concrete evidence that Aafia was being held by the CIA. She said it didn't but that news reports of Aafia's disappearance in 2003 seemed to fit a larger pattern of CIA abductions. "We just found it hard to believe," Mariner told me, "that she could have gotten away when KSM and all the other big guys they were looking for at the same time got picked up."

From Amsterdam, I noted that Khalid Khawaja, the former ISI man who had discouraged me from pursuing Aafia's case, had helped form a new group to lobby on behalf of the missing. The Deobandis at the Lal Mosque also had joined the campaign.

Musharraf's government initially stonewalled the Supreme Court, refusing to say whether it had arrested any of those on the commission's list of forty-one missing persons. Then Chief Justice Chaudhry began summoning the heads of Pakistan's intelligence agencies to testify. Chaudhry said his goal was to see suspected terrorists tried in court. But Pakistan's spies weren't about to let that happen. Like the CIA, they preferred to release suspected terrorists rather than let them testify in open court about their dealings with the "invisible establishment."

Under pressure from the court, the government eventually released more than a hundred people. Freed with them were many secrets about where the ISI had been holding prisoners. Musharraf was furious and ordered Chaudhry to resign. The judge refused. Musharraf suspended him anyway. The country's lawyers responded with widespread demonstrations.

Musharraf claimed that his decision had had nothing to do with missing persons—most of whom, he said, had simply run away to join the jihadis and some of whom had been killed in Afghanistan. But the president had lied so many times before that no one believed him, and, as the spring of 2007 ended and Pakistan's monsoon season approached, his troubles mounted.

Sixteen

Ayaan occasionally tripped in her new political world.

In Holland, it had been important to pretend, at least, to dislike all religions equally. But her new American colleagues reacted with dismay when she criticized Christianity and Judaism alongside Islam. Interviewed by the British newspaper *Metro*, Ayaan said that asking her whether she saw a positive side to Islam was like asking if she saw anything positive in "Nazism, Communism, or Catholicism." Robert Spencer, a Catholic critic of Islam who had called Ayaan his "hero" on his blog Jihad Watch, was taken aback by her "offhand remark with which I could not disagree more." Ayaan told the *Jerusalem Post* in 2006 that Israel's biggest problem was that ultra-Orthodox Jews were "fanatics" who were breeding faster than other Jews. Beila Rabinowitz, a Dutch-speaking writer for Militant Islam Monitor, responded with an angry blog asking why Ayaan likened "Israel's most devout Jews" to terrorists. Rabinowitz and the Monitor appealed to AEI to rescind its offer to Ayaan, "since she has neither the temperament nor the intellectual gravitas necessary for successful scholarship—in our opinion Ali is a train wreck just waiting to happen."

AEI, however, stood by its offer. And Ayaan learned to direct her ire at Islam.

She spoke and wrote less about women's issues. In fact, during her first two years at AEI, she dedicated only three of twenty-one opinion pieces written in English to women's issues. She wrote nothing at all in English during those years about gay rights, abortion, or the theory of evolution—all of which she had championed in Holland. Politically, she was shifting.

Her attacks on Islam, meanwhile, were often so harsh that they startled even the neocons, who frequently assailed the Bush administration and others for failing to recognize the danger of "Islamofascism." (The term seemed to encompass not only Islamism but also Baathism and other thuggish ideologies emanating from the Muslim world.) Ayaan said flatly that the West was at war not with Islamism or "Islamofascism" but with Islam itself.

"It's not a war on terror," she told journalists soon after she arrived in the United States. "It's a war on Islam." That, of course, was what the jihadis said.

Interviewing her in London again in early 2007, David Cohen of the *Evening Standard* noted that—though her nails were nicely manicured and she looked as lovely as ever in a gray flannel suit and pearl earrings—her "explosive rhetoric" was "even more inflammatory and hard line now" than it had been when he had interviewed her two years earlier.

"Violence is inherent in Islam—it is a destructive, nihilistic cult of death," she told Cohen.

She warned him that Great Britain was "sleepwalking" into a very different culture, one that could eventually be ruled by Islamic law and that Muslims would soon dominate. "We risk a reverse takeover," she said. "In 50 years, a majority Muslim society could democratically vote for Sharia law, and then what you face is that Britain will slowly start to look like Saudi Arabia. Women will be veiled, driven away from the public sphere, polygamy will be rife."

Cohen gave her a skeptical look, but Ayaan went on. She claimed to base her argument on "current projections of immigration growth and birth rates," as well as on a newspaper poll in which 40 percent of young Muslims said they would prefer to live under Muslim law.

She had said similar things in Holland. But for English speakers who had thought Ayaan was controversial only because of "Submission" and some petty lies, her cataclysmic predictions and casual disregard for civil liberties came as a surprise. I found her claims of a Muslim takeover ludicrous: Muslims made up only 4 percent of Britain's population, and Muslim birth rates and immigration rates were both falling. But powerful elements in the media kept promoting her opinions.

"Islam, even in its non-violent form, is dangerous," Ayaan told the editor of the *Wall Street Journal*'s editorial page, Joseph Rago. She went on to hector Rago about the weakness and passivity of the West in the face of what she called "an external enemy that to a degree has become an internal enemy, that has infiltrated the system and wants to destroy it." In her view, strong measures were needed, and she was no more swayed in the United States by arguments about freedom of religion or Muslims' right to equal legal protection than she had been in the Netherlands. "It's easy to weigh liberties against the damage that can be done to society and decide to deny liberties," Ayaan said. "As it should be. A free society should be prepared to recognize the patterns in front of it, and do something about them."

The *Journal* would never have endorsed a political figure who proposed denying civil liberties to Jews, Christians, or any other religious group, and even Rago seemed uneasy with her opinions, writing that he could understand why some people found Ayaan "disturbing or even objectionable." Still, he rallied to her defense, concluding that "Society, after all, sometimes needs to be roused from its slumbers by agitators who go too far so that others will go far enough."

"In person, she is modest, enthralling," Rago wrote. "Intellectually, she is fierce, even predatory." She was known as a champion of free speech, but she urged him and other Westerners to punish Muslims even for peacefully expressing their antipathy to the West. She wrote in *Newsweek* that veiled Muslim women who were harassed got what they deserved. "To every woman who decides to walk out the door looking like Batman and then complains of being ridiculed, I say, you are inviting it. Bear it or shed it." In the *New York Times* she urged the West to defend its "honor" against Muslim students who had burned effigies of Salman Rushdie and Queen Elizabeth II after the queen knighted Rushdie. "The West," she said, "should join together to vigorously defend its symbols and civilization that, with all its flaws, still offers the best life to the most people."

Just what the essence of that civilization was remained unclear, except that it did not and could not include Islam. Democracy itself and even the rule of law were secondary, in her view. She argued in the *Los Angeles Times* that the European Union should stop demanding that Turkey place its army under the control of its elected government as a condition of admission to the European Union. Since Turkish voters had made the mistake of electing a moderately Islamic government, she seemed to be saying, they had lost the right to control their army.

She maintained that Iraq was better off since the U.S. invasion, though it was becoming clear that more than 100,000 Iraqis had been killed and that Islamists were gaining rather than losing power there. Nor did she respond to studies like the one published in 2009 by the British researchers Nadje Al-Ali and Nicola Pratt, *What Kind of Liberation?*, showing that women's rights in Iraq had been set back for decades. Instead, she pushed tirelessly for the Bush administration to attack Iran. "Talking to Iran is a sheer waste of time," she told *Reason* magazine in a long interview with Rogier van Bakel published in October 2007. The West should be fighting Iran, and the United States and Europe would have to keep fighting until "Islam, period," was defeated.

"We have to crush the world's 1.5 billion Muslims under our boot?" van Bakel asked, seemingly caught off guard. "In concrete terms, what does that mean, 'defeat Islam'?"

"I think that we are at war with Islam," Ayaan replied, "and there's no middle ground in wars. Islam can be defeated in many ways. For starters, you stop the spread of the ideology itself; at present, there are native Westerners converting to Islam, and they're the most fanatical sometimes. There is infiltration of Islam in the schools and universities of the West. You stop that. You stop the symbol burning and the effigy burning, and you look them in the eye and flex your muscles and you say, 'This is a warning. We won't accept this anymore.' There comes a moment when you crush your enemy."

"Militarily?" van Bakel asked.

"In all forms, and if you don't do that, then you have to live with the consequence of being crushed," Ayaan answered.

Her prescription was the opposite of what the leaders of Iran's burgeoning human rights movement—including the Nobel Peace Prize winner Shirin Ebadi and the journalist and former political prisoner Akbar Ganji—were urging. Earlier in the year, the diminutive Ebadi had told the Italian Web site Reset DOC what secular Muslims in Holland had been saying for a long time: that Ayaan and others who called Islam incompatible with human rights simply gave license to the Islamists.

"Intellectuals like Ayaan Hirsi Ali play into the mullahs' hands," Ebadi said. "They end up presenting Muslims with an ultimatum: either accept Islam, and with it all the injustices which you are suffering, or abandon the religion of your fathers in favor of democracy. It is not fair to force such a decision. I propose another way—that Islam be interpreted in a way which allows for democracy."

Ebadi had been warning since 2004 that a U.S. attack on Iran would be a disaster for women's rights. "When a society is in danger of attack, its government feels itself authorized to limit civil liberties in order to strengthen national security," she told Reset DOC. "This has always been true, and the case of Iran is no exception."

In the end, the Bush administration did not attack Iran. Its credit with the Pentagon was running low, and in a National Intelligence Estimate released at the end of 2007, the CIA and its associated agencies reported that Iran had halted its nuclear weapons program in 2003. The estimate undermined a key argument that the administration had made for embarking on a third war against a Muslim country. Under the military command of General David Petraeus and with the political guidance of Ambassador Ryan C. Crocker, the U.S. "surge" in Iraq was beginning to have an effect. But just as Iraq seemed headed toward relative stability, the Taliban made a comeback in Afghanistan and Pakistan. The military warned Bush that the United States couldn't handle another war.

The military attitude taking root was in many ways the opposite of the administration's initial approach—and not just toward Iraq but also toward the war on terror. One key to the new strategy was to avoid, at all costs, defining the conflict as a war against Islam. Instead, the United States needed to emphasize the differences among Muslims rather than to blur them and to protect Muslims willing to abide by democratic rules against other Muslims intent on ruling by violence.

It has yet to be seen whether the United States is capable of stabilizing governments in Iraq, Afghanistan, Pakistan, and elsewhere. But the new strategy in Iraq, which was put together partly by people at AEI, did allow the neocons to avoid or postpone the meltdown that they had helped start. The new strategy also meant that, even as Ayaan was becoming widely known as a commentator on the Muslim world, those in Washington actually charged with policy making toward Muslims had already stopped listening to her type of advice.

Seventeen

Umme Hassan, the headmistress of the female seminary connected to the Lal Mosque, which the former spy Khalid Khawaja had recommended I visit, embarked with her students on a campaign against "vice" in Islamabad. Dressed in black cloaks and face veils, this "burka brigade" prowled the capital terrorizing the owners of CD shops, burning "un-Islamic" videos, ordering female drivers to wear Islamic dress, and condemning the "sexually immoral" policies of the Pakistani government.

The students had already occupied a children's library. And in June 2007, they kidnapped seven Chinese women working at a massage parlor that the madrassa girls claimed was really a brothel.

Musharraf's government ignored the vigilantes for months, while officials such as Ijaz ul-Haq enlisted Khawaja to negotiate. But the Lal Mosque leaders refused to back down, and with support from jihadi groups and even al-Qaeda they seemed determined to undermine the government. Finally, on July 10, government troops attacked the mosque. The government reported afterward that 102 people had been killed. The militants claimed that more than a thousand men, women, and children had burned to death. The whole capital city could hear the explosions.

Like everyone else in Pakistan, Aafia's former husband, Amjad, followed the dramatic news. He could only wonder what Aafia must be thinking. Umme Hassan, after all, had become the sort of national symbol of jihad that his ex-wife had aspired to be. Amjad had felt a few months earlier, after Chief Justice Chaudhry had ordered the government to report on her case, that he might learn where she and the children were. But before the law could take its course, Musharraf had suspended the judge, ending Chaudhry's inquiries.

Indirect evidence later surfaced that Aafia may somehow have been involved in the disastrous insurrection. At any rate, she told the FBI that she and Mufti Muhammad Rafi Usmani had had a terrible falling out over what had happened at the Lal Mosque. She claimed that the mufti had blamed her for the disaster—though I wonder if he said such a thing or if he simply meant that angry female rebels like her were to blame. Aafia denied it, claiming darkly that she had been "caught in the game of the American-Israeli-Russian alliance" and that an "Indian agent" had incited the fervor at the madrassa. Among the papers later found on Aafia was a flier urging Pakistanis to recognize the injustice of Musharraf's decision to attack. "When those in charge repeatedly failed to fulfill their duties, then is providing shelter to raped women, helping the downtrodden, providing speedy justice, closing down a couple of brothels without causing harm—are these 'crimes' per se? And if so, are they so great, that their punishment is death?"

The storming of the Lal Mosque became a turning point for Pakistan. The long-standing alliance between the Deobandi jihadis and the military seemed to break down. Many of the militant Pakistanis in Waziristan and on the border with Kashmir had had young relatives in the shattered mosque, and they began attacking the army in revenge. In the five years after Jaish-e-Muhammad had organized Pakistan's first suicide bombing in 2002, the country had suffered twenty-two such attacks. But after the Lal Mosque disaster, suicide bombers carried out fifty-six attacks, killing 2,729 Pakistanis in just five months. Most of them were orchestrated by two groups associated with KSM and al-Qaeda, namely Jaish-e-Muhammad and Lashkar-e-Jhangvi.

In theory, Musharraf might have looked to Pakistan's secular middle class for support. But the country's professionals were up in arms over his suspension of the chief justice. The United States tried to prop him up by working out a compromise in which Benazir

Bhutto would return from exile and govern with him. After months of negotiations, Bhutto returned on October 19. A joyous parade in Karachi welcomed her home. Then suicide bombers set off two huge truck bombs, killing 139 people and barely missing the former prime minister. Bhutto would write in her posthumously published memoir that she thought a longtime jihadi named Qari Saifullah Akhtar, a man with close ties to the Deobandi establishment, had organized that bombing.

President Musharraf declared martial law and placed the chief justice under house arrest. Then on December 27, Bhutto, the first woman elected to lead a Muslim country, was murdered in a second attack, at a rally in Rawalpindi. Within hours, Musharraf said that telephone intercepts showed that Baitullah Mehsud, the leader of a new group in Waziristan calling itself the Pakistani Taliban, was to blame. Al-Qaeda also tried to take credit: "We have terminated America's most precious asset, who had vowed to defeat the mujahideen." But a yearlong UN investigation later determined that Pakistan's military-intelligence establishment also probably played a role in Bhutto's murder.

The glamorous Harvard graduate, who had inspired Aafia's mother to send her abroad to study, was dead. And now thousands of Pakistani women were competing to become that other kind of leader, the one that Aafia dreamed of resurrecting: the strong mujahida who dared to stand up for Islam as had the Prophet's wives, "mothers of the believers."

But the Deobandi clerics and officers who had formerly applauded such radicals had grown angry. The women of the Lal Mosque had gone too far. It was said that women created dissension, and that was what those women had done: they had divided the military from its longtime allies, the jihadis.

Perhaps Aafia fell out with her secret government protectors over her support for the jihadi women. In any case, toward the end of 2007, she appears to have decided to leave Pakistan.

Eighteen

The Dutch government had agreed to fund Ayaan's protection when she left for Washington. But the Ministry of Justice soon warned her that if she planned to stay in America she would have to start paying for her own bodyguards.

The Hague had spent $3 million a year to hire a private U.S. firm to guard her while she lived in the United States and traveled the world to promote her book, and the Dutch didn't want to keep paying now that she was neither a public official nor a resident of Holland. Dutch officials also doubted that she required so much protection in the United States. Unlike Salman Rushdie, they argued, Ayaan had never been threatened by a head of a state or even by a particular religious or political group, only by an amorphous collection of individuals, several of whom had been tried and imprisoned. Nor did she stand out in the United States as she had in Holland, where she was the most famous black woman in a country with very few of them.

Soon the ministry refused to pay for her travel by armored car, and it asked her to pay to maintain the alarm and video systems it had installed in her apartment. Ayaan complained—and was furious when she heard the ministry had made its decision without asking the FBI to evaluate the threat against her.

In December 2006, the Dutch justice minister, Ernst Hirsch Ballin, informed Ayaan by letter that payment for her two armed bodyguards would end in July. "While you are living in the U.S. the Dutch government has no responsibility for your protection," Ballin wrote. Not long after that, Ayaan received what Dutch security officials considered credible death threats. The minister extended her protection. But he warned that payments would stop on October 1, 2007.

Ayaan refused to accept it. She said she still felt unsafe and that the Liberal Party and other officials had never told her she would forfeit her guards if she moved to Washington. In a tense meeting in the Netherlands, she told the ministry that even her American guards underestimated the danger to her life. She said they had once let her ride in a taxi alone, even though many taxi drivers in Washington were Eritreans or Somalis who might recognize her.

The officials retorted that she needed a psychiatrist more than she needed guards, and they volunteered to get her an appointment with one at the University of Amsterdam. Ayaan coldly declined, telling them, according to the minutes of the meeting, that "if she were in an emotional mood, she would talk with a good friend."

The U.S. secretary of state Condoleezza Rice, whom Ayaan had first met at the *Time* gala in 2005, put her on the fast track to get a coveted green card that let her stay and work in the United States. But not even Rice could change the law barring the U.S. government from providing private citizens with protection beyond ordinary police services.

Ayaan made no plans for Holland's impeding cutoff. When October 1 arrived, she seemed stunned to discover that her guards were gone. She flew to the Netherlands to fight the decision from a safe house, complaining to reporters that she had been forced to cancel several speaking engagements.

Her friends accused the Dutch, in extreme terms, of abandoning her to Muslim fanatics. Leon de Winter was quoted in the October 3 *New York Times* as saying, "Canceling Ayaan's bodyguards is a death sentence." Christopher Hitchens in *Slate* compared the government's refusal to pay for guards to the abandonment of Srebrenica's Muslims by Dutch peacekeepers and the subsequent massacre of eight thousand Bosnian boys and men and the ethnic cleansing of more than twenty-five thousand refugees in 1995. Anne Applebaum, also in *Slate*, called the Dutch decision "a truly fundamental turning point, maybe even a test, for that part of the world which is known as the West." And in a piece for the *Los Angeles Times*, Sam Harris and Salman Rushdie argued that Ayaan might be the first refugee from Western Europe since the Holocaust. "There is not a person alive," Rushdie and Harris wrote, "more deserving of the freedoms of speech and conscience we take for granted here in the West, nor is there anyone making a more courageous effort to defend them."

None of those overwrought arguments changed the Dutch government's mind. In the Netherlands, Ayaan's once-potent symbolism had evidently lost its charge.

Applebaum claimed that The Hague had withdrawn its protection because "many in Holland find her too loud and too public in her condemnation of radical Islam." This was not the case. Some Dutch citizens did think that Ayaan went too far in condemning Islam in general. Ayaan herself, of course, had rejected the distinction between Islam and radical Islam. But her beliefs had nothing to do with the government's decision.

Ayaan's old friend and former Liberal Party colleague Geert Wilders, for example, condemned Islam even more loudly than Ayaan did. Wilders had left the Liberals to form his own political party, centered solely on opposition to Islam. He was also making a movie saying that the Quran ought to be banned. The Dutch prime minister and the entire government opposed Wilders's film project, which they feared would lead to attacks on Dutch citizens and businesses abroad. Yet the government continued to provide Wilders with guards twenty-four hours a day. It also provided guards for five other Dutch critics of Islam, including several private citizens. But Ayaan's case was different: the government didn't want to set the precedent of guarding private citizens who lived outside Holland.

The media attacks by Ayaan's friends only alienated her further from the Dutch. In an article called "Friends of Ayaan Heckle the Netherlands," the newspaper *Eindhoven Dagblad* noted with sour amusement that the same neoconservatives who mocked the Dutch welfare state were now demanding that Holland spend millions of euros to provide Ayaan with a level of security overseas that the U.S. government refused to provide its own citizens even inside the United States. Other articles asked why—if Ayaan was planning to live permanently in the United States and was "filled with great pride and gratitude" to be an immigrant there, as she had told the magazine of the U.S. immigration service, she didn't ask the United States to protect her.

The Dutch government said that it would continue to guard her in Holland. But public distaste was clearly rising, and Prime Minister Balkenende advised her to return to the United States and take responsibility for her own safety. The advice prompted Ayaan to comment bitterly that Balkenende would be personally responsible "if anything goes wrong."

Elsevier magazine, which had named her Person of the Year in 2005, ran an article asking, "Why can't the Dutch stand Ayaan?" The author concluded that they saw her as "an ungrateful adopted child" who, having milked their system, now wanted them to pick up the bills for her self-promotion elsewhere. Opinion polls showed that less than 40 percent of Dutch citizens favored paying for her overseas protection. When the Green Left party proposed a law that would extend her overseas protection, only one tiny party and one Labor parliamentarian voted for it. Even Geert Wilders's new party opposed the measure.

The battle of the bodyguards spilled into France, and a lineup of French intellectuals, including Bernard-Henri Lévy and Caroline Fourest, appealed to President Nicolas Sarkozy to protect her. A few months earlier, Ayaan had nominated the conservative Sarkozy for *Time* magazine's Person of the Year, "in recognition for his services to women around the world." Now she told the French newspaper *Le Journal du Dimanche* that she hoped to become a French citizen.

Sarkozy seemed receptive at first. But when it turned out that Ayaan wasn't proposing to live in France but merely wished the French to pay her guards while she worked in the United States for the American Enterprise Institute, his government's support evaporated.

She and her friends next tried the European Union. Benoît Hamon, a French MP in the European Parliament, launched the campaign. Ayaan told the European Parliament in Brussels that since October, she had been forced to spend her time raising money for her own protection. "The threats to my life have not subsided and the cost is beyond anything I can pay," she told the lawmakers. "I don't want to die. I want to live and I love life."

Hamon proposed that the European Union create a 50-million-euro fund to guard her and other threatened European intellectuals wherever they lived. But other members called the idea unworkable. Only 85 of the European parliament's 785 members supported it, and the proposal died.

So she returned to Washington and resumed speaking around the world, reportedly for $25,000 per speech plus the cost of her security. Friends such as Sam Harris helped her set up various funds to raise money to pay her guards. In the United States they established a tax-exempt fund in 2007; it was located in Washington and called the Foundation for Freedom of Expression. Since U.S. law doesn't allow tax-exempt contributions to benefit just one person, the foundation's stated mission was to support Ayaan and other Muslim dissidents. The Wikipedia entry for the group said, "Donating to the Foundation for Freedom of Expression is a way to help Ayaan Hirsi Ali and others under similar circumstances, while allowing tax benefits to the contributor."

Harris campaigned vigorously for the funds, receiving help even from his *Newsweek* sparring partner Rick Warren, the popular Christian evangelist and author of *The Purpose-Driven Life.* (Harris joked that if Warren raised more money than he did, he might yet be convinced that Christians were morally and socially more engaged than atheists.) In October 2008, Harris wrote to thank the contributors to Ayaan's fund and to announce that her security costs were "now being met on an ongoing basis."

Ayaan and a group of wealthy women friends had already formed another group at the end of 2007 that they called the AHA Foundation. According to the U.S. Internal Revenue Service, Bruce Kovner's wife, Suzie Kovner, chaired the group. The wife of John Bolton, Bush's former ambassador to the United Nations, became treasurer. Two other Republican donors, Gwendolyn van Paasschen of Darien, Connecticut, and Brenda Boone of Houston, Texas, sat on the board. Still another charity, Haweya BV, was set up in Holland, and Ayaan herself was president of both Haweya BV and of the AHA Foundation. Soon a Web site, www.theahafoundation.org, began inviting donors to contribute regularly by PayPal to the AHA Foundation. The Web site said the group's mission was "to help protect and defend the rights of women in the West against militant Islam."

It was the first time in several years that Ayaan had proposed doing anything practical to support the cause of Muslim women. Certainly there was plenty to do. All over Europe, women's groups and others were examining the issues of honor-related violence and forced marriages. In the United Kingdom, for example, the Centre for Social Cohesion, founded the same year as the AHA Foundation with a grant of $428,000, produced eleven meticulously documented studies of how Islamism and other extreme ideologies were eroding British law, plus numerous briefing papers and several public debates—all by 2010. One of the center's studies was a 169-page report, "Crimes of the Community," dealing with honor killings, genital mutilation, and domestic violence among UK Muslims, for which the center conducted more than eighty interviews with women's groups, community activists, and victims of violence. The AHA Foundation, by contrast, produced no original research.

IRS records showed that AHA raised a total of $90,042 in 2008. Some $52,470 of that went toward "professional services." An additional $31,432 went unspent. The AHA Foundation had no paid employees. No one answered the telephone number listed on its tax return. The group's address appeared as 1735 Market Street,

Philadelphia, but Pennsylvania authorities said they had no such organization incorporated in the state. AHA's tax number turned out to be the same as the number for the Foundation for the Freedom of Expression in Washington, D.C.

In 2009, according to IRS filings, the AHA Foundation received a grant of $375,000 to cover the costs in 2010 of setting up an office and hiring staff. (The IRS doesn't require nonprofits to name donors.) Adding several new board members—including the AEI scholar and critic of feminism Christina Hoff Sommers and AEI's former president, Christopher DeMuth—AHA moved its headquarters to New York and hired an operations coordinator and Elise Jordan, a former speechwriter for Condoleezza Rice, as director of strategic initiatives. The group began producing more material, including a report on freedom of expression and the rights of women and a resource directory for Muslim women in the United States. Its output nonetheless remained puny compared to that of the United Kingdom's Centre for Social Cohesion, for instance, or of international rights groups such as the London-based Women Living Under Muslim Laws.

Nineteen

The perplexing story that Aafia's uncle S. H. Faruqi tells about the visit she paid him in early 2008 is typically Pakistani. By that I mean that important parts appear to be missing, other parts seem quite incredible, and further inquiries hit a brick wall. The persistence of such stories is one reason Pakistani history is littered with mysteries such as "Who killed President Zia ul-Haq?" Yet one needs to *try* to get to the bottom of them or admit defeat.

Here's how Faruqi told the story, to me and to other journalists, in a series of e-mails and interviews.

On the evening of January 22, 2008, the doorbell rang at his two-story bungalow in the F-7 Sector of Islamabad.

Faruqi went to the door and found a man waiting for him who said he was a driver for the Ministry of Foreign Affairs using his white government Suzuki to moonlight as a taxi driver. He said that inside his car sat a woman he had picked up at the Karachi Company Bus stand who wanted to see the geologist.

Puzzled, Faruqi approached the car. A woman got out wearing a black niqab and burka covering her entire body except her eyes. "O Uncle, I am Aafia," she said, and, to Faruqi's amazement, she was.

She told him she had come with a request. She wanted him to escort her to meet the Taliban in Afghanistan. "She said she wanted to get away, to go back to Afghanistan, where she said the Taliban would protect her," Faruqi told the British daily the *Independent*. "According to her," he told me, "they would not hand her over to her enemies." He added that he assumed that Aafia's enemies were American.

The woman refused to take off her niqab, but Faruqi had no doubt that she was Aafia.

Above her face veil, Aafia's wide-set brown eyes and thick, sweeping eyebrows were unchanged. Moreover, "I recognized the voice to my complete satisfaction," Farqui wrote me. "I was greatly surprised and perplexed, too, but soon regained my normalcy and welcomed her and embraced her."

He invited his niece to come inside, but she refused, asking him instead to take her to some place where they could talk alone. When he tried to insist, she became very agitated. "Do not insist," she screamed, "as that would simply result in the destruction of your house as well as of myself."

Flustered, the geologist got into the white car and asked the driver to take him and Aafia to the Jinnah Super Market, an upscale strip mall around the corner. There, Faruqi says, he and Aafia talked for more than two hours, first at the Taj Mahal restaurant and later at Captain Cook's.

Based on his conversation with her, Faruqi later claimed in the Pakistani newspaper the *Nation* that Aafia and her three children had been arrested on March 30, 2003, on Karachi's University Road, as she and the children were on their way to the airport and while the United States was rolling up KSM's network. He claimed that she and the children had been separated that same day and that she had never seen them again.

He said Aafia told him that after she was arrested, she was taken to Afghanistan, where she was held at Bagram Airfield until mid-2007. Faruqi claims she was tortured during that period and was finally given a new identity. He told the *Guardian*'s Declan Walsh that her keepers wanted her to act as a double agent and infiltrate extremist groups for Pakistani intelligence. She was then returned to Islamabad.

Faruqi later wrote me that Aafia was held at first in "the private jail of the American Embassy" in Islamabad and later handed over to the ISI. (The United States strenuously denies holding her anywhere during this period, and human rights officials I spoke to knew of no other reports of a "private jail" at the U.S. Embassy in Islamabad.)

Toward the end of 2007, the geologist says, Aafia was transferred—by whom she didn't say—to Lahore. There, she said, Pakistan's Federal Investigation Agency (FIA) had taken her into custody. She showed him a false national identity card that she said the FIA had issued to her in a different name. The card described her as a research scholar at a university, and it gave a Karachi address. The name on the ID card was different, but the photograph was of her. She said the FIA had given her money to go out occasionally in her concealing black burka under the pretext of gathering information about al-Qaeda. That morning, she told her uncle, she had seized the opportunity of just such an excursion to catch a bus to Islamabad and make her way to his house. "That was her main point, that she will be safe with the Taliban," Faruqi told Walsh in 2009.

Faruqi found Aafia's story extraordinary. He says he told her he would take her to the Taliban—he says he had contacts with them from his years in mineral exploration—but he needed time to make the arrangements. Meanwhile, he wanted Aafia to tell some local journalists about her imprisonment. "She very seriously opposed it and remarked that it would simply be killing her." Eventually she allowed him to check her into a nearby guesthouse, the Islamabad Inn, and the following day, he convinced her to come and stay with him and his wife at his house, where she spent the night on the floor, praying. By this time he had called his sister, Ismat, in Karachi, and Ismat flew up to see her daughter. But on the morning of January 24, Aafia insisted on returning to Lahore.

Aafia's uncle also described her behavior during her visit. She always carried a large black bag with her. Noticing how heavy it was, Faruqi tried to carry it for her, but she wouldn't let anyone look inside it. When he asked what was in the bag, she said her captors had let her keep a few books.

As she left for Lahore, her mother, Ismat, tried to give her 5,000 rupees. Aafia refused at first but eventually took the money.

When I tried to ask Faruqi more about this tale, he became irritated and asked me not to contact him about it again. He seems to have been more forthcoming with Declan Walsh, and Walsh speculated that Aafia might have decided to go to Afghanistan to avoid being forced to spy on jihadis for Pakistani intelligence.

Twenty

The book tour that was supposed to end in the spring of 2006 went on and on. It helped Ayaan fashion a career for herself as a professional critic of Islam. She attended conferences and gave speeches all over the world. Television news shows asked for her comments on a succession of crises, such as the uproar over Geert Wilders's anti-Islamic short film "Fitna," the continuing threats to the lives of the Danish cartoonists, and later the controversy over a proposed mosque near the ruins of the World Trade Center.

She debated Hassan al-Banna's grandson Tariq Ramadan and the British ex-Islamist Ed Husain. She continued to be a useful symbol and figurehead for the kinds of publicists and politicians who liked to accuse their opponents of being soft on Islam. The American writer Paul Berman and the French philosopher Pascal Bruckner tapped out tens of thousands of words and engaged half a dozen other writers in a strange debate conducted on the German Web site Sign and Sight and in magazines such as *The New Republic* and *The New York Review of Books*. The argument (which resembled earlier fights in Holland) revolved around whether the writers Ian Buruma and Timothy Garton Ash—by qualifying their praise of Ayaan, and calling her, as Ash had, "a brave, outspoken, slightly simplistic Enlightenment fundamentalist"—had thereby taken Ramadan's side against Ayaan and thus opposed the Western Enlightenment. Bruckner even claimed, memorably, if hysterically, that the two mild critics had written in "the spirit of the inquisitors who saw devil-possessed witches in every woman too flamboyant for their tastes." Buruma and Ash protested that they had nothing against Ayaan at all; indeed, they admired her greatly, and Ash apologized in public to her for calling her an "Enlightenment fundamentalist." But Berman seems not to have accepted their apologies. Eventually he wrote an entire book, called *The Flight of the Intellectuals*, that a friendly reviewer called "an outraged attack on Ayaan Hirsi Ali's attackers." (A less friendly reviewer, Lee Siegel of the *New York Observer*, characterized Berman's book as an "onanistic tour du force" and a barely sublimated attempt to get back at Buruma and Ash for having taken Berman to task for cheerleading the U.S. invasion of Iraq.)

It was left to the German-Syrian philosopher of Islamic liberalism Bassam Tibi to point out that Muslim thinkers trying to reconcile Islam with universal human rights didn't take Ayaan *or* Ramadan seriously. "What Hirsi Ali says about Islam is an affront to Muslims and to anyone who knows anything about Islam," Tibi wrote on Sign and Sight. Tibi, a professor at Göttingen and Cornell universities and the author of nine books and dozens of articles about political Islam, had warned since the 1990s of the danger the jihadis posed to the West. And though he drew no attention to it, he, too, had been threatened with murder and forced to live under guard in Germany. (In truth, thousands of accomplished people have come under threat from violent Islamists—in Afghanistan, Egypt, Pakistan, Somalia, and other countries.) Yet Tibi continued to write and lecture to Muslims and non-Muslims around the world, and he received only quiet recognition for his pains. Ayaan, by contrast, was named by both *Foreign Policy* in the United States and *Prospect* in the United Kingdom in 2008 as one of the world's leading public intellectuals despite her output of one ghostwritten memoir, one collection of heavily edited journalism, and some op-ed pieces.

Ayaan was on the road so long that she didn't bother to rent an apartment, though eventually she found one in New York. She lived on planes and in hotel rooms and occasionally at the homes of friends—always accompanied by her bodyguards. Her travels were coordinated with the police, sometimes weeks ahead of time. She had not spoken with anyone in her family for years.

In June 2008, Claudia Anderson, the managing editor of the conservative *Weekly Standard*, wrote a cover story called "Parallel Lives" comparing Ayaan to Frederick Douglass, the famous former slave and abolitionist whose nineteenth-century autobiography had helped crystallize Americans' opposition to slavery in the South. The article suggested that Ayaan's "flight to freedom" from her family in Nairobi had been similar to Douglass's escape from slavery in Maryland. It also included a postscript that hinted at changes in Ayaan's life.

Anderson recounted the story of how Douglass had written an open letter warning his former master, Thomas Auld, that he intended to use the story of their relationship as a "weapon with which to assail the system of slavery." Three decades later, Auld, by then over eighty and dying, sent for Douglass to see him. "Douglass records that he was ushered straight into the bedroom, and the two old men were overcome with emotion," Anderson wrote. "Neither showed malice. Each acknowledged ways he had wronged the other. They 'conversed freely about the past' and parted reconciled."

The article did not mention it, but Ayaan had recently received a similar summons regarding her own seventy-three-year-old father, whom she had portrayed as masterlike and the story of whose relationship with her she had used to assail Islam. Earlier that month, Ayaan's twenty-four-year-old half sister Sahra (the daughter of her father's third wife) had managed to track down Ayaan's former boyfriend Marco and asked him to tell Ayaan that Hirsi was dying of leukemia in the East End of London.

Ayaan wrote that she called her father as soon as she heard, though it was late in the evening in London. Her hands were shaking, and when Hirsi picked up the phone, tears welled up in her eyes at the sound of his voice, "strong and excited." "I said the only thing I wanted to convey, that I loved him, and I heard his smile, so powerful that it seemed to come through the telephone."

"Of course you love me!" he exclaimed in reply. "And of course I love you."

They began to talk, and Ayaan says she told her father that she wanted to see him. But then the conversation went wrong. Ayaan offended Hirsi by saying she would have to bring the police if she visited. Her father started preaching to her about how she ought to return to Islam, and after a while she told him she had to run and catch a plane.

Twenty-one

The British television presenter Yvonne Ridley had never forgotten about the screams of the woman that Moazzam Begg, the Briton later released from Guantánamo, had described hearing at the CIA's secret prison at Bagram in his memoir *Enemy Combatant*. In 2008, while putting together a program on Guantánamo, Ridley asked Begg who he thought the woman might have been.

"I put it to him that she didn't really exist and that the screams he had heard were on a tape recorder as part of a mental torture process used by his interrogators at Bagram," Ridley wrote me later. But Begg replied that other detainees at Guantánamo had told him they had seen a woman at Bagram, and he directed Ridley to a video on YouTube in which four al-Qaeda detainees who escaped from Bagram in July 2005 expressed their disgust at the way a female prisoner was being treated there.

Ridley found the video. She also learned that another prisoner at Bagram had seen such a woman, and he said that the Americans had given her a number: 650.

Ridley hasn't identified her source. But some months later, Binyam Mohamed, an Ethiopian-born British resident who was captured in 2002 trying to fly out of Karachi with the former American gang member Jose Padilla, and who was later imprisoned at Bagram and Guantánamo, said in public interviews with Begg and Ridley that he had encountered a female prisoner at Bagram who wore a shirt with the number 650 on it.

Neither Binyam Mohamed nor Begg could be called a disinterested witness. According to U.S. officials, anyway, Binyam Mohamed was working for the same circle of al-Qaeda operatives around KSM in 2001 that Aafia was later accused of working with. The thin, soft-spoken Ethiopian claimed to have left London for Afghanistan in June 2001 to kick a drug habit, but he also admitted that he had trained in Afghanistan at al-Qaeda's al-Farouq camp that summer. He was arrested on April 4, 2002, trying to use a false passport at the Karachi airport. U.S. military prosecutors later charged him with participating in KSM's plot to blow up American apartment buildings—the same "dirty bomb plot" involving Jose Padilla that may have led the FBI in Boston to question Aafia and Amjad in May 2002. But Binyam Mohamed denied having had anything to do with such a plot. The charges against him were later dropped, and he was released in 2008.

According to Binyam Mohamed, he was flown to Morocco after his arrest in Karachi and tortured in an effort to make him confess that he had met with al-Qaeda leaders such as KSM and bin Laden. From Morocco he was taken to the so-called "dark prison" that the Americans ran in the Afghan capital, Kabul. He arrived at Bagram in June 2004. He said that was when he saw a female prisoner who he heard was a Pakistani who had studied in the United States.

Binyam Mohamed said that the woman was kept in isolation and that the Americans in charge of the prison told the other prisoners she was a spy working for "the governments." (He didn't say which ones.) In an interview filmed for Cageprisoners, Begg showed Binyam Mohamed a picture of Aafia. He identified her as the woman he had seen at Bagram.

Ridley says she doubted at first that Aafia could be prisoner 650. As she wrote me, "I thought to myself, 'If it is her, what the hell has the United States done with her baby and two young children?' " But whoever prisoner 650 was, Ridley wanted to find out more.

In late June 2008, she contacted Lieutenant Colonel Mark

Wright, a spokesman for the Pentagon. Wright denied that there was any prisoner 650, and he said the United States was holding no female prisoners at Bagram. (Later a spokeswoman for U.S. forces in Afghanistan said that a female prisoner had been held in Bagram from 2003 to 2005 but she wasn't Aafia Siddiqui.) Ridley, however, felt sure of her source, and she refused to drop the story.

She says she told Wright, "Mark, we can do this the easy way or, if I have to, I will go and get some sworn affidavits which will prove that you are being lied to and passing on wrong information to me. Do you really want another Abu Ghraib on your hands?" Shortly after that, Ridley says, Wright stopped answering her calls, and the YouTube film made by the Bagram escapees—which had appeared on the Internet for two years—was pulled down.

Ridley decided to go public with her suspicions. On July 5, 2008, she and the director of Cageprisoners, Saghir Hussain, flew to Islamabad to hold a press conference with Imran Khan, the politician and ex-cricketer who had become the champion of Pakistan's disappeared.

The next day was the first anniversary of Operation Silence, the Pakistani military's assault on the Lal Mosque the year before.

Striking the themes that Aafia herself had used to rouse Boston's Muslims to jihad, Ridley called on the *ummah* to protect a Muslim woman threatened by unbelievers. "Today," she told more than a hundred Pakistani journalists who showed up at the conference, "I am crying out for help, not for myself but for a Pakistani woman whom neither you nor I have ever met. She has been held in isolation by the Americans for more than four years and she needs help." Ridley said she called Aafia the Gray Lady "because she is almost a ghost, a specter whose cries and screams continue to haunt those who hear her."

Ridley's press conference attracted enormous coverage. Reading about the hubbub in Amsterdam, I thought she might actually have solved the mystery of Aafia's whereabouts. In Pakistan, of course, the idea that Aafia had been handed over to the Americans fit in nicely with the claims of Umme Hassan and Khalid Khawaja that Musharraf's government had joined a grand conspiracy against Islam and was willing to imprison Muslim women and children in return for U.S. dollars.

The agitation was still growing when, a few days later, a strange incident took place in Afghanistan that struck many Pakistanis as further proof of Aafia's plight.

Twenty-two

Ayaan often said that she missed her father more than her mother. Even as a child she felt Hirsi was the parent who lifted her out of the ordinary, the one who called her pretty, the one who called her his only son. She was also angry, though, that he had abandoned her again and again, first as a child, then as a young woman alone in Europe, and finally as a novice politician in danger of her life. When she first sat down to write her autobiography in 2004, she found herself instead composing an open letter to her father. She accused him of offering his children only conditional love. "Every time he has had to make a choice between the community and his children, he has chosen the former," she wrote. "This hurts." In many ways, her imperious father was her audience of one. Yet before their brief telephone call in the summer of 2008, they hadn't spoken in four years.

Why didn't she go to him now? She wrote in *Nomad* that when she phoned him, she was on her way to a conference in Brazil. She says she planned to visit him later in the summer. She says she was afraid to go to his apartment in Tower Hamlets, a largely Muslim development in an immigrant section of London, without taking the police with her, though she knew that doing so would cause offense. Yet even if she rejected going to Tower Hamlets, she could have tried to meet him somewhere else. Or she could have phoned him again from Brazil. But she didn't.

Why not? One had to think—or at least I do after reading what Ayaan has written and said, and talking to so many people who know her—that she was still afraid to confront him. Just as her tongue had "stuck in my throat" the time her mother had begged her to tell her father about her secret marriage and instead she had run away to the Netherlands, this time she also ran away—first to the conference in Brazil and after that to another conference, in Australia.

Twenty-three

It was just getting dark on July 17, 2008, in the bazaar district of the ancient walled city of Ghazni, Afghanistan, when a shopkeeper noticed a woman and a boy of about twelve sitting on the ground in front of a closed shop.

The woman wore the all-concealing powder blue burka of an Afghan woman, and she was holding the boy's hand. She had a large black handbag by her side. As the shopkeeper later told the FBI, the Ghazni police had recently alerted him and other merchants to a tip they had received: that a woman and child might be coming to Ghazni to cause some kind of trouble. The shopkeeper decided to use his phone to tell the police about the pair.

The Afghan government at the time controlled Ghazni, a provincial capital south of Kabul, but little else in the area. The war was going badly for the Americans and their ally, President Hamid Karzai. As the violence in Iraq subsided, war was surging in Afghanistan. For the first time, more U.S. soldiers were being killed there than in Iraq. In the first two weeks of July alone, sixty people had been killed in a suicide attack on the Indian Embassy in Kabul, twenty-four more had died in a suicide attack on a police patrol in Uruzgan, and a ferocious Taliban assault on a U.S. military outpost had left nine Americans dead. The Afghan and U.S. governments said that Pakistani groups such as Jaish-e-Muhammad and Lashkar-e-Taiba were helping the Taliban, and they had telephone intercepts showing that Pakistan's intelligence agencies were directing the attacks. A separate UN study showed that more than half of Afghanistan's suicide bombers originated in Pakistan.

Traditionally, the Afghans didn't draft women into their ceaseless warfare. But that was changing—under Pakistani influence, according to Karzai's government. In May, a woman in a burka had blown herself up, killing twenty-eight people. Across the border in Pakistan's tribal areas, Islamist militants had shut down dozens of girls' schools in the areas they ruled, replacing them with madrassas where girls as well as boys were indoctrinated to become suicide bombers. Only days before the woman in the blue burka appeared in Ghazni's bazaar district, the governor of Ghazni, Muhammad Usman, had received a report that the Taliban were sending a Pakistani woman and a young boy to circulate in Afghanistan, urging Afghan women to volunteer for suicide missions. "We heard they are saying, 'This foreigner is willing to give her life for Islam. What about you?' " the governor told me later by telephone.

Police commander Ghani Khan and another officer arrived at the shop and began questioning the woman. They spoke in the Afghan languages of Dari and Pashto, but the woman didn't understand and replied to them in Urdu, the Pakistani tongue. A passing man who knew Urdu later told the FBI that he had stepped in and offered to help. The woman told him she was looking for her husband and needed no help. Then she walked away. When the police tried to stop her, she and the boy began kicking the officers and calling them infidels. "Allahu Akhbar!" the boy cried, while the woman shouted that the officers were "Americans, not Afghans."

A wind blew up, and the woman threw a bunch of papers out of her bag, causing the men to chase after them. To the Urdu-speaking man's amazement, the papers turned out to include maps of Ghazni's Jihad Mosque, the governor's house, the airport, and the Afghan National Police compound, plus drawings of materials used in bombs.

"Back up!" one of the policemen shouted. "This woman is dangerous!"

The police opened her bag. Inside, they found chemical substances and gels in sealed bottles. They also found hundreds of pages of tiny handwritten notes and diagrams for making explosives, maps of Afghan army and police posts, and some photocopied excerpts from *The Anarchist Arsenal.* Some of the papers were written in English, others in Urdu or Pashto. Police commander Khan took the woman to the police station and delivered her bag to the governor himself.

Governor Usman examined the woman's belongings and decided she must be an international terrorist. He went to the police station, a walled collection of adobe buildings in the Ghazni city center, to get a look at her. Small and slight though she was, with enormous, frightened eyes, she refused to sit still. Even handcuffed she kept fighting and trying to get away, screaming, "Allahu Akhbar! Allahu Akhbar!"

When the governor approached her, she spat at him and cursed him in Urdu. "She called me very bad, very terrible names," Governor Usman told me. "She said I am a dog of the Americans. She said I will die like a dog and I will go to hell."

He telephoned Captain John-Caleb Threadcraft, a U.S. infantry officer from Alabama who acted as the liaison between the Afghan national forces and the Americans stationed in Ghazni, and asked if he could visit the captain right away.

Threadcraft later testified that the governor had burst into his unit around 8 p.m. "I've captured a female bomb-maker," he told the American. The governor showed Threadcraft the woman's bag and its contents, exclaiming excitedly, "You see? You see?" The two men started going through the papers. Threadcraft saw notations in English concerning dirty bombs, the Ebola virus, and bioweapons, as well as something that looked like a fuse. He called his superior, the U.S. battalion commander at Ghazni. The battalion commander agreed that Threadcraft should try to take the woman into custody and find out who she was.

Threadcraft drove to the police station, and the police chief took him to the building that housed the jail. They found the woman still shouting, "Allahu Akhbar! Allahu Akhbar!" When she saw Threadcraft, she began yelling even more loudly that the Afghans would go to hell if they gave her to the Americans. For two hours, Threadcraft tried to persuade the police captain to release the woman into his custody, but the chief refused. He said he needed permission from the interior ministry in Kabul. Governor Usman said the Afghans planned to hold a press conference the next day to exhibit their important captive. After that, he would give her to the Americans.

Threadcraft went back to his unit, gathered the woman's things, and took them to the military intelligence unit at Ghazni Forward Operating Base. By now it was almost 2 a.m. The military intelligence officer, Captain Robert Snyder, had to be woken up by his aides. Threadcraft and the governor had found a thumb drive in the woman's bag; he now plugged it into his computer. Flipping through the documents stored there, he came across one in English titled "Why I Am Not a Terrorist." Its author described attending MIT. She wrote about living in a dorm where she claimed American women were regularly raped. She decried the way women were treated in America and said Islam offered a far superior alternative.

Threadcraft had never heard of Aafia Siddiqui, and he couldn't imagine the small, scared woman in the police station being the person who had written the fiery statement on the thumb drive. But when Snyder appeared and read the document, he decided she might be a U.S. citizen and that the FBI unit at Bagram Airfield should know about her.

The response from the FBI was electric. The special agent in charge let Snyder know he was sending two FBI agents to Ghazni first thing in the morning to interview the woman.

Snyder and his team continued translating, photographing, and cataloging the items they found. Among them was a plastic container filled with white briquettes that the FBI later identified as more than two pounds of sodium cyanide, an extremely toxic industrial chemical. There were writings about a "mass casualty attack," maps and diagrams of the Empire State Building, Wall Street, the Brooklyn Bridge, and other famous New York sites, even a discussion of how to build a dirty bomb.

At the Ghazni police station, some policemen and an Afghan named Abdul Qadeer, a counterterrorism official, were beating the woman with sticks. "People say she was a suicide bomber so we are all hitting her," Qadeer later testified. Qadeer was informed that two Afghan officials would be arriving from Kabul to take the woman to the capital, so he led her out of the jail and into another building to wait in a second-floor meeting room with a shiny yellow polyester curtain strung across it.

The governor's office held its news conference as advertised. The governor's spokesman told gathered Afghan reporters that the two had been attaching explosives to their bodies when they were spotted and had planned to kill the governor with a suicide bomb. "They both were attempting to get into the governor's compound and target the governor and high-ranking officials," the governor's spokesman said. He handed out photographs of Pakistani military figures, and he claimed that the woman had been carrying the pictures.

In a video of the press conference, the woman and boy are shown covering their faces while officials and reporters shout questions at them. "We didn't do anything," the woman keeps saying in a high, soft voice. "We didn't do anything, and we didn't come to do anything." The governor's spokesman said the woman's name was Saliha and the boy's name was Ali Hasan. He said the woman was twenty-five years old and the boy thirteen. They both spoke English, Urdu, and Arabic. Apparently the woman told them that they came from Pakistan and the boy was an orphan she had adopted.

The governor's spokesman said "Saliha" told them she had left Pakistan from Quetta (in Baluchistan), entered Afghanistan at Chaman, and traveled to Kabul before continuing on to Ghazni two days later. He said she had confessed to having three other accomplices, who were not captured.

After the press conference, another officer took the boy into a separate room to question him, and Abdul Qadeer, the Afghan antiterrorism official, called the Interior Ministry for further instructions. He later testified that, while he was on the phone, the woman leaped over some chairs onto a bed behind the curtain and tried to jump out the window.

His officers restrained her. She fought back, biting one man on the wrist deeply enough to draw blood and hitting and kicking at the others. Finally they tied her to the bed. Qadeer then took the boy to another office and questioned him.

While Qadeer was dealing with the captives, the two FBI agents and a U.S. Army expert in chemical weapons arrived by helicopter at the U.S. base outside town. Threadcraft was told to accompany them to the governor's house and ask the governor to release the woman into the agents' custody. He took Captain Snyder with him on the mission, together with a female medic, a Special Forces team led by a warrant officer, and several Afghan interpreters. To the Americans' disappointment, however, Governor Usman told Threadcraft that the prisoner couldn't be given to them as promised. He said that the president of Afghanistan, Hamid Karzai, had called him personally to say that he had decided to take charge of her case.

The U.S. group returned to its base. Threadcraft went to bed, and Snyder called headquarters for further orders. He was told to go back to the Ghazni police station with the rest of the party and at least try to question the woman and find out who she was.

They piled into a couple of Humvees and drove back to the police station. Since the press conference, several Afghan officials from the Interior Ministry had arrived from Kabul. When the Afghan officials saw that Qadeer and his men had tied the woman to a bed, they ordered him to untie her. "What can she do? She is a woman," Qadeer recalled them saying.

The woman sat down on the bed, and someone closed the yellow polyester curtain, presumably to protect her modesty.

Curious Afghans were now milling around the police compound.

As usual in Afghanistan, most of them were armed. The U.S. soldiers and FBI agents arrived. They were tired and cranky after being up all night and felt frustrated at not being allowed to take the woman into custody. The armed crowd of Afghans struck them as menacing.

The police chief told the Americans that they could talk to the woman, but first they needed to meet with the Interior Ministry officials from Kabul.

So Captain Snyder, the FBI agents, the chief warrant officer, their interpreters, and the female medic were led across the courtyard, into another building, and upstairs to the meeting room with the yellow curtain where the officials from Kabul were waiting. Sergeant Kenneth J. Cook and Pat MacDonald, a civilian investigator on loan to military intelligence, stayed outside to keep an eye on the increasingly surly Afghans in the courtyard, who were now huddling in small groups and pointing their weapons at the building. Some men in the crowd carried rocket-propelled grenade launchers.

"Something bad is going to happen," Cook told MacDonald.

"Relax," said MacDonald.

"I know something bad is about to happen," Cook repeated.

Just then the two Americans heard shots inside the building. Afghans and Americans came tumbling down the stairs and out the door. MacDonald dashed up the stairs to see what had happened; Cook dropped to one knee with his automatic rifle to guard the entrance. After a few minutes, MacDonald, Snyder, and the medic came out carrying a small, struggling woman. Snyder ordered Cook to fetch a litter from the Humvee. When he brought it back, the sergeant saw that the woman's feet were tied and that she was handcuffed and bandaged around the abdomen. But she was still kicking and, to Cook's astonishment, yelling in English.

"Cover my feet!" Cook heard her say as he and the others tried to maneuver her onto the litter. "Cover my fucking feet! Cover my feet, you motherfucker!"

The Americans picked up the stretcher with the woman on it and ran for their Humvees.

From Ghazni, the woman was flown to another base, called Organ-E, where military surgeons operated on her to save her life. From Organ-E, she was flown to Bagram. With the woman now hospitalized, restrained, and under guard, the FBI at last took her fingerprints. It was only then that the United States confirmed her identity.

She was Aafia Siddiqui.

Twenty-four

Ayaan wasn't exaggerating when she told her father she was afraid to visit him without the police. She had told the Dutch Justice Ministry that of all possible assassins, she feared Somalis most.

It was true that many Somalis couldn't stand her. A lot of her own relatives, for example, refused to read anything written by or about her. They would turn off the TV rather than watch her being interviewed. They had heard enough.

Her cousin Omar Osman Haji, an influential clan leader and businessman, absolutely would not forgive her. I first met Omar in Kenya in 2006 at a hotel in Ayaan's childhood neighborhood of Eastleigh. It was easy to see, watching the man, where Ayaan got her regal manners. He wore leopard-skin slippers and a pale linen suit jacket over his spotless white gown. A tall, commanding figure, Omar stood out among the skinny Somalis lounging around that marbled lobby like a lion surveying a herd of gazelles.

We sat down in the deserted hotel restaurant. It was Ramadan, and Omar was fasting. I asked him about Ayaan's autobiography. He hadn't read it. As I nervously described Ayaan's account of Haweya's abortions and the days leading up to her death, he stroked his beard and tapped his cane against the floor.

His voice had thickened when he spoke again, and I saw that his eyes had misted over. "I don't know about any of that," Omar said shortly. "I don't know how Haweya died. I only know that it was very tragic. But if Ayaan would talk this way about her own sister, maybe it is not so surprising that she would talk the way she had about our Prophet."

Evidently more comfortable talking about Ayaan's perfidy than about his dead niece, he warmed to his topic.

"It is amazing," he said. "A child, born from a Muslim family, educated in Muslim schools, a relative who knows a lot about Islam—you can hardly believe that she would say such things. You know, if it's an illiterate person, if it's a convert, we say they got bad information. But she knows a lot.

"I wonder who put her up to it," he continued. "This is craziness, to insult a billion people. She just insults us like this. It's not fair. You are insulting 1.5 billion people. You have to respect the religion of Islam. You have to respect the people."

But what made him angrier than what Ayaan had said was the way the West applauded her.

"The West! We don't insult their religion. You must not insult the deepest beliefs of other people. I respect your beliefs. You should respect mine. This is what we are looking for."

His voice grew louder. "You talk about freedom of expression. To say, 'You are ugly, you are dirty,' is that freedom of expression?" He was shouting now.

"If I shit on your face, is that freedom of expression? It is not! It is an insult! You can't criticize what you don't know. Do you know me? Do you know Africa? Do you know Islam? If you don't know me, how can you criticize me?"

He dismissed Ayaan's book with the same aristocratic wave that had so irritated people in Holland when Ayaan used it on the abused women who didn't like her film "Submission." Omar said he didn't need to read the book to know that her family had the right, perhaps even the duty, to kill her.

"She is bringing problems between Muslims and the West. When others do it, we think maybe they don't know, it's ignorance. But she knows. A close relative can kill her now. And I must say, I am a close relative to her."

Ever since 2002, Ayaan's father had refused to discuss her with journalists, and he had ordered other family members to follow the same rule. He told Westerners that despite everything Ayaan had done, she was still his daughter and he didn't want to run her down. To other Somalis, he said he believed that she had gone mad, like her sister.

"It's tragic because he loved her so much," one of their cousins in London said. "He held her in very high regard."

Other members of the family said angrily that Ayaan had stopped sending money to her mother, who now lived in poverty in Somalia, and to her brother, who suffered from mental illness. Her formidable stepmother and stepsisters had disowned her long ago. A relative who was present in London when her stepsister Ijaabo first read the passages about herself in Ayaan's autobiography told me that Ijaabo had begun trembling so violently she had to leave the room to compose herself.

I called Ayaan's stepmother, Maryan Farah Warsame, not long after the Bush administration backed an Ethiopian invasion of Somalia in 2007. She was anxious to speak out about the killing of civilians. But Maryan's tone turned icy when I asked about her stepdaughter.

"There is just one thing I have to say," she interrupted. "I have nothing to do with *Al-i*. Do I make myself clear?" Her voice dripped with contempt as she pronounced the two syllables of the name that Ayaan had adopted when she moved to the Netherlands.

Ayaan rarely mentioned the torments of her homeland. She told David Pryce-Jones of *National Review* that she foresaw nothing but violence and war for Somalia. Pryce-Jones wrote, "The only way to prevent and cure these self-inflicted Third World injuries, Ayaan says, is Western intervention."

Her parents and other educated Somalis who remained connected to their homeland considered that attitude a way of writing Somalia off. To those who had lived through the U.S. "intervasion" of 1992–1994, it was clear that the West had neither the desire nor the means to fix Somalia. Indeed, as the country's agonies spilled into Western consciousness in the form of an al-Qaeda plot hatched there or a Somali pirate attack on a foreign ship, the United States no longer bothered to send soldiers or aid workers but used unmanned drones to hunt for suspects from the skies. The only thing the West wanted from Somalia was for the country to disappear. A good many Somalis seemed to think that Ayaan felt the same way.

Twenty-five

The U.S. government said nothing at first about its capture of Aafia Siddiqui. But word got back to Pakistan, setting off another maddening series of unexplained events.

Three days after Aafia was shot, Pakistan's Urdu press reported that her mother, Ismat Siddiqui, had died. Aafia's ex-father-in-law, Aga Naeem Khan, thought he might mend the rift between the families by visiting the Siddiquis' house and offering Fowzia his condolences. But as he and his driver entered the gate, they were shocked to see a young girl that they recognized as Maryam—Aafia and Amjad's daughter—playing in the garden.

Aga Naeem called to his granddaughter; Maryam saw him and ran inside. Then a servant came out and informed the visitors that Ismat was *not* dead but away in Islamabad.

Islamabad was already buzzing with fresh rumors that Aafia was being held at Bagram, just as Yvonne Ridley had said at her press conference two weeks earlier. Almost nobody, however, yet connected her presence there to the incident in Ghazni, which involved an alleged suicide bomber called "Saliha" and a boy called "Ali Hasan." Instead, the assumption was that Aafia had been at Bagram since she had disappeared in 2003.

Both Great Britain's Lord Nazir Ahmad and, independently, the nongovernmental Asian Human Rights Commission appealed to the U.S. government on July 24 to tell the truth about "Prisoner 650." That same day, a Pakistani barrister named Javed Iqbal Jaffree received two or three calls from a source who was supposedly inside

Bagram. The source said that Aafia was badly hurt and if someone didn't get her out of Bagram soon, the Americans were going to kill her. A Shiite from Lahore, Jaffree had attended Harvard Law School and was known for his willingness to challenge just about anyone. Jaffree didn't know the Siddiquis, and they didn't return his telephone calls, but, persuaded by his source's urgency, he went ahead on July 29 and filed a habeas corpus petition for Aafia Siddiqui—a petition her own family had long declined to file—before the Islamabad High Court. Meanwhile, another prominent Pakistani—Ansar Burney, a former federal minister and a member of a UN advisory committee on human rights—asked permission from both the U.S. and Afghan ambassadors to visit Aafia and other Pakistanis being held at Bagram.

It was a perfect storm of publicity, and it seemed to confuse the Siddiquis at first. Fowzia tried to discourage Jaffree from pursuing the case, telling him, as she had told others, that she didn't dare approach the court because the Americans were holding Aafia's children hostage. "Fowzia has stated that the U.S. is safekeeping the children," Jaffree told me when I phoned him. "She says the government of Pakistan is trying to help and that I should be careful." But he decided that Fowzia was naive to think that the United States and Pakistan were on her side, and he went ahead with his petition.

In the meantime, Yvonne Ridley and Lord Ahmad scheduled another demonstration on Aafia's behalf. It would be staged in London on August 1.

As for Aafia, she had been talking for almost ten days in Bagram to a pale young FBI agent named Angela Sercer, while CIA and FBI analysts in Washington were examining the documents, phone numbers, chemicals, and other items she had been found carrying. They were looking for anything they could use in the hunt for al-Qaeda.

A few hours before dawn on July 28, a barrage of U.S. missiles sailed across the border from Afghanistan and into a mud-walled madrassa in Pakistan's South Waziristan, near the village of Azam

Warsak. Among the bodies found in the rubble was that of al-Qaeda's famed chemical and biological weapons expert, fifty-four-year-old Abu Khabab al-Masri, and four other high-ranking Egyptians in al-Qaeda. Apparently al-Qaeda's second in command, Ayman al-Zawahiri, was among those wounded. A day after the strike, the same Pakistani Taliban leader, Baitullah Mehsud, who had been accused of murdering Benazir Bhutto, sent a message to Peshawar that was intercepted. Mehsud was urgently requesting a doctor for Zawahiri, who, Mehsud said, was suffering from infected wounds and severe pain.

Whether Aafia's statements or belongings had directed the Americans to Abu Khabab and his colleagues remains unknown, but the timing is intriguing.

The Siddiquis still hadn't made any public statement. On July 30, I e-mailed their American lawyer, Elaine Whitfield Sharp, to ask about Jaffree's petition, the London demonstration, and the reports of Ismat's death. Sharp wrote back the same day that "thankfully Ismat is not dead" (no one ever explained why the Urdu press had reported that she was) and that the family had had nothing to do with the legal moves or the demonstration. "It's been initiated by a human rights group, and the best thing to do is to call them with any questions. The family knows nothing about any of this."

Then on Sunday, August 3, Sharp, still at home north of Boston, announced the stunning news to the press that the FBI had notified the family that Aafia was "injured but alive" in Afghanistan. On Monday, before anyone could digest that, the U.S. Department of Justice released its own statement: Aafia had been arrested, announced U.S. Attorney Michael J. Garcia, and had already been flown from Afghanistan to New York. She was charged not with terrorism but with attempting to murder U.S. personnel on July 18 at the police station in Ghazni. Garcia said she had picked up a rifle that one of the U.S. soldiers had left lying on the floor and fired it at the Americans and Afghans who came to interview her.

The most wanted woman in the world was no longer wanted. If convicted, she could face life in prison.

Twenty-six

Ayaan attended a dinner in Australia with Prime Minister Kevin Rudd, afterward correcting him in an interview with Rebecca Weisser of the *Australian* for what she said was his misunderstanding of the Austrian economist Friedrich Hayek on the free market.

She hadn't talked much lately about *Shortcut to Enlightenment*, her proposed book about the Prophet debating Friedrich Hayek, John Stuart Mill, and Karl Popper, but in the admiring presence of Weisser, who had written an earlier article about Ayaan called "The Dangerous Odyssey of a Muslim Voltaire," Ayaan spoke with zest about her favorite project. "The great thing about Hayek is his proposition that the individual's life is here on earth, not in the hereafter," she told the reporter, beaming as she spoke.

Ayaan was stopping over in Los Angeles, on her way back from this pleasant trip, when Marco called her again. He had received another message from her half sister Sahra. Their father had slipped into a coma, and Ayaan needed to hurry to London if she wanted to see him.

So Ayaan called the twenty-four-year-old half sister whom she hadn't seen since Sahra was eight and Ayaan stopped in Ethiopia on her way to Germany. To Ayaan's surprise, Sahra didn't seem hostile to the family's most famous rebel. She assumed that Ayaan wanted to visit their father, and she seemed to take a furtive pleasure in helping to arrange it. She volunteered that Ayaan might feel more comfortable if she avoided the Royal London Hospital's normal visiting hours, when many other Somalis went to see her father and seek his blessing.

Ayaan phoned "a number of friends in Europe who might be influential" in helping her get to his bedside fast. A large black car from the Dutch Embassy was waiting for her when she reached London's Heathrow Airport. Behind it, Scotland Yard had positioned a smaller vehicle full of armed policemen. Whisked by this convoy through the darkened streets of London, Ayaan arrived at the hospital and went straight to the intensive care unit.

She found her father lying in bed. The family says he was already in a coma. Ayaan says he smiled at her.

She says he grasped her hand and made kissing gestures with his lips, gasping and struggling to speak. She wrote that she felt he was using his last strength to say something to her, but she didn't know what it was. She told him again that she loved him. She felt she saw in his eyes and in his gestures that he had forgiven her.

"He ultimately allowed his feelings of fatherly love to transcend his adherence to the demands of his unforgiving God," Ayaan wrote of what she sensed.

But visiting hours were quickly approaching. And despite the presence of her bodyguards and Scotland Yard, she wrote, she couldn't bear to meet any Somalis. So she slipped out of the hospital into Whitechapel Road, got into a car with her guards, and returned to Heathrow and the United States.

Twenty-seven

More than five years after her disappearance, Aafia limped into the same federal court in Manhattan where Ramzi Yousef and his Al-Kifah associates had been tried and found guilty of conspiring to bring down the World Trade Center fifteen years earlier. It was now August 5, 2008. Spectators craned their necks to get a look at the tiny thirty-six-year-old woman with the burgundy scarf over her hair. The judge read out the charges of attempted murder and assault; Aafia shook her head slowly and decisively. She seemed to be saying she wasn't guilty.

Pakistani and Western journalists agreed that her case was one of the most mysterious in a secret war dense with mysteries. Few believed the Bush administration when it claimed that the Afghan police had simply found her loitering in Ghazni on July 17, less than two weeks after Yvonne Ridley's press conference. Some suspected, rather, that the United States had set her up in Ghazni to conceal the fact that it had secretly imprisoned her for more than five years. The Pakistani press reinforced that suspicion by continuing to report it as a fact that Aafia and her children had been kidnapped on March 30, 2003, and later turned over to the FBI.

To U.S. civil rights attorneys, Aafia's case looked like the one they had been waiting for since the terror war had begun—the one that would reveal to everyone what the administration had been doing with its secret prisoners. If Aafia really had been locked up since 2003, she would be the first of the administration's ghost prisoners to be charged in a U.S. court. "You could have a judicial inquiry into how someone was treated at a black site—it would be incredibly valuable," said Jonathan Hafetz, the director of litigation for the Liberty and National Security Program at New York University's Brennan Center for Justice.

A mass of secret U.S. cables, released by WikiLeaks in 2010, showed that even the U.S. Embassy in Islamabad had been asking other U.S. government departments whether Aafia had been in secret custody. "Bagram officials have assured us that they have not been holding Siddiqui for the last four years, as is alleged," the embassy wrote on July 31, 2008, in a confidential cable about the case.

By chance, one of America's most celebrated civil litigators, Elizabeth Fink, happened to be on duty when Aafia was brought into court, and Fink was appointed to defend her. A large, untidy woman with a wild halo of gray curls, Fink was known to relish nothing more than highly political fights like this one. Her late law partner, William Kunstler, had defended the blind sheikh Omar Abdel Rahman in the World Trade Center trials in the mid-1990s. Since the 9/11 attacks, Fink herself had defended another of Sheikh Omar's lawyers, Lynne Stewart, against charges of aiding terrorists. American and Pakistani lawyers alike commented on how lucky Aafia was to have Fink on her side. Fink quickly declared that the charges against her new client were "patently absurd" and asked that the case be dismissed.

The next day, Elaine Whitfield Sharp flew to New York to join Fink and one of her associates for a meeting with Aafia at the Metropolitan Detention Center, the same high-security Brooklyn jail in which Uzair Paracha and Ramzi Yousef had been held.

Aafia was in a wheelchair. She said her wound, which stretched from her sternum to her pubic bone, still hurt. But she spoke to the lawyers for almost three hours through a food slot in the reception area while they crouched down to hear her.

Sharp came out of the meeting seething with indignation. She told reporters that Aafia had said she had been imprisoned at Bagram for a long time. "She doesn't know how many years, but it was the same location, and her captors were Americans, and the treatment was horrendous," Sharp told the *Boston Globe*. Fink claimed that the United States or its allies had planted the documents and other suspicious items that were found on Aafia: "She is the ultimate victim of the dark side."

But U.S. officials told a very different tale. They insisted that they had been looking for Aafia for years and had had no idea where she was before they took her into custody in July. They said the only time she had spent at Bagram was the two-week period after her surgery and before she was arrested and flown to the United States. "For several years, we have had no information regarding her whereabouts whatsoever," said Gregory Sullivan, a State Department spokesman on South Asian affairs. It was "our belief," Sullivan said, that she "has all this time been concealed from the public view by her own choosing."

As for the CIA, its people said they were delighted to have her at last.

"She is the most significant capture in five years," John Kiriakou, a retired CIA officer, told ABC News. Kiriakou had led the team that had caught the first key al-Qaeda figure, Abu Zubaydah. "We know that she's extremely bright. She's radicalized. We knew that she had been planning or at least involved in the planning of a variety of operations, whether they involved weapons of mass destruction or research into chemical or biological weapons, whether it was a possible attempt on the life of the president. We knew that she was involved with a great deal."

In interviews, as well as in the formal complaint against her, U.S. Justice Department officials cited the notes found in Aafia's bag that Captain Snyder and his people had started sorting out in Ghazni. They said the notes listed U.S. targets, including the Statue of Liberty, the New York City subway system, and the Plum Island Animal Disease Center, a U.S. government facility off the northeast coast of Long Island. The notes also speculated on how many people might die in "mass casualty attacks" and described ways not only to build a dirty bomb but also to bring down reconnaissance drones. Officials added that Aafia's thumb drive contained the names of specific terrorist cells and planned attacks.

U.S. prosecutors scoffed at Fink's claim that the notes might have been planted on her. "Hundreds of pages—in her own handwriting?" one terrorism expert who was close to the government's case told me. "She's going to have a hard time convincing a jury of that."

But Aafia's supporters found it equally unlikely that she would be carrying all those maps, substances, and recipes for bombs if she really was a terrorist. "A terrorist carrying manuals in [her] bag?" wrote "Uzair" from Islamabad to the *Times* Online. "That's the most ridiculous story I've heard from the Americans for a while! She was held hostage at one of FBI's dungeons for five years without charge, tortured."

Those who knew more were also mystified. Aafia's uncle S. H. Faruqi noted uneasily that the bag described in the complaint sounded very similar to the heavy bag that Aafia had been carrying when she had paid her secretive visit to his house in January. Her ex-husband, Amjad, was struck by the reported detail that Aafia had been carrying pages from *The Anarchist Arsenal.* Was it possible, he wondered, that she still had the photocopies she had made before they left Boston in 2002?

Amjad and his parents had been in shock since hearing of Aafia's capture. Despite everything, Amjad had always believed that wherever she was, she would take care of his children. Surely she understood her obligation to them. Now he didn't know what to think.

For the time being there was no news at all about the boy captured with Aafia in Ghazni. But a videotape had appeared on YouTube of their press conference in Ghazni, and Amjad recognized the boy as his son Ahmad. Remembering the mysterious and inaccurate reports in July of Ismat's death, he even wondered if the Siddiquis had concocted some dramatic plan to make Aafia reappear and the plan had gone drastically wrong. He could imagine his former wife being inspired by Yvonne Ridley's "Prisoner 650" press conference to want to emerge from hiding and show the world who the real Aafia Siddiqui was. Amjad guessed that she had been traveling with Ahmad—on whatever mission she thought she was on—so that the boy could act as her male guardian. For Amjad still couldn't believe that Aafia would become a suicide bomber, let alone turn her son into one.

Yet the more he read, the angrier he got, thinking of the danger in which she had placed the boy.

Aafia's family sprang into clamorous action. They finally began making the sort of eloquent appeals that the families of other Pakistani "missing persons" had been making for several years now. After five years of refusing to give interviews, Fowzia held a press conference on August 5 with the president of the Human Rights Commission of Pakistan. "I have decided to break my silence to say that one is innocent until proven guilty," she told reporters. "My sister is innocent and has never actually been accused of a crime. . . . Aafia was tortured for five years until one day the U.S. authorities announced that they have found her in Afghanistan."

Fowzia went on to assert that the United States had imprisoned Aafia because "she covers her hair and says her prayers." She claimed that the family hadn't previously reported Aafia missing because they had received death threats from self-described intelligence agents. Three weeks after she had told the Lahore lawyer Iqbal Jaffree that the United States was "safekeeping" Aafia's two younger children, Fowzia now announced that she didn't know where Maryam and Suleman were.

That statement, like several others Fowzia made, was laced with inaccuracies. For example, Aafia *had* been accused of a crime: she had been charged with attempted murder and assault. Moreover, the United States was hardly arresting every Muslim woman who covered her hair. Yet with the eager approval of the Pakistani establishment, the country's press swallowed her performance whole.

The Asian Human Rights Commission, on August 8, released a photo of a crumpled Aafia, lying down with her eyes closed and what appeared to be a swollen lip and broken nose. The governor of Ghazni later said the photo had been taken on July 17, after the police had beaten her. But in the press release that accompanied the photo, the Asian Human Rights Commission claimed that it "showed evidence of years of physical abuse." The same release claimed that she had been tortured to force her into testifying against KSM at his eventual trial for directing the 9/11 attacks. But rather than asking about the link between Aafia and KSM, Pakistan's press and political parties seized on the photo as proof that she was a victim of American torture. For Pakistanis, the image of the beaten Aafia would become as iconic as the picture of the scarecrow-hooded prisoner at Abu Ghraib was in Iraq.

Aafia attended a bail hearing on August 11 in a wheelchair. Dozens of Pakistanis bearing placards demonstrated outside, and the courtroom itself was filled with her supporters. Islamist groups appeared to be organizing many of the protests.

Aafia had told the FBI that the boy she had been captured with was an orphan she had brought to Afghanistan because she did not want to travel unaccompanied. (She also said that her family had told her not to go to Afghanistan but she hadn't been thinking clearly.) When agents confronted her with the boy's statement that the two of them had been living in the Pakistani town of Multan with Aafia's mother, Ismat, before traveling to Afghanistan, Aafia "vehemently denied" it, according to the FBI's report of her interrogation.

In August, however, U.S. officials informed the Siddiquis that DNA tests in Afghanistan had revealed that the boy really was Aafia's oldest son, Ahmad.

Aafia appeared to shut down after she learned that the FBI had discovered Ahmad's real identity and that the Afghan authorities were still holding the boy. She refused to see her lawyers, talk with them on the phone, or even receive mail. At the Metropolitan Detention Center, officials reported that she cried a great deal. She had asked them, they said, to put turkey from her meal in the refrigerator for her son, who she feared was being starved or tortured.

Aafia's mother provided a hint of what might have been preying on Aafia's mind. U.S. officials had found eleven-year-old Ahmad's birth certificate in Boston, and they knew he would turn twelve in November. Under U.S. law, a child over the age of twelve can be required to testify against his parents. According to a memo later filed by Aafia's defense, Ahmad had told investigators that he believed that he and his mother were on a suicide mission in Ghazni. And Ismat told Pakistan's *Frontier Post* that she feared that U.S. officials planned to hold the boy without charge until he was old enough to testify against Aafia.

The Pakistani public followed each twist of the drama with breathless sympathy. No matter what the news about Aafia, Geo TV ran the same banner: "Aafia Siddiqui—A Human Rights Tragedy." The *Daily Times* reported that sources in the Sindh government had said that official documents proved that Aafia and her children had been arrested on March 30, 2003—but the documents were never produced. It became an article of faith, though, that Aafia had been handed over to the FBI after this often-cited arrest. Moreover, despite everything that Pakistanis had seen of gun-toting jihadi women during the Lal Mosque crisis, most professed to find it impossible to believe that an upper-middle-class Pakistani woman could have picked up a military rifle and fired it at a U.S. soldier.

A Pakistani journalist in Washington was one of the few among his country's commentators to express some skepticism about the nimbus of martyrdom surrounding Aafia. Khalid Hasan, the longtime Washington correspondent for the *Daily Times*, reported on August 20 that the United States planned to bring additional and more serious charges against Aafia, ranging from money laundering to attempting to procure military equipment—both on behalf of al-Qaeda. He said the United States believed she had been underground for five years and that her children had been with her. A few days later, Hasan, who was dying of cancer, wrote a despairing column in which he described Pakistan's uncritical embrace of Aafia as another example of a suicidal unwillingness to face reality. "There is little interest in or scant regard for facts," Hasan wrote. "What matters are opinions, which are held with such vehemence that those in disagreement should be prepared for an assault or, at the very least, denunciation as this or that foreign power's agent."

But no one listened to him. Pakistan's government was teetering on the brink of collapse. A few days after Aafia was charged, Musharraf's turbulent reign ended with his resignation. Elections were called for September. Citing the example of the eighth-century Muslim conqueror of Aafia's home province of Sindh, Aafia's supporters lamented that her case proved once again how low Muslims and their secular rulers had sunk. The great Muhammad bin Qasim, they cried, had seized all of Sindh to rescue a Muslim woman! Now Muslims and Pakistanis like Musharraf openly sold pious women like Aafia to the enemies of Islam.

After years of tactfully praising Musharraf's government for its help, the Siddiquis now accused Pakistan's intelligence agencies of betraying the nation by handing her over to the Americans. "Without the active help of the agencies," Fowzia told reporters, it wouldn't have been possible to move Aafia out of the country. She also claimed (without evidence or even a relevant statement from Aafia or her lawyers) that her sister had been raped and tortured in prison and that the United States was denying her medical treatment. Her charges appeared on Pakistan's front pages.

Anne Patterson, the U.S. ambassador to Pakistan, wrote a letter to *Dawn* denouncing "erroneous and irresponsible media reports" and denying that the United States was mistreating Aafia in any way. Fowzia denounced Patterson's letter as "a pack of lies." On August 21, three days after Musharraf's resignation, Fowzia addressed the Pakistani Senate: "A few months back I felt I was alone with an ailing mother, but today I feel I have millions of family members with me in this plight to stand up to defend the ultimate symbol of purity and innocence—my sister, Aafia Siddiqui."

The National Assembly passed a unanimous resolution calling for Aafia's repatriation. The Senate voted to send a delegation to meet her.

Benazir Bhutto's widower, Asif Ali Zardari, who had been elected prime minister, now became president. Zardari's new interior minister, Rehman Malik, understood better than most that Aafia's marriage to Ali, KSM's nephew, linked her to the single most violent and extreme faction in all of jihad. As head of Pakistan's Federal Investigation Agency in the 1990s, Malik had tracked down Ramzi Yousef and his accomplices for Benazir Bhutto, including KSM's elusive older brother Zahid al-Sheikh. Malik knew that KSM's family operated at the intersection of Pakistan's jihadi groups, al-Qaeda, and the ISI; and Malik and President Zardari both believed that the dark forces behind that family were the same ones that had killed Benazir Bhutto.

Yet these new top officials did not challenge the Siddiqui family's claims. Instead, they promised their support for Aafia's defense.

The Bush administration had stepped up its drone attacks on the Taliban's tribal areas, killing hundreds of civilians in addition to some militants and inflaming Pakistani public opinion. Meanwhile, the Taliban and their allies seized bigger and bigger chunks of territory. They had extended their reach deep into Pakistan's North-West Frontier Province, where they busied themselves blowing up girls' schools, enlisting boys as suicide bombers, and murdering policemen and elected officials. More than a million Pakistanis in the north had been driven from their homes. Even in the country's normally placid capital, the horror of Taliban-backed suicide bombs kept people on edge.

I decided I badly needed to go back.

Twenty-eight

Ayaan's father died about a week after her visit, on August 25, 2008.

The British press took no notice. But Somali Web sites and newspapers everywhere ran the great man's three-page obituary with the same youthful, optimistic photograph of him in a pin-striped suit that Ayaan carried in her wallet. Somalis flocked to his funeral from all over the United Kingdom and Europe. For many, his death marked the final passing of that moment when the newborn Somali state had first stood on its wobbly legs and men like Hirsi had imagined that they would build "America in Africa." All that was gone now, smashed in "the apocalypse," as Somalis called the multisided civil war that continued to burn in Somalia.

Ayaan and her father never had the emotional reconnection that *The Weekly Standard* said Frederick Douglass and his former master had enjoyed—that last parting in which "each acknowledged ways he had wronged the other . . . conversed freely about the past and parted reconciled." For some reason, Ayaan hadn't called, hadn't gone to London sooner. At the time she had told herself that the trip was simply not convenient; but now that her father was dead, she wondered whether she had been afraid to open the door to the past. "If I had gone to his side and spoken truthfully to him before he died, I might have had to open an emotional closet I have nailed shut," she wrote. She was filled with regret.

Twenty-nine

This time in Islamabad, I stayed with friends rather than at the Marriott. Pakistan would soon overtake Iraq as the world capital of suicide bombing, and by September 2008 it was too dangerous to hang around a hotel that the jihadis had already tried twice to bomb. In the first eight months of that year, more than 471 Pakistanis had been killed in suicide attacks, most of them the work of the Pakistani Taliban. The United States, meanwhile, continued firing missiles at the militants in Waziristan, and ordinary Pakistanis, angry and terrified, felt caught in the middle.

Some of Pakistan's newspapers made the situation even more confusing. If the English-language papers seem to reflect the country's ego, its Urdu papers are like its id. The latter print lurid conspiracy theories involving malignant agents of the Dajjal—India, Israel, and the United States. Now they were also telling convoluted tales about how Blackwater, the U.S. mercenary company, was responsible for the suicide attacks and how Pakistan's secular government had sold Aafia ("Daughter of the Nation") to be raped and tortured in a U.S. jail.

The rallies for her were massive. There were no rallies for the thousands of Pakistanis being killed by bombs and assassinated in the tribal areas. Most people were too fearful of the militants and their hidden backers in the Sunni elite to take a stand. "Please don't quote me saying anything against them," an elderly member of the ruling family of Swat, a pristine mountain area once beloved of tourists, told me when I visited him in his Islamabad bungalow. "Those chaps would think nothing of cutting my head off."

Even liberal Pakistanis preferred to turn their rage against the United States. If it weren't for the Americans—who had nurtured the jihadis to fight the Soviets in Afghanistan, then gotten into a fight with them and were now bribing Pakistan's rulers to do the same—the country wouldn't be on the brink of civil war. Or so I heard, over and over. "We don't know who these people are," said a young woman whose affluent family had moved from Peshawar to Islamabad for safety. "We used to think they were part of us, but now we don't know. We think the CIA or RAW"—India's intelligence agency—"is behind them." The backing that Pakistan's government had given the militants for twenty years seemed to have vanished from their minds.

Aafia was the perfect emblem of this mood. Despite the unanswered questions about where she had been and despite the unmistakable hand of the religious parties in whipping up daily protests on her behalf, Pakistanis of every description latched on to the cause of this "Daughter of the Nation"—desperate, perhaps, for something to unite them.

"Free Dr. Aafia" began appearing on walls even in remote areas. Retired generals published poems about her on the Internet. "To filthy scum they sold the bride," ran one typical offering. "Yet the mighty Creator, seeing it all, unveils the gruesome act they hide!" She became the new symbol of Islamic victimhood. Mass-printed by the thousands, the picture of her crumpled figure became the latest bloody flag to wave, a new scab to be ripped from the wound, a new proof of Pakistan's impotence against America—and of the need for an Islamist takeover.

Just as the question of whether the Dutch government had been wrong to stop paying for Ayaan's bodyguards became a political litmus test in the West, so the question of whether the Pakistani government was wrong to let the United States go unpunished for brutalizing "Dr. Aafia" became a test of Pakistani pride and nationalism.

The former ISI agent Khalid Khawaja, with his Defense of Human Rights group, was especially busy in rallying support for

Aafia. The mysterious Khawaja, who seemed to have plenty of money, had left the apartment where I first met him four years earlier for a larger neoclassical house farther away from town. Still dressed in his cotton gown and skullcap, he had smoothed his edges a bit. He ranted less about the angelic qualities of Osama bin Laden and more about how the United States and its Pakistani "slaves and puppets" were violating the human rights of Muslim prisoners. But as we began to talk about Aafia, Khawaja openly admitted that he had been trying to steer me away from trying to find her when I had visited him and Zaynab Khadr, the daughter of the Canadian al-Qaeda man, back in 2004. "There was a feeling," he said, tapping his foot, "that maybe Aafia has gone underground herself, and so why take up this case. . . . Now, of course, I see that I was wrong. Aafia's case is one of the worst crimes in history."

Aafia, he said, was no ordinary person. "She was unique, standing out from the whole block. She was like an angel." He said he had come to believe that Pakistani intelligence had picked up Aafia in 2003 and held her until 2008. "I think it is probably not the Americans but our government that has done the worst to Aafia," he continued. "I am quite sure that most of the blame is going to fall on Pakistan." He said he had heard that she had been separated from her children, and that her youngest, Suleman, had died while in custody.

But when I asked who had told him that, he waved away my question and began slapping his knee. "I don't know exactly. It is just a strong hearsay."

It struck me again that Khawaja—who was now building up Aafia as a holy martyr—seemed to be in awfully close contact with the same jihadi groups for which Aafia was accused of working. When I asked if he would help me reach the relatives of Aafia's second husband, Ali, and the relatives of Majid Khan, the man for whom U.S. prosecutors claimed that Aafia had rented that post office box, he simply whipped out his telephone and began calling them. None wanted to speak to a reporter on the telephone, but he had their numbers on speed dial. I asked if he also knew Khalid Sheikh Mohammed. He answered with a diatribe on how KSM had *not* directed 9/11. The real mastermind, Khawaja said, had been the "Satanic rule which is behind Bush and all of this." As for KSM's family, he said, "You know, you call them the worst people, but we call them the best people. That family is really outstanding. We get inspiration from them."

Who did Khawaja really work for? Al-Qaeda? The ISI? Himself? All of them—at least that was my guess.

And now he had taken up the quest, like much of the rest of Pakistan, of making sure that Aafia's son Ahmad was brought back from Afghanistan and reunited with Aafia's sister and parents. The U.S. government had originally planned to take Ahmad to the United States, where he would stay with Aafia's brother, Ali. But after politicians had denounced the United States in Parliament for illegally detaining a Pakistani minor who had committed no crime, and after the Pakistani embassies in Kabul and Washington had demanded his return, the U.S. and Afghan governments had agreed to release him to Fowzia.

According to the *New York Times*, the boy had admitted to Afghan intelligence that he belonged to Jaish-e-Muhammad. Under Pakistani law, custody would normally have gone to his father, Amjad, because his mother was in jail. But with the whole country rooting for Fowzia to get him, Amjad decided not to interfere.

Much of the Pakistani press corps turned out at the Islamabad airport to record the reunion of the shy, black-haired boy and his veiled, tearful aunt, who was staying in the capital at the home of her uncle S. H. Faruqi. Fowzia had scheduled another news conference at the Islamabad Press Club for the following day. About eighty journalists waited for an hour for her to arrive and tell them where Ahmad said he had been for the past five years, but she failed to show up. Finally a businessman friend of hers appeared with the news that Pakistan's intelligence agencies had surrounded Faruqi's bungalow and ordered Fowzia not to meet with reporters.

Since many news reports were still calling the boy Ali and others said he might actually be an orphan, I later asked Fowzia's friend, who said he preferred to remain anonymous, if he was sure the boy was Aafia's son.

"Even I can see it!" he told me. "All you have to do is to look at the eyes." He added that the boy had also recognized Fowzia. But he said a shadow had come over the boy's face when the businessman asked him what name he preferred to be called. "I don't like to talk about my name," the boy replied. "Every time I change my name, something bad happens."

I asked Fowzia's friend why the boy's name might have been changed. He shrugged. "Maybe he has been hiding, and his mother changed his name," he told me, "or maybe whoever has been holding her has changed his name."

The next day, Fowzia took the boy back to her mother's house in Karachi. Soon she told the press that he was "mentally unfit" and so traumatized that he didn't remember his own name. Khalid Khawaja and others began to say that maybe he wasn't Ahmad after all. "The child doesn't even know about Aafia," Khawaja told me, shaking his head sadly, when I went to see him the next day. Fowzia herself declined my requests for an interview.

I left Islamabad for Karachi. This time no one bothered me about a travel permit. The Siddiquis still wouldn't see me when I got there. But some of KSM's family did.

I contacted them through the lawyer who had filed the missing persons petition before the Supreme Court for KSM's sister Maryam. Maryam herself was in Iran, but KSM's uncle, Mohammed Hussein Abid Baluch, and his wife and Ali's sister Amna all came to meet me at the lawyer's office in the dimly lit old sandstone building across from the British-era Karachi courthouse. They told me I was the only foreign journalist to meet with them, and as far as I know I still am.

KSM's uncle had a clever, hawkish face, but the al-Baluchi were in general less polished than the Siddiquis. I could imagine Aafia's mother disapproving of her marrying into their family. The uncle wore a simple cotton skullcap. The two women in their black polyester abayas and niqabs—including Aafia's sister-in-law Amna—twisted and turned in their chairs and tucked up their feet. They didn't speak English and evidently were more comfortable sitting on the floor. In previous interviews with the Pakistani press, other members of the KSM clan had cheerfully admitted that Ali and Aafia had been married. Ramzi Yousef's older brother, Abdul Qadeer, had even described how the pair had used to argue. By the time I met them, the family had grown more cautious. They told me they didn't know for sure whether Aafia had married Ali before he was captured. But they said they wouldn't have objected if he had. "It is a blessing to marry divorced women," Ali's sister Amna said. "Our Prophet did it, peace be upon him."

I wanted to go on talking with KSM's relatives and learn more about this extraordinary family, whose members had been involved in nearly every serious al-Qaeda attack on the United States over the past two decades—attacks that had killed thousands. What made them do it? But KSM's uncle was getting restless. It was late in the afternoon. He said they needed to get home in time to break the Ramadan fast. So we said our good-byes, and I went back to the small Karachi hotel where I was staying.

The hotel's televisions and computers were down when I reached my room. So it wasn't until my husband phoned me from Amsterdam that I learned that a suicide bomber in a dump truck had finally succeeded in blowing up the Marriott Hotel in Islamabad. The attack coincided with the time of day when the maximum number of upper-crust Pakistanis would be attending parties there to break the Ramadan fast. Sixty people were killed, not counting the bomber. All that night, Pakistani television broadcast scenes of firemen slipping and sliding in blood as they tried to douse the burning building.

Later, an investigation traced the attack to the same conglomerate of Deobandi jihadi groups—Lashkar-e-Jhangvi, Jaish-e-Muhammad, and the Pakistani Taliban—that were so closely associated both with KSM's family and with Aafia.

Might KSM's relatives have wanted to go home because they

knew the blast was coming and planned to watch the aftermath on television? I had no way of finding out. When I suggested to the Pakistani colleague who had accompanied me to my interview that we visit the family again—but in Lyari this time, at their house—he begged me so earnestly not to do it that I took his advice. Soon afterward, I left the country.

Thirty

Ayaan got a call from her cousin Magool after her father died. Magool was the Somali girl who had lived briefly with Ayaan and Marco in Leiden. She had done well in the years since Ayaan had seen her and was now studying law at a British university.

Magool said she wanted to ask a favor.

Instantly Ayaan was suspicious. "From the old days," she wrote, "I know that Somali relatives ask—no, demand—money, immigration papers, the smuggling of people and goods; they request to be allowed to camp in your home for three days only, which stretch into forever."

But Magool just wished that Ayaan would call her mother, Asha.

Ayaan protested that she didn't think her mother wanted to talk to her. But Magool said that Asha did want to hear from her, and she gave Ayaan her cell phone number in the remote hamlet of Las Anod where she was living. "She is all alone now and she talks about you all the time," Magool said.

Ayaan wrote in *Nomad* that she could imagine how her mother was living: a cinder-block house with a dirt floor surrounded by "thorn bushes and endless dust." Just thinking about it made her feel guilty. She knew that in Somali eyes it wasn't her parents who had abandoned her but she who had abandoned them—and to poverty and disease.

For a while, she couldn't get through to the number. But then one day as she was driving along in a car with an American friend, she tried again, and her mother answered.

They spoke for a few minutes about the death of Ayaan's father. Then her mother asked if Ayaan prayed and fasted and read the Quran. Ayaan replied that the Quran didn't appeal to her. Her mother hung up the phone.

If Ayaan had been alone, that might have been the end of it. But the American friend who had overheard the conversation talked Ayaan into calling her mother back and apologizing. Mother and daughter began to talk, albeit in a distant and sometimes hurtful way. And Ayaan says she started sending her mother and brother money.

Thirty-one

Aafia remained stubbornly, bafflingly silent. She refused to attend her arraignment, and she refused to attend a hearing in September. Nor would she meet with visitors. Cut off from contact, her lawyers backed away from their early assertions that she had been held and tortured by the Americans in Bagram. Fink began saying that Aafia had been held by "somebody—American or Pakistani intelligence—on the dark side."

But in Pakistan's peculiar way, the public there absorbed such vague statements without letting it dent their conviction that Aafia was innocent. It seemed to me that they knew and didn't know at the same time that Aafia was a jihadi, and they preferred to keep it that way.

After Aafia missed several of her own hearings, Fink wrote to the court in September suggesting that her client was suffering from post-traumatic stress disorder. She said that she had not been able to develop a relationship of trust with Aafia and she did not think Aafia was mentally competent to assist in her own defense. The Justice Department agreed that Aafia should be evaluated, and an early-psychiatric report by the Bureau of Prisons diagnosed her as psychotic.

In October, Judge Richard M. Berman ordered that she be sent to the only specialized medical facility in the U.S. prison system for women, the Federal Medical Center, Carswell—in Fort Worth, Texas—for further evaluation.

The Pakistani Senate sent a delegation to meet with her at FMC, Carswell, in December. The senators found her in good spirits. She still wasn't able to explain exactly where she had been for the past five years; all she remembered, she said, was getting into a taxi after her fight with her mother in 2003 and then waking up at Bagram. (She warned the senators that she had made some statements to the FBI that might not look good to the Pakistani public, but she said she had done it only because her children had been threatened.) Apparently that was good enough for the Pakistani Senate, which voted to allocate $1.8 million to her defense.

Aafia's ex-husband, Amjad, had not wanted to tangle with the Siddiquis either in court or in the media since returning from Saudi Arabia in 2004. But as time passed and the Siddiquis denied him access to Ahmad, and no one came forward to say where Maryam and Suleman were, he felt he had no choice.

In December, he wrote a letter to *Dawn* announcing that he had decided to sue the Siddiquis for custody of Ahmad. In February 2009, he agreed to an interview with the *News*. "Aafia's mother and Dr Fowzia had warned me at the time of our divorce that they would take revenge by not letting me meet the children," Amjad said, adding, "but now they are discouraging a meeting with Ahmad because they fear Ahmad will reveal the truth about Aafia's activities and the whereabouts of his siblings over these years."

The Jamaat-e-Islami party rushed to defend the Siddiquis. Anwar ul-Haq, a U.S.-educated pathologist who had announced after the September 11 attacks that the Mossad had done it, now wrote letters to *Dawn* denouncing Amjad as a "sadistic extremist" and a sexual pervert.

Pakistan's spy agency, meanwhile, cautioned Amjad's family that if they went forward with their custody suit, it might hinder Aafia's possible repatriation, and they might also put themselves in danger from Ali Abdul Aziz Ali's family—that is, KSM's relatives. Some people would have taken that as a serious government threat, but after many delays Amjad filed his suit anyway.

The Siddiquis didn't respond directly to his allegations; instead, Ismat's brother S. H. Faruqi wrote to *Dawn* to say the boy whom

Amjad called his son might not be Ahmad after all. Faruqi claimed that Ahmad continued to insist he was an orphan from Balakot whose family had died in the 2005 earthquake; now Ahmad supposedly told Faruqi that he had been held by U.S. and Italian soldiers and given a new name every few months and that he had been scolded and sometimes physically punished if he failed to remember the new story.

In Faruqi's account, the boy said he had been ordered to travel to Ghazni with Aafia. Faruqi said he didn't know who had given the order.

When I asked Faruqi about this complicated letter to *Dawn*, he wrote me back that Fowzia had commissioned two DNA tests on Ahmad and that she remained dissatisfied with the results. (Evidently she claimed not to believe the result of the U.S. test that identified the boy as Aafia's son.) Amjad, meanwhile, who was certain just by looking at his pictures that the boy was his son, volunteered to have his DNA tested to prove it; the Siddiquis ignored him.

Only Aafia herself, if her continued silence was any clue, may have realized that the days of doublethink were over. So far she had been charged only with shooting at some U.S. soldiers. But even if she were found innocent on that charge, the U.S. prosecutor had filed a statement leaving open the possibility that she might also be charged with providing support to terrorism in connection with opening the post office box in Maryland for Majid Khan.

Thirty-two

Ayaan kept lecturing—especially at universities, Jewish groups, and conservative organizations such as the Goldwater Institute, which had given her an award in 2007. "Islam is not a religion of peace," she told a Palm Beach audience in March 2008. "It is a political theory of domination that seeks conquest by any means it can."

But the surging popularity of the Democratic presidential candidate, Barack Obama, in the fall of 2008 suggested that most Americans favored a more nuanced approach to the war on terror.

Obama's stated desire to mend relations with the Muslim world was completely at odds with Ayaan's penchant for confrontation. Yet it wasn't as easy for Ayaan to dismiss Obama as she had dismissed other Western politicians. As the son of an African Muslim economist and a white American anthropologist who had spent years in Indonesia as a boy, Obama could lay claim to knowing more about Islam than most Americans. He also had a large political following, which Ayaan and the neoconservatives lacked—and not just among Muslims but among Americans generally, who told pollsters they agreed with Obama when he said, "The United States is not at war with Islam and never will be."

Ayaan had seemed receptive at first to America's new master of cool. "I think he is very smart," she reported enthusiastically to the *Australian* in June 2008. "I don't think it matters that he has, in his very short career, a left-liberal record. I think that just shows consistency."

But it was too late for Ayaan to make another switch, and from her perch at the American Enterprise Institute she began to snipe at the Democratic candidate. At first she made the unusual claim that Obama and the Republican candidate, Senator John McCain, wouldn't be very different presidents. Then, in a more conventional taunt from the right, she accused Obama of boosting the jihadists by planning to "cut and run" in Iraq.

In November, America's voters elected Obama as the country's first African-American president. Ayaan remained publicly silent about this historic election. She said and wrote nothing for the press about what such a vote might mean for Africans, for Muslims—or for Americans after centuries of slavery and racial prejudice. Nor did she comment on Obama's promise to close Guantánamo and open up at least some of the files on the Bush administration's record of torture and imprisonment outside any legal system. When the new president made a speech in Cairo reaching out to Muslims, she said he had disappointed moderate Muslims by failing to emphasize human rights. "According to the President," she told the Web site New Majority, "we are only fighting a very small number of extremists, but it's not Islam, so if that's the case then there really isn't much to reform." She also pointed out, correctly, that he had failed to address sharia law in relation to women.

She kept writing op-eds, often for the *Wall Street Journal*, assailing liberals for their blindness to the dangers of Islam. But the audiences she attracted were getting smaller, and her American critics seemed bolder. At Scripps College in Claremont, California, a female rabbi complained after hearing Ayaan that she couldn't imagine the college inviting a speaker who called for the annihilation of Judaism or Christianity to address its students. In the Netherlands, critics panned *Adan and Eva*, the book that she and a children's author (writing under the name Anna Gray) produced in 2008 about the friendship between a Muslim boy and a Jewish girl. As for her often-promised sequel to "Submission," she eventually became persuaded that the plan was too risky.

She still grew animated when talking about *Shortcut to Enlightenment*, the book she planned to write about the Prophet Muhammad waking up in the New York Public Library. But the book didn't happen, and to keep her career going she needed something new. She had always had her greatest success telling her own story—of her family and how the West had delivered her from Islam—but in the five years she had gone without speaking to her relatives she had been cut off from that source of material.

Perhaps her telephone conversations with her family after her father's death suggested a new angle.

In any case, the publishers Free Press and Knopf Canada announced in February 2009 that Ayaan would be coming out with another memoir. According to Louise Dennys, the executive publisher of Knopf Random Canada Publishing Group, this sequel to *Infidel* would again explore Ayaan's feelings about Islam. "It will be a blend of personal narrative and reportage, weaving together Ayaan Hirsi Ali's ongoing story, including her reconciliation with her father who disowned her, addressing the situation of girls and women in the world today, and speaking openly about her own efforts to reconcile Islamic and Western values." Dennys did not say whether Ayaan planned to use a ghostwriter again.

Thirty-three

Aafia's psychiatric evaluation provided the first strong evidence that she was in the grip of an obsessive anti-Semitism.

Her attorney, Elizabeth Fink, had been eager to expose what she expected would be Aafia's tale of torture, but after one interview, Aafia refused to see Fink or speak to her on the phone. Later court documents revealed that Aafia not only didn't want to deal with the celebrated civil rights lawyer because she was Jewish but also refused to talk to anyone else at the Metropolitan Detention Center whom she suspected of being Jewish.

At FMC, Carswell, Aafia seemed to relax. She said later that she thought the Bureau of Prisons' assessment that she was psychotic would be enough for her to be found incompetent to stand trial. The Pakistani senators and embassy officials who visited told her to be patient while they worked to get her released on humanitarian grounds.

She was therefore shocked when a new set of psychiatrists appeared to evaluate her. When one of them tried to question her, she put her hands over her ears and screamed for the woman to go away.

She seems to have believed she could trade information for her release, asking several times to speak to the FBI agents who had questioned her at Bagram, Angela Sercer and Bruce Kammerman. She wrote what she described as a "highly confidential letter" to Carswell's warden, which she asked the warden to share only with "loyal African-Americans" and to give to President Obama. The letter claimed that the U.S. wars against Pakistan and Afghanistan were "designed to 'benefit' Israel at the expense of the very existence of the USA."

"Study the history of the Jews," Aafia wrote. "They have always back-stabbed everyone who has taken pity on them and made the 'fatal' error of giving them shelter. This was the 'crime' of the Palestinian Arabs and this is the 'crime' of the USA—and it is this cruel, ungrateful back-stabbing of the Jews that has caused them to be mercilessly expelled from wherever they gain strength. This is why 'holocausts' keep happening to them repeatedly! If they would only learn to be grateful and change their behavior!! But they will not! And history will repeat itself as it always does!"

She wrote to Judge Berman, who she evidently believed was Jewish, quoting to him from the Quran about the duty of women to "stay quietly in your houses" and asking to let her follow the example of the Prophet's wife Aisha in the seventh century; Aisha "once left her city to try to settle matters in a political dispute among Muslims, but her action was in error and resulted in a horrible war between Muslims," Aafia wrote. "She regretted and repented all her life for what she did and she shunned politics thereafter. I fear similarly for my 'peace efforts' and would much rather leave men's world to GOD and obey his commands regarding women as quoted above."

She claimed that she wasn't against all "Israeli-Americans," and she brought up the example of the wise associate dean at Brandeis who had allowed her to graduate despite the "nasty game" someone else in authority had played that had almost forced her to "go after Brandeis" and "open a can of worms." She warned the judge that "prison here is not my 'house'" and that if the "Zionist elements seeking to harm me" insisted upon a trial, she would "open a BIG can of worms and expose a lot of unpleasant facts about many, possibly Israeli Americans."

But Aafia was disappointed again. The government's psychiatrists found her mentally capable of standing trial, and Judge Berman appointed a new defense attorney, Dawn Cardi, to replace Fink. A hearing on her competency was scheduled for June 7, 2009.

I saw Aafia myself for the first time at that competency hearing in Judge Berman's oak-paneled courtroom on Pearl Street in Manhattan. She entered wearing a cream-colored polyester scarf across her face and a long beige gown. Only her flashing dark eyes were visible, but her fiery personality soon became obvious as she interrupted her lawyers and harangued the court about her desire to make peace between the Taliban and the United States.

She wanted nothing to do with Cardi, a pleasant-looking woman wearing a shiny gold jacket. When Cardi spoke, Aafia would turn away or put her head down on the table, behavior, Cardi said, that demonstrated her mental illness. Cardi and the defense psychologist, Thomas Kucharski, argued that Aafia's political convictions—"her beliefs that Israel, the United States and India are conspiring to invade Pakistan, that Jews are responsible for 9/11 and have infiltrated American political and nongovernmental organizations"—were so bizarre as to amount to insanity. Sitting in the courtroom, I couldn't help reflecting on how common such views are in Pakistan. They're literally talk show staples.

Kucharski spoke of the "satchel of strange writings" that Aafia had been carrying in Afghanistan. "Some of her writings are frankly psychotic," he said. "I find it hard to believe that a trained neuroscientist can believe in these half-baked ideas. She talks about explosions or instructions for chemical weapons. These are grandiose ideas. They are delusional. . . . She has a factual but not a rational understanding of the world around her. She is not capable of assisting her defense."

Aafia sat up at this point. "I was trying to make peace!" she cried out. "I am a student of Noam Chomsky! All I ever wanted was to end the war, and I didn't shoot anyone!" She was led out of the courtroom.

Kucharski said that Aafia's claims that her children were dead and that she had seen them in hallucinations, that she herself was dead, and that the Bureau of Prisons had released a video on the Internet of her being strip searched were evidence of her disorder.

But the government psychiatrist Dr. Sally Johnson said Aafia was faking.

Johnson had stayed in FMC, Carswell, for several days, watching Aafia both when Aafia was aware of her and sometimes when she wasn't. Johnson also interviewed prison staff there and in Brooklyn about Aafia's behavior. Aafia refused to speak to Johnson. Often she would act as if she were sobbing, sometimes crying out that she had been told her still-missing daughter would be raped if she talked. But Johnson observed that Aafia's eyes remained dry and that as soon as she thought Johnson was out of sight she would begin to act normally.

"I disagree that she suffers from delusional disorder and I don't believe she's suffering from major depression," Johnson testified. "Many of the ideas Dr. Kucharski has put down to delusional thinking are not abnormal in radical groups. These things are accepted within her peer groups."

Cardi tried to argue that Aafia might be suffering from post-traumatic stress disorder due to the torture she and her children had endured during the years she was missing. But Johnson pointed out that Aafia herself had never given anyone—not her brother, not her lawyers, not the Pakistani senators or the embassy personnel who came to visit, not the prison staff, and not the psychiatrists—a clear account of any torture or imprisonment.

Personally, I found this vagueness very damaging to Aafia's case. By contrast, KSM and the other "high-value" detainees who had been held in secret CIA prisons were capable of giving the Red Cross elaborate descriptions of waterboardings and other tortures they had suffered, and they described them as soon as they got the chance.

Moreover, both government and defense psychiatrists who had access to the FBI's secret interrogation reports noted that Aafia had told the agents at Bagram that she had spent her missing years not as a prisoner at Bagram but hiding in Pakistan.

Judge Berman found Aafia competent to stand trial. The date was set for November.

Thirty-four

Ayaan Hirsi Ali had been telling reporters for years that she wanted to have a child, but so far she hadn't done it. She gravitated toward wealthy, older intellectuals such as Herman Philipse, but her relationships never seemed to last.

But at the 2009 *Time* gala, Ayaan seems to have found the love she was waiting for.

She was first introduced to the boyishly handsome British historian Niall Ferguson at a conference put on by a conservative Australian think tank called the Centre for Independent Studies. Later the two really clicked, it's said, when they met again at the *Time* party in Lincoln Center.

Like Ayaan, the forty-five-year-old Ferguson was invited because he had been named earlier as one of the hundred most influential people in the world. He was making a reputation for himself as a rather blunt defender of Western imperialism, past and present, and he had first landed on *Time*'s list in 2004 under the title "Theorist of Liberal Imperialism." As *Time* noted in the article explaining its choice, "Timing is everything," and, as the United States was invading Iraq, Ferguson had published *Empire*, "a book whose central thesis was a defense of the 'liberal imperialism' that Britain purported to practice toward the end of its time as a great power. Moreover, Ferguson argued that the United States, whether it wanted to admit the fact or not, had become an imperialist power itself" and ought to do the job properly.

A superb storyteller and astonishingly prolific, Ferguson dealt in ideas that went down well in large segments of Great Britain and America. Not just *Empire* but also *The War of the World* (2006) and *The Ascent of Money* (2008) became British television series. Ferguson, meanwhile, collected academic posts at Oxford, New York University, Harvard—and later other famous schools. He wrote that he had come to love the empire as a child in Kenya, where his Scottish father had briefly worked as a doctor and which he recalled in *The War of the World* as much better run in those days. Ferguson considered decolonization to have been mostly a mistake. Particularly in Africa, he wrote, "some form of imperial governance" might have been better than independence.

Ayaan, of course, had grown up on the other side of Nairobi from Ferguson, and she would never have been accepted in the semicolonial British society of the 1960s that he remembered so wistfully. Yet she wasn't bothered by what critics called Ferguson's failure to present the viewpoints of the colonized. She herself had been charged with the same failing, and she had long shared his belief that many parts of the Third World would benefit from Western rule.

Ferguson was married with three children to the former publishing executive Susan Douglas, but the chemistry between him and Ayaan prevailed. Photographs from the *Time* party record their attraction. Ayaan was wearing a short cobalt blue satin dress. In one picture, Ferguson stands with his arm wrapped around her shining waist, looking thunderstruck. Soon he and Ayaan were spending as much time together as their travel schedules allowed.

Among many other talents, Ferguson was a leading historian of finance. His ability to explain the origins of the Western financial system—and his conviction that it, too, was basically a good thing—had helped make him a wealthy man, with earnings sometimes estimated at more than $4 million a year. Ferguson also had the reputation of being tight-fisted, however, and some of his friends wondered whether the "intense dislike of spending money" to which he confessed might clash with Ayaan's free-spending habits. Yet the relationship flourished.

Ferguson's marriage was apparently in trouble before he met Ayaan. His wife, Susan, a fifty-two-year-old former Fleet Street newspaper editor and magazine executive, lived in England with their children. She and Ferguson had met when she was an editor at the *Daily Mail*, and he had briefly moonlighted there. She had supported him financially when he was a young don at Oxford. But his and Ayaan's lawyers later wrote to the *Independent* of London that he had already "moved out of the marital home" before he met Ayaan. (Actually, Ferguson and his wife owned three houses, a working farm in Oxfordshire, an eleventh-century castle near the Welsh border, and a town house in Boston, the oldest on Beacon Hill.)

With Ayaan's fortieth birthday approaching in November, he agreed to help sponsor her birthday party at a five-star Manhattan hotel, reportedly picking up a bar tab for many thousands of dollars. The party was a celebration of how far Ayaan had come since arriving in the United States three years earlier. Old friends from the Netherlands, including her Dutch foster mother and Marco van Kerkhoven, were on hand to watch as more than a hundred guests, including some of the wealthiest people in the world, lined up to have their photos taken with Ayaan, dressed in a long brown evening gown. That evening she gave an interview to Steffie Kouters, the reporter who had first put her into the Dutch national eye in 2002. Although Ferguson's wife still didn't know about Ferguson and Ayaan (by one account, he invited his wife to the party and then, after she flew to New York, told her it was happening elsewhere after all), Ayaan regaled Kouters with the story of her love affair. "This is him," she said, pointing to a picture of Ferguson. "Most of the time, I think: this is the man I belong with," she said. But there were also "big problems" because Ferguson was married and Ayaan said she didn't intend to be polygamous. In a speech to the guests, Ferguson said he had never met anyone as sharp as Ayaan.

The pair went public in January 2010. Ayaan was flown secretly to make a surprise appearance at India's Jaipur Literature Festival, an important event for the global literary set. Ferguson was giving another talk there, and they were photographed kissing on the grounds of the opulent Hotel Diggi Palace. Two weeks later, on February 12, the *Daily Mail* broke the news that Ferguson was leaving his wife for Ayaan. The story's impudent headline read, "The History Man and the Fatwa Girl."

Thirty-five

If Aafia had listened to her lawyers, she might have been found not guilty.

She still hadn't been charged with terrorism. The Justice Department thought it safer and easier to try to keep her behind bars for the attempted murder of U.S. soldiers in Ghazni than to charge her in connection with KSM's plot to blow up gas stations. Trying her for terrorism would open the door to testimony from KSM, Ali Abdul Aziz Ali, and Majid Khan, all of whom claimed to have been tortured in the CIA's secret prisons.

Prosecutors believed they had a strong case for attempted murder of U.S. personnel, which, under a law passed by the U.S. Congress after the 1998 embassy bombings, carries even heavier penalties than ordinary murder charges. They had nine eyewitnesses, including three decorated U.S. soldiers, ready to testify that they had seen or heard Aafia fire the gun at Captain Robert Snyder on July 18, 2008. They also had the evidence of the documents and the nearly two pounds of sodium cyanide she was carrying, plus her own statements that she wanted to kill Americans, to show that she had a motive to shoot.

Yet, as Aafia's lawyers pointed out, the government had no forensic evidence to support their witnesses' statements—no bullets, no fingerprints, no shell casings, no gunshot residue. And no one had been hurt in the incident except Aafia. The government's refusal, moreover, to address her lawyers' claims that she might have been held in a secret prison before being dumped in Ghazni and that she might have been set up could have created a reasonable doubt about just what had happened. After all, the defense only needed one dubious juror to get a hung jury.

The Pakistani taxpayers paid the $2 million bill for Aafia's brother to hire what Judge Richard Berman called a "dream team" of defense lawyers. There was Charles D. Swift, the former U.S. Navy litigator who had won *Hamdan v. Rumsfeld*, in which the Supreme Court had ruled that the U.S. prison at Guantánamo was subject to U.S. and international law. There was Linda Moreno, the Florida-based attorney who had won acclaim for her defense of various Islamist groups in the Holy Land Foundation case in Texas, and there was Elaine Whitfield Sharp, the Marblehead, Massachusetts, lawyer whom Aafia's family had first hired in 2004. The judge also ruled that the court-appointed Dawn Cardi should continue to defend Aafia.

This legal team had a simple plan: all Aafia had to do was keep quiet while they pointed out holes in the government's case. But Aafia refused mostly even to look at them, much less take their advice. Sharp, who knew her best, genuinely believed that her client was mentally ill. She said that when Aafia deigned to speak to her, which wasn't often, she made grandiose proclamations, such as her plans to reconcile the United States and the Taliban. When Sharp tried to talk to Aafia about the case, the prisoner would wave her away, claiming that greater powers would resolve her problem behind the scenes. After jury selection began in January 2010, Aafia stood up in court and demanded that Jews be kept off her jury. "If they have a Zionist or Israeli background . . . they are all mad at me," she told Judge Berman. "I have a feeling everyone here is them—subject to genetic testing."

As the trial began, the government's witnesses took the stand one by one while Aafia often sat with her head on the table. To my mind, at least, the witnesses explained many things about the prosecution's case that had initially seemed implausible. I had wondered whether a U.S. Special Forces chief warrant officer really would leave his M-4 assault rifle on the floor, where Aafia could reach it. But the warrant officer said he always put his rifle aside as a gesture of respect when meeting with Afghans. "You don't talk to somebody with an assault rifle around your neck," he said. And all the soldiers testified that they had had no idea when they entered the room in Ghazni and sat down that Aafia was behind the yellow curtain.

A few minutes later, however, they had found themselves looking down the barrel of a gun. So said the warrant officer, his Afghan interpreter, an FBI agent, a U.S. medic, and Captain Snyder. The Afghan interpreter told the court that as he lunged for her, Aafia had fired several shots. The warrant officer then pulled out his pistol and shot her in the abdomen.

Pakistani commentators had scoffed at the idea that a "frail woman" like Aafia could have lifted an assault rifle, much less fired several shots at heavily armed Americans before they fired back. The jury seemed to share this concern. But when prosecutors brought in the warrant officer's rifle (which could also be used as a machine gun) and the jurors passed it around, the deadly M-4 was shown to be almost as small and light as a child's toy. U.S. Attorney Jenna Dabbs was a woman about Aafia's size. She demonstrated how easy it was to hold.

The defense was on firmer ground when it pointed to the absence of physical evidence. But there, too, prosecutors called expert witnesses who testified that it wasn't unusual for fingerprints and other forensic evidence to be missing, especially considering that the shooting had taken place in a war zone, where the FBI had no control over the crime scene.

The government's silence, however, about where Aafia had been since she disappeared in 2003 still seemed suspicious. Aafia's lawyers also showed that Afghan police had beaten her badly the night before the shooting, and it seemed possible that her lawyers could have persuaded at least one juror that, even if she had seized the gun, she had done so in self-defense.

But before her legal team could unfurl its full case, and against their vehement advice, Aafia insisted on testifying.

Up on the stand, she looked so small and harmless that some of the Pakistani reporters who were present thought at first that she had made the right decision. As defense lawyers gingerly led her through the story of her life, she told the court in her high-pitched voice about how much she loved New York City, about the many awards she had won at MIT for public service, and how worried she was for her children. She claimed she had not even picked up the rifle at Ghazni but had just peeked from behind the curtain to see what was happening when she was shot. When asked if she had fired the gun, she answered that the charge was such a joke she had "sometimes been forced to smile under my scarf." She added that she had not even known what an M-4 rifle looked like until she saw the one in court. She presented herself as exactly the sort of gentle middle-class Pakistani girl that most Pakistanis believed her to be. I could just picture how she must have charmed her professors at MIT and the University of Houston.

Yet, with the courtroom packed and the media listening carefully, Aafia avoided the question of where she had been for the five years before she was picked up in Ghazni. The judge had warned Aafia to stick to the subject of the shooting, but Sharp, who was questioning her, later conceded that once Aafia got onto the stand there was nothing to stop her from saying anything she wanted. Aafia made the same hazy claims she had made all along, but they lacked the punch and plausibility of many other prisoners' accounts. She didn't supply any details a jury could follow. "If you have been in a, I don't know, secret prison, abused, you become more modest," she said at one point when Sharp was asking her why she wore a veil. Then Sharp, who knew that the FBI's Angela Sercer was standing by to testify that Aafia had told her at Bagram that she had spent the five years leading to her arrest in hiding, steered her back to the events at the Ghazni police station.

Under cross-examination, Dabbs caught Aafia telling what appeared to be one lie after another. Dabbs asked if the boy she was with was her son, Ahmad. Aafia claimed she didn't know who the boy was. "I was in a daze at that time," she said. At first she claimed that the documents in her bag had been given to her. Pointing out that many of the documents were in Aafia's own handwriting, Dabbs put one up on an overhead screen that concerned the construction of a dirty bomb. In a vague and halting manner, Aafia claimed that she had been forced to copy it out of a magazine so that her children would not be tortured in front of her in a secret prison. Then she let the subject drop.

Dabbs asked Aafia why, if she had been imprisoned, she had told the FBI that she had been in hiding. Aafia claimed she had thought the FBI was playing the same "game" with her that the "fake Americans" who had held her in the secret prison had played, and therefore she had just told them what she thought they wanted to hear.

Finally Dabbs asked if it wasn't true that she knew how to fire a gun because she had taken a pistol safety course at Braintree Rifle & Pistol Club while studying at MIT in 1993. At first Aafia said she probably had—"everybody used to take it." Then she said she couldn't remember. The next day, Dabbs produced her instructor from the club, Gary Woodworth. He testified that he remembered teaching her how to fire "hundreds of rounds."

In his closing arguments, U.S. Assistant Attorney Christopher La Vigne pointed out that Aafia had not even given a straight answer when Dabbs had asked her if she was born in 1972, replying instead, "If you say so." "She raised her right hand and she lied to your face," La Vigne said. "She lied and lied and lied."

Defense attorney Linda Moreno tried to persuade the jury to focus on the absence of physical evidence, but after deliberating for three days, the jurors returned with their verdict on February 3, 2010. Aafia was convicted on all seven counts of attempted murder and assault of U.S. personnel.

Her quiet brother, who had attended the trial every day, slumped over on his bench. Aafia herself twisted around to wag her finger at the spectators. "This is a verdict coming from Israel and not from America," she cried. "Your anger should be directed where the anger belongs."

Thirty-six

Ayaan's new memoir, *Nomad: From Islam to America: A Personal Journey Through the Clash of Civilizations*, came out in the United States and United Kingdom in the spring of 2010.

In it, she used the slight opening of her renewed family contacts to flay them again for their failure to embrace modernity, by which she meant Western ways, as thoroughly as she had. For her pains in tracking Ayaan down to inform her that their father was dying, her half sister Sahra became the subject of a chapter that criticized her decision to remain a devout Muslim, wear the hijab, and live in the fold of her family. Ayaan admitted that she hadn't seen Sahra since the girl was eight; she didn't even pretend to know whether Sahra's choices were her own, and she produced no evidence that Sahra was dangerous or anti-Western. Nevertheless, she wailed for our very civilization—at Sahra's expense: "For how long will Western societies, whose roots drink from the rational sources of the Enlightenment, continue to tolerate the spread of Sahra's way of life, like ivy on their trunks, an alien and possibly lethal growth?"

Once again, Islam was monolithically evil while the West was monolithically good with the exception of the feminists and liberals too cowardly to confront Islam. The only hope for Muslims, once again, was to trade their faith and culture for that of the West—including, if necessary, Christianity, Ayaan now wrote.

The reviews this time were decidedly mixed, though Ayaan still got plenty of praise. Her friend Christopher Hitchens wrote, "For me, the three most beautiful words in the emerging language of secular resistance to tyranny are Ayaan Hirsi Ali." In the *Christian Science Monitor* Nathan Gardels described *Nomad* as "the most powerful book you will read in a long time."

In the Netherlands, by contrast, reviewers were taken aback by the celebrated atheist's surprise call for the Roman Catholic Church to embark on a missionary campaign for the souls of Muslim immigrants as a way of stemming what she called "the rising tide of jihad." In the United States, Nicholas Kristof of the *New York Times* chided her for "excoriating a varied faith that has more than a billion adherents," and Bob Drogin of the *Los Angeles Times* dismissed the book as an "anti-Islamic screed" and "a tough jeremiad to read." In Britain, the book's reception was perhaps colored by what the celebrity Web sites persisted in calling the "Famously Snobby Divorce Scandal" between Ayaan's new love, Niall Ferguson, and his wife, Susan Douglas.

Meeting Ayaan at the Algonquin Hotel in Manhattan, Tony Allen-Mills of the *Times* of London wrote that he actually wanted to ask her about her circumcision. But he settled for inquiring about the "odd epilogue at the end of *Nomad* titled 'Letter to My Unborn Daughter.'" Was Ayaan pregnant? She said she wasn't. In the *Guardian*, Emma Brockes wrote that Ayaan was almost "coyly glamorous, moving with fawn-like grace." "It's a combination," Brockes said, "that works particularly well on male polemicists of the muscular left, who can't do enough to defend her: her gentle charm, her small wrists, her big eyes—oh, and her brave commitment to Enlightenment values—in the face of all that extremism." The *Telegraph* took an even tougher line: "The tone of this feverish, self-justifying tome reminded me of a Dutch social worker I met once," wrote Cristina Odone in a review headlined "Ayaan Hirsi Ali Reminds Me of Richard Dawkins—Obsessive and Simplistic." "The only difference is that Hirsi Ali, unlike the frumpy, solid and sandaled social workers the world over, has made rather a lot of money out of promoting her grim philosophy." Under Ayaan's photo, the caption read, "Ayaan Hirsi Ali: one-track mind."

This coolness notwithstanding, Ayaan and Ferguson announced at the Hay Festival that they were moving to England for a year. "History Man Heads Home with His Girl," said the *Daily Mail*, adding that the move came "much to the chagrin of his estranged wife." Ferguson told reporters he would be advising his friend, Britain's new Tory prime minister David Cameron, on how British schools should teach history—as well as lecturing at the London School of Economics. Ayaan would be writing books. Ever since breaking the news of their romance, the *Daily Mail* had reported relentlessly on Ferguson's previous affairs, on Ayaan's confession to being "enormously in love," and on her yearning to have a baby with the historian. Ayaan herself wrote an article in the *Sunday Times* titled "I'm a Nomad, But I Want to Be a Mother." Ferguson's wife was reported to be pained by what the *Telegraph* called Ayaan's "excruciatingly tactless statements." "She clearly feels no compunction," the *Telegraph* said of Ayaan, "to play down her joy as Ferguson's family attempt to adjust to their abrupt change in domestic circumstances."

The new couple were apparently undeterred. The *Daily Mail* claimed that Ferguson and Ayaan had planned to hold a festive "coming out" party at the thousand-year-old castle that Douglas had renovated as a weekend retreat for the family until Douglas had scotched the idea. Ayaan and Ferguson didn't let the media criticism stop them from dancing the night away at Hay, and Ferguson even referred to his divorce in his lecture at the festival: "Henry VIII's marital troubles, of course, led to the Reformation. I wish my own were as productive." Ayaan, of course, was used to controversy. Tony Allen-Mills of the *Times* found her "radiant."

In early 2011, Ferguson dedicated his book, *Civilization: The West and the Rest*, to Ayaan. Ayaan, the historian wrote, "understands better than anyone I know what Western civilization really means and what it still has to offer the world." Soon afterward Ayaan's fondest wish was granted when she learned that she was pregnant with Ferguson's child.

Thirty-seven

After Aafia's conviction, Pakistani politicians of every stripe assailed what they called the "false U.S. justice," and thousands of her supporters burned American flags in demonstrations across Pakistan and beyond. Prime Minister Yousaf Raza Gilani again declared Aafia "a Daughter of the Nation" while the opposition leader, Nawaz Sharif, promised to keep pushing for her release.

As for the Pakistani Taliban, they vowed revenge.

The Pakistani media covered the trial but mostly passed over Aafia's statements to the FBI about spending her missing years in hiding and being watched by the country's intelligence agencies, to focus instead on her nebulous but sensational claims in court to have been in a secret prison. Nobody tried to find the Karachi Institute of Technology, where she had told the FBI's Angela Sercer she had worked. And no one interviewed Abu Lubaba, who Aafia said had given her the fatwa to conduct research on unconventional weapons. (I contacted Abu Lubaba through an intermediary to see if he would talk with me. He replied that he didn't meet with women. When I e-mailed questions to him, he didn't answer them.)

Aafia's sister, Fowzia, toured the country, leading rallies and accusing the U.S. and Pakistani governments of kidnapping and torturing Aafia and her children. Yet she failed to bring legal charges against either government. A *Daily Express* columnist, Mubashir Lucman, raised questions about Fowzia's account, and soon graffiti appeared all over Karachi insulting Lucman. "It takes great courage to question Fozia [*sic*] Siddiqui's certified truth," wrote the columnist

Shakil Chaudhry on the Pakistani Web site Viewpoint. "There is a mass hysteria on the Aafia Siddiqui issue in Pakistan and rationality has been totally pushed aside."

Most disturbing was the silence over the fate of Aafia's children. The Siddiqui family continued to waffle, sometimes saying that the boy living with them was Aafia's son Ahmad and sometimes that he wasn't. The politicians and journalists backing the Siddiquis never questioned this discrepancy, nor did they suggest that the boy take a DNA test to determine whether he was Amjad's son. The Siddiquis also claimed that the two younger children were still missing. Amjad called on the U.S., Pakistani, and Afghan governments to investigate their disappearance. U.S. ambassador Anne Patterson wrote to tell him that the United States had never had custody of his children. The Pakistani and Afghan governments ignored him.

Then, in another of those weird Pakistani happenings, Fowzia and Ismat announced that they had found a twelve-year-old girl standing outside their door with a placard around her neck that had Ismat Siddiqui's address printed on it. The Siddiquis claimed not to recognize the girl but told the press they planned to adopt her anyway. Pakistan's Justice Ministry asked Amjad for a DNA sample; the tests showed that she was his daughter. Yet the Siddiquis refused to let him see her. A senator from the Deobandi religious party who was one of their biggest promoters told the press that the girl had been a prisoner of an American named "John" at Bagram. Once again no one asked for any evidence or proposed to find this "John."

Aafia and Amjad's youngest child, Suleman, still had not been found, but Amjad believed that he was alive and living under an assumed name with members of the Siddiquis' extended family. But, by the end of 2010, Amjad and his family were so exhausted by battling the Siddiquis that they decided to abandon their custody suit. "The children are by now of a mindset that is not compatible with us," Amjad wrote me. "We will welcome them if they want to come meet us but we are not going to the Siddiquis' place to meet them.

And if they don't want to meet us, that's okay too. I am, and always have been, willing to fulfill my obligations towards them."

As for al-Qaeda and Pakistan's jihadi groups, they used Aafia's case as a rallying cry, accusing the Pakistani government and military of failing in their religious duty to protect and avenge her. "If a Muslim woman is arrested in the east, it is the duty of every Muslim in the west to save her," Jaish-e-Muhammad declared in its online magazine, *al-Qalam*.

Even before Aafia's trial began, the new leader of the Pakistani Taliban, the long-haired Hakimullah Mehsud, had released a video in which he revealed that a Jordanian doctor had killed seven CIA operatives and a Jordanian intelligence agent in a suicide bombing at Khost, Afghanistan, partly in revenge for Aafia's imprisonment. Now that she had been convicted, the Pakistani Taliban announced, Aafia's family had approached them for help and they had agreed to add Aafia to a list of twenty-one Afghan prisoners for whom it had agreed to swap one U.S. soldier it had taken prisoner, twenty-three-year-old Private Bowe Bergdahl of Idaho.

The Siddiquis, however, denied having made the request, and the Americans refused to swap anybody.

In early March, Khalid Khawaja, the ex-spy who in 2004 had advised me to drop Aafia's story, traveled to Waziristan to try to make peace between the Pakistani Taliban and the Pakistani army. He carried a letter from Hakimullah Mehsud to Fowzia on his way back. "You are my sister and I share the pain and grief that you are undergoing," Hakimullah wrote to Aafia's sister. "And God willing we will teach a lesson to the U.S. and cruel rulers of Pakistan—a lesson to be remembered by them." He told Fowzia she could reach him through Khalid Khawaja.

Fowzia later told *Dawn* that the letter had never been delivered. "Mr. Khawaja called me and said he had some letter for me," she explained. "He wanted to personally hand over the letter to me, but I avoided meeting him."

Khawaja returned to Waziristan on March 25. Toward the end of

April, a group calling itself the Asian Tigers announced that it had kidnapped him and his companions. The group delivered a series of videos to the press in which Khawaja confessed to being a double agent.

Masked men subsequently dumped Khawaja's body beside a stream in North Waziristan. He had been shot through the head and chest. The men left a letter on his corpse stating that he had been killed for associating with the ISI and the CIA, and for his role in the army's assault on the Lal Mosque.

The next day, Hakimullah Mehsud released another video. It promised to avenge Aafia. The day after that, May 1, a thirty-year-old man left a car running in New York's Times Square. The car was crudely fitted with propane gas tanks, fertilizer, gasoline, and explosives. If it had gone off as intended, it could have killed dozens or even hundreds of people. Police soon tracked down the would-be bomber, Faisal Shahzad, to Bridgeport, Connecticut. He proved to be a recently naturalized U.S. citizen and the son of a Pakistani Air Force officer. On his Facebook page he had posed wearing fashionable sunglasses. Raised in Karachi and educated in the United States, Shahzad's background resembled Aafia's. The trail of his contacts soon led back to Jaish-e-Muhammad—and to Hakimullah Mehsud.

Thirty-eight

A picture of Khalid Khawaja, wrapped in a white shroud, with his eyes closed and a bullet through his head, appeared on the Internet. I wouldn't have expected it, but I felt a wave of regret. Khawaja had been an enigmatic figure, infected by the same evil fantasies as Aafia; now he had been devoured by the same nightmare forces he had helped to set into motion.

After his death I also discovered that, in a circuitous way, Khawaja had shown me a link between Aafia and Ayaan—the sixth degree of separation, perhaps, that I had sensed in their stories that very first day in 2004, when, on my way to Pakistan, I had read about the beheading of Theo van Gogh.

Back in 2004, when Khawaja had asked me to tell Daniel Pearl's widow, Mariane, that he had nothing to do with Pearl's murder, I had contacted Pearl's friend Asra Nomani with a request that she pass along the message. Nomani and I began to talk, and I learned about her plans to unravel the conspiracy that had led to Pearl's killing. Eventually she went to work on an investigation called the Pearl Project, which was staffed by students and teachers at Georgetown University.

In January 2011, Nomani and a professor at Georgetown, Barbara Feinman Todd, released the results of their research on Pearl's murder. U.S. officials, they had learned, believe that on the last day of Pearl's life three men arrived at the shed where he was being held captive on property owned by the patron of the al-Rashid Trust. One of the men was KSM. Another was the cousin who had studied with KSM in North Carolina, Ramzi Yousef's brother Abdul Karim, also known as "Musab Aruchi." The third man, Nomani and Feinman Todd said, was KSM's nephew—Aafia's future husband, the handsome young Ali Abdul Aziz Ali.

The men had entered the shed to make a movie.

Ali set up the video camera. The men interviewed Pearl about his Jewish ancestry. Then Abdul Karim and another man, who had been guarding Pearl, held the bucking and struggling journalist while KSM cut his throat—not once but twice, to be sure Ali captured it on camera. It was twenty-four-year-old Ali who U.S. investigators believe shot the film "The Slaughter of the Spy-Journalist, the Jew Daniel Pearl."

It was just a horrible coincidence, but what struck me was the impact—almost like the butterfly effect—that Ali's film had on Ayaan Hirsi Ali's rise to stardom as an Islam critic. For it was "The Slaughter of the Spy-Journalist, the Jew Daniel Pearl" and the many copycat versions that followed it that had inspired Mohammed Bouyeri and taught him how to murder Theo van Gogh. And it was Bouyeri's murder of van Gogh that had made Ayaan and her film, "Submission," internationally famous.

Then in 2011 another event showed how tragically these opposites, Ayaan and Aafia, had become mirror images of each other in the eyes of some of their adoring followers. That summer Anders Behring Breivik, a thirty-two-year-old Norwegian who shared Ayaan's fears of an Islamic takeover of Europe, slaughtered seventy-seven government officials and youthful Labor Party campers whom he blamed for Muslim immigration to Norway. In the 1,500-page manifesto Breivik left behind before setting off on his "martyrdom operation," he claimed to belong to an al-Qaeda-like organization of the "Knights Templar" that would expel Muslims, punish "multiculturalists," and restore Europe to cultural purity. He also proposed Ayaan for the Nobel Peace Prize.

Thirty-nine

On September 23, 2010, I joined the same Pakistani and American spectators who had attended Aafia Siddiqui's trial and filed through the now-familiar security checks into Judge Richard Berman's courtroom for her sentencing.

Lawyers and aides for both sides made their way to the tables in front of the bench. Aafia was led in by U.S. marshals. After looking around the courtroom for her brother, she took a seat in her usual garb of long beige gown and white polyester head scarf tied across her face.

Judge Berman arrived in his robes, and all rose.

The judge warned that the sentencing could take some time. For one thing, there were certain mysteries surrounding Aafia's case that had never been resolved.

Despite having followed her case for six years, I had to agree.

It had never been definitively established, Berman observed, why Aafia and her son had turned up in Afghanistan on July 17, 2008. "Speculation," said the judge, "has ranged from the following, that, one, she was looking for Ammar al-Baluchi [also known as Ali], who I understand she is married to, and who is currently being held, along with his uncle Khalid Sheikh Mohammed, at the United States base in Guantánamo Bay, Cuba. Other speculation is that she was on a mission to attack Americans. Another speculation is that she was there to distribute documents instructing the Taliban how to make explosives to destroy the foreigners and the government army."

He added that the court lacked the evidence to confirm Aafia's whereabouts between 2003 and 2008. But he had not found any credible evidence that any U.S. agency had detained her before she was captured on July 18, 2008.

The trial had been a complicated one, partly because Aafia had disrupted the proceedings with her outbursts. The judge had found her competent, but "this was most definitely a situation in which the defendant's political beliefs and perspectives blur the line between mental health issues and political advocacy." Overall, he said, she had been able to confront her accusers and participate in her own defense. The result was that the jury determined that Aafia picked up the chief warrant officer's rifle in Ghazni, "aimed at the Americans and pulled the trigger, firing several shots."

Dawn Cardi spoke for the defense. She told the court that Aafia's had been one of the most difficult cases of her career, most of all because Aafia remained "an enigma." "I don't think in this time we really know what the truth is and what happened in the life of Dr. Siddiqui," Cardi said. She agreed that "there were no facts in front of the court to corroborate or to aid us in knowledge," but she said she believed that the CIA and other government agencies knew and that someday the truth would come out. She argued that Aafia had been frightened and just trying to escape that day at Ghazni. She asked for mercy for a woman whose children were missing and whose mind was clearly impaired. She asked the court not to give in to "fear" but to settle for a sentence of twelve years.

In his turn, U.S. Attorney Christopher La Vigne urged the judge not to forget fear but to remember the fear that the members of the U.S. interview team had felt when Aafia picked up the gun and fired it at them. "That's the fear in this case. That's what this case is about. That's what the jury found."

Aafia then gave a long, rambling statement in which she said she loved America and claimed she had proof that Israelis had masterminded 9/11. She said she had only been trying to stave off a catastrophe because "big wars are being planned and they are involved in it." Once again, she advised Americans to use genetic testing to determine who was loyal and who was not. But she said several times that she did not want Muslims to think that she had been tortured.

Then Judge Berman read out her sentence. He recommended that she be allowed to serve it at the FMC, Carswell, where she could receive psychiatric treatment and her brother would be nearby. But he sentenced her to eighty-six years in prison.

There were gasps from the audience. "Shame, shame, shame on this court!" one man cried out.

Aafia stood up again. "I just want to say one thing," she said. She spoke about how the Prophet Muhammad had forgiven all of his personal enemies. "Forgive everybody in my case, please. . . . Don't get angry. If I'm not angry, why should anyone else be? Just, I mean the world is so full of injustices. You can strive in many ways to make the world a more livable, peaceful place."

Judge Berman thanked her, and she thanked him in return.

There was talk of an appeal. Aafia said she didn't want one, but her lawyers said they would file for one anyway.

At last Judge Berman said, "It's been a long day, Dr. Siddiqui. I wish you the very best going forward."

Aafia nodded back to him. The U.S. marshals got to their feet, and she was led away.

Forty

And so it was over. The six years I had spent following these two women, both so ambitious and dramatic in their different ways, had come to an end. What had I learned?

Just as there are layers of stories about Islam, so there are layers to the tale of the war on terror—including the important story of women in general and many tales of individual women as different as Ayaan Hirsi Ali and Aafia Siddiqui.

When I began, I felt that the control of women was as fundamental to radical Islam as racism was to the old American South or as anti-Semitism was to Nazi Germany. I learned that this was true, depressingly so. But I also learned that Westerners who want to keep the Muslim world under Western rule also have used Islamic attitudes toward women not so much to help free Muslim women as to justify the West's continued domination of Muslim men.

In the mirror symmetry operating here, the jihadis claimed that they weren't really fighting to maintain their control over women but rather to throw off Western dominance. Right-wing Westerners, meanwhile, claimed that they weren't fighting to maintain Western dominance but to liberate Muslim women. Women like Ayaan and Aafia became symbols in battles that were really about other things.

I thought when I began that, by following Aafia and Ayaan, I could get close to what was driving the war on terror, and I believe I did.

Both these women are products of our migratory times. Like many others of their generation, they grew up on the move between countries and cultures, and they took refuge in universal identities. Ayaan chose the West and Aafia chose Islam; both women became symbols in what they defined as an inexorable clash of civilizations. Ayaan's sweeping criticism of Islam and Muslims led her to be threatened and her collaborator Theo van Gogh to be murdered. The help that Aafia gave al-Qaeda and, more particularly, Khalid Sheikh Mohammed and his family led the United States to hunt her in its shadowy war against jihad. And despite the muddiness of the truth each woman came to be seen by her camp as a pure victim who embodied everything that was wrong with the other side.

In the lands of European descent, Ayaan appeared as heroic proof of the barbaric essence of Islam. Shaped and molded by Ayaan and her packagers, her story seemed to prove that Muslims everywhere, but for the power of the West, would be mutilating women's genitals, forcing them to marry strangers, justifying their treatment in the name of Islam, and killing them when they dared to resist. The complexities within modern Islam, its indigenous struggles for justice, the history of Western imperialism in the region—all these were lost in the version of Ayaan's tale fed to the public.

In the lands of Islam, Aafia came to be widely viewed as living proof of the emptiness and hypocrisy of the Western concept of universal human rights and of the West's continuing designs on Muslim territory. Aafia's defenders said that the problem with the Muslim world wasn't that it mistreated women but that it failed to protect them from a West that respects no law, not even its own—a West that kidnaps, tortures, and kills Muslims at will. They closed their eyes to the paranoia, the willful disregard for the truth, and the sheer bloodlust of Aafia and her jihadi friends even as it threatened above all their own society.

In each case, the woman's legend was false enough to convince her critics that her supporters were either liars or completely irrational. Important bits of each side's sweeping complaint, however—whether against the oppression of Muslim women or against the frequent lawlessness of the war on terror—were true enough to persuade each woman's supporters that her critics were toadies, traitors, or hopelessly naive. Ayaan and Aafia both proved to be powerfully polarizing; as such, they became useful to the real drivers of conflict in their countries, whether the ISI and the Islamists in Pakistan or anti-Muslim pundits and politicians in the United States and Holland.

That is not to say they are equivalent figures, morally or otherwise. They are not. Ayaan, as her friend Herman Philipse pointed out long ago, "fights only with words," whereas the evidence leads me to conclude that Aafia was almost certainly plotting murder during her missing years and perhaps prepared to further a biological or chemical attack on the United States on a scale to rival that of 9/11. For all its faults, the system that Ayaan espouses provides for the happiness and freedom of hundreds of millions of people. Aafia's apocalyptic visions, by contrast, can only bring destruction. Accordingly, perhaps, their recent fortunes have been as dissimilar as their thinking, at least for now. Ayaan, as I write these words, is looking forward to marriage and the birth of her child with Ferguson. Aafia, meanwhile, faces life in a federal prison.

Yet Aafia's grim failure won't lead her ardent followers to give up their faith in her innocence any more than Ayaan's worldly success will convince her most passionate supporters that her concept of the war on terror was dangerously overblown. To her followers, each woman is an icon; her legend will always be more alluring than her reality.

Acknowledgments

My deepest thanks are owed to my wise and supportive agents, Toby Eady and Jennifer Joel, whose enthusiasm launched this book and who steered the project past many shoals; to my editor, Claire Wachtel, in the United States and to Jan Mets in the Netherlands, both of whom stuck by it with fierce loyalty; and especially to Jamie Coleman at Toby Eady and Associates, a brilliant young agent who labored mightily to put it in shape.

At *Vogue*, my editors, Eve MacSweeney and Laurie Jones, set me off on this journey when they assigned me to write a profile of Aafia Siddiqui in 2004. Roane Carey at *The Nation* then introduced me to Ayaan Hirsi Ali's story by agreeing to let me write about her in 2005.

My friends Tom Lansner, Jan Michael, and Javaid Aziz took time to read the manuscript and provided crucial comments and suggestions.

Among those who provided advice and hospitality along the way, I am especially grateful to Karl Meyer and Shareen Brysac, Julie and Elliott Taylor, Petra Bartosiewicz, Joanne Mariner, Marnie Henricksson, Russell Shorto, Tom Lansner and Joanne Nagano, Mary Lee and David Owen, Pat Michaelson and Joel Bowman, David Lewis and Danica Kombol, Tom Milo, the late Gritta Weil, William Shawcross, Sheila Dillon and Peter Koenig, Ralitsa Ivanova and Mumchil Ivanov, Mischa Alexander, Dunya Verwey and Jurn Buisman, Roland Spek, Alex de Waal and Nimco Mahamud-Hassan, and Stephen Ellis and Gerrie Ter Haar.

No one sacrificed more to see this book become a reality than my husband, Colin Campbell, and our two daughters, Anna and Elizabeth. Colin went through the entire manuscript three different times, adding immeasurably to the final product. His confidence and good cheer sustained me during a difficult process. I can never thank him enough.

Note on Sources

Since 2004 I have interviewed dozens of people about the events described in this book. Some of those who informed the chapters about Ayaan are Abdullahi An'Naim, Karima Belhaj, Frits Bolkestein, Sam Cherribi, Cisca Dresselhuys, Jocelyne Cesari, Margreet Fogteloo, Theodor Holman, Geert Mak, Fadime Örgü, Annelies Moors, Eveline van Dijk, Herman Philipse, Bram Peper, Paul Kalma, Marco van Kerkhoven, Joris Luyendijk, Janny Groen, Albert Benschop, Ruud Peters, Jytte Klausen, Nimco Mahamud-Hassan, Sinan Can, Jos van Dongen, Elma Verhey, Guled Ahmed Yusuf, Yassin Musse Boqor, Omar Osman Haji, Maryan Farah Warsame, Asha Hagi Elmi, Alies Pegtel, Huib Pellikaan, Leo Louwé, Juha-Pekka Tikka, and the late Gijs van der Fuhr.

Some of those who informed the chapters about Aafia are Salma Kazmi, Aga Naeem Khan, Mohammed Amjad Khan, Zahera Khan, Fowzia Siddiqui, Elaine Whitfield Sharp, Imran Khan, C. Christine Fair, Pervez Hoodbhoy, Rolf Mowatt-Larssen, Hamid Mir, Zaynab Khadr, Ijaz ul-Haq, Hamid Gul, Aamir Latif, Mohammed Hussein Baloch, Iqbal Jaffrey, Evan Kohlmann, Tamar Tesler, Thomas Joscelyn, Lorenzo Vidino, and the late Khalid Khawaja.

Quite a few others interviewed about both women prefer not to be named. I am grateful to all of them for their time and trust.

I have not cited material drawn from these personal interviews. Quotations and other information taken from books, articles, and other published materials are listed in the notes.

Notes

Part I: Regarding the West

One

3 When Aafia Siddiqui's name: In addition to interviews, my account of Aafia's upbringing is taken from her testimony in *United States of America v. Aafia Siddiqui*, January 28, 2010, pp. 1696–1697, as well as the forensic evaluations conducted by Sally Johnson, M.D., March 16, 2009, pp. 5–6; Thomas L. Kucharski, Ph.D., June 20, 2009, pp. 2–4; Gregory B. Saathoff, M.D., March 15, 2009, pp. 4–6.

5 The Deobandis: Barbara Metcalf, *Perfecting Women: Maulana Ashraf 'Ali Thanawi's* Bihishti Zewar (Berkeley: University of California Press, 1990); Charles Allen, *God's Terrorists: The Wahhabi Cult and the Hidden Roots of Modern Jihad* (New York: Da Capo Press, 2006).

6 Most Indian Muslims: For a biography of Mufti Muhammad Shafi, see http://en.wikipedia.org/wiki/Mufti_Muhammad_Shafi and www.classicalislamgroup.com/index.php?view=tafseer/s17-v61to65.

6 Western intellectual historians: On Abu al-A'la al-Maududi and women, see Lamia Rustum Shehadeh, *The Idea of Women in Fundamentalist Islam* (Gainesville, Fla.: University of Florida Press, 2003), pp. 23–48.

7 Asked what had set him: Ibid., p. 31.

7 When Aafia was two: Aafia describes the United Islamic Organisation and its work in two e-mails sent out to Muslim newsgroups on July 25, 1995, and September 18, 1995, copy in author's files plus at www.qucis.queensu.ca/home/fevens/UIO/html.

Two

9 Ayaan's mother: Ayaan Hirsi Ali has described her childhood and upbringing in her three books, *The Caged Virgin: An Emancipation Proclamation for Women* (New York: Free Press, 2006); *Infidel: My Life* (New

York: Free Press, 2007); and *Nomad: From Islam to America: A Personal Journey Through the Clash of Civilizations* (New York: Free Press, 2010), as well as in many interviews and news reports.

9 Even today, a typical Somali child: See Lee V. Cassanelli, *The Shaping of Somali Society: Reconstructing the History of a Pastoral People, 1600–1900* (Philadelphia: University of Pennsylvania Press, 1982); David D. Laitin and Said S. Samatar, *Somalia: Nation in Search of a State* (Boulder, Colo.: Westview Press, 1987); and I. Lewis, *A Pastoral Democracy: A Study of Pastoralism and Politics among the Northern Somali in the Horn of Africa* (Oxford, England: Oxford University Press, 1961) on Somali history and culture.

10 Both Asha and Hirsi belonged: Some details of Hirsi Magan Isse's life are taken from his obituary, "Tariikhii Dr. Xersi Magana 1935–2008," August 25, 2008, www.garoweonline.com/artman2/publish/Islam_28/Tariikhii_Xersi_Magana.shtml. Others are taken from Mahmoud Yahye's unpublished manuscript, "A Short Biography of Mr. Hirsi Magan," copy in author's files.

12 As Ayaan's half sister Arro later wrote: *IAW Newsletter*, no. 5 (June 2002), www.womenalliance.org/pdf/June2002.pdf; "Le Mutilazioni Genitali Femminili: Una Tradizione da Abbandonare per Sempre," www.migranti.torino.it/Documenti%20%20PDF/MutItal.pdf.

13 Hirsi, however, like his first wife: Transcript of Jos van Dongen, interview with Mahad Hirsi Magan, March 30–April 1, 2005.

14 "Something inside": Hirsi Ali, *Infidel*, p. 40.

14 "Ma saw us": Ibid., p. 41.

14 "You are my only son": Hirsi Ali, *Nomad*, p. 52.

15 "There were two examples": Kathy Brewis, "On a Jihad Against the Faith She Cast Off," *Sunday Times*, December 4, 2004.

15 Banna later described: Quoted in Richard P. Mitchell, *The Society of the Muslim Brothers* (New York: Oxford University Press, 1969), p. 7.

15 "Allah is our way": Quoted in Matthias Kuntzel, *Jihad and Jew-Hatred: Islamism, Nazism and the Roots of 9/11* (New York: Telos Press, 2007), p. 14.

16 At the time, Wahhabis: Lawrence Wright, *The Looming Tower: Al Qaeda and the Road to 9/11* (London: Penguin, 2006), p. 149; Alexi Alexiev, "The End of an Alliance," *National Review*, November 26, 2002.

Three

19 "the modernity": Quoted in Muhammed Taqi Usmani, *Islam and Modernism* (trans. Muhammad Sualeh Siddiqui), www.fahmedeen.org/books/islamandmodernism.pdf.

19 The implications: Afshan Jafar, "Women, Islam and the State in Pakistan," *Gender Issues* 22, no. 1 (2005), 35–55.

21 There was plenty for a woman: Aafia Siddiqui, e-mails to Muslim newsgroups on July 25, 1995, and September 18, 1995, copy in author's files plus at www.qucis.queensu.ca/home/fevens/UIO/html.

22 The *zakat* money helped support: Khalid Baig, "Yeh Tere Pur Asrar Bande, Author: Mufti Muhammad Rafi Usmani," www.urdustan.com/nuqta/warriors.htm.

22 A few numbers: International Crisis Group, "Pakistan: Karachi's Madrassas and Violent Extremism," March 29, 2007, http://www.crisisgroup.org/~/media/Files/asia/south-asia/pakistan/130_pakistan_karachi_s_madrasas_and_violent_extremism.ashx.

22 Back in 1981: Baig, "Yeh Tere Pur Asrar Bande."

23 The girl's hobby: Fowzia wrote me about Aafia's pets, and *Der Spiegel* describes her pulling out the family albums in Juliane von Mittelstaedt, "The Most Dangerous Woman in the World," November 27, 2008.

23 As Aafia later summarized: www.qucis.queensu.ca/home/fevens/UIO/html.

Four

26 Hirsi had installed her: Ayaan Hirsi Ali, *Nomad: From Islam to America: A Personal Journey Through the Clash of Civilizations* (New York: Free Press, 2010), p. 51.

26 *Chicken Licken*: Jean Westmoore, "A Flight from Radical Islam's Oppression," *Buffalo News*, October 6, 2009.

27 Mahad could do well: Jos van Dongen, interview with Mahad Hirsi Magan, March 30–April 1, 2005.

27 "fighting practice": Hirsi Ali, *Nomad*, p. 188.

27 But Somalia's confrontational methods: Ibid., pp. 53–55.

28 In January 1983: Van Dongen, interview with Mahad.

28 "It was the ideal home": Ibid.

29 "She began to beat us": Ayaan Hirsi Ali, *Infidel: My Life* (New York: Free Press, 2007), p. 40.

29 "as a family": Van Dongen, interview with Mahad.

29 "angry at everyone": Jutta Chorus and Ahmet Olgun, *In godsnaam: Het jaar van Theo van Gogh* (Amsterdam: Contact, 2005), p. 92.

29 "Sometimes in those": Hirsi Ali, *Infidel*, p. 90.

30 "What we learned was": Westmoore, "A Flight from Radical Islam's Oppression."

30 A new teacher: Ayaan has described her relationship with Sister Aziza in *Infidel*, pp. 83–124, as well as in many interviews. See, e.g., Christopher

Caldwell, "Daughter of the Enlightenment," *The New York Times Magazine*, April 3, 2005.

31 "it sent a message": Hirsi Ali, *Infidel*, p. 85.

31 "I never reached": Ibid., p. 130.

31 "Suddenly we hated Israel": Caldwell, "Daughter of the Enlightenment."

31 "I must confess": Rogier van Bakel, "The Trouble Is the West," *Reason*, November 2007.

31 "It was when I was most devout": Mary Wakefield, "We Are at War with Islam," *The Spectator*, December 1, 2007.

32 Ayaan finished high school: Ayaan describes the period between her graduation from high school and her departure for Somalia in *Infidel*, pp. 114–122.

Five

34 It was snowing: *United States of America v. Aafia Siddiqui*, January 28, 2010, p. 1697.

34 Aafia's architect brother: Muhammad A. Siddiqui is mentioned as the architect of the Islamic Society of Greater Houston in "Islamic Architecture, Art and Urbanism: Vital Resources," http://libraries.mit.edu/guides/subjects/islamicarchitecture/visual/usamosqueslist.html.

35 Several other: "Who was Dr. Aafia Siddiqui? An Eyewitness Account," www.draafia.org/2009/07/23/who-was-dr-aafia-an-eyewitness-account/.

35 Her only extracurricular: Lorenzo Vidino details the history of the Muslim Students Association in *The New Muslim Brotherhood in the West* (New York: Columbia University Press, 2010).

37 The prayer leader: Catherine Criss, "Area Muslims Fear the World Is Going to War," *Houston Chronicle*, January 12, 1991.

37 The Siddiquis' spiritual guide: Muhammad Taqi Usmani, *Islam and Modernism* (trans. Muhammed Sualeh Siddiqui), www.fahmedeen.org/books/islamandmodernism.pdf, p. 22.

Six

39 Somalia in the spring: Ayaan describes the period she spent in Somalia in 1990 in *Infidel: My Life* (New York: Free Press, 2007), pp. 123–144.

40 "I always felt": Hirsi Ali, *Infidel*, p. 125.

40 "Our relationship": Maaike Beekers, "Ayaanlaanse Toestanden," *Red*, June 2010.

41 "I was violating": Hirsi Ali, *Infidel*, p. 131.

41 "a rather bewildered Englishman": Ibid., p. 133.

41 Somalia was so poor: See, e.g., Haley Sweetland Edwards, "Somalis Risk Passage to Yemen," February 10, 2010, on the terrifying annual rite by which Somalis try to make it to the poorest Arab country.

42 "utterly gorgeous": Hirsi Ali, *Infidel*, p. 138.

43 "As for my father's family": Hirsi Ali, *Infidel*, p. 140.

43 Mohamud, for his part: See Juha-Pekka Tikka, "Ayaan Hirsi Alin outo Suomi-yhteys," *Ilta-Sanomat*, October 9, 2007; Tikka, "Rajatarkastus selvittaa Hirsi Ali–mysteeria," *Ilta-Sanomat*, October 15, 2007.

Seven

45 Aafia had requested: *United States of America v. Aafia Siddiqui*, Document 258-1, August 19, 2010, p. 5.

45 "She was religious": Katherine Ozment, "Who's Afraid of Aafia Siddiqui?" *Boston Magazine*, May 15, 2006.

45 Aafia gravitated toward: *United States of America v. Aafia Siddiqui*, January 28, 2010, pp. 1699–1700.

46 One MSA member: A former Wellesley student reminisced about Aafia at http://muslimmatters.org/2010/12/30/aafia/.

46 By the time: MIT MSA's recommendation can be found at http://msa.mit.edu/life/housing/.

46 The MSA's executive board: The package of materials Aafia and Suheil Laher contributed is part of the "MSA Starter's Guide: A Guide on How to Run a Successful MSA," 1st ed., March 1996.

47 "First make sure the intention": Ibid.

47 Another recalled: Syed Shoaib Hassan, "Mystery of Siddiqui Disappearance," BBC News, August 14, 2008.

Eight

49 For the first time: Ayaan gives the fullest account of the events leading up to her departure for Germany in *Infidel: My Life* (New York: Free Press, 2007), pp. 145–180. However, she gave different accounts in her earlier book, *The Caged Virgin: An Emancipation Proclamation for Women* (New York: Free Press, 2006) and in many interviews. See Marlise Simons, "Behind the Veil: A Muslim Woman Speaks Out," *New York Times*, November 9, 2002, in which Simons says Ayaan's father forced her to marry "a man she had never seen before." More recently Ayaan told Joseph Rago that her marriage would have been "an arranged rape" if it had gone forward. See "Free Radical; The Weekend Interview: Ayaan Hirsi Ali Infuriates Muslims and Discomfits Liberals," *Wall Street Journal*, March 9, 2007.

49 The Somali refugees: See Ilse van Liempt, *Navigating Borders: Inside Perspectives on the Process of Human Smuggling into the Netherlands* (Amsterdam: Amsterdam University Press, 2007), for a discussion of how and why Somalis began arriving in the Netherlands in the early 1990s. Elizabeth H. Campbell, "Formalizing the Informal Economy: Somali Refugee and Migrant Trade Networks in Nairobi," *Global Migration Perspectives*, no. 47 (2005), describes the situation of Somali refugees in Nairobi after the fall of Siad Barre. Lucy Hannan, "A Gap in Their Hearts: The Experience of Separated Somali Children," *IRIN,* 2003, details how the smugglers' network brings Somalis to Europe.

50 "If you could raise": Ayaan Hirsi Ali, *Nomad: From Islam to America: A Personal Journey Through the Clash of Civilizations* (New York: Free Press, 2010), p. 179.

51 Finnish immigration records: Juha-Pekka Tikka, "Ayaan Hirsi Alin outo Suomi-yhteys," *Ilta-Sanomat*, October 9, 2007.

52 She says: Hirsi Ali, *Infidel*, p. 161.

52 according to Mahad: Jos van Dongen, interview with Mahad Hirsi Magan, March 30–April 1, 2006.

53 "fed on North American beef": Jos van Dongen, interview with Ayaan, April 27, 2006.

53 Osman himself: "The Holy Ayaan," *Zembla*, VARA Television, May 11, 2006. Osman and Faduma were interviewed by *Zembla* in 2006. In 2009, I interviewed Faduma and her son, Mahad. I reached Osman Musse Quarre in Toronto, but he would not talk to me.

54 "Mahad's goal now": Hirsi Ali, *Infidel*, p. 176.

54 Ayaan would later confess: For instance, in *The Caged Virgin*, p. 87, she wrote that she "mastered the art of lying." In *Nomad*, p. 182, she wrote, "I lie to . . . apologize."

55 "I personally": Van Dongen, interview with Mahad.

56 Osman, on the other hand: "The Holy Ayaan," May 11, 2006.

56 Like everyone else: *Zembla* was the first to expose in "The Holy Ayaan" the fact that Ayaan already had refugee status in Kenya when she applied for asylum in the Netherlands.

57 "my tongue": Hirsi Ali, *Infidel*, p. 180.

Nine

58 Aafia spent: Aafia is listed as a recipient of a Carroll L. Wilson award at http://entrepreneurship.mit.edu/clw-award-recipients.

58 The two largest: "Double Jeopardy: Police Abuse of Women in Pakistan," Human Rights Watch, 1992.

59 MIT has never released: Aafia spoke to the FBI about the book she wrote and her views of American feminism in *United States of America v. Aafia Siddiqui*, Document 256, August 19, 2010, p. 4.

60 "was that of an Islamic state": Hassan Abbas, *Pakistan's Drift into Extremism: Allah, the Army, and America's War on Terror* (Armonk, N.Y.: M.E. Sharpe, 2005), p. 148.

60 Under Nasir: Ibid.

60 Less famous: In addition to my interview with members of the family, this account of the al-Baluchi clan's origins is taken from Terry McDermott, *Perfect Soldiers* (New York: HarperCollins, 2005), pp. 107–126, and Yosri Fouda and Nick Fielding, *Masterminds of Terror: The Truth Behind the Most Devastating Terrorist Attack the World Has Ever Seen* (New York: Arcade Publishing, 2003), pp. 88–104.

Ten

62 "I wanted to be": Ayaan Hirsi Ali, *Infidel: My Life* (New York: Free Press, 2007), p. 187.

62 Staying in Germany: Lucy Hannan, "A Gap in Their Hearts: The Experience of Separated Somali Children," *IRIN*, 2003, p. 22.

63 "You had to go": Hirsi Ali, *Infidel*, p. 190.

63 "If you just told them": Van Dongen, interview with Ayaan, April 27, 2006.

63 She has never said in detail: What follows is taken from *Infidel*, pp. 192–193.

64 The first Somali refugees: Ilse van Liempt, *Navigating Borders: Inside Perspectives on the Process of Human Smuggling into the Netherlands* (Amsterdam: Amsterdam University Press, 2007), pp. 79–80.

64 There were so many other: Scott Peterson, *Me Against My Brother: At War in Somalia, Sudan, and Rwanda* (New York: Routledge, 2001), p. 45.

64 "For months": "Airlift for Humanity," *Time*, August 10, 1992.

66 Until she found work: Ayaan discusses her unemployment benefits in *Nomad: From Islam to America: A Personal Journey Through the Clash of Civilizations* (New York: Free Press, 2010), p. 166.

Eleven

67 Blinded as a child: Peter Waldman, "Bully Pulpit: Egyptian Jihad Leader Preaches Holy War to Brooklyn Muslims—Sheik Omar Abdel-Rahman Blessed Slaying of Sadat, Now Operates from U.S.—Murder in the Neighborhood," *Wall Street Journal*, January 7, 1993.

68 The group vehemently opposed: Mark Fineman, "A Death Threat:

Afghan Women Fear for Rights in the Future," *Los Angeles Times*, February 12, 1989.

68 Although most Muslim men: Peter Bergen, *The Osama bin Laden I Know* (New York: Free Press, 2006), pp. 17–18.

68 Yet despite all this: Evan F. Kohlmann, "Expert Report—*United States of America v. Muhamed Mubayyid, Emadeddin Muntasser, and Samir Al-Monla*," Criminal Action no. 05-40026-FDS, 2007, p. 38.

69 Back in 1985, Kanj: Bernard Rougier gives the best capsule biography of Bassam Kanj in *Everyday Jihad: The Rise of Militant Islam Among Palestinians in Lebanon*, trans. Pascale Ghazaleh (Cambridge, Mass.: Harvard University Press, 2007), pp. 231–254.

69 As Abdullah Azzam's widow: Mohammed Al Shafey, "Asharq Al-Awsat Interviews Umm Mohammed: The Wife of Bin Laden's Spiritual Mentor," *Asharq Al-Awsat*, April 30, 2006.

70 The MSA in Chicago: Evan Kohlmann, "Relief International (R.I.)—Chicago, IL," copy in author's files.

70 Aafia was eager: Shakat Ali Bhatti to Aafia on Muslim newsgroups, March 27, 1993, copy in author's files; Aafia Siddiqui, e-mail to Muslim newsgroups, March 15, 1993, copy in author's files.

Twelve

73 Back in Eastleigh: Ayaan Hirsi Ali, *Infidel: My Life* (New York: Free Press, 2007), p. 197.

74 If the Islamists feared: "The Guns of August Echo," *Time*, August 17, 1992.

74 The same month the Americans: Hirsi Ali, *Infidel*, pp. 203–205.

74 Osman's account: The interview with Osman Musse was in "The Holy Ayaan," *Zembla*, VARA Television, May 11, 2006.

75 According to Ayaan: Ayaan describes this in *Infidel*, pp. 204–205.

76 Ayaan wrote her father: Ibid., pp. 209–211.

Thirteen

77 His uncle KSM: John R. Schindler, *Unholy Terror: Bosnia, Al-Qa'ida, and the Rise of Global Jihad* (St. Paul, Minn.: Zenith Press, 2007), p. 280.

77 Ramzi Yousef had set: Simon Reeve, *The New Jackals* (Boston: Northeastern University Press, 1999), p. 24.

78 On February 23: Steve McGonigle and Gayle Reaves, "Texas Ties: Texas Linked Network of Suspects in World Trade Center Bombing," *Dallas Morning News*, June 8, 1997.

78 Mohammed Salameh: Colum Lynch, "Few Fans of Sheik Among Local Muslims," *Boston Globe*, March 7, 1993.

78 Yet the commitment: The quote from al-Hussam is taken from Evan

F. Kohlmann, "Expert Report—*United States of America v. Muhamed Mubayyid, Emadeddin Muntasser, and Samir Al-Monla,*" Criminal Action no. 05-40026-FDS, 2007, pp. 41–42.

79 A few days later: Lynch, "Few Fans of Sheik Among Local Muslims"; Aafia Siddiqui, e-mail to Muslim newsgroups, March 15, 1993, copy in author's files.

Fourteen

80 The word that Ayaan most: Ayaan Hirsi Ali, *Infidel: My Life* (New York: Free Press, 2007), pp. 198, 216.

80 Every refugee: Ibid., p. 202.

80 But with everyone: Ibid., pp. 197–198.

81 The Dutch system: Ilse van Liempt, *Navigating Borders: Inside Perspectives on the Process of Human Smuggling into the Netherlands* (Amsterdam: Amsterdam University Press, 2007), pp. 79–80.

81 "meant, above all": Ayaan Hirsi Ali, *Nomad: From Islam to America: A Personal Journey Through the Clash of Civilizations* (New York: Free Press, 2010), p. 178.

Fifteen

83 The FBI: Alison Mitchell, "After Blast, New Interest in Holy War Recruits in Brooklyn," *New York Times*, April 11, 1993.

83 A few days later: *United States of America v. Muhamed Mubayyid, Emadeddin Muntasser, and Samir Al-Monla*, superseding indictment, March 8, 2007, pp. 1–28.

83 The FBI had quickly traced: Yosri Fouda and Nick Fielding, *Masterminds of Terror: The Truth Behind the Most Devastating Terrorist Attack the World Has Ever Seen* (New York: Arcade Publishing, 2003), pp. 95–96.

84 In Cambridge: *United States of America v. Muhamed Mubayyid, Emadeddin Muntasser, and Samir Al-Monla*, pp. 1–28.

84 Care International distributed: Evan F. Kohlmann, *Al-Qaeda's Jihad in Europe: The Afghan-Bosnian Network* (Oxford, England: Berg, 2004), p. 40.

Sixteen

86 Finnish immigration records: Juha-Pekka Tikka, "Ayaan Hirsi Alin outo Suomi-yhteys," *Ilta-Sanomat*, October 9, 2007; Tikka, "Rajatarkastus selvittaa Hirsi Ali—mysteeria," *Ilta-Sanomat*, October 15, 2007.

86 She worked as a cleaner: Ayaan Hirsi Ali, *Nomad: From Islam to America:*

A Personal Journey Through the Clash of Civilizations (New York: Free Press, 2010), pp. 170–174.

87 Her Dutch had improved: Ayaan Hirsi Ali, *Infidel: My Life* (New York: Free Press, 2007), pp. 218–223.

Seventeen

88 An Internet newsgroup: Haider Ali Qazilbash, e-mail to Muslim newsgroups, June 5, 1993 (Aafia's reply is attached), copy in author's files.

88 Mercy International's Pakistani director: Simon Reeve, *The New Jackals* (Boston: Northeastern University Press, 1999), p. 190; William K. Rashbaum, "For Ireland and U.S., a Lost Chance on a Terror Plot," *New York Times*, January 22, 2000; *United States of America v. Usama bin Laden et al.*, March 20, 2001.

Eighteen

91 Ayaan's Dutch foster father: Jutta Chorus and Ahmet Olgun, *In Godsnaam: Het jaar van Theo van Gogh* (Amsterdam: Contact, 2005), pp. 99–100.

91 Somalia could use: George J. Church, "Somalia: The Anatomy of a Disaster," *Time*, October 18, 1993.

92 Ayaan and Yasmin: Ayaan Hirsi Ali, *Infidel: My Life* (New York: Free Press, 2007), p. 225.

Nineteen

93 Aafia returned to MIT: *United States of America v. Aafia Siddiqui*, January 28, 2010, p. 1701.

94 Just up the street: Samuel Huntington, *The Clash of Civilizations and the Remaking of World Order* (New York: Simon and Schuster, 1996); Bernard Lewis, "The Roots of Muslim Rage," *The Atlantic*, September 1990.

94 Salman al-Ouda: Jonathan D. Halevi, "Al Qaeda's Intellectual Legacy: New Radical Islamic Thinking Justifying the Genocide of Infidels," *Jerusalem Viewpoints*, no. 508 (December 1, 2003).

95 Non-Muslims almost never: Katherine Bullock, "How to Plan a Lecture for a Muslim and Non-Muslim Audience," in "MSA Starter's Guide: A Guide on How to Run a Successful MSA," 1st ed., March 1996.

96 The anonymous writers: Quoted in Evan F. Kohlmann, "Expert Report—*United States of America v. Muhamed Mubayyid, Emadeddin Muntasser, and Samir Al-Monla*," Criminal Action no. 05-40026-FDS, 2007, pp. 41–42.

96 Arguing that women: *United States of America v. Aafia Siddiqui*, January 28 and 29, pp. 1732–1733, 1770.

96 Yet according to Aafia's family: Aafia Siddiqui, "Starting and Continuing a Regular Dawah Table," in "MSA Starter's Guide"; Aafia Siddiqui, letter to FMC, Carswell, Warden Elaine Chapman, filed on July 7, 2009.

Twenty

98 One day in January 1994: Ayaan Hirsi Ali, *Infidel: My Life* (New York: Free Press, 2007), p. 226.

98 In her collection of essays: Ayaan Hirsi Ali, *The Caged Virgin: An Emancipation Proclamation for Women* (New York: Free Press, 2006), p. 72.

98 Later, in her autobiography: Hirsi Ali, *Infidel*, p. 226.

98 She told Haweya: Ibid., p. 227.

99 Yet, to Ayaan's irritation: Ibid., pp. 226–228.

99 Haweya was shocked: Ibid., pp. 227–235.

100 Somalis who made it: Yaccub Enum and Angela Yphantides, "Tower Hamlets Mental Health Promotion Strategy, 2008–2011," NHS, July 2008; and Edmund Sanders, "Snow, Malls and Stoves, Oh My: Somalis Get a Crash Course on Living in America," *Los Angeles Times*, September 19, 2006.

Twenty-one

101 Benevolence International Foundation: *United States of America v. Enaam M. Arnout*, Government's Evidentiary Proffer, no. 02 CR 892, pp. 48–56.

101 The director of operations: "Two UNL Students Freed in Croatia," Associated Press, July 25, 1993; John Mintz, "U.S. Tries to Link Activist to Al Qaeda; Evidence May Not Be Usable in Trial," *Washington Post*, February 9, 2003.

Twenty-two

103 Even their pious: Ayaan Hirsi Ali, "Why They Deny the Holocaust," *Los Angeles Times*, December 16, 2006.

103 It was while: Interview with Ayaan Hirsi Ali, *Voices on Antisemitism—A Podcast Series*, U.S. Holocaust Museum, January 4, 2007.

103 At home she tried: Hirsi Ali, "Why They Deny the Holocaust."

Twenty-three

105 From Ahmer, Aafia had heard: Suleman Ahmer tells the story of Kamila in *The Embattled Innocence: Recollections of a Muslim Relief Worker*, www.timelenders.com/download/embattledinnocence.pdf.

105 The wives of these knights: Mohammed Al Shafey, "Asharq Al-Awsat Interviews Umm Mohammed: The Wife of Bin Laden's Spiritual

Mentor," *Asharq Al-Awsat*, April 30, 2006. Rabiah Hutchinson describes the life of the wives in this period in Sally Neighbor, *The Mother of Mohammed* (Philadelphia: University of Pennsylvania Press, 2010), pp. 189–197.

107 She suspected them: Lee Hammel, "Jihad Noted in Wiretaps," *Worcester Telegram and Gazette*, December 11, 2007.

107 Meanwhile, Benazir Bhutto: Steve Coll, *Ghost Wars: The Secret History of the CIA, Afghanistan, and Bin Laden, from the Soviet Invasion to September 10, 2001* (New York: Penguin, 2005), p. 292; Yosri Fouda and Nick Fielding, *Masterminds of Terror: The Truth Behind the Most Devastating Terrorist Attack the World Has Ever Seen* (New York: Arcade Publishing, 2003), p. 96.

107 A South African student: Simon Reeve, *The New Jackals* (Boston: Northeastern University Press, 1999), pp. 97–101.

107 Bhutto appealed: John F. Burns, "Pakistan Asks for U.S. Help in Crackdown on Militants," *New York Times*, March 22, 1995.

108 Aafia read: Aafia Siddiqui, e-mail to Muslim newsgroups, April 4, 1995, copy in author's files.

109 A few weeks later: Evan Kohlmann, "U.S. v. Muntasser et al—The Evidence Behind the Convictions," *Counterterrorism Blog*, January 11, 2008, http://counterterrorismblog.org/2008/01/us_v_muntasser_et_al_the_evide.php.

109 The *nikhah* ceremony: Juliane von Mittelstaedt, "The Most Dangerous Woman in the World," *Der Spiegel*, November 27, 2008.

Twenty-four

111 Ayaan rented a room: Ayaan Hirsi Ali, *Infidel: My Life* (New York: Free Press, 2007), pp. 238–239.

111 The Dutch students: Ibid., p. 243.

112 "Imagine," she said: Alexander Linklater, "Danger Woman," *Guardian*, May 17, 2005.

112 "big blue innocent eyes": Hirsi Ali, *Infidel*, p. 251.

113 The photographer Marc de Haan: Alies Pegtel's eight-part series on Ayaan in *HP/De Tijd* began in the Christmas issue 2006 and continued for eight weeks into 2007. Marc de Haan was quoted in the third part, "Helemaal ingeburgerd," January 12, 2007.

113 "Most women are a little": Ibid., p. 42.

Twenty-five

114 But he noticed: Declan Walsh, "The Mystery of Aafia Siddiqui," *Guardian*, November 24, 2009.

Twenty-six

116 By the time Ayaan: Ayaan Hirsi Ali, *Infidel: My Life* (New York: Free Press, 2007), pp. 247–249.

117 Haweya joined them: Ibid., pp. 252–254.

117 She had been smashing: Ibid., pp. 252–253.

118 One night the phone rang: Ibid., p. 255.

Twenty-seven

119 Aafia's parents: *United States of America v. Aafia Siddiqui*, Document 256, filed August 19, 2010, p. 7.

120 When she started: See Thomas Feven's Web page, www.qucis.queensu.ca/home/fevens/UIO/html.

121 She bitterly resented: *United States of America v. Aafia Siddiqui*, letter to Judge Richard Berman, August 18, 2009.

122 It was perhaps unfortunate: Marco Iacoboni describes the discovery of mirror neurons in *Mirroring People: The New Science of How We Connect with Others* (New York: Farrar, Straus and Giroux, 2008).

122 "do for psychology": V. S. Ramachandran, "Mirror Neurons and Imitation Learning as the Driving Force Behind 'the Great Leap Forward' in Human Evolution," Third Culture, http://www.edge.org/3rd_culture/ramachandran/ramachandran_p1.html.

123 An Orthodox Jewish professor: Farah Stockman, "Alleged Pakistani Miliant Stands Trial Today," *Boston Globe*, January 19, 2010.

Twenty-eight

125 After Haweya left: Ayaan Hirsi Ali, *Infidel: My Life* (New York: Free Press, 2007), p. 255.

125 Her brother says: Jos van Dongen, interview with Mahad Hirsi Magan, March 30–April 1, 2005.

Twenty-nine

127 The top woman: Farhat Haq, "Militarism and Motherhood: The Women of the Lashkar-i-Tayyabia in Pakistan," *Signs: Journal of Women in Culture and Society* 32, no. 4 (2007).

127 The Western world: Ahmed Rashid, *Taliban: Islam, Oil and the New Great Game in Central Asia* (New York: I. B. Tauris, 2001), pp. 105–120.

128 "This is a big infidel policy": Ahmed Rashid, *Taliban* (New Haven: Yale University Press, 2000), p. 111.

128 Usually the lesson: "No Parallel to Islamic Emirate on Earth: An In-

terview with Sheikh ul-Hadith Maulana Saleem Ullah Khan," *Zarb-e-Momin*, 2001.

Thirty

131 In Kenya, Haweya: Jos van Dongen, interview with Mahad Hirsi Magan, March 30–April 1, 2005.

131 "She would be talking": Ibid.

131 Ayaan wrote later: Ayaan Hirsi Ali, *The Caged Virgin: An Emancipation Proclamation for Women* (New York: Free Press, 2006), p. 73.

131 Their brother, Mahad, said: Van Dongen, interview with Mahad.

131 Ayaan talked with Haweya: Ayaan Hirsi Ali, *Infidel: My Life* (New York: Free Press, 2007), p. 257.

131 In *The Caged Virgin*: In *The Caged Virgin*, p. 76, Ayaan wrote, "Presumably she died from exhaustion, but I will never be sure because no autopsy was performed. In our culture it is taboo to ask questions about the cause of death. Every time I brought up the subject, I was dismissed as a tiresome child." In *Infidel*, p. 258, she wrote, "Ma told me how Haweya died. . . . She saw Alah in the lightning and ran out the door. She ran barefoot into the road in the dark, sprinting across the potholes and when Ma screamed for help, two Somali men ran after her. When they brought Haweya back, she was bleeding from her knees and between her legs. She died a week after her miscarriage. I supposed it was an infection."

131 the lowest point of her life: Jutta Chorus and Ahmet Olgun, *In Godsnaam: Het jaar van Theo van Gogh* (Amsterdam: Contact, 2005), p. 103.

131 Ayaan found: Hirsi Ali, *Infidel*, p. 259.

132 "You drive around": Ayaan Hirsi Ali, *Nomad: From Islam to America: A Personal Journey Through the Clash of Civilizations* (New York: Free Press, 2010), p. 63.

132 In truth, Ayaan: Hirsi Ali, *Infidel*, p. 259.

Thirty-one

133 She taught: Farah Stockman, "Activist Turned Extremist," *Boston Globe*, August 12, 2008.

133 "She shared with us": Ibid.

136 "at various times": *United States of America v. Aafia Siddiqui*, Document 256, August 19, 2010, p. 34, and Document 258–1, August 19, 2010, p. 2.

Thirty-two

140 And when Marco lent her: Ayaan Hirsi Ali, *The Caged Virgin: An Emancipation Proclamation for Women* (New York: Free Press, 2006), p. 68.

Thirty-three

141 The new year also brought: Bernard Rougier, *Everyday Jihad: The Rise of Militant Islam Among Palestinians in Lebanon*, trans. Pascale Ghazaleh (Cambridge, Mass.: Harvard University Press, 2007), pp. 239–246; Stephen Kurkjian and Judy Rakowsky, "FBI Terrorism Probe Tracks Ex-Cabdrivers," *Boston Globe*, February 5, 2001.

141 Aafia visited Marlene: Dan Malone, "Cells Without Numbers," *Fort Worth Weekly*, May 9, 2002.

142 For the next year: Aafia Siddiqui, "Separating the Components of Imitation," unpublished dissertation, on file at MIT; Robert Sekuler, Aafia Siddiqui, Nikhil Goyal, and Rohin Rajan, "Reproduction of Seen Actions: Stimulus-Selective Learning," *Perception* 32 (2003), 839–854.

142 She finished her thesis: John A. Cooley, M.D, "Fair Winds and Following Seas," *ASA Newsletter*, February 2001, vol. 65.

143 With the millennium: Safar Ibn 'Abd Al-Rahman Al-Hawali, *The Day of Wrath: Is the Intifadha of Rajab only the Beginning?* http://thetruth.hypermart.net/wrath/0_preface.htm.

Thirty-four

144 Leiden's student magazine: Quoted in Alies Pegtel, "Helemaal Ingeburgerd," HP/De Tijd, January 12, 2007.

144 In *Infidel*: Ayaan Hirsi Ali, *Infidel: My Life* (New York: Free Press, 2007), pp. 264–265.

145 In 1991: Ian Buruma explores Frits Bolkestein's and Pim Fortuyn's contribution to the rise of immigration as a political issue in *Murder in Amsterdam: The Death of Theo van Gogh and the Limits of Tolerance* (New York: Penguin, 2006), pp. 37–70. Christopher Caldwell offers a different point of view in *Reflections on the Revolution in Europe* (New York: Doubleday, 2009), pp. 307–323. See also Aranka Klomp and John Kroon, eds., *The Netherlands 2006: The Mood after the Hysteria* (Amsterdam: Prometheus, 2005).

146 Ayaan found: Hirsi Ali, *Infidel*, p. 262.

147 "My dear fellows": Unpublished letter from Hirsi Magan to members of Osman Mahamoud clan, undated, copy in author's files, printed with permission of Guled A. Yusuf.

Thirty-five

148 Another time Aafia quarreled: *United States of America v. Aafia Siddiqui*, Document 258-1, August 19, 2010, pp. 12–13.

149 Aafia told: *United States of America v. Aafia Siddiqui*, Document 256, August 19, 2010, p. 14.

Thirty-six

151 The pharmaceutical company: Ayaan Hirsi Ali, *Infidel: My Life* (New York: Free Press, 2007), pp. 264–265.

151 She and Marco were: Ayaan Hirsi Ali, *The Caged Virgin: An Emancipation Proclamation for Women* (New York: Free Press, 2006), p. 77.

153 Ayaan sat down: Hirsi Ali, *Infidel*, p. 266.

Thirty-seven

154 A few weeks after: Peter Bergen, *The Osama bin Laden I Know* (New York: Free Press, 2006), pp. 290–294.

155 The Al-Kifah circle: Dan Malone, "Cells Without Numbers," *Fort Worth Weekly*, May 9, 2002.

156 Police in Boston: Kevin Cullen, "Task Force Probing Hub Link to Attacks," *Boston Globe*, September 11, 2001.

156 Amjad tried to calm her: Ron Nordland, "Prejudice in Pakistan," *Newsweek*, September 13, 2001; Kenneth Timmerman, *Preachers of Hate: Islam and the War on America* (New York: Three Rivers Press, 2003), pp. 12–13.

Thirty-eight

157 Ayaan had been working: Ayaan Hirsi Ali, *Infidel: My Life* (New York: Free Press, 2007), pp. 267–269.

Part II: Acting

One

161 "I felt that I knew him": Ayaan Hirsi Ali, *Infidel: My Life* (New York: Free Press, 2007), p. 269.

161 "Did the 9/11 attacks": Ibid., pp. 270–271.

161 She read bin Laden's statements: Ibid., pp. 270–273.

162 It doesn't seem to have occurred: The highly respected International Institute for the Study of Islam in the Modern World (ISIM) was established in 1998 in Leiden by the University of Amsterdam, Leiden

University, Utrecht University, and Radboud University Nijmegen. Before it closed in 2009, it produced *The ISIM Review* and the ISIM paper series that often discussed or featured the work of Islamic scholars such as Abdullahi An'Naim and others seeking to integrate Islam and the modern human rights movement.

162 Psychological studies have shown: See, e.g., Sheldon Solomon, Jeff Greenberg, and Tom Pyszczynski, "Fatal Attraction: A New Study Suggests a Relationship Between Fear of Death and Political Preferences," *Association for Psychological Sciences Observer*, October 2004.

162 But for Muslims: Hirsi Ali, *Infidel*, p. 280.

Two

164 The week after: Ahmed Rashid, *Taliban: Islam, Oil and the New Great Game in Central Asia* (New York: I. B. Tauris, 2001), p. 77; Kathy Gannon, *I Is for Infidel: From Holy War to Holy Terror: 18 Years Inside Afghanistan* (New York: PublicAffairs, 2005), pp. 92–96; Bernard-Henri Lévy, *Who Killed Daniel Pearl?* trans. James X. Mitchell (South Yarra, Australia: Hardie Grant Books, 2005), pp. 298–299.

169 Jaish-e-Muhammad: "Al-Rasheed Trust—From a Welfare Trust to a Terrorist Empire," *Hindustan Times*, September 27, 2001.

Three

171 The title of this: Ayaan calls it "The West or Islam: Who Needs a Voltaire?" in *Infidel: My Life* (New York: Free Press, 2007), p. 274.

171 Vice President Dick Cheney: Jane Mayer, *The Dark Side: The Inside Story of How the War on Terror Turned into a War on American Ideals* (New York: Doubleday, 2008), pp. 9–10.

171 Ayaan has said: Ayaan Hirsi Ali, "Infidel: My Journey from Somalia to the West," *Cato's Letter*, The Cato Institute, Spring 2007.

172 "She spoke Dutch": Jutta Chorus and Ahmet Olgun, *In godsnaam: Het jaar van Theo van Gogh* (Amsterdam: Contact, 2005), p. 106.

172 After the debate: Hirsi Ali, *Infidel*, p. 275.

172 Ayaan wasn't a polished writer: Chorus and Olgun, *In godsnaam*, p. 107.

172 It was published: Ayaan Hirsi Ali, "Laat ons niet in de steek, gun ons een Voltaire," *Trouw*, November 24, 2001. An expanded version of the article appears in English in *The Caged Virgin: An Emancipation Proclamation for Women* (New York: Free Press, 2006), pp. 35–41. The quotes here are taken from *The Caged Virgin*.

173 In the years that followed: See, e.g., Ayaan's debate with Farid Esak, NIO Dutch Muslim Television, April 4, 2002; Joel Voss, " De Verlich-

ting dicteert niet, ze ziet nuance," *Trouw*, May 25, 2006; and Pankaj Mishra, "Islamism: How Should the West Respond to Muslim Scholars?" *The New Yorker*, June 7, 2010.

174 "To say that 'Islam is the problem'": "Do Western Europeans Hold a Grudge Against Muslims: A Debate," NMO, August 4, 2002.

174 She appeared: George Packer tells Mahmoud Mohammed Taha's story in "The Moderate Martyr," *The New Yorker*, September 11, 2006.

174 She also seemed not to know: Nasr Hamed Abu Zeid described his exile in Leiden to Nadia Abou El-Magd in "When the Professor Can't Teach," *Al-Ahram Weekly*, June 15–21, 2000.

175 Human rights activists: For more about the activists mentioned, see Fatima Mernissi, *The Veil and the Male Elite: A Feminist Interpretation of Women's Rights in Islam*, trans. Mary Jo Lakeland (New York: Perseus, 1991); Khalida Messoud and Elisabeth Schemla, *Unbowed: An Algerian Woman Confronts Islamic Fundamentalism*, trans. Anne C. Vila (Philadelphia: University of Pennsylvania Press, 1998); and Shirin Ebadi with Azada Moeveni, *Iran Awakening: A Memoir of Revolution and Hope* (New York: Random House, 2006).

Four

177 Osama bin Laden and his fighters: National Commission on Terrorist Attacks Upon the United States, *9/11 Commission Report: Final Report of the National Commission on Terrorist Attacks Upon the United States* (New York: W. W. Norton, 2005), pp. 276–277.

177 As the various foreign jihadis: Mohammed Shehzad, "Al-Qaeda Next Door," *Hindustan Times*, August 24, 2004.

177 She had been a speaker: *United States of America v. Aafia Siddiqui*, Document 256, August 19, 2010, p. 22.

177 Jose Padilla: David Adams, "U.S. Charges Long-Detained Citizen," *St. Petersburg Times*, December 22, 2005.

178 Another American resident: Manuel Roig-Franzia and Dan Eggen, "From Bookish Boy to Focus of FBI Manhunt; Terror Suspect Labeled Worst Threat to U.S.," *Washington Post*, April 14, 2003.

Five

179 Ayaan's article about Voltaire: Ayaan Hirsi Ali, *Infidel: My Life* (New York: Free Press, 2007), pp. 276–277.

179 Job Cohen: See Russell Shorto's profile of Job Cohen, "The Integrationist," *The New York Times Magazine*, May 28, 2010.

180 "I was learning": Hirsi Ali, *Infidel*, p. 277.

180 "He blew me away": Ibid., p. 278.

180 "looks like a fashion model": Andrew Anthony, "Taking the Fight to Islam," *Observer*, February 4, 2007.

180 Polls show: In a study of a series of worldwide polls, the social scientists Pippa Norris and Ronald Inglehart found that Muslims and Westerners disagreed more about sexuality than any other issue. See their book *Sacred and Secular: Religion and Politics Worldwide* (Cambridge, England: Cambridge University Press, 2004). See also Paul M. Sniderman and Louk Hagendoorn, *When Ways of Life Collide: Multiculturalism and Its Discontents in the Netherlands* (Princeton, N.J.: Princeton University Press, 2006), p. 29.

Six

184 A few days before: Daniel Pearl, "Militants Still Operate Despite Pakistan's Efforts—Groups Suspected in Attack on India's Parliament Keep Going—Government's Limited Actions Fuel Tensions with New Delhi," *Wall Street Journal*, December 31, 2001; Kathy Gannon, "Al Rashid Trust Where Body Believed to Be Daniel Pearl's Found Has a History with Al Qaida, Jaish-e-Mohammed," Associated Press, May 17, 2002.

184 Soon the ghastly video: Vince Horiuchi, "Grisly Site: Pearl Video on Web Stirs FBI Interest," *Salt Lake Tribune*, May 21, 2002.

184 Aafia usually followed: Justin Pope, "Software Company Tries to Survive Terrorism Investigation," Associated Press, January 5, 2003; Farah Stockman, "Roxbury Address Eyed in Terrorism Probe," *Boston Globe*, April 10, 2004.

185 The Americans finally captured: George Tenet with Bill Harlow, *At the Center of the Storm: My Years at the CIA* (New York: HarperCollins, 2007), p. 251.

185 Abu Zubaydah also told them: Thomas Joscelyn, "The Zubaydah Dossier," *The Weekly Standard*, August 17, 2009.

186 Three or four weeks: "Remarks of Deputy Attorney General James Comey Regarding Jose Padilla," U.S. Department of Justice, June 1, 2004.

Seven

190 A filmmaker: Karin Schagen, "Door het leven: Met de angst in het achterhoofd," VPRO, November 1, 2002.

190 Ayaan later wrote: Ayaan Hirsi Ali, *Infidel: My Life* (New York: Free Press, 2007), p. 285.

191 As the journalist Alies Pegtel: Alies Pegtel, "Schatje van de Grachtengordel," *HP/De Tijd,* February 2, 2007.

191 Steffie Kouters: Steffie Kouters, "Durf te Botsen," *De Volkskrant*, April 11, 2002.

193 On May 6, 2002: Quoted in Bruce Bawer, *While Europe Slept: How Radical Islam Is Destroying the West from Within* (New York: Doubleday, 2006), p. 169.

193 Ayaan continued to wrap: Hirsi Ali, *Infidel*, pp. 280–281.

194 "I would no longer": Ibid., p. 282.

194 Jaffe Vink had introduced: Pegtel, "Schatje van de Grachtengordel."

195 In early August: Hirsi Ali, *Infidel*, pp. 285–286.

Eight

199 Aafia recalled . . . in 2008: *United States of America v. Aafia Siddiqui*, Document 256, August 19, 2010, p. 15.

Nine

200 On the first anniversary: Ayaan Hirsi Ali, *Infidel: My Life* (New York: Free Press, 2007), pp. 287–289.

201 On September 18: "Hirsi Ali weg uit publiciteit na dreigementen," *De Volkskrant*, September 18, 2002.

204 Labor itself had: Alies Pegtel, "Schatje van de Grachtengordel," *HP/De Tijd,* February 2, 2007.

204 A day after: Ayaan Hirsi Ali, "PvdA onderschat het lijden van moslimvrouwen," *NRC Handelsblad*, October 3, 2002.

205 Soon after she left: Elma Verhey, "Tussen bedreigen en bedriegen," *Vrij Nederland*, October 12, 2002.

206 On October 16: "Hirsi Ali kandidaat Kamerlid voor VVD" and "Waarom ik de VVD verkies boven de PvdA," *De Volkskrant*, October 31, 2002.

206 Ayaan answered: Alies Pegtel, "Van links naar rechts," *HP/De Tijd,* February 9, 2007.

207 A Dutch reporter: Ibid.

Ten

210 She signed a statement: Divorce decree, Mohammed A. Khan and Aafia Siddiqui, October 21, 2002, issued by Karachi Town Union Council, copy in author's files.

Eleven

211 She wrote: Ayaan Hirsi Ali, "Waarom ik de VVD verkies boven de PvdA," *De Volkskrant*, October 31, 2002.

211 Karin Schagen's sympathetic portrait: Karin Schagen, "Door het leven: Met de angst in het achterhoofd," VPRO, November 1, 2002.

212 On November 9: Marlise Simons, "Behind the Veil: A Muslim Woman Speaks Out," *New York Times*, November 9, 2002.

212 Lea was making a name: Susanna Lea's publishing successes are chronicled on her Web site, www.susannaleaassociates.com.

213 She often bonded: Jutta Chorus and Ahmet Olgun, *In godsnaam: Het jaar van Theo van Gogh* (Amsterdam: Contact, 2005), p. 112.

213 Kroes was smitten: Alies Pegtel, "Van links naar rechts," *HP/De Tijd,* February 9, 2007.

214 Ayaan has never made: Ayaan Hirsi Ali, *Infidel: My Life* (New York: Free Press, 2007), p. 298.

215 The filmmaker Eveline van Dijk: Eveline van Dijk's home videos of Ayaan and her friends were later made into a documentary, "Ik ben Ayaan," *Profiel*, May 19, 2006.

217 "Those who fail to see": Frits Bolkestein, "Integration," a speech delivered at Rotterdam, January 5, 2003, www.fritsbolkestein.com/docs/speeches/20030105-integration_en.pdf.

Twelve

218 She later told the FBI: *United States of America v. Aafia Siddiqui*, Document 256, August 19, 2010, p. 11.

218 The al-Rashid Trust: Pepe Escobar, "Anatomy of a 'Terrorist' NGO," *Asia Times*, October 26, 2001.

218 Aafia told the FBI: *United States of America v. Aafia Siddiqui*, Document 256, August 19, 2010, p. 22.

219 Ali had been in touch: "Remarks of Deputy Attorney General James Comey Regarding Jose Padilla," U.S. Department of Justice, June 1, 2004.

219 Clean-shaven: "'Ali 'Abd 'al-Aziz 'Ali" (capsule biography released by the White House in September 2006), www.nefafoundation.org/miscellaneous/FeaturedDocs/DNI_Ammar_al-Baluchi_Bio.pdf.

220 Starting in the spring of 2000: "Summary of Evidence for Combatant Status Review Tribunal—al-Baluchi, Ammar," Combatant Status Review Tribunal, March 28, 2007, www.defense.gov/news/ISN10018.pdf; National Commission on Terrorist Attacks Upon the United States, *9/11 Commission Report: Final Report of the National Commission on Terrorist Attacks Upon the United States* (New York: W. W. Norton, 2005), pp. 236–237.

220 After the 9/11 attacks: "'Ali 'Abd 'al-Aziz 'Ali"; Vikram Dodd, "Former Grammar School Boy Gets 13 Years for Shoe Bomb Plot: Repentant Islamist Broke with Militants and Confessed," *Guardian*, April 23, 2005.

220 Khan had moved to Baltimore: Katherine Shrader, "An Immigrant's Journey from the Maryland Suburbs to a Cell at Guantanamo Bay," Associated Press, March 21, 2007; Eric Rich and Dan Eggen, "From Baltimore Suburbs to a Secret CIA Prison; Family Learned Last Week That Man Was Among 'High-Value' Terrorism Suspects Moved to Guantanamo," *Washington Post*, September 10, 2006.

221 According to a secret assessment: U.S. Department of Defense, JTF-GTMO Detainee Assessment, June 13, 2008, http://wikileaks.ch/gitmo/pdf/pk/us9pk-010020dp.pdf.

222 She told the FBI: *United States of America v. Aafia Siddiqui*, Document 256, August 19, 2010, p. 8.

223 Given Aafia's intense fear: *United States of America v. Uzair Paracha*, November 14, 2005, pp. 598–632.

Thirteen

225 The newspaper *Trouw*: Arjan Visser, "Ayaan Hirsi Ali: Politiek schadelijk voor mijn ideal," *Trouw*, January 25, 2003. Ayaan's replies to Visser's questions are reprinted in English in Ayaan Hirsi Ali, *The Caged Virgin: An Emancipation Proclamation for Women* (New York: Free Press, 2006), pp. 79–87.

226 She had been asked: Hirsi Ali, *The Caged Virgin*, p. 80.

227 Gerrit Zalm and his: Alies Pegtel, "Van links naar rechts," *HP/De Tijd*, February 9, 2007.

228 "Because it's true": Ayaan Hirsi Ali, *Infidel: My Life* (New York: Free Press, 2007), p. 305.

228 "She spoke Dutch well": Jutta Chorus and Ahmet Olgun, *In godsnaam: Het jaar van Theo van Gogh* (Amsterdam: Contact, 2005), p. 117.

228 Theodor Holman held: "Ik ben Ayaan," *Profiel*, May 19, 2006.

230 "Gore and porn": Rachel Halliburton, "Teenage Cults: Blood and Gore on the Web," *New Statesman*, March 28, 2005.

230 That night: Chorus and Olgun, *In godsnaam*, p. 23.

Fourteen

231 Like Aafia: David Rohde, "Pakistani Detainee Enjoyed Deep U.S. Roots," *New York Times*, August 18, 2003.

232 "We had friendly talks": Ibid.

232 Paracha later told: "Summary of Evidence for Combatant Status Review Tribunal—Paracha, Saifullah," Combatant Status Review Tribunal, November 12, 2004, http://projects.nytimes.com/guantanamo/detainees/1094-saifullah-paracha/document, pp. 1–19.

233 U.S. military prosecutors: U.S. Department of Defense, "JTF-GTMO Detainee Assessment," December 1, 2008, http://projects.nytimes.com/guantanamo/detainees/1094-saifullah-paracha.

233 Paracha's oldest son: *United States of America v. Uzair Paracha*, November 17, 2005, pp. 1060–1067.

234 "A good sister": Ibid., p. 1190.

234 Uzair seems to have been: Ibid., p. 1243.

234 Khan offered Uzair a lift: Ibid., p. 1243.

Fifteen

237 In her interview: Ayaan Hirsi Ali, *The Caged Virgin: An Emancipation Proclamation for Women* (New York: Free Press, 2006), p. 84.

237 When a Belgian newspaper: Merlijn Doomernik, "Ayaan Hirsi Ali: Rede Gaat Altijd voor op Geloof," *De Standaard*, September 30, 2006.

238 From the day: Sam Cherribi, *In the House of War: Dutch Islam Observed* (Oxford, England: Oxford University Press, 2010), pp. 188–189.

238 On April 12, 2003: Ayaan Hirsi Ali and Geert Wilders, "Het is tijd voor een liberale jihad," *NRC Handelsblad*, April 12, 2003.

239 Only a few dozen: The AIVD spelled out its position on the jihadist threat facing the Netherlands in a series of reports available in English at www.aivd.nl/english/publications-press/aivd-publications.

239 With its surveillance power: Ministry of the Interior and Kingdom Relations, "From Dawa to Jihad: The Various Threats from Radical Islam to the Democratic Legal Order," December 2004, www.fas.org/irp/world/netherlands/dawa.pdf.

240 The AIVD had recently: Janny Groen and Annieke Kranenberg, *Women Warriors for Allah: An Islamist Network in the Netherlands*, trans. Robert Naborn (Philadelphia: University of Pennsylvania Press, 2010), pp. 47–59; European Union, "The 'Hofstadgroep,'" April 15, 2007, www.transnationalterrorism.eu/tekst/publications/Hofstadgroep.pdf. The EU report concluded that the political, as opposed to personal, trigger cause of Bouyeri's radicalization was the U.S. invasion of Iraq and the "(perceived) critique of Islam by politicians and opinion makers" in the Netherlands.

240 The police were first called: Albert Benschop, "Jihad in the Netherlands: Chronicle of a Political Murder Foretold," trans. Connie Menting, University of Amsterdam, first published 2004, modified 2007, www.sociosite.org/jihad_nl_en.php. The account of Bouyeri's activities is taken from this source.

242 A childhood friend: Ibid.

242 Much later some women: Groen and Kranenberg, *Women Warriors for Allah*, p. 48.

Sixteen

243 Aafia didn't know it: Dr. Hamid Manzoor, "Aafia Siddiqui Mystery—Extracting the Hard Facts," *Daily Times*, July 10, 2010.

243 The arrests began: George Tenet with Bill Harlow, *At the Center of the Storm: My Years at the CIA* (New York: HarperCollins, 2007), p. 253; and Jane Mayer, *The Dark Side: The Inside Story of How the War on Terror Turned into a War on American Ideals* (New York: Doubleday, 2008), p. 270.

243 Within hours: *United States of America v. Uzair Paracha*, November 21, 2005, p. 1285.

243 Ali took one of those: Saifullah Paracha, *Administrative Review Board Round One Transcripts*, p. 44, http://projects.nytimes.com/guantanamo/detainees/1094-saifullah-paracha/documents/search?document_query=paracha.

244 Or maybe: *United States of America v. Aafia Siddiqui*, Document 256, August 19, 2010, p. 13.

244 Her husband: Christina Lamb, "Was Khalid Arrested Where the FBI Said He Was?" *Sunday Times*, March 9, 2003.

244 The CIA found: Barton Gellman, "Al Qaeda Near Biological, Chemical Arms Production," *Washington Post*, March 23, 2003.

245 Majid Khan was arrested: Ali Khan, "Statement of Ali Khan," in *Verbatim Transcript of Combatant Status Review Tribunal Hearing on ISN 10020*, p. 12.

245 On March 10: American Civil Liberties Union, "Sanctioned Bias: Racial Profiling Since 9/11," February 2004, p. 14, www.aclu.org/national-security/racial-profiling-911-report.

245 The news that: *United States of America v. Aafia Siddiqui*, Document 256, August 19, 2010, p. 8; Document 258-1, August 19, 2010, p. 6.

245 Aafia told Ismat: Ibid., 258-1, pp. 12–13, 15.

246 "His female family members": *United States of America v. Aafia Siddiqui*, Document 256, August 17, 2010, p. 8.

246 On March 17: "Sanctioned Bias: Racial Profiling Since 9/11," pp. 14–15.

247 The FBI posted pictures: Ralph Ranalli, "FBI Seeks to Question Former MIT Student," *Boston Globe*, March 20, 2003.

247 Majid Khan's friend: Eric Rich, "Terrorism Suspect Alleges Mental Torture," *Washington Post*, May 16, 2007.

247 Five days later: Colin Miner, "FBI Hunts Down Suspected Terrorist," *Sun*, March 21, 2003; Dave Wedge, "Hub Doctor's Wife Sought as Suspect," *Boston Herald*, March 22, 2003; David Weber, "Suspect's Neighbors Quizzed," *Boston Herald*, March 23, 2003; Allen Lengel,

"FBI Seeking Pakistani Pair over Possible Al Qaeda Link," *Washington Post*, March 26, 2003; "FBI: Terrorists Can Make Simple, Deadly Chemical Weapons," Dow Jones International News, March 26, 2003.

247 On March 28: *United States of America v. Uzair Paracha*, November 17, 2005, pp. 1006–1012.

248 After two days: *United States of America v. Uzair Paracha*, November 14, 2005, pp. 364–412.

248 The very next day: Deborah Scroggins, "The Most Wanted Woman in the World," *Vogue*, March 2005.

248 On March 31: "Pak Police Arrest Woman for Suspected al-Qaida Links," Press Trust of India, March 31, 2003.

248 In 2011, lawyers: International Justice Network, "Aafia Siddiqui: Just the Facts," February 14, 2011, www.ijnetwork.org/ijn-news-newsroom-53/240-ijnetwork-releases-report-aafia-siddiqui-just-the-facts.

249 In the United States: "FBI Wary That al-Qaida May Start Using Women in Attacks," Dow Jones International, April 1, 2003; Jerry Seper, "FBI Steps Up Hunt for Pakistani," *Washington Times*, April 2, 2003.

249 On April 9: Azfar-ul-Ashfaque, "Mystery Surrounds Disappearance of Pakistani Doctor," *News*, April 9, 2003.

250 The next mention: B. Muralidhar Reddy, "Pak Promised More to Help Fight Terrorism," *Hindu*, April 17, 2003.

250 Ismat quickly called: Chitra Ragavan, "All in the Family: A Missing Mom, an Estranged Husband—and Al-Qaeda?" *U.S. News & World Report*, April 21, 2003; "Pakistani Woman Accused of Ties with al-Qaeda," *NBC Nightly News*, April 21, 2003; "U.S. Officials Doubt Pakistani Woman Is in Custody," Associated Press, April 22, 2003.

251 After the FBI arrested: David Rennie, "Captured al-Qaida Man was FBI Spy," *Telegraph*, June 23, 2003; "Summary of Evidence for Combatant Status Review Tribunal—al-Baluchi, Ammar," *News*, May 1, 2003; Azfar-ul-Ashfaque, "11 Al-Qa'idah Suspects Arrested, Arms Recovered," *News*, May 1, 2003.

253 One of KSM's uncles: Mansoor Khan, "Mystery Still Shrouds Dr. Afia's Whereabouts," *Nation*, August 6, 2008.

253 Aafia described: *United States of America v. Aafia Siddiqui*, Document 256, August 19, 2010, p. 8.

Seventeen

254 The Liberal Party asked: Alies Pegtel, "Van links naar rechts," *HP/De Tijd*, February 9, 2007.

255 She seemed to regard: Gerald Traufetter, "The Odyssey of Ayaan Hirsi Ali," *Der Spiegel*, May 12, 2007.

256 Ayaan initially asked: Sam Cherribi, *In the House of War: Dutch Islam Observed* (Oxford, England: Oxford University Press, 2010), pp. 191–192; Deborah Scroggins, "The Dutch-Muslim Culture War," *The Nation*, June 27, 2005.

256 "proxies put forward": Andrew Anthony, "Ayaan Hirsi Ali: Taking the Fight to Islam," *Observer*, January 29, 2007.

256 "I called it": Alexander Linklater, "Danger Woman," *Guardian*, May 17, 2005.

Eighteen

258 Family lawyers later claimed: International Justice Network, "Aafia Siddiqui: Just the Facts," February 14, 2011, www.ijnetwork.org/ijn-news-newsroom-53/240-ijnetwork-releases-report-aafia-siddiqui-just-the-facts, p. 7.

259 Her son took her: The redacted text of the report on Ismat's interviews with the FBI on May 24, 2003, and July 1, 2003, is in *United States of America v. Aafia Siddiqui*, Document 258-I, filed August 19, 2010, pp. 6–11.

260 Ismat was still: Evan Thomas, "The Enemy Within," *Newsweek*, June 23, 2003.

Nineteen

264 Ayaan often spoke of: Ayaan Hirsi Ali, *The Caged Virgin: An Emancipation Proclamation for Women* (New York: Free Press, 2006), pp. 82–83.

264 Ayaan would later tell: Maaike Beekers, "Ayaanlaanse Toestanden," *Red*, June 2010.

265 Ayaan sometimes seemed: Alexander Linklater, "Danger Woman," *Guardian*, May 17, 2005.

265 FGM had been illegal: Bertine Krol, "Fighting Mutilation," Radio Netherlands, May 12, 2004.

266 For several years: Ilse van Liempt, "Then One Day They All Moved to Leicester," *Population, Space and Place,* December 30, 2009.

Twenty

270 The Bush administration knew: Adrian Levy and Catherine Scott-Clark, *Deception: Pakistan, the United States and the Global Nuclear Weapons Conspiracy* (London: Atlantic Books, 2007), pp. 357–379; Ahmed Rashid, *Taliban: Islam, Oil and the New Great Game in Central Asia* (New York: I. B. Tauris, 2001), pp. 236–237.

271 Aafia's uncle: S. H. Faruqi, "Letters to the Editor," *Dawn*, March 30, 2004, and May 2, 2004.

272 On May 26, 2004: Dale Lezon, "Former Houston Resident Sought as

al-Qaida 'Fixer,'" *Houston Chronicle*, May 27, 2004; Daniel Klaidman, Evan Thomas, and Michael Isikoff, "Suspect Motives," *Newsweek*, June 7, 2004.

273 The following day: Muhammed Anis, "Pakistan Interior Minister Denies Terror Suspect Turned Over to U.S.," *News*, May 30, 2004.

273 Then, on June 1: Mac Daniel, "Suspect's Kin Seek Help Finding Her," *Boston Globe*, June 2, 2004.

273 The fog of rumors: Glenn Simpson, "The UN Ties al-Qaeda Figure to Diamonds," *Wall Street Journal*, June 28, 2004.

Twenty-one

274 Ayaan's political party made good: Sam Cherribi, *In the House of War: Dutch Islam Observed* (Oxford, England: Oxford University Press, 2010), pp. 192–198.

275 Ayaan opposed the decision: Alies Pegtel, "Van Zomergast to onderduiker," *HP/De Tijd*, February 16, 2007.

275 She often said: Ayaan Hirsi Ali, *The Caged Virgin: An Emancipation Proclamation for Women* (New York: Free Press, 2006), p. 26.

275 "In reality": Ayaan Hirsi Ali, *Infidel: My Life* (New York: Free Press, 2007), p. 307.

275 Her battles in Parliament: Jutta Chorus and Ahmet Olgun, *In godsnaam: Het jaar van Theo van Gogh* (Amsterdam: Contact, 2005), pp. 115–117.

275 One day Ayaan was invited: "Ebru Umar to Muslim Politician Hirsi Ali: 'You turned your Private War into a National War' and said 'To Hell with the VVD,'" Militant Islam Monitor, May 15, 2006, www.militantislammonitor.org/article/id/1911.

276 Theo van Gogh: Assaad E. Azzi, Xenia Chryssochoou, Bert Klandermans, and Bernd Simon, *Identity and Participation in Culturally Diverse Societies* (New York: Wiley, 2010), p. 232.

276 A bit later she flew: Chorus and Olgun, *In godsnaam*, p. 28.

276 The filmmaker had just left: Ian Buruma, *Murder in Amsterdam: The Death of Theo van Gogh and the Limits of Tolerance* (New York: Penguin, 2006), pp. 100–101.

276 When Ayaan got back: Chorus and Olgun, *In godsnaam*, p. 35.

277 Ayaan knew the film: Ibid., p. 148.

278 While still working: Ibid., pp. 151–152.

278 A *De Volkskrant* poll: "Griezelen uit onbegrip. Angst voor Moslims," *De Volkskrant*, June 23, 2004.

278 Now when Ayaan: Chorus and Olgun, *In godsnaam*, p. 54.

279 A rap song: "Ayaan Hirsi Ali doelwit Haagse rapgroep," *Algemeen Dagblad*, June 30, 2004.

279 In Amsterdam West: Albert Benschop, "Jihad in the Netherlands: Chronicle of a Political Murder Foretold," trans. Connie Menting, University of Amsterdam, first published 2004, modified 2007, www.sociosite.org/jihad_nl_en.php.

279 The videos: Rudolph Peters examined the videos found in Bouyeri's computer and apartment for his report to the court, "De Ideologische en Religieuze Ontwikkeling van Mohammed B.," www.sociosite.org/jihad/peters_rapport.pdf. Groen and Kranenberg also interviewed members of the group about the effect of the videos; see Janny Groen and Annieke Kranenberg, *Women Warriors for Allah: An Islamist Network in the Netherlands*, trans. Robert Naborn (Philadelphia: University of Pennsylvania Press, 2010), pp. 74–81.

280 He wrote tract after tract: Albert Benschop, "Jihad in the Netherlands: Chronicle of a Political Murder Foretold."

280 Bouyeri narrowed his options: Ibid.

281 All the members: Groen and Kranenberg, *Women Warriors for Allah*, p. 67.

281 Bouyeri had fallen: Ibid., pp. 51–53.

282 Ayaan has said: See, e.g., "Dutch MP to Make Gay Islam Film," BBC News, November 17, 2005.

283 "He simply asked": Hirsi Ali, *Infidel*, p. 315.

283 But the press: Three articles appeared on August 28, 2004, in *NRC Handelsblad*: Jutta Chorus, "Nieuwe provocatie Hirsi Ali"; Jutta Chorus, "Ze zullen zien dat ik gelijk heb Een half jaar met Ayaan Hirsi Ali"; and Daniela Hooghiemstra, "Ongekroonde koninginnen."

283 Then, in September: Benschop, "Jihad in the Netherlands."

Twenty-two

284 "It seems that this family": Kamran Khan, "Al-Qaeda Arrest in June Opened Valuable Leads," *Washington Post*, August 4, 2004.

285 Aafia almost certainly knew: Jarret Brachman, *Global Jihadism: Theory and Practice* (New York: Routledge, 2009), details Babar Ahmad's role in the establishment of www.azzam.com on pp. 122–123.

285 Noting that the Pakistani government: Syed Saleem Shahzad, "Pakistan Produces the Goods, Again," *Asia Times*, August 4, 2004.

Twenty-three

287 Ayaan went to see: Jutta Chorus and Ahmet Olgun, *In godsnaam: Het jaar van Theo van Gogh* (Amsterdam: Contact, 2005), pp. 210–211.

287 Back in Holland: Marc de Leeuw and Sonja van Wichelen, " 'PLEASE, GO WAKE UP!': Submission, Hirsi Ali, and the 'War on Terror' in the Netherlands," *Feminist Media Studies* 5, no. 3 (2005).

288 But as the journalist: Ian Buruma, *Murder in Amsterdam: The Death of Theo van Gogh and the Limits of Tolerance* (New York: Penguin, 2006), p. 183.

288 On the Internet: Albert Benschop, "Jihad in the Netherlands: Chronicle of a Political Murder Foretold," trans. Connie Menting, University of Amsterdam, first published 2004, modified 2007, www.sociosite.org/jihad_nl_en.php.

289 It isn't certain: Ibid.

289 Bouyeri wrote a farewell letter: Ibid.

290 On the night of November 1: Ibid.

291 Ayaan was in Parliament: Janny Groen and Annieke Kranenberg, *Women Warriors for Allah: An Islamist Network in the Netherlands*, trans. Robert Naborn (Philadelphia: University of Pennsylvania Press, 2010), pp. 67–68.

292 While Cohen attended: Arthur Max, "Dutch Cabinet Gets Its First Muslims," *Guardian*, February 21, 2007.

292 Bouyeri reserved: Benschop, "Jihad in the Netherlands."

292 In the days after: Jaap van Donselaar and Peter R. Rodrigues, "Ontwikkelingen na de moord op Van Gogh," Anne Frank Stichting, Onderzoek en Documentatie, Universiteit Leiden, Departement Bestuurskunde, Leiden, December 2004.

292 Ayaan was told: Ayaan Hirsi Ali, *Infidel: My Life* (New York: Free Press, 2007), pp. 326–327.

Part III: Being Regarded

One

297 Big, brash Karachi: *United States of America v. Aafia Siddiqui*, January 28, 2010, p. 1696.

299 Pearl's horrible murder: Bernard-Henri Lévy, *Who Killed Daniel Pearl?* trans. James X. Mitchell (South Yarra, Australia: Hardie Grant Books, 2005), pp. 298–299, 342–351.

300 I had also read: Asra Q. Nomani, "Who Really Killed Danny Pearl?" *Salon*, October 22, 2004, www.asranomani.com/Writings.aspx?p=P.

302 In the days after: Asra Q. Nomani, "The Taliban Ladies' Auxiliary," *Salon*, October 25, 2001, http://dir.salon.com/story/news/feature/2001/10/25/mujahida/.

Two

311 With mosques and churches: Anthony Browne, "Hatred Engulfs a Liberal Land," *Times*, November 13, 2004.

311 She stayed long enough: "Ayaan Hirsi Ali: Ik ga me absoluut niet aanpassen (Gerectificeerd)," *NRC Handelsblad*, November 29, 2004; "Dutch Politician Plans New Film Criticizing Islam—Report," Reuters, November 29, 2004.

312 When she finally returned: David Rennie and Joan Clements, "Dutch Muslim MP Out of Hiding After Death Threats," *Daily Telegraph*, January 19, 2004.

312 At first everyone vied: Deborah Scroggins, "The Dutch-Muslim Culture War," *The Nation*, June 27, 2005.

313 When a group of Muslims: Paul Gallagher, "Dutch Court Rules in Row over MP's Film on Islam," Reuters, March 15, 2005.

313 In a series of open letters: Tom Lanoye et al., *Brieven van Ayaan Hirsi Ali* (Amsterdam: Prometheus, 2005).

313 Herman Philipse was so infuriated: Herman Philipse, *Verlichtingsfundamentalisme? Open brief over Verlichting en fundamentalisme aan Ayaan Hirsi Ali. Mede bestemd voor Piet Hein Donner* (Amsterdam: Bert Bakker, 2005).

314 Holland's best-loved historian: Geert Mak, *Gedoemd tot kwetsbaarheid* (Amsterdam: Johan Blaauw, 2005).

316 Donner, the minister of justice: "Threatened Dutch MP Reveals Living on Navy Base," Reuters, February 18, 2005.

317 Donner accused Ayaan of ingratitude: Andrew Higgins, "Taking Leave: Islamist Threats to Dutch Politician Bring Chill at Home—Ms. Hirsi Ali Quits Parliament, Plans to Resettle in U.S.," *Wall Street Journal*, May 17, 2006.

317 Van Gogh's friend: "Ebru Umar to Muslim Politician Hirsi Ali: 'You Turned your Private War into a National War' and Said 'To Hell with the VVD,' " Militant Islam Monitor, May 15, 2006, www.militantislammonitor.org/article/id/1911.

318 The police continued to arrest: Janny Groen and Annieke Kranenberg, *Women Warriors for Allah: An Islamist Network in the Netherlands*, trans. Robert Naborn (Philadelphia: University of Pennsylvania Press, 2010), pp. 87–91, 108.

318 Ayaan's own Liberal Party: Christopher Caldwell, "Daughter of the Enlightenment," *The New York Times Magazine*, April 3, 2005.

318 Jozias van Aartsen: Sam Cherribi, *In the House of War: Dutch Islam Observed* (Oxford, England: Oxford University Press, 2010), pp. 191–192.

319 Hans Wiegel: Marc Peeperkorn and Raoul du Pré, "Hans Wiegel of Ayaan Hirsi Ali?" *De Volkskrant*, November 25, 2005.

319 She later compared: Steffie Kouters, "Ayaan Hirsi Ali: In die VS moet ik drie keer nadenken voor ik wat roep," *Volkskrant Magazine*, September 23, 2006.

319 In public she never lost: Gitit Ginat, "Freedom Fighter," *Haaretz*, June 3, 2006.

Four

322 Marlise Simons: Marlise Simons, "Dutch Filmmaker Is Killed," *New York Times*, November 3, 2004.

322 He had an abiding fear: Christopher Caldwell, *Reflections on the Revolution in Europe: Immigration, Islam and the West* (New York: Doubleday, 2009).

322 In an early article: Christopher Caldwell, "Holland Daze," *The Weekly Standard*, December 27, 2004.

323 "Hirsi Ali had been dealt": Christopher Caldwell, "Daughter of the Enlightenment," *The New York Times Magazine*, April 3, 2005.

323 Within days: Derek Rose, "The World Players," *New York Daily News*, April 11, 2005.

323 Like Cinderella: Gerald Traufetter, "The Odyssey of Ayaan Hirsi Ali," Der Spiegel Online, May 12, 2007, www.spiegel.de/international/world/0,1518,521546,00.html.

324 Mohammed Bouyeri's trial: Gregory Crouch, "Man on Trial Accepts Blame for Filmmaker's Killing," *New York Times*, July 13, 2005.

324 In Denmark the editors: See Jytte Klausen, *The Cartoons That Shook the World* (New Haven, Conn.: Yale University Press, 2008), for an analysis of the events leading up to the cartoon crisis.

325 In February 2006: Ibid., p. 41.

326 For months, various think tanks: Glenn Greenwald discusses how Richard Perle and others on the Hudson Institute and American Enterprise Institute boards were agitating for war against Iran in 2006 in *A Tragic Legacy: How a Good vs. Evil Mentality Destroyed the Bush Presidency* (New York: Random House, 2008), pp. 174–175.

Six

331 Holland's minister of immigration and integration: See "Dutch Judge Rejects Refugee Bid," BBC News, April 24, 2006, http://news.bbc.co.uk/2/hi/europe/4938568.stm.

Seven

336 The Justice Department had attempted: Michele Garcia, "Terror Suspect Can Use Operatives' Statements," *Washington Post*, November 9, 2005.

337 Once in court: *United States of America v. Uzair Paracha*, November 17, 2005, p. 1059, and November 21, 2005, pp. 1326–1327.

337 In the end: "Pakistani Gets 30 Years for Aiding al-Qaeda Operative," *New York Times*, July 21, 2006.

Eight

339 A Somali-born reporter: Rageh Omaar describes his attempts to contact Ayaan in *Only Half of Me: Being a Muslim in Britain* (New York: Viking, 2006), pp. 50–59.

339 For months she had been: Twan Huys, "The Fortune Hunter," *Nova*, May 2006.

339 Van Dongen began: What follows is taken from the transcript of van Dongen's interview with Ayaan on April 27, 2006.

341 The ex-husband: Osman Musse Quarre can be heard on tape in "The Holy Ayaan," *Zembla*, VARA Television, May 11, 2006.

342 Later that same day: Mischa Cohen, Sander Donkers, Carolina Lo Galbo, and Rober van de Griend, "Bij de buren van mevrouw Magan," *Vrij Nederland*, May 27, 2006.

342 She was already talking: Huys, "The Fortune Hunter."

Nine

343 Where was Aafia?: The main court documents are the FBI's FD-302 reports of their interrogations of Aafia contained in *United States of America v. Aafia Siddiqui*, document 256, August 19, 2010, plus the psychiatric evaluations by Thomas L. Kucharski, Leslie Powers, and Sally Johnson.

343 She said that in 2004 or 2005: *United States of America v. Aafia Siddiqui*, document 256, August 19, 2010, pp. 16–17.

343 Abu Lubaba was then writing: Abu Lubaba's columns can be read in Urdu at http://zarbpk.blogspot.com/search/label/Boltay%20Naqshay%20-%20Authentic%20Researched%20Articles.

344 He comes across: The Internet discussion about Mufti Abu Lubaba Shah Mansoor is at www.sunniforum.com/forum/showthread.php?46694-Dajjal-by-Mufti-Abu-Lubaba-Shah-Mansoor&p=386644&viewfull=1.

344 Aafia told the FBI: *United States of America v. Aafia Siddiqui*, Document 256, August 19, 2010, p. 11.

344 At Abu Lubaba's request: Ibid., pp. 9–10.

345 Perhaps the coconspirators' paranoia: Ibid., pp. 9, 17.

345 She said that to get away: Ibid., p. 17.

345 Among the papers: Ibid., p. 30.

Ten

346 Ayaan's first Sunday in New York: Brendan Bernhard, "An Enlightenment Fundamentalist," *New York Sun*, May 3, 2006.

347 On hand to hear: Nathan Guttman, "Bush: US Ties to Israel 'Unshakable.' Annan, Merkel Also Address Centennial Gathering of American Jewish Committee," *Jerusalem Post*, May 7, 2006.

347 With their playful: Jim Lobe, "Iran Showdown Tests Power of 'Israel Lobby,'" Interpress News Service, April 12, 2006.

347 Ayaan began her speech: An audiotape of Ayaan's acceptance speech is available at www.ajc.org/site/apps/nl/content2.asp?c=ijITI2PHKoG&b=1591361&ct=2387665.

348 Five days before: Gary Shapiro, "Celebrating Bernard Lewis's 90th," *New York Sun*, May 9, 2006.

348 Ayaan later said: Gerald Traufetter, "Settling Scores with Old Europe," *Der Spiegel*, May 22, 2006.

348 The British-born writer: Christopher Hitchens, "The Caged Virgin: Holland's Shameful Treatment of Ayaan Hirsi Ali," *Slate*, May 8, 2006, www.slate.com/id/2141276/.

349 *Zembla*'s documentary: "The Holy Ayaan," *Zembla*, VARA Television, May 11, 2006.

349 "Just watched an interesting report": The debate about Ayaan on Expatica after the *Zembla* program can be read at www.expatica.com/nl/news/local_news/ayaan-hirsi-alibr-hero-or-phony-29962_28335.html. There were hundreds of exchanges like this on Dutch Web sites. I choose this one because it was in English.

350 "Iron Rita" Verdonk: "Lying Can Lead to Loss of Asylum: Expert," Expatica, May 12, 2006, www.expatica.com/nl/news/local_news/lying-can-lead-to-loss-of-asylum-expert-29978_28350.html.

350 The following day: "MP Faces Inquiry over Naturalisation Lies," Expatica, May 15, 2006, www.expatica.com/nl/news/local_news/mp-faces-inquiry-over-naturalisation-lies-29989_28358.html.

350 To the astonishment: "MPs Order Verdonk to Reconsider Hirsi Ali's Status," Expatica, May 17, 2006, www.expatica.com/nl/news/local_news/mps-order-verdonk-to-reconsider-hirsi-alis-status-30073_28432.html.

353 For at least a little while: Mak later wrote me that the fever had not broken for long, though, as Ayaan broke the intellectual ground for radical anti-Muslim and xenophobic movements everywhere in Europe and especially Geert Wilders's Freedom Party in the Netherlands. "We are still in the middle of it."

Eleven

354 Even in her previous incarnation: Yvonne Ridley, "Pop Culture in the Name of Islam," DailyMuslims, April 24, 2006, http://yvonneridley.org/index2.php?option=com_content&do_pdf=1&id=15.

354 Ridley wrapped herself: Yvonne Ridley, "How I Came to Love the Veil," October 31, 2006, http://yvonneridley.org/index2.php?option=com_content&do_pdf=1&id=29; Rachel Cooke, "Free Radical," *Observer*, July 6, 2008.

355 Ridley was also: Richard Kerbaj, "Amnesty Is Damaged by Taliban Link," *Sunday Times*, February 7, 2010.

355 The star of "Torture Week": Moazzam Begg, *Enemy Combatant: A British Muslim's Journey to Guantanamo and Back* (New York: Free Press, 2006); Tim Golden, "Jihadist or Victim: Ex-Detainee Makes a Case," *New York Times*, June 15, 2006.

Twelve

357 One of the favorite: Robert Kagan, *Of Paradise and Power: America and Europe in the New World Order* (New York: Knopf, 2003).

358 George Will dined: George Will, "Muslim Dissident Has Warning for the West," *Chicago Sun-Times*, September 21, 2006.

358 Ayaan's most influential: One of many books dedicated to unraveling the history of the neoconservative movement and the links among its leaders is Justin Vaïsse, *Neoconservatism: The Biography of a Movement*, trans. Arthur Goldhammer (Cambridge, Mass.: Belknap Press, 2010).

359 She told *De Volkskrant*: Steffie Kouters, "Ayaan Hirsi Ali: In die VS moet ik drie keer nadenken voor ik wat roep," *De Volkskrant*, September 23, 2006.

Thirteen

360 Five years had passed: Jane Mayer, *The Dark Side: The Inside Story of How the War on Terror Turned into a War on American Ideals* (New York: Doubleday, 2008), pp. 324–326.

361 "In 2002, Ammar directed": "'Ali 'Abd 'al-Aziz 'Ali," at www.defense.gov/pdf/detaineebiographies1.pdf .

Fourteen

362 Starting in January 2007: Ayaan's conversation with Clive Crook took place on July 26, 2007, at the Aspen Ideas Festival; see www.youtube.com/watch?v=HLmkHMBsls4.

362 With very few exceptions: Anne Applebaum, "The Fight for Muslim Women: A Feisty Memoir by a Controversial Champion of Female

Rights," *Washington Post*, February 4, 2007; William Grimes, "No Rest for Feminist Fighting Islam," *New York Times*, February 14, 2007; Anita Quigley, "Female Rushdie Slams Sheik," *Daily Telegraph*, May 31, 2007; Natasha Walter, "Women: Life Force," *Guardian*, March 3, 2007; Caroline Glick, "Our World: Ayaan Hirsi Ali's Challenge to Humanity," *Jerusalem Post*, May 7, 2007.

363 Only a handful: Ian Buruma, "Against Submission," *New York Times Book Review*, March 4, 2007; Timothy Garton-Ash, "Islam in Europe," *The New York Review of Books*, October 5, 2006; "A Critic of Islam: Dark Secrets," *The Economist*, February 8, 2007.

363 The few Muslims: Lorraine Ali, "The Controversial Memoir of a Muslim Woman," *Newsweek*, February 26, 2007; Irfan Yusuf, "Islam and the West: An Unreliable Narrator," *New Matilda*, July 25, 2007; Taslima Nasreen, "A Long Journey to Be Herself," *Outlook India*, April 2, 2007; "Three Cheers for Ayaan," *Outlook India*, August 28, 2006.

364 In Hollywood: Diane Clehane, "Ayaan Hirsi Ali: Author's Memoir Receives Critical Kudos," *Variety*, July 30, 2007.

364 "The issue of freedom": Ibid.

365 Some members of the clan: Juha-Pekka Tikka, "Ayaan Hirsi Alin outo Suomi-yhteys," *Ilta-Sanomat*, October 9, 2007; Tikka, "Rajatarkastus selvittaa Hirsi Ali–mysteeria," *Ilta-Sanomat*, October 15, 2007.

365 "I am a happy individual now," Neely Tucker, "'Infidel' Author Ayaan Hirsi Ali Brings Her Incendiary Views to Washington," *Washington Post*, March 7, 2007.

Fifteen

367 In Karachi the families: "Petition Seeks Information When and How al-Qaeda Leader Shifted to U.S.," *Baluchistan Times*, April 20, 2007.

367 The CIA was still: Carlotta Gall, "Freed Suspects in Pakistan Point to Secret Detentions; About 400 Men Still Missing, Lawyers Say," *New York Times*, December 20, 2007.

368 From Amsterdam: Jane Perlez, "Pakistani Wife Embodies Cause of 'Disappeared,'" *New York Times*, July 19, 2007.

368 Musharraf's government initially stonewalled: "Pakistan Judge Rejects Bail for Man Opposing Detentions by Spy Agencies," Associated Press, February 3, 2007.

368 Then Chief Justice Chaudhry: Munir Ahmed, "Pakistan Says 10 of 41 Missing Men Are Free Amid Complaints of Disappearances," Associated Press, December 1, 2006.

Sixteen

369 In Holland, it had been: Andrew Williams, "Sixty Seconds: Ayaan Hirsi Ali," *Metro*, February 6, 2007. Robert Spencer published his comments at www.jihadwatch.org/2007/02/agreeing-and-disagreeing-with-ayaan-hirsi-ali.html; see also Manfred Gerstenfeld, "Interview with Ayaan Hirsi Ali," *Jerusalem Post*, August 3, 2006; Beila Rabinowitz's comments for Militant Islam Monitor, www.militantislammonitor.org/article/id/2207.

370 "It's not a war on terror": See Ayaan's interview with Clive Crook, July 26, 2007, at the Aspen Ideas Festival; see www.youtube.com/watch?v=HLmkHMBsl/4s.

370 Interviewing her in London: David Cohen, "Violence Is Inherent in Islam—It is a Cult of Death," *Evening Standard*, February 7, 2007.

371 "Islam, even in": Joseph Rago, "Free Radical: Ayaan Hirsi Ali Infuriates Muslims and Discomfits Liberals," *Wall Street Journal*, March 11, 2007.

371 She wrote in *Newsweek*: Ayaan Hirsi Ali, "Setting Themselves Apart," *Newsweek International*, November 27, 2006.

371 In the *New York Times*: Ayaan Hirsi Ali, "An Honor Worth Defending," *New York Times*, June 25, 2007.

372 She argued in: Ayaan Hirsi Ali, "Hearts and Minds in Turkey," *Los Angeles Times*, May 9, 2007.

372 She maintained that Iraq: Joel Whitney, "Infidel," *Guernica*, February 2007.

372 Nor did she respond: Nadje al-Ali and Nicola Pratt, *What Kind of Liberation? Women and the Occupation of Iraq* (Berkeley: University of California Press, 2009).

372 "Talking to Iran": Rogier van Bakel, "The Trouble Is the West," *Reason*, November 2007.

373 Her prescription: Shirin Ebadi, interviewed by Danielle Castellani Perelli, "Intellectuals like Hirsi Ali Play into the Mullahs' Hands," Reset DOC, March 9, 2007, www.resetdoc.org/story/00000000350. Another Iranian intellectual who advocated a different approach was Akbar Ganji, "Half a Man: Notes on Gender Apartheid in Iran," *Boston Review*, November–December 2007.

373 In the end: Thomas E. Ricks describes the AEI's role in coming up with a new strategy in *The Gamble: General David Petraeus and the American Military Adventure in Iraq, 2006–2008* (New York: Penguin, 2009), p. 159.

Seventeen

375 And in June 2007: Jane Perlez, "Islamic School Taunts Authorities," *New York Times*, June 25, 2007.

375 Musharraf's government ignored: Ali Dayan Hasan, "Pakistan's Moderates Are Beaten in Public," *New York Times*, June 15, 2005.

376 Indirect evidence later surfaced: L. Thomas Kucharski, "Forensic Evaluation: Aafia Siddiqui," July 2, 2009, p. 6.

376 Among the papers later found: *United States of America v. Aafia Siddiqui*, Document 256, August 19, 2010, p. 29.

376 The storming of the Lal Mosque: Ahmed Rashid, *Descent into Chaos: The United States and the Failure of Nation Building in Pakistan, Afghanistan, and Central Asia* (New York: Viking, 2008), p. 379.

376 In theory, Musharraf: Benazir Bhutto, *Reconciliation* (New York: HarperCollins, 2009), p. 323.

377 President Musharraf declared: United Nations, "Report of the United Nations Commission of Inquiry into the Facts and Circumstances of the Assassination of Former Pakistani Prime Minister Mohtarma Benazir Bhutto," April 15, 2010.

377 The glamorous Harvard graduate: Qandeel Siddique, "The Red Mosque Operation and Its Impact on the Growth of the Pakistani Taliban," Norwegian Defense Research Establishment, October 8, 2008.

Eighteen

378 The Dutch government had agreed: Ayaan's lawyer, Britta Bohler, released the letters Minister of Justice Ernst Hirsch Ballin wrote to Ayaan revoking her security to the press. See Marlise Simons, "Critic of Islam Confronts Dutch over Guards," *New York Times*, October 4, 2007; David Charter, "Bodyguards Taken from Former MP Who Fled After Islamic Death Threats," *Times*, October 3, 2007.

379 The U.S. secretary of state: "Noted Author Ayaan Hirsi Ali Receives Her Green Card," U.S. Citizenship and Immigration Services. www.uscis.gov/files/pressrelease/HirsiAliRlease25Sep07.pdf.

379 Her friends accused the Dutch: Christopher Hitchens, "The Price of Freedom: If the Dutch Government Abandons Ayaan Hirsi Ali, America Should Welcome Her," *Slate*, October 8, 2008, www.slate.com/id/2175458; Marlise Simons, "Critic of Islam Confronts Dutch over Bodyguards"; Anne Applebaum, "Double Dutch: The Dutch Government Once Again Threatens to Abandon Ayaan Hirsi Ali," *Slate*, www.slate.com/default.aspx?id=3944&qt=ayaan; Sam Harris and Salman Rushdie, "Abandoned to Fanatics," *Los Angeles Times*, October 9, 2008.

380 The media attacks: Alies Pegtel, "De creatie van een mythe," *HP/*

De Tijd, Christmas 2006; "Morning Newspapers," Expatica, October 11, 2007; Gerald Traufetter, "The Odyssey of Ayaan Hirsi Ali," Der Spiegel Online, May 12, 2007, www.spiegel.de/international/world/0,1518,521546,00.html.

381 The Dutch government said: "Parliament Angry with Hirsi Ali's Lawyer," Expatica, October 10, 2007; "Security of Hirsi Ali Not Extended," Expatica, October 11, 2007, www.expatica.com/nl/common/search.html?page=2&phrase=ayaan%20hirsi%20ali&nl=on.

381 *Elsevier* magazine: Traufetter, "The Odyssey of Ayaan Hirsi Ali."

381 The battle of the bodyguards: "Make Hirsi Ali an Honorary French Citizen," Expatica, October 23, 2007; "Ayaan Hirsi Ali Seeks Protection in France," Expatica, November 2, 2007; "France Won't Protect Hirsi Ali," Expatica, February 21, 2008, www.expatica.com/nl/common/search.html?page=2&phrase=ayaan%20hirsi%20ali&nl=on.

382 She and her friends: "EU Politicians Make Empty Promises to Hirsi Ali," Expatica, February 15, 2008; "The Netherlands Not Being Petty Towards Hirsi Ali," Expatica, February 12, 2008, www.expatica.com/nl/common/search.html?page=2&phrase=ayaan%20hirsi%20ali&nl=on.

382 So she returned: "Three Funds for Hirsi Ali," Expatica, October 17, 2007, www.expatica.com/nl/common/search.html?page=2&phrase=ayaan%20hirsi%20ali&nl=on; "Foundation for the Freedom of Expression," http://en.wikipedia.org/wiki/Foundation_for_Freedom_of_Expression.

382 Harris campaigned vigorously: Jerry Adler, "Bankrolling Ali's Asylum," *Newsweek*, December 3, 2007; Sam Harris, "Security Trust," October 15, 2008, www.samharris.org/site/security_trust/.

383 Ayaan and a group: The list of board members is taken from the AHA Foundation's 2007 IRS Form 902. The AHA Foundation's Web site is www.theahafoundation.org.

383 It was the first time: The Centre for Social Cohesion's studies can be found at www.socialcohesion.co.uk. Its founding grant is described at "Centre for Social Cohesion," http://en.wikipedia.org/wiki/Centre_for_Social_Cohesion.

383 The AHA Foundation, by contrast: "What Do We Know? Facts and Figures on the Circumstances Affecting Muslim Girls and Women in the United States," The AHA Foundation, December 18, 2009, www.theahafoundation.org/system/include/resources/files/AHA2009WhatDoWeKnow.pdf.

383 IRS records showed: AHA's 2008 and 2009 tax returns are available at www2.guidestar.org/organizations/33-1185369/aha-foundation.aspx#.

384 Adding several new board members: The new board members are listed on the foundation's 2009 tax returns. Elise Jordan's position is mentioned in Pamela Paul, "The Party, in Exile," *New York Times*, June 11, 2010.

384 Its output nonetheless: Studies and other materials published by Women Living Under Muslim Laws (WLUML) are available at www.wluml.org.

Nineteen

385 On the evening of January 22, 2008: S. H. Faruqi, "Salient Features of the Visit of Dr. Aafia Siddiqui at the Residence of Her Uncle Mr. S. H. Faruqi at Islamabad, Pakistan on 22st to 24th of January, 2008," e-mailed to the author October 11, 2008.

385 "She said she wanted": Robert Fisk, "The Mysterious Grey Lady of Bagram," *Independent*, March 19, 2010.

386 He told the *Guardian*'s: Declan Walsh, "The Mystery of Aafia Siddiqui," *Guardian*, November 24, 2009.

387 "That was her main point": Ibid.

Twenty

389 She continued to be: Paul Berman waged a crusade against Ayaan's alleged critics that began with his 28,000-word article "Who's Afraid of Tariq Ramadan?" *The New Republic*, June 4, 2007, and culminated in a book, *The Flight of the Intellectuals: The Controversy over Islamism and the Press* (Brooklyn, NY: Melville House, 2010). Pascal Bruckner, "Enlightenment Fundamentalism or Racism of the Anti-racists?" and other contributions to the debate about Ayaan can be seen at www.signandsight.com/features/1146.html.

390 Eventually he wrote: Ron Rosenbaum, "Bonfire of the Intellectuals: Paul Berman's Outraged Attack on Hirsi Ali's Attackers," *Slate*, March 25, 2010, www.slate.com/id/2248809/; Lee Siegel, "Who's Right? Who's Left? Who Cares?" *New York Observer*, May 11, 2010.

390 It was left: Bassam Tibi, "Europeanisation, Not Islamisation," March 22, 2007, www.signandsight.com/features/1258.html.

390 Ayaan, by contrast: Joshua Keating, "Turkish Cleric Gulen Tops Intellectuals List," *Foreign Policy*, June 23, 2008, http://blog.foreignpolicy.com/posts/2008/06/23/turkish_cleric_guelen_tops_intellectuals_list.

391 In June 2008: Claudia Anderson, "Parallel Lives: Frederick Douglass, Ayaan Hirsi Ali and the Flight to Freedom," *The Weekly Standard*, June 23, 2008.

391 Ayaan had recently received: Ayaan Hirsi Ali, *Nomad: From Islam to America: A Personal Journey Through the Clash of Civilizations* (New York: Free Press, 2010), pp. 5–6.

Twenty-one

393 Ridley hasn't identified: "Binyam Mohamed in Conversation with Moazzam Begg," March 26, 2009, http://old.cageprisoners.com/articles.php?id=28464.

394 Neither Binyam Mohamed: Thomas Joscelyn, "The False Martyr," *The Weekly Standard*, February 20, 2009.

394 Binyam Mohamed said: "Binyam Mohamed in Conversation with Moazzam Begg."

395 Striking the themes: "Unidentified Pak Woman Detained at Bagram Airbase for More Than Four Years," Asian News International, July 7, 2008.

Twenty-two

397 Ayaan often said: Ayaan Hirsi Ali, *The Caged Virgin: An Emancipation Proclamation for Women* (New York: Free Press, 2006), p. 62.

397 She wrote in *Nomad*: Ayaan Hirsi Ali, *Nomad: From Islam to America: A Personal Journey Through the Clash of Civilizations* (New York: Free Press, 2010), pp. 5–6.

Twenty-three

399 It was just getting dark: *United States of America v. Aafia Siddiqui*, Document 258-2, August 19, 2010, pp. 13–22. This document contains portions of the FBI reports on their interviews with witnesses to Aafia's arrest and imprisonment at Ghazni. I have also drawn on the testimony of eyewitnesses given at the trial.

399 The Afghan government: "Suicide Bomber Kills 16 in Southwest Afghanistan," Ria Novosti, May 5, 2008; Ashfaq Yusufzai, "Becoming a Suicide Bomber," Interpress News Service, July 21, 2008.

400 Police commander Ghani Khan: *United States of America v. Aafia Siddiqui*, Document 258-2, August 19, 2010, pp. 15, 22.

401 Threadcraft later testified: *United States of America v. Aafia Siddiqui*, January 19, 2010, pp. 239–256.

403 At the Ghazni police station: Ibid., pp. 86–87.

403 The governor's office: The videotape of the press conference is at www.youtube.com/watch?v=23yT7soyV48.

404 After the press conference: *United States of America v. Aafia Siddiqui*, January 19, 2010, pp. 131–143.

404 While Qadeer was dealing: *United States of America v. Aafia Siddiqui*, January 25, 2010, pp. 1363–1399.

405 Sergeant Kenneth J. Cook: Ibid., p. 1,200.

Twenty-four

409 Ayaan rarely mentioned: David Pryce-Jones, "Europe's Loss, America's Gain," *National Review*, August 28, 2006.

Twenty-five

411 Both Great Britain's: Asian Human Rights Commission, "Pakistan/ USA: A Lady Doctor Remains Missing with Her Three Children Five Years After Her Arrest," Urgent Appeals Case AHRC-UAC-167-2008, www.ahrchk.net/ua/mainfile.php/2008/2947/.

412 As for Aafia: *United States of America v. Aafia Siddiqui*, Document 256, August 19, 2010, pp. 1–34.

412 A few hours before dawn: "Al-Qaeda Leader Ayman al-Zawahiri May Be Dead," *CBS News: The Saturday Early Show*, August 2, 2008.

413 Then on Sunday: Farah Stockman, "Pakistani Scientist Alive, in Custody; FBI Linked Her to Al Qaeda in Hub," *Boston Globe*, August 3, 2008.

413 On Monday: Christine Kearney, "Pakistani Woman in US Court for Assault on Troops," Reuters, August 5, 2008.

Twenty-six

414 afterward correcting him: Rebecca Weisser, "Prophet Faces a Polemic," *Australian*, August 2, 2008.

414 Ayaan was stopping: Ayaan Hirsi Ali, *Nomad: From Islam to America: A Personal Journey Through the Clash of Civilizations* (New York: Free Press, 2010), pp. 7–8.

415 She found her father: Ibid., pp. 10–12.

Twenty-seven

416 Pakistani and Western journalists: Alison Hoffman, "NY Terror Trial of Pakistani Woman May Lead to First Investigation of US Secret Intelligence Techniques," *Jerusalem Post*, September 7, 2008.

417 A mass of secret: "US Embassy Cables: Bagram Officials Deny Detaining Aafia Siddiqui," *Guardian*, December 1, 2010.

417 By chance: Tom Hayes, "NY Charges for Woman in Afghan Military Shooting," Associated Press, August 5, 2008.

417 Sharp came out: Farah Stockman, "Activist Turned Extremist, US Says; Ex-Hub Woman Tied to Al Qaeda," *Boston Globe*, August 12, 2008.

418 But U.S. officials: Brian Ross, "Alleged Mata Hari of al-Qaeda Indicted," ABC News, "The Blotter," September 2, 2008; James Bone, "Neuroscientist 'Had List of New York Targets,'" *Times*, September 4, 2008.

418 "She is the most significant": Alison Gendar, Jose Martinez, and Stephanie Gaskell, "Pakistani Scientist Busted, Called Most Significant Capture in Five Years," *New York Daily News*, August 12, 2008.

420 Aafia's family sprang: Hasan Mansoor, "Pakistani Mum Extradited to US on Terror Charges," Agence France-Presse, August 5, 2008.

420 The Asian Human Rights Commission: Asian Human Rights Commission, "Dr. Afia's Health Is in Serious Condition and Two of Her Children Remain Missing," Urgent Appeal Update AHRC-UAU-049-2008, August 8, 2008.

421 Aafia had told the FBI: *United States of America v. Aafia Siddiqui*, Document 256, August 19, 2010, p. 18.

422 Aafia's mother provided: *United States of America v. Aafia Siddiqui*, Document 314, October 7, 2010, p. 14.

422 Khalid Hasan: Khalid Hasan, "Aafia Siddiqui's 'al-Qaeda Links' to Come Up in Court," *Daily Times*, August 20, 2008; "Postcard USA: Where Do We Go from Here?" *Daily Times*, August 24, 2008.

423 But no one listened to him: One of many commentaries contrasting Musharraf's behavior to that of Muhammed bin Qasim is "Dr. Aafia and Mohammed bin Qasim," https://azkaarali.wordpress.com/2010/09/26/dr-aafia-and-mohammed-bin-qasim/.

423 After years of tactfully praising: "Dr Aafia's Sister Fears US Security Agencies May Kill Her," *Daily Times*, August 13, 2008.

423 Anne Patterson: Anne Patterson, "Aafia Siddiqui: US Envoy's Version," *Dawn*, August 16, 2008.

423 On August 21: "Dr. Fowzia Siddiqui's Address to the Pakistani Senate," www.draafia.org/2008/08/22/dr-fowzia-siddiquis-address-to-the-pakistani-senate-2/.

Twenty-eight

425 The British press: "Tariikhii Dr. Xersi Magana 1935–2008," August 25, 2008, www.garoweonline.com/artman2/publish/Islam_28/Tariikhii_Xersi_Magana.shtml.

425 "each acknowledged ways": Claudia Anderson, "Parallel Lives: Frederick Douglass, Ayaan Hirsi Ali and the Flight to Freedom," *The Weekly Standard*, June 23, 2008.

425 "If I had gone": Ayaan Hirsi Ali, *Nomad: From Islam to America: A Personal Journey Through the Clash of Civilizations* (New York: Free Press, 2010), p. 26.

Twenty-nine

429 According to the *New York Times*: Carlotta Gall and Abdul Waheed Wafa, "Afghans Repatriate Son, 12, of Pakistani Indicted in U.S.," *New York Times*, September 16, 2008.

Thirty

433 Ayaan got a call: Ayaan Hirsi Ali, *Nomad: From Islam to America: A Personal Journey Through the Clash of Civilizations* (New York: Free Press, 2010), pp. 29–31.

Thirty-one

435 Aafia remained stubbornly: Larry Neumeister, "Pakistani Scientist Is Deemed Unfit to Stand Trial," Associated Press, November 18, 2008.

435 The Pakistani Senate: "Report of the Functional Committee on Human Rights on Dr. Aafia Siddiqui," presented by Senator S. M. Zafar, Chairman, Functional Committee, January 2009.

436 In December, he wrote: "Dr. Aafia's Children: Father's Plea," *Dawn*, December 12, 2008; Aroosa Mansoor, "Dr. Aafia Siddiqui's Husband Breaks His Silence After Six Years," *News International,* February 18, 2009.

436 Pakistan's spy agency: "Dr. Aafia's Ex-Husband Seeks Children's Custody," *Dawn*, July 8, 2009.

437 Only Aafia herself: John Hawkinson, "Aafia Siddiqui's Son Released; DOJ Hints at Conspiracy Charges," *Tech*, September 16, 2008.

Thirty-two

438 Ayaan kept lecturing: Jan Sjostrom, "Author, Activist Condemns Muslim Faith at Palm Beach Talk," *Palm Beach Daily News*, March 21, 2009.

438 Ayaan had seemed receptive: Rebecca Weisser, "Prophet Faces a Polemic," *Australian*, August 2, 2008.

438 But it was too late: "A Symposium: On the U.S. Election, Viewed Abroad," *World Affairs*, September 22, 2008; Ayaan Hirsi Ali, "Cut and Run Won't Do," *Australian*, November 4, 2008.

439 In November: Ayaan Hirsi Ali, "Obama Let Down Moderate Muslims," American Enterprise Institute for Public Policy Research, June 5, 2009, www.aei.org/article/100582.

439 She kept writing: Charles Johnson, "A Few Preliminary Thoughts on Ayaan Hirsi Ali," *Claremont Conservative*, February 6, 2009, www.claremontconservative.com/2009/02/few-preliminary-thoughts-on-ayaan-hirsi.html; "Islam Critic Ayaan Hirsi Ali Writes Children's Book," Expatica, May 30, 2008.

439 She still grew animated: Weisser, "Prophet Faces a Polemic."

440 In any case: "Ayaan Hirsi Ali Signs with Knopf Canada," *Globe and Mail Blog Post*, February 25, 2009, www.theglobeandmail.com/books/in-other-words/ayaan-hirsi-ali-signs-with-knopf-canada/article973264/.

Thirty-three

441 Aafia's psychiatric evaluation: L. Thomas Kucharski, "Forensic Evaluation: Aafia Siddiqui," July 9, 2009, p. 11; Sally C. Johnson, "Forensic Evaluation," March 16, 2009, p. 15; *United States of America v. Aafia Siddiqui*, Aafia Siddiqui, letters to Judge Richard Berman and FMC, Carswell, Warden Elaine Chapman, July 7, 2009, pp. 1–4.

441 At FMC, Carswell: *United States of America v. Aafia Siddiqui*, "Camille Kempke," transcript of deposition taken July 1, 2009, Defense Exhibit DX7, pp. 78, 142.

441 She seems to have believed: Aafia Siddiqui, letter to FMC, Carswell, Warden Elaine Chapman, July 7, 2009.

441 She wrote what she described: Aafia Siddiqui, letter to Judge Richard Berman, July 7, 2009.

Thirty-four

445 Like Ayaan: Michael Elliott, "Niall Ferguson: Theorist of Liberal Imperialism," *Time*, April 24, 2004.

445 A superb storyteller: Niall Ferguson, *The War of the World: Twentieth-Century Conflict and the Descent of the West* (New York: Penguin, 2007); Ferguson, *Colossus: The Price of America's Empire* (New York: Penguin, 2004), p. 170.

446 She herself had been charged: David Pryce-Jones, "Europe's Loss, America's Gain," *National Review*, August 28, 2006.

447 But his and Ayaan's lawyers: "Niall Ferguson and Ayaan Hirsi Ali," *Independent*, February 25, 2010.

447 With Ayaan's fortieth birthday: Steffie Kouters, "Ik ben de moeder van chaos," *De Volkskrant*, March 13, 2010; Katie Nicholl, Miles Goslett, and Caroline Graham, "The History Man and Fatwa Girl: How Will David Cameron Take News That Think-Tank Guru Niall Ferguson Has Deserted Wife Sue Douglas for Somali Feminist?" *Daily Mail*, February 12, 2010; "Profile: Niall Ferguson," *Sunday Times*, February 14, 2010; Richard Kay and Geoffrey Levy, "Naughty Niall Ferguson: The Dashing TV Historian and the String of Affairs That Could Cost Him Millions," *Daily Mail*, February 20, 2010.

447 The pair went public: Nicholl, Goslett, and Graham, "The History Man and Fatwa Girl."

Thirty-five

450 After jury selection began: Alison Gendar, "'Lady Al Qaeda' Cries Foul: Accused Terrorist Aafia Siddiqui Says Toss Jews from Jury Pool," *Daily News*, January 14, 2010.

450 As the trial began: *United States of America v. Aafia Siddiqui*, January 25, 2010, p. 1074, and January 19, 2010, p. 76.

451 Up on the stand: *United States of America v. Aafia Siddiqui*, January 28, 2010, p. 720.

452 Yet, with the courtroom: Ibid., pp. 1726–1733, and January 29, 2010, p. 2027.

453 In his closing arguments: *United States of America v. Aafia Siddiqui*, January 29, 2010, p. 1947.

Thirty-six

454 In it, she used: Ayaan Hirsi Ali, *Nomad: From Islam to America: A Personal Journey Through the Clash of Civilizations* (New York: Free Press, 2010), pp. 13–22.

454 The reviews this time: Hirsi Ali, *Nomad*, jacket cover; Nathan Gardels, "Want to Know What Makes a Jihadist Tick? Read Ayaan Hirsi Ali's *Nomad*," *Christian Science Monitor*, May 27, 2010; Arita Baijens, "Bij nomaden heeft de vrouw soms de broek aan," *NRC Handelsblad*, March 22, 2010; Anet Biech, "Ayaan Hirsi Ali, woelig nomade," *De Volkskrant*, March 19, 2010; Nicholas Kristof, "The Gadfly," *New York Times Sunday Book Review*, May 28, 2010; Bob Drogin, "Book Review: *Nomad*, by Ayaan Hirsi Ali," *Los Angeles Times*, June 7, 2010; "Fabulously Snobby Divorce Scandal of the Week: Niall Ferguson's Fatwa Mistress Two-Step," http://gawker.com/5466433/fabulously-snobby-divorce-scandal-of-the-week-niall-fergusons-fatwa-mistress-two+step.

455 Meeting Ayaan: Toby Allen-Mills, "In Love . . . and on an Islamist Death List," *Sunday Times*, May 9, 2010; Emma Brockes, "Why Are Muslims So Hypersensitive?" *Guardian*, May 8, 2010; Cristina Odone, "Ayaan Hirsi Ali Reminds Me of Richard Dawkins—Obsessive and Simplistic," *Daily Telegraph*, June 6, 2010.

456 This coolness notwithstanding: Richard Kay, "History Man Heads Home with His Girl," *Daily Mail*, June 2, 2010; Judith Woods, "Has the Face of Adultery Changed?" *Daily Telegraph*, May 11, 2010.

456 Ayaan herself wrote: Ayaan Hirsi Ali, "I'm a Nomad, but I Want to Be a Mother," *Sunday Times*, May 9, 2010; Woods, "Has the Face of Adultery Changed?"

456 The *Daily Mail* claimed: Kay, "History Man Heads Home with His Girl"; Allen-Mills, "In Love . . . and on an Islamist Death List."

456 In early 2011: Niall Ferguson, *Civilization: The West and the Rest* (London: Allen Lane, 2011).

Thirty-seven

457 After Aafia's conviction: Declan Walsh, "Pakistan Erupts After US Jailing of 'Daughter of the Nation' Aafia Siddiqui," *Guardian*, September 24, 2010.

457 A *Daily Express* columnist: Shakil Chaudhry, "Aafia Siddiqui: Hysteria Grips Pakistan," *Viewpoint*, February 25, 2011.

458 Then, in another: "DNA Proves Girl as Aafia's Daughter: Malik," *News International,* April 11, 2010.

459 As for al-Qaeda: Qandeel Siddique, "Aafia Siddiqui," February 24, 2010, www.jihadica.com/aafia-siddiqui/.

459 Even before Aafia's trial began: Megan Chuchmach, Nick Shifrin, and Luis Martinez, "Martyrdom Video from CIA Base Bomber Links Deadly Attack to Pakistani Taliban," ABC News, January 9, 2010; Mushtaq Yusufzai, "Taliban to Execute US Soldier if Aafia Not Released," *News International,* February 5, 2010.

459 In early March: Azaz Syed, "Hakeemullah Writes Letter to Afia's Sister," *Dawn*, May 5, 2010.

459 Khawaja returned to Waziristan: Nadir Hassan, "Who Killed the Ex-ISI Official?" The AfPak Channel, April 30, 2010, http://afpak.foreignpolicy.com/posts/2010/04/30/who_killed_the_ex_isi_official.

460 The next day: Laith Alkhouri, "Flashpoint Exclusive: Video of Times Square Bomber Faisal Shahzad with Taliban Commander Hakimullah Mehsud," Flashpoint Global Partners, July 22, 2010, www.globalterroralert.com/library/pakistan/631-flashpoint-exclusive-video-of-times-square-bomber-faisal-shahzad-with-taliban-commander-hakimullah-mehsud.html.

Thirty-eight

461 In January 2011: Asra Q. Nomani and Barbara Feinman Todd, "The Pearl Project: New Findings in the Unsolved Murder of Journalist Daniel Pearl Expose the Secret Network of Terrorism, Militancy and Islamic Extremism Inside Modern Pakistan," The Center for Public Integrity, January 3, 2011.

Thirty-nine

463 It had never been: *United States of America v. Aafia Siddiqui*, Document 314, October 7, 2010, p. 13.

464 The trial had been: Ibid., p. 19.

464 Dawn Cardi spoke: Ibid., pp. 21–24.

464 In his turn: Ibid., p. 20.

464 Aafia then gave: Ibid., pp. 24–30.

465 Aafia stood up again: Ibid., p. 49.

465 At last Judge Berman said: Ibid., p. 53.

Index

About the Author

Deborah Scroggins is the author of *Emma's War*, which was translated into ten languages and won the Ridenhour Truth-Telling Prize. Scroggins has written for *The Sunday Times Magazine, The Nation, Vogue, Granta,* and many other publications, and she has won two Overseas Press Club awards and a Robert F. Kennedy Journalism Award as a foreign correspondent for the *Atlanta Journal-Constitution*. She lives with her family in Massachusetts.